DUE DATE			

ELLEN J. HAMMER

A Death

in

November

AMERICA IN VIETNAM, 1963

Oxford University Press
New York   Oxford

Oxford University Press
Oxford   New York   Toronto
Delhi   Bombay   Calcutta   Madras   Karachi
Petaling Jaya   Singapore   Hong Kong   Tokyo
Nairobi   Dar es Salaam   Cape Town
Melbourne   Auckland

and associated companies in
Berlin   Ibadan

94334

Lines on page v from Poem No. 90 by Nguyen Binh Khiem
in *Heritage of Vietnamese Poetry*, edited and translated by
Huynh Sanh Thong. Copyright © 1979 Yale University Press.
Reprinted by permission of Yale University Press.

First published in 1987 by E. P. Dutton, a division of
New American Library, 2 Park Avenue, New York, N.Y. 10016.

First issued as an Oxford University Press paperback, 1988

Oxford is a registered trademark of Oxford University Press

Library of Congress Cataloging-in-Publication Data
Hammer, Ellen J. (Ellen Joy)
A death in November.
Bibliography: p.
Includes index.
1. Vietnam—Politics and government—1945–1975.
2. Ngô Dinh Diêm, 1901–1963. 3. United States—
Foreign relations—Vietnam. 4. Vietnam—Foreign
relations—United States. I. Title.
DS556.9.H346   1986   327.730597   86-16724
ISBN 0-525-24210-4

ISBN 0-19-520640-1 (PPBK.)

2   4   6   8   10   9   7   5   3   1

Printed in the United States of America

The seats of state lie ready for high skills.
Must one let vulgar hands draw Heaven's sword?
Should wicked rascals hone the crescent-ax?

—Nguyen Binh Khiem
1491–1585

Translation by
Huynh Sanh Thong

Contents

Contents

Illustrations follow page 160.

Acknowledgments

Hundreds of people, living and dead, have helped in the writing of this book, which in a sense has been in preparation ever since 1963, when I was witness in Vietnam to many of the events described here. Some of those to whom I am indebted are named in the notes at the end. I am grateful to them all.

I should like particularly to thank Paul T. De Angelis, my editor, for his understanding, his patience, and his skill.

Tran Van Dinh, Arthur J. Dommen, Ruth Leon, and Michael D. Mosettig have made valuable contributions to the manuscript, and I wish to express my heartfelt gratitude.

I am indebted to Martin F. McGann and Suzanne K. Forbes, archivists at the John Fitzgerald Kennedy Library, for their assistance since 1982 in the lengthy process of declassifying official documents and for providing access to documents declassified at the request of other researchers. I also want to thank David C. Humphrey, archivist at the Lyndon Baines Johnson Library, and Henry J. Gwiazda, Supervisory Curator of the Robert F. Kennedy Collection. •

Author's Note

The political division of Vietnam into North and South in 1954 was superimposed on a country that the French had divided administratively into three parts (Tonkin, Annam, and Cochin China), known to Vietnamese as simply the north, the center, and the south: the Bac Bo, the Trung Bo, and the Nam Bo.

I have capitalized *South* to refer to the territory of the Republic of Vietnam under Ngo Dinh Diem, as distinguished from *south,* the southern part of that country, the Nam Bo. Even at that time, when the Trung Bo was divided between the governments of Saigon and Hanoi, the northern part of the territory of the Republic of (South) Vietnam was described as the central provinces.

A
Death
in
November

Vietnam After the 1954 Geneva Agreement

CHINA

BURMA

Lang Son

Dien Bien Phu

HANOI
Hon Gay
Haiphong

Black River
Red River

Sam Neua

Gulf of Tonkin

Mekong River

Luang Prabang

Plaines des Jarres

NORTH VIETNAM
Hon Me Island

HAINAN (CHINA)

LAOS

VIENTIANE

Vinh ○ Hon Niem Island

Udorn

Mekong River

Con Thien

1954 DEMARCATION LINE (17th Parallel)

Tchepone
Quang Tri
Khe Sanh
Hue

Savannakhet

THAILAND

HO CHI MINH TRAIL

Da Nang

SOUTH CHINA SEA

Ubon
Pakse

Chu Lai
My Lai
Quang Ngai
Dak To

Kontum
Pleiku

SOUTH VIETNAM

BANGKOK

Qui Nhon

CAMBODIA

Ban Me Thuot

Nha Trang

Gia Nghia

Dalat

Cam Ranh Bay

Gulf of Thailand

Mekong

PHNOM PENH

Loc Ninh
Song Be
An Loc
Tay Ninh

Bien Hoa
SAIGON

Sihanoukville

River

Long Xuyen
My Tho

Mekong Delta

Prologue

The monsoon that originated far to the northeast in central Asia blew across Hue as it did every winter, breaking its force against the pine-covered hills that overlooked the city and lashing it with torrential storms. Peasants covered their clothes with cloaks woven of heavy leaves to keep off the gusts of cold rain that made the climate of this region of Vietnam with its alternating seasons so different from the monotonous heat in the lowlands farther south. From the distance, these peasants resembled giant birds scattered about the wet fields outside the city. In Hue the Perfumed River overflowed the grassy embankment stretching along the walled city known as the Citadel, the heart of the imperial capital of Vietnam, and the level of water rose in the lotus-covered moats, submerging the low, narrow streets lined with omnipresent litchi and longan trees. Besieged by the waters, people remained at home. They squatted on the beds—built of planks of precious wood in the tile-covered residences of the mandarins and of bamboo in the leaf-roofed houses of the poor—on which they worked as well as rested, to attend to the sedentary routine of their daily chores. These city dwellers had already made their provision of dried fish, rice, and pickles to tide themselves through the period of floods when markets could not be reached and the sampans that brought their daily catch of fresh fish up the Perfumed River from Thuan An lagoon became rare.

Beyond this lagoon that protected the imperial city from invasion by sea—one of the reasons the Nguyen dynasty that ruled Vietnam had chosen Hue as their capital—the waters of the South China Sea were wild when in December 1832 the American warship *Peacock* arrived off the Vietnamese coast. Short of attempting to reach Hue, the *Peacock* set its course for Da Nang, some seventy miles to the south, a port long used by other navigators from both Europe and Asia. The American ship neared Da Nang on New Year's Day 1833, but there too the turbulent seas made landing impossible, and the Americans continued southward to drop anchor at last off Phu Yen province, not far from the mountains and coral reefs of Cam Ranh Bay. Aboard the *Peacock* was Edmund Roberts from New Hampshire, appointed by President Andrew Jackson as his envoy to "the courts of Cochinchina [Vietnam], Siam and Muscat" for the purpose "of effecting treaties which should place our commerce in these countries on an equality with that enjoyed by more favored nations."

The ship *Fame* under Captain Jeremiah Briggs from Salem had reached Vietnam as early as 1803. Sixteen years later the brig *Franklin* and the ship *Marmion* were, in the words of Lieutenant John White aboard the *Franklin,* "the first American ships that ever ascended the Don-nai River and displayed the stars and stripes before the city of Saigon." But no Western power had yet managed to persuade the Vietnamese to enter into continuing official relations, although both the French and the British had already tried to do so. A few months before the arrival of Edmund Roberts and the *Peacock,* a young Frenchman whom the imperial court had refused to accept as French consul, tried to console the minister of foreign affairs in Paris by reporting that the United States had also been rebuffed the previous year. The prospective American consul was refused, he said, despite his "artful insinuations" that the intentions of the United States were peaceful in character and purely mercantile in nature, and that in this his countrymen differed from the French and the English, "who were always ready to take by force what they could not get by influence."

Certainly Roberts's intentions were both peaceful and "mercantile." The problem was to reach the emperor so that these intentions could be expounded at the highest level. As the ship lay at anchor in Vung Lam Bay, a local official came aboard to find out what the Americans wanted. He wrote down his questions in Chinese, and they replied in the same language, also in writing. The *Peacock* finally succeeded in putting ashore a lieutenant who carried a letter written in both Chinese and English that announced Roberts's arrival to the Vietnamese sovereign. The American handed it over on the beach to two mandarins who were attended by soldiers, their pikes fixed in the sand, accompanied by three elephants with small riding boxes on their backs, palanquins, and several ponies. Shortly afterward, when a Vietnamese Catholic priest acting as an interpreter visited the *Peacock* with more questions, they communicated again in writing, but this time in Latin. Foreigners would have a difficult time gaining admission to this country, Roberts later noted, if they were not Chinese.

He could not know, of course, that the elaborate chain of command in the Vietnamese administration required that the documents that explained his mission be placed in the hands of a succession of mandarins beginning with the *tri phu,* or district administrator, of Tuy An, who had to bring Roberts's letter to his superior, the governor of the province of Phu Yen. From him they went to the governor of the neighboring and larger province of Binh Dinh in his capital at Qui Nhon to whom, for such important matters, this official was subordinated. Only then could Roberts's papers be conveyed on horseback or by palanquin northward to Hue, where they were delivered to the minister of the interior, who traditionally acted as prime minister. Because the country had few diplomatic relations with other nations and little commerce, no minister was specially charged with the conduct of foreign affairs, and it was the minister of the interior who studied all such documents before they could be brought to the august attention of the emperor.

Thus only on January 11 did two representatives of the imperial court arrive from Hue. They came across the Mandarin Road, built by the father of the reigning emperor, Minh Mang, along the narrow coastal plains and over the mountains where steps were cut into solid rock to link his capital with the ancient city of Hanoi in the north, and with Saigon, which had been settled only recently, in the south. To requests for more details about the mission that could be submitted to the emperor, the Americans replied that they had no more information to give. They found it intensely frustrating dealing with these ceremonious Vietnamese mandarins who seemed to haggle interminably over details. It was almost impossible to extract any concrete information from them, and whenever they were questioned on subjects about which they did not wish to reply, they said they could not remember. This device, which Roberts recorded, was of course only one among a variety of verbal defenses thrown up by the Vietnamese in particular and the people of the Far East in general to protect themselves against the curiosity of outsiders. The Americans had entered into contact with a world of circumlocution and nuance where language was used as much to conceal as to communicate and was permeated by an acute sensitivity to the effect a reply might have on the questioner.

To give Minh Mang his proper title of emperor (and not simply king as they had first written), the Roberts mission corrected the letters they wished to send to Hue. But then the mandarins asked that the Chinese translations of both—President Jackson's letter to the emperor and Roberts's to the chief minister—include forms of politeness involving American expressions of their inferiority. The Americans refused, apparently unaware that these were simply meaningless formulas of courtesy derived from Chinese practice. In February 1833 they left the country in disgust to find a more hospitable welcome in Siam.

They had departed too soon for anyone to inform them that Minh Mang had not only been told of their visit but was willing to have the United States open commercial relations with Vietnam, on condition that the Americans obey the laws of the country, not attempt to set up a trading settlement, and stay in a specified area on the Gulf of Da Nang.

When Roberts and the *Peacock* returned to Vietnam three years later, this time anchoring off Da Nang, he and his men were no longer in any shape to carry out a diplomatic mission. Aside from some hard salted meat and rice, there was no food left. A quarter of the crew were confined to their hammocks by illness, and those who were not under medical treatment had been weakened by previous disease. Roberts himself, still unaware of the emperor's earlier favorable decision, was dying.

Again the emperor in Hue discussed with his mandarins whether he ought to see the American envoy. One of his advisers argued against it, urging that the frontiers be kept sealed against the West as the ancestors had always insisted. But the other was in favor of receiving Roberts, and Minh Mang agreed. The Americans, he said, having come more than forty thousand leagues across the ocean, deserved as much, and he ordered an important delegation to greet them in Da Nang. But it was too late—three years too late. Roberts's illness prevented him from receiving the dignitaries from Hue when they arrived. He died a few weeks later, on July 12, in Macao.

According to the annals of the imperial court, the Vietnamese were not convinced that Roberts really had been ill and had not deliberately snubbed them. Even less of the true facts was known to the Americans. Exactly a century later, a leading American historian, Samuel Flagg Bemis, in a standard work of diplomatic history, dismissed the episode in these words: "The rulers of Cochin-China refused to treat with him [Roberts] except after the preliminary kowtow—a gesture of prostration in obeisance—which, of course, Roberts refused to give."

In the memoirs that were assembled from his journals and letters after his death, Roberts had little good to say of Vietnam. Presumably he described what he thought he had seen and heard, just as many other Americans—officials and writers—would do from the 1950s to the 1970s. Their influence was infinitely greater, for they succeeded in intervening in Vietnamese internal affairs. Yet many of these Americans had more in common than they imagined with Andrew Jackson's special envoy. Like Roberts, they would not only fail to bridge the gap in communication between the two cultures; they would not even realize that such a gap existed.

1.
The
President's
Birthday

JANUARY 1, 1963

The city was still suspended in time that January. Stories of killings in isolated villages filtered in from the troubled countryside. But within the city, all that seemed remote. Parts of Saigon still had the look of a provincial town in southern France of an earlier era—the tree-lined boulevards laid out by Frenchmen before World War I, the quiet residential streets of pleasant villas. The president's brother, a professional archivist, had stripped most of the streets of their old French names. The new street names were a roll call of Vietnamese heroes from other times and places far removed from this lively commercial city turned in on itself and its own immediate concerns.

Saigon had become the capital of an independent nation only a few years earlier. It was easy to forget that the main avenue leading from the cathedral square to the river was no longer the rue Catinat but Freedom Street, and people still spoke of Radio Catinat, the gossip of the cafés where they exchanged old rumors and invented new scandals about the president's family, where they complained about the government and whispered of plots. Where there was smoke there was fire, they said with equanimity as they had for years, of even the wildest rumor. But the fire when it finally came in the summer would be of a different sort.

The wooden stalls were up again along the main shopping streets and people crowded around them in a festive mood, to buy cakes that were special to the season, sprays of peach blossoms and other flowers, clothing, gifts. They were preparing for Tet, the lunar New Year, that time when Vietnamese families reaffirmed their ties with their ancestors and celebrated their oneness with this land and its centuries-old traditions.

Officials went to Gia Long Palace to offer the president their good wishes that January 1. The usual residence of the president, Independence Palace, was still under repair. It had been damaged the previous February when two disaffected air force pilots bombed it.

It was the eighth January 1 that Ngo Dinh Diem received the New Year's greetings of the diplomatic corps. A stocky man about to turn sixty-two, with a smooth and surprisingly young face, he was flanked by members of his cabinet and the national assembly, all, like him, on this formal occasion, in national dress: turban and dark high-necked tunic over white trousers. To some of Diem's critics who preferred western suits (or the Chinese-style jackets of the Communists) this choice of traditional garb was a sign of the conservatism of the Diem regime; his supporters saw it simply as an assertion of the national identity. On other occasions Diem wore white sharkskin suits, the costume Vietnamese had adopted from the French in colonial times, in the days of his youth.

The American ambassador stood among his colleagues at Gia Long Palace that day. Diem was on excellent terms with Frederick E. Nolting, as he had not been with his predecessor who had passed on many disagreeable messages from Washington. True, Nolting had come to Vietnam in May 1961, with instructions from President John F. Kennedy "to build a bridge of confidence strong enough to carry the load of advice and aid which we were giving." But the relationship between the two men went deeper than that. Mutual esteem had grown rapidly between the courtly Virginian and the reserved mandarin from Hue. Nolting accompanied the president on trips around the country and spent hours with him in deep, private conversation. He liked and admired Diem as a person, Nolting had cabled Washington two months after his arrival in Vietnam. Diem was no dictator, he could not be, because he did not relish power for its own sake. "On the contrary, he seems to me to be a man dedicated to high principles for himself and his people." Nolting advised the American government to back Diem to the hilt.

A network of American advisers now covered South Vietnam, American planes and helicopters supported the Vietnamese armed forces and Diem's brother, Ngo Dinh Nhu, the archivist, was in regular contact with the Central Intelligence Agency chief of station John Richardson. It was a good thing there were so many American experts in the country, Diem had once told President Dwight D. Eisenhower, because they could control the use of American aid. But that was before 1961, when Diem was forced to appeal for increased military help against the spreading Communist-led insurgency.

President Kennedy had given him help: more, it turned out, than Diem had bargained for. Now that Americans had their own direct, and costly, investment in the defeat of the insurgency, they were growing impatient of whatever seemed to stand in the way of a government victory. Some Americans had begun to think a major obstacle to success might be the Saigon regime itself.

For years Diem, although profoundly nationalistic and dedicated to the independence of his people, had behaved as if he had no choice but this close relationship with the United States, a country totally unlike his own and one with which the Vietnamese had little in common, not even a shared colonial history. He had only recently come to see the advantages of making other friends as well.

One of them appeared to be the French ambassador, by seniority dean of the diplomatic corps in Saigon. Roger Lalouette stepped forward on behalf of the others that morning, January 1, with words of praise for Diem, his resoluteness and his faith. Lalouette spoke with feeling; he had worked hard to expunge the bitterness and suspicion that had marked Diem's dealings with France over three decades. When Vietnam was still part of the French empire, Diem had resigned as chief minister at the court of Emperor Bao Dai because colonial officials refused to grant his countrymen a greater voice in their own affairs. He was reputed to be an enemy of France by the time he returned in 1954 as head of an independent government of South Vietnam. His regime and its press were then vociferously anti-French, and it was Diem who ordered France to remove its last remaining troops from South Vietnamese soil in 1956.

In 1963 the French imprint was still strong in South Vietnam. The Western culture best known to the Vietnamese was French, and families who could afford to sent their children to French schools. A large colony of Vietnamese lived in France, and there were some fifteen thousand French citizens (many of them naturalized Vietnamese) in Vietnam, where French economic interests ranged from rubber plantations to trade and banking. But the French colonial era was over. As Diem chafed under the encroaching presence of the Americans, he found he could speak freely to the urbane ambassador from Paris who expressed sympathy for his problems.

The previous summer, when the French cruiser *De Grasse* had stopped over at the port of Saigon for several days, Diem made a point of going on board to stay for an hour and drink champagne. When relations between Saigon and Washington were particularly strained, in April 1963, Diem would actually remark to Lalouette, "If the French would send us only two battalions, people would dance on the rue Catinat."

The diplomats who headed the International Control and Supervisory Commission (commonly known as the ICC) also came to pay their respects at Gia Long Palace on January 1. Their presence was a sobering reminder that this was a partitioned country. The ICC had been established by the great powers meeting in Geneva in 1954, to oversee the precarious cease-fire between North and

South Vietnam. A newly appointed officer directed the South Vietnamese mission accredited to the ICC. The post was not without danger; the man he replaced had been kidnapped and tortured to death by a band of insurgents.

Once a mission from the Ho Chi Minh government had been tolerated in Saigon. Appointed in 1955 at the request of the International Control Commission to deal with the French forces still in the South, its job had been to implement the armistice provisions of the Geneva Accords. It remained, accredited to the ICC, when the French left in 1956, its security guaranteed by the Saigon government, its offices and members guarded by Southern police. It was a rare and little-known link between the two unfriendly governments of this divided country.

But the Saigon regime soon had had enough of this delegation from the North. Hanoi appealed to the ICC to intervene on its behalf. But all the International Control Commission could do was evacuate its members in May 1958.

In January 1963 the Ho Chi Minh government protested to the ICC that Diem had again refused, as he did every year, to let people living in the demilitarized zone on both sides of the Ben Hai River cross the river that marked the border between North and South, to exchange visits during the forthcoming Tet celebrations for the Year of the Cat.

This was the latest in a series of rejections to other proposals from the North over the years, to open the frontier to trade and to the free movement of people and mail. The argument for the rejection was that the South had to keep the border closed for its own protection because there was no reciprocal freedom in the Communist North.

During the years following the Geneva Accords doctors of the Southern veterinary service had still crossed the border at the Ben Hai River to give inoculations against bovine plague. Rice was sold unofficially to the North as late as 1959.

Even so, contacts of the population across their common border gradually died, until by 1963 partition had become the basic fact of Vietnamese life.

This partition caused Ho Chi Minh in the North to require extensive aid from his Communist allies for survival. He was therefore balanced precariously between China and the Soviet Union.

Partition had also forced the South away from its natural interdependence with the North into apparent dependence on the United States. But in 1963 Saigon, like Hanoi, was nonetheless an independent nationalist regime. The government was entirely in Vietnamese hands.

Now, only members of the International Control Commission traveled freely between North and South.

Of the three ambassadors on the ICC, the Canadian, Gordon E. Cox, like his countrymen who held the post before him, got on well with the pro-American, anti-Communist government of South Vietnam. The Indian ambassador was president of the ICC, but his country, one of the leading members of the nonaligned bloc of countries, had been highly critical of the Diem regime. Indian diplomats had not been popular in South Vietnam and generally kept to themselves. But Saigon government circles had changed their ideas about at least some Indians, and the present Indian ambassador, the ebullient Ramchundur Goburdhun, had played a vital part in changing them; he had actually become a friend of Ngo Dinh Nhu and his family. The third member of the ICC, the Pole, who would soon be replaced by his government, was the only Communist ambassador stationed in Saigon. The Poles were generally not welcome at the presidential palace.

Greetings arrived for President Diem from more countries than ever before during that last January—from the Third World as from the West. Diem was unalterably opposed to communism, but he had ceased to regard the nonaligned countries of Asia and Africa with automatic suspicion, and these countries in turn no longer dismissed him as an American puppet. In fact the Third World countries had supported Prince Buu-Hoi, Diem's ambassador, for election to the Board of Governors of the International Atomic Energy Agency in Vienna. He defeated the American candidate from Taiwan.

That the Saigon regime had been so widely accepted abroad was a considerable achievement, and not only because of its close ties to the United States—but because the government of South Vietnam was founded on a basic contradiction. It had existed for only a few years and had no history apart from Ngo Dinh Diem, but it was nonetheless the direct heir of the French colonial regime and owed its independence to another man in another place.

Just after Tet in 1941, a frail middle-aged Vietnamese of unremarkable aspect but for his startlingly brilliant eyes made his way across the Chinese border into the jungle of North Vietnam. Less than a mile from the frontier in the mountains of Cao Bang province, he took up residence in a grotto protected by dense vegetation. The man we now know as Ho Chi Minh, the founder and undisputed leader of the Indochinese Communist Party, had come home after thirty years abroad.

As a young man he had decided, like other Vietnamese patriots before him, that only from outside the country could he work to liberate his occupied homeland. By the time he was born in 1890, Vietnam had already lost its independence to France. He studied at the school in Hue founded by Ngo Dinh Diem's father. Some years later, Diem would study there, too. Ho's name then was Nguyen Tat Thanh. In 1911 he shipped out of Vietnam as a cook's helper on a French liner. He worked his way around the world and lived under different aliases wherever revolutionaries gathered. In France, where he wrote bitter articles against the evils of colonial rule and became a founding member of the French Communist Party, in the Soviet Union, and in China.

It was first patriotism and not yet communism, which gave him confidence in Lenin, Ho would recall shortly before his death in 1969. But he studied Marxism-Leninism and worked with the party and came to the conclusion that "only socialism and communism can liberate from slavery the oppressed nations and the working class of the entire world." Westerners would speculate in later years whether Ho Chi Minh was a nationalist or a Communist, but the question would have been meaningless to this dedicated man for whom, like many other Asian Communists, patriotism had become indissolubly linked with the Third International.

World War II was raging when Ho returned to Vietnam. France, defeated in Europe, was defeated in Asia too and was obliged to accept Japanese hegemony over the colony of Indochina that included Vietnam, Laos, and Cambodia. The French colonial administration collaborated with the Japanese and was ruthless in pursuit of Vietnamese revolutionaries. The Communists had taken heavy losses, yet managed to salvage enough of their cadres to regroup in the northern mountains and in south China. In May 1941, Ho Chi Minh presided over a meeting of the Central Committee in his jungle hideout. He brought them, in their desperate need, a new strategy that would transform them from a handful of hunted men into the leaders of an independent Vietnam.

Ho's message was that the war had opened new prospects of freedom in colonial Asia and the time was right to put off talk of social revolution in favor of a broadly based popular movement to rally all patriots regardless of class. Around the nucleus of the Communist Party, he founded the Vietnam Independence League —the Viet Minh. He issued a manifesto calling on his countrymen to unite against the invader as their ancestors had against the Mongols in the thirteenth century, to follow the example of all the heroes who had revolted against the colonial regime, and rise against both the Japanese and the French.

The following year Ho was back in China, a country that Vietnamese revolutionaries usually found more hospitable than colonial Indochina. But it was still the Nationalist China of Chiang Kai-shek, and this time Ho was arrested. He was held prisoner for more than a year, dragged about from prison to prison, and forced to cover many miles on foot.

The American Office of Strategic Services (OSS), forerunner of the Central Intelligence Agency, intervened with his Chinese captors on Ho's behalf because they wanted to use him in their operations against Japan. So, too, did two conservative Vietnamese nationalists in China, who guaranteed in writing that Ho was not a spy but a Vietnamese patriot.

These two men, who traced their nationalist lineage back to an earlier period of the twentieth-century struggle for independence, belonged to an uneasy and shifting alliance of Vietnamese groups and individuals that looked to the China of Chiang Kai-shek for help in liberating Vietnam. Now that victory was so close, the Vietnamese gathered in south China did not want its fruits snatched from them by this new breed of revolutionaries belonging to the Communist Party, whose appetite for power, in their own hands and for their own ends, left little room for outsiders. But they were outmaneuvered by Ho, who, once released, won a coveted subsidy from the Chinese because he had at his command—as these other Vietnamese did not—an organization capable of operating effectively against the Japanese.

Ho did not stop at this triumph over his nationalist rivals. He looked beyond the disintegrating outlines of Nationalist China for American support for the Viet Minh. He finally achieved it in March 1945, when Japan decided the French colonial administration had outlived its usefulness and seized Indochina outright. American officials refused to give a hearing to Vietnamese nationalists in Paris who called at the embassy in the avenue Gabriel to volunteer to serve in any Allied army that would liberate Indochina, provided it did not attempt to restore French rule. But the OSS needed anti-Japanese allies on the territory of Vietnam, and it welcomed Viet Minh offers of collaboration against their common enemy.

The Viet Minh, which had resisted efforts by French colonial troops to drive it out of the northern highlands and launched a series of attacks on French military posts, now joined the Americans in military and sabotage missions against the Japanese, saved the lives of pilots from downed American planes, and collected valuable intelligence.

While this was going on, the Viet Minh pursued another kind of action, radical and far-reaching in its effects, which had nothing to do with the Americans. Month after month, the Viet Minh steadily enlarged the region under its control. It established a proliferating network of people's committees and popular "salvation associations" and perfected in the villages techniques of organization that enabled it to dominate wide areas of the countryside long before it was strong enough to march on any town. Where local opposition existed, it was eliminated by force.

By June 1945, the Viet Minh had extended its authority over one million people in the northern provinces lying east of the Red River and declared them a single liberated zone. Americans arrived to join the first, newly formed units of the Vietnam Liberation Army under Vo Nguyen Giap and to train the Vietnamese in the use of American weapons and in techniques of guerrilla warfare.

The Americans who encountered Ho Chi Minh during this period, in the hut where he had established his headquarters at Tan Trao in the Thai Nguyen "middle region" north of Hanoi, were impressed by his simplicity and his gentle manners. These young OSS agents seem to have treated Ho as no more than a charming, elderly native leader, unaware that they were dealing with a highly intelligent professional revolutionary who had a wide experience of the world and of men (and who was skillful enough to project the image of himself as a humble old man at a time when he was only in his midfifties and at the height of his powers). Despite recurrent attacks of tuberculosis and malaria, he had already spent twenty-five years as one of the major Communist organizers of the Comintern and had personally recruited and trained a large number of followers among his own people by the sheer force of his own personality. Austere and didactic, he followed in the footsteps of scholars from his impoverished native province of Nghe An, which had furnished 90 percent of Vietnam's teachers before the French colonial period (and a great many revolutionaries during it). To his close associates, Ho was said to be fearsome, authoritarian, an extreme autocrat.

In August 1945 Japan surrendered. Allied troops were coming to disarm the defeated enemy. The British, who were expected in the South, did not hide their sympathies for their fellow Europeans, the French. Vietnam north of the Sixteenth Parallel (Da Nang was included) was assigned to the Chinese, who had no friendship for France as a white colonial power and meant to use their occupation of the North to extort concessions from Paris for themselves. The Viet Minh did not feature in Nationalist Chinese calculations about the region any more than it did in those of imperial Britain.

But Ho and his followers had their own plans for the immediate future. At his Tan Trao headquarters, Ho Chi Minh, barely recovered from a serious illness, presided over a meeting of the Communist Party Central Committee.

After he had made clear his directives for action, a congress of sixty delegates was convened on August 16 at Tan Trao. It represented a spectrum of political groups and ethnic minorities and was convened to approve an embryo national government for Vietnam and to confirm Ho Chi Minh as president.

In Hanoi, the Viet Minh organized a series of mass demonstrations that rallied the people behind the new regime and against the French. On August 19 the Viet Minh took over the city.

The Viet Minh moved to seize power in other urban centers throughout the country. In Hue, in central Vietnam, Bao Dai, the last of the Vietnamese emperors, was assured that Ho Chi Minh had the support of the victorious Allies and abdicated in his favor. Bao Dai responded to Ho's summons to Hanoi, where he was given the title of Supreme Advisor to the government, strengthening its claim to legitimacy among the population and the Allies. But the former emperor soon tired of this role and retired to Hong Kong.

Further south, the nationalist movement was splintered. Politico-religious sects and political groups whose opposition to the French had led them to collaborate with the Japanese tried to seize the city of Saigon. But they were displaced by Communist militants who claimed Allied backing for the new anti-Japanese Viet Minh regime in Hanoi that they represented in the South. They assumed power in Saigon as the Committee of the South, in the name of the Ho Chi Minh government.

The nationalist politicians Ho had left in China were still there with troops that had been training in guerrilla warfare and political action under the Chinese and unable to get home. Some Vietnam Nationalist Party (VNQDD) armed forces, though cut off from their leaders in China, did manage to seize territory within Vietnam near the Chinese frontier, but they rapidly lost the initiative to the Viet Minh.

The key center of political action had shifted to Hanoi. On August 22, an official representative of General Charles de Gaulle and a small entourage reached the Northern capital by plane from

China to reclaim North Vietnam for France. The Viet Minh leaders, recalled General Vo Nguyen Giap years afterward, were shocked by the arrival of this French mission.

Pham Van Dong, the mandarin's son who was one of Ho's most devoted followers, had taken the precaution of remaining behind at the secret Tan Trao base north of Hanoi with another member of the Central Committee. But Ho Chi Minh himself was already in the capital, installed in a private house on Hang Ngang Street, one of Hanoi's oldest and busiest thoroughfares, with Giap and several others of his closest associates. From the balcony of the house on Hang Ngang Street, they watched the advance guard of the Chinese army march through the city. Even though the Americans did not seem in any hurry to have the French return to Indochina, the Vietnamese would not be left alone much longer to determine their own future. The Viet Minh had to act. On September 2, some half a million Vietnamese responded to the call to gather at Ba Dinh Square and there heard Ho proclaim their country independent.

The Vietnamese yearning for independence guaranteed wide support to the new government in Hanoi and throughout the country. It was a triumph of organization and the manipulation of symbols by the Communist Party, operating through the Viet Minh, and gave a foretaste of similar successes on a far greater scale that lay ahead.

News of these stirring days in Hanoi roused the countryside in the southern provinces, too, the region Vietnamese called quite simply the Nam Bo, the southern part of the country. The cradle of the Vietnamese nation was in the far north around Hanoi, and it was from the north that the Vietnamese had worked their way southward, fighting and colonizing over a thousand years until they reached the southern delta, then a part of the Khmer Empire (Cambodia). The hardworking and intelligent Vietnamese, impregnated with the influence of Confucian civilization, had impressed their own image on the south, and thereby set it apart from the neighboring plains of Cambodia, whose inhabitants' lives were also regulated by the even tempo of the monsoons, and the rise and fall of the waters of a great river.

If the Vietnamese had succeeded in making the Nam Bo their own, they had not remained entirely unchanged in the process. The equable waters of the Mekong eliminated the need for the kind of dikes that controlled the frightening and unexpected floods of the Red River in the North Vietnamese delta; the land was more fertile than in the central provinces; and wide expanses were still undeveloped. Southern Vietnamese gradually developed distinctive regional characteristics as they adapted over generations to this easier way of life in a region where Cambodia was much closer than Hanoi and more accessible than even the former imperial capital in Hue. It was easy for foreigners to exaggerate the difference between the southern population and the rest of the country, especially since it had long been French policy to insist on the separateness of the Nam Bo. And after 1954, when tightly knit communities of northerners led by Catholic priests arrived in the far south, fleeing from the Communist regime in Hanoi, they were in fact regarded with a hostility that they returned with interest; they remained strangers in the Nam Bo.

But other Vietnamese refugees received a different welcome in the fall of 1945, in the aftermath of World War II. They were peasants, fishermen, businessmen, officials, longtime residents of neighboring Cambodia who fled that country to avoid persecution. These Vietnamese piled all their movable possessions on sampans and set off down the Mekong River. They passed the Cambodian frontier and reached the Nam Bo, where the inhabitants of this tropical world of interlocking canals and rich rice fields greeted the refugees simply as fellow countrymen, even though most spoke with the accents of northern Vietnam. People opened their homes to the newcomers and questioned them eagerly. Had they heard about the new government proclaimed in Hanoi? Was it really true that Vietnam was independent once again? In remote southern villages peasants gathered around those of the refugees who could read and asked them about the signs that were beginning to appear, tacked up on walls. They were directives issued by the southern branch of the Hanoi government that signed its proclamations, "Committee of the Nam Bo."

The revolutionary government had been expelled from Saigon

on September 23 after only a few weeks in power, when the French took over the city with British help. The Vietnamese response was to launch a guerrilla war against the French in the countryside.

In the north, the fledgling Ho Chi Minh government was able to hold Hanoi for fifteen months until French troops drove it out of that city, too, in December 1946. The Viet Minh would regroup in the northern hinterland. It was the start of a war between the Viet Minh and the French fought mostly on Vietnamese territory but also in Laos and Cambodia out of sight and sound of the ancient city of Hanoi, and won—and lost—on these distant battlefields.

SAIGON, JANUARY 3, 1963

The festivities of the season continued at Gia Long Palace, and representatives of the government, the national assembly, the army, and others came to congratulate President Ngo Dinh Diem on his sixty-second birthday.

Their praise was fulsome. For Nguyen Dinh Thuan, Secretary of the Presidency, the most important official in the administration after the president, Diem was "born to be a hero, contrary to the popular saying that heroes are made not born. He snatched Vietnam from total destruction in 1954." Vice-President Nguyen Ngoc Tho, for his part, offered "thanks to the Almighty for having given the country a leader whose genius was outweighed only by his virtue." Later that day Tho, a Buddhist, accompanied Diem to the Catholic Redemptorist Church to join in prayers for the president.

"The Diem regime was not just a single man; it was an entire administration," Secretary Thuan would insist long afterward. "The trouble was not that Diem was a dictator but that he wasn't enough of a dictator. And also, he was a poor judge of men and at the mercy of his informants."

There had been a time when American officials, impatient with their difficult ally, the Vietnamese president, had considered both Secretary Thuan and Vice-President Tho and wondered whether one of them had the stuff to replace Diem.

Thuan, a native of the North, intelligent and efficient, already held several important posts such as deputy secretary of defense (Diem kept the Defense portfolio for himself) and administrator of the American economic aid program. Thuan was one of the few people to whom the president, notoriously reluctant to delegate power, did allow responsibility; and when there was a special mission to be performed in the United States, it was usually entrusted to Thuan. In later years he would wonder whether events might have turned out differently in 1963 had Diem allowed him to go to the meeting of the International Monetary Fund in Washington that spring, giving him the chance to discuss the widening crisis between Saigon and Washington with officials in the American capital.

Vice-President Tho had made clear his own opinion of the regime he served in private contacts with American officials in Saigon, and his language belied his obsequious public admiration for Diem. He complained of the president's reliance on his brother Nhu for advice, his attempt to control the extensive bureaucracy through the secret Can Lao party, his inability to put down the Viet Cong insurgency.

But Vice-President Tho, though a native of the Nam Bo, had no political following among his own people, and even knowledgeable Americans dismissed him as "unimpressive" (General Maxwell Taylor), a "nonentity" (State Department official Paul Kattenberg).

In the months ahead, Diem's difficulties with the Americans would highlight Tho's scarcely hidden lack of enthusiasm for the president and would strain Thuan's personal loyalty to him. As Diem's vice-president, only Tho could bring a semblance of legality to any regime that replaced Diem (and before the year was out Tho would be called upon to do just that). But other men would overthrow the South Vietnamese government; by 1963 American officials did not doubt that only the military could dislodge Ngo Dinh Diem from power.

This tense relationship with the United States would force Diem to a reconsideration of the policies of his government, a government that came into existence in 1954 only because the Viet Minh had finally succeeded in defeating the French.

Some people in South Vietnam, however, continued to look for leadership not to Saigon but to Hanoi.

In October 1954, in the small town of Tra Bong deep in the mountains of the south-central province of Quang Ngai, the population gathered to say farewell to the soldiers and political cadres —their husbands, brothers, and sons—who were about to leave for the North. Together they swore, "We will be faithful at any cost to the revolution, to Uncle Ho."

In the months after the Geneva armistice accords, similar scenes were enacted throughout those areas south of the Ben Hai River occupied by the Viet Minh. Just as the evacuation of the French army from the North had been accomplished in stages, so Viet Minh forces in the South were gathering in regroupment zones from which they would be evacuated over a period of months to the North. It had not been easy for Hanoi to persuade many Southerners to lay down their arms. But Northern leaders sent messages assuring them that this was only a tactical withdrawal; they would return. Had not Ho Chi Minh himself said, "North, Center and South make up integral parts of the country which must be united and liberated"? And, "South Vietnam is our own flesh and blood." Frenchmen were astounded by the discipline of these disappointed Southerners, who had fought so long in apparent autonomy, as they responded to orders from the North to respect the timetable for their evacuation established by the armistice arrangements.

Some troops departed from the Plain of Reeds and sections of the south-central provinces in October 1954. As others awaited their turn to leave, they used the time to instruct the local population in what the Viet Minh radio called "their new mission of political struggle." The Viet Minh army continued to dominate the southernmost part of Vietnam, the Ca Mau Peninsula, as they had for ten years, until February 1955. Before they left they held a festival with the people they were leaving behind, where a message of solidarity from Ho Chi Minh was read aloud.

South of the Seventeenth Parallel, Viet Minh troops remained longest in parts of south-central Vietnam—called Interzone V by the Viet Minh during the war—and continued their work of popular indoctrination until the day of their departure. In November 1954, four months after the end of the Geneva Conference, the Communist radio reported that the port town of Qui Nhon, capital of the South Vietnamese province of Binh Dinh, was the scene of the greatest festival of arts, letters, and sports ever held in Interzone V. The festival concluded with a unanimous resolution protesting alleged violations of the armistice accords by French troops and "the Ngo Dinh Diem band." That January 1955 a Russian ship brought Chinese rice and clothing to the people of Qui Nhon. During the early months of 1955 as Viet Minh troops in the province of Binh Dinh still waited for transport, public meetings were organized to exchange messages with Hanoi in support of Ho Chi Minh and his government. To one such meeting a delegation from Hanoi reported on the health of Ho and on political activities in the Northern capital and attacked Diem and "the American imperialists." Later, the town of Bong Son, where this meeting was held, would become an operations base on a Communist infiltration route.

On May 16, 1955, at Qui Nhon, the last elements of the Vietnam People's Army remaining in South Vietnam boarded Russian and Polish ships for their trip to the North.

Thus the Hanoi government had removed from South Vietnam its regular army units and some political cadres that were too well known to stay hidden. It had satisfied the requirements of the Geneva armistice accords.

At the very same time, the Communist Party was spreading the slogan "To go North means victory, to remain in the South is to bring success." In striking contrast to the Diem regime and its American allies, Hanoi did not encourage refugees. Its policy was to persuade its supporters to remain in the South, where they could be most useful, and preserve their clandestine organization, to make ready for the coming struggle against the Diem government, whatever the form that struggle might assume.

The troops of Ngo Dinh Diem moved in to take over the areas evacuated by the Communists. When they reached southern

Quang Ngai province in October 1954, three weeks after the Viet Minh had left, the Saigon army acted as if it were occupying enemy territory in time of war. Later, the Diem regime extended its authority over other areas with less brutality. Even so, there were old scores to be settled between enemies of the Viet Minh and its supporters, between those who had suffered from the revolutionary regime and those who profited from it. Hanoi filed a series of complaints with the International Control Commission that its adherents were being murdered, some of them buried alive—often in the very same villages that in earlier years had witnessed other such murders, and people buried alive, by the other side.

It was not enough to place the former Viet Minh areas officially under the civil administration of the Diem government. The real problem was to integrate their inhabitants into the South Vietnamese state. But the Saigon regime lacked both the policy and the responsible officials to deal justly and imaginatively with the newly recovered regions and with former members of the Viet Minh in general.

The Diem government did prove surprisingly effective in rooting out elements of the underground revolutionary apparatus, more effective than most observers realized at the time. But too often local officials failed to distinguish between hard-core revolutionary cadres and people who had collaborated with the Viet Minh out of simple patriotism and now asked only to return to normal peacetime life in an independent South Vietnam. From indifference or prejudice, the Saigon regime tolerated the persecution of numerous patriots for no other reason than that they had once served in the Communist-led resistance, and it thereby alienated many in the Southern countryside.

JANUARY 1963

Few Tet celebrations were held in the southwestern areas of the Nam Bo that were inhabited largely by ethnic Cambodians. For them the New Year came only in April when the Vietnamese Communist-led guerrillas operating in the region would announce a truce so that the local bonzes (who professed a different Buddhism from that practiced in most of Vietnam) could travel to the frontier and visit their religious superiors in Cambodia.

The frontier with Cambodia was officially closed before 1963 began. This was one country of the Third World with which Ngo Dinh Diem's relations were bad. The very existence of Prince Norodom Sihanouk of Cambodia and his government in Phnom Penh seemed a challenge to Saigon because Sihanouk maintained good relations with Communist as well as non-Communist countries, an even-handedness that was anathema to Ngo Dinh Diem.

The two men had little in common. Sihanouk was the grandson of a king and had been a king himself until this volatile man decided to abdicate and become actively involved in the Cambodian political life that he now dominated. Among the peasant masses he still commanded the allegiance due a hereditary monarch, a god-king.

Cambodia, unlike Vietnam, was not a partitioned country, so the Khmers were spared the political pressures and economic distortions inherent in the situation of South Vietnam. Sihanouk, in January 1963, seemed to have the best of both worlds. From the Americans he received aid, as he did from the Communist powers. He had escaped the dangers that hung over the Ngos, of dependence on a single, too powerful ally.

There were some Khmer Communists in the country, and others in North Vietnam and in Paris. But they were a small minority. The only threat Sihanouk feared that January was from outside the country, from the Vietnamese.

Sihanouk ended 1962 by thanking Hanoi prime minister Pham Van Dong for recognition of Cambodia's neutrality and borders—assurances he had been unable to extract from Diem, who shared a common (and disputed) frontier with Cambodia as Hanoi did not. For the time being, South Vietnam, however unfriendly, was a buffer between Phnom Penh and Communist Hanoi, and Pham Van Dong could permit himself a generosity he would not show after 1975 when Hanoi had taken over the South, even when Cambodia itself was Communist. But Sihanouk, like many of his countrymen, did not have much confidence in the Vietnamese, any Vietnamese, and in February 1963 he set off on a state visit to Communist China, where he received strong assurances of support.

He had no illusions even then. The future of Cambodia depended on the course of events in South Vietnam.

And in South Vietnam, on January 2, 1963, which happened to be the eve of the birthday of Ngo Dinh Diem, two thousand South Vietnamese soldiers, supported by helicopters and amphibious personnel carriers, failed to dislodge a Communist-led force one-tenth its size from a fortified village near the western extremity of the Plain of Reeds, still a Communist stronghold. The Saigon troops ignored the instructions of their American military advisers and took heavy casualties. Three Americans were killed. The Communist-led 514th Local Force Battalion escaped during the night.

This was the encounter at Ap Bac that was to assume a significance out of all relation to its true importance and precipitate the events leading to the overthrow of the Diem government.

2.
The
Eager
Americans

In retrospect, it would seem that Diem's "American problem" had been inevitable ever since the day Secretary Thuan arrived in Washington nearly two years earlier carrying a message from President Diem. It was June 1961, and Diem wanted to build up his armed forces to counter the growing threat from the Viet Cong. He needed increased American military aid to add more men to the South Vietnamese army, and he asked for American advisers to train them. He did not want U.S. combat forces—he was opposed to American troops' fighting on Vietnamese soil (unless there were an open invasion from the North). He specifically requested "a considerable expansion of the United States Military Advisory Group [MAAG]" in the South. "We have not become accustomed to being asked for our own views as to our needs," he had noted dryly in a letter to President Kennedy.

Diem's confidence in the new American president had been shaken by Kennedy's decision to give up trying to impose a pro-American regime across the border in Laos. The rugged highlands of that isolated kingdom lying south of China were part of the same mountain range that stretched along the length of Communist North Vietnam and the non-Communist south-central provinces of South Vietnam. Farther west, the Mekong River marked the frontier between the Laotian lowlands and Thailand.

During the Eisenhower years, the ruling lowland Lao elite had splintered into warring factions; Americans had intervened to back rightist elements against neutralists and Communists. The only winner had been the Pathet Lao—the Laotian offshoot of the Indochinese Communist Party founded by Ho Chi Minh in 1930.

Before leaving the White House Eisenhower had warned Kennedy he might have to go to war in Laos, and he would have to fight alone if America's allies in the Southeast Asia Treaty Organization (SEATO) refused to help: the royal government had to be defended against the Pathet Lao.

The outgoing president had decided Laos was "the key to the entire area" because American military planners assumed that if North Vietnam, China, or both launched an attack, they would move through the Mekong River valley from Laos into Thailand and perhaps Burma. South Vietnam was seen, in the words of General Maxwell Taylor, as "only a secondary theater in which the campaign would probably take the form of a thrust by North Vietnamese divisions down the Vietnamese littoral toward Saigon."

American strategists, in their concern for Thailand (a member of the SEATO alliance), had obviously discounted the militant nationalism of the Hanoi government and misjudged its priorities; and SEATO military planning, as Taylor wrote, "had little bearing on the situation which was arising from the salami tactics of the Pathet Lao in Laos and the clandestine infiltration of guerrilla reinforcements into South Vietnam by way of the Laotian panhandle."

Kennedy would have had Eisenhower's personal support if he decided to fight in Laos. But the young president was chastened by one disaster—the rout of the invasion he had authorized against Fidel Castro at the Bay of Pigs—and did not want to risk another. When Kennedy put hard questions to the chiefs of staff, he found them ready to go to war in Laos but unable to promise an easy victory, or any victory at all, without the right to use nuclear weapons.

Was there no way to avoid turning Laos into an international battlefield? Kennedy decided to adopt the course the French and British governments had urged for years: accept the neutrality of Laos and abandon the impossible attempt to create an American satellite on the border of Communist China. The veteran diplomat W. Averell Harriman became the architect of the new policy. The warring Laotian factions were to be pressed to make peace among themselves and form a coalition government headed by the neutralist Prince Souvanna Phouma. Laotian neutrality was to be guaranteed by international treaty.

Even the Soviet Union was ready to accept a neutral Laos, the Soviet chairman Nikita Khrushchev told Kennedy when they met in Vienna. The Geneva Conference on Laos opened in May 1961 and dragged on for fourteen months until three Laotian princes representing the rival factions agreed on a coalition government led by Prince Souvanna Phouma, and the nations assembled in Geneva recognized its neutrality.

For Harriman, once Franklin Roosevelt's ambassador and now Kennedy's, the conference was a personal triumph. He had wished to give Kennedy an alternative to military intervention in Laos and had succeeded. An old hand at negotiating with the Russians, he worked out an agreement with the Soviet deputy foreign minister G. M. Pushkin whereby the Russians accepted responsibility for assuring the compliance of their Communist allies with the accord that neutralized Laos: the North Vietnamese would remove their troops and refrain from using Laotian territory for military or subversive action against the South. (Harriman would have liked to arrange a peaceful settlement in Vietnam, too, and had approached the delegation from Hanoi about that and been rebuffed. He did not consult the South Vietnamese, who had strict instructions to reject any and all proposals for international negotiations on Vietnam, something many other delegates expected to follow the conference on Laos.)

Diem was not impressed with Harriman's triumph. He had sent a delegation to Geneva to oblige the Americans, but he was at a loss to understand how the Americans could talk about the neutrality of Laos while pursuing the opposite policy in South Vietnam. Hanoi, for one, regarded the two countries as part of the same strategic area, as had other Vietnamese over the centuries, at least in wartime. At the start of the war against France, Viet Minh troops had been ordered out of Hue westward into the mountains and jungles of Laos, far from the unprotected Vietnamese coast that was vulnerable to air and sea attack. Other Viet Minh forces, the fierce Ba To guerrillas, had preceded them. These troops sought out the pathways needed by the Ho Chi Minh government to maintain its lifeline with the safe Laotian hinterland and with the Vietnamese south. It was the beginning of the network of trails and roads that would enable the Communists to supply and reinforce the Viet Cong and come to be known as the Ho Chi Minh Trail.

In 1961, Diem might have accepted a partitioned Laos if that were the only way to cut the Ho Chi Minh Trail, even (he said) a hostile Laos where he would have been free to harass Communist bases and communication lines. But not this "neutrality" preached by Harriman that would stigmatize South Vietnamese forces as aggressors if they entered Laos, while leaving the North Vietnamese free to use Laotian territory as they chose because the treaty lacked any enforceable safeguards.

The Saigon government under pressure from the Americans reluctantly signed the treaty neutralizing Laos in July 1962. The Hanoi government also signed, under pressure from the Soviet Union. Foreigners could decide what they liked at Geneva; Diem knew as well as the Northern leaders themselves that the heirs of the Viet Minh were not going to surrender their hard-won positions in Laos.

Averell Harriman, who had argued with Diem before about the advantages of neutrality, had returned to Saigon to see the

Vietnamese president when he balked at signing the Geneva treaty. The meeting, according to Ambassador Nolting, was "stormy."

"They took a violent dislike to each other from their first meeting in 1961," Secretary Thuan said years later. "It was very unfortunate. Diem did not understand Harriman's role in the Democratic Party and Harriman did not understand Diem."

Thuan traced back to the first encounter of the two men in 1961 Harriman's open hostility to President Diem that took on much greater consequences by 1963.

The traffic of men and supplies along the Ho Chi Minh Trail increased after the Geneva Conference. "Some people called it the Harriman Memorial Highway," Ambassador Nolting noted. In the highlands of Laos and North Vietnam, where the same ethnic minority groups lived on both sides of the border, the frontier was more theoretical than real. And in the two northeastern provinces it had occupied ever since the end of the war with France, the Pathet Lao remained entrenched as ever. Many of the six to ten thousand men the Hanoi regime had in Laos stayed on; only forty of them departed through international checkpoints.

By 1963 a de facto partition existed in Laos, and CIA-led tribesmen were fighting Communists on Laotian soil and local factions were at war with each other. Harriman went to Moscow to ask for help in April 1963, but it seemed the Russians had no control over their Communist allies after all; they could do nothing.

However, Harriman had found a way for President Kennedy to avoid sending American troops to Laos, and his work in Laos raised him even higher in the president's esteem. In 1963 he was promoted to the post of under secretary of state for political affairs, the third most important post in the State Department, and he had excellent connections with the White House staff, which were useful in an administration where the president liked to act as his own secretary of state and did not think much of some other members of the State Department.

Nothing had happened to lessen Harriman's dislike of Diem —a dislike both personal and unforgiving—and he was soon well placed to translate that dislike into policy. He would lead the fight for a coup against Diem, said Robert Kennedy, the brother of the president. "It became an emotional matter . . . and in fact, his advice was wrong. In fact, he started us down a road which was quite dangerous."

Harriman was only one of Kennedy's men who were having second thoughts about Ngo Dinh Diem. There had been a new mood in Washington since 1961, when the Kennedy administration had taken office with a flourish of high-sounding rhetoric. They were men of action—"a new generation of Americans," Kennedy had called them, "born in this century, tempered by war, disciplined by a hard and bitter peace."

These new cold warriors were eager to use the great power at their command, confident of their ability to deal with crisis abroad, never questioning their right to intervene in Vietnam as they chose. Kennedy had been galvanized by a speech of Khrushchev in January 1961, which the young president read as a declaration that the Soviet Union intended to promote wars of liberation in the Third World; from this it followed that the Americans had no choice but to intervene wherever Communist guerrillas emerged in the developing countries. Unfortunately, Khrushchev's speech was misunderstood in Washington; in fact, it had been meant as a call for peaceful coexistence, a rebuttal of the militant line preached by the Chinese Communists.

The eager men of the Kennedy administration were fascinated by the challenge of revolutionary warfare. Kennedy himself, according to General Maxwell Taylor, "repeatedly emphasized the desire to utilize the situation in Vietnam to study and test the techniques and equipment related to counterinsurgency, and hence he insisted that we expose our most promising officers to the experience of service there."

The Kennedy men were out to prevent Communist domination of South Vietnam and proposed to do nothing less than "create in that country a viable and increasingly democratic society." In May 1961, the president had ordered "a series of mutually supporting actions of a military, political, economic, psychological and covert character . . ." and the Defense Department was directed to examine "the size and composition of forces which would be desirable in case of a possible commitment of U.S. forces to Vietnam." At the same time, the Americans were going to try "to strengthen President Diem's popular support within Vietnam by reappraisal and negotiation, under the direction of Ambassador Nolting. . . ."

The Americans were more directly involved in Vietnamese affairs than ever before by 1963, and they expected more from the Vietnamese in return.

A local newspaper, writing about tensions between the Saigon regime and American officialdom, quoted a Vietnamese saying: "Daily friction leads to no more love left."

To Diem and his brother Nhu, the Geneva settlement had meant that South Vietnam could not have any firm bases in Laos to defend itself against the Communists. Diem and Nhu had begun to think the unthinkable, that they might have to make some sort of accommodation with the North.

The delegation from Saigon had walked out of the Geneva Conference before the signing of the accord on Laos in July 1962. They had returned only when John Kennedy sent a letter to Ngo Dinh Diem assuring him the Americans did not intend to abandon South Vietnam.

Laos was a special case requiring "concessions," Kennedy had written, because of "the complete ineffectiveness of the Royal Laotian Army, as demonstrated again in the recent action [against the Pathet Lao] at Nam Tha. It is only the threat of American intervention that has enabled us to come as far as we have in Laos." But American strategy in Vietnam "is based on the fierce desire of your people to maintain their independence and their willingness to engage in an arduous struggle for it . . . our policy toward Vietnam must and will continue as it has been since my administration took office. We have helped and shall continue to help your country defend itself."

The additional aid authorized by Kennedy had already affected the balance of forces in the South, and the situation was no longer so dramatic as it had seemed to Brigadier General Edward G. Lansdale when he visited the country in January 1961 and found that the "Viet Cong have the initiative and most of the control in the region from the jungled foothills of the High Plateau north of Saigon all the way south down to the Gulf of Siam, excluding the big city area of Saigon-Cholon." Lansdale had reported that the South was in critical condition and should be handled "as a combat area of the cold war, as an area requiring emergency treatment." He believed a coup d'état would be attempted against Diem soon "unless the United States makes it clear that we are backing him as the top elected man."

It had been Lansdale's first visit to Vietnam since 1956. Diem wanted his old friend and supporter to return, and Lansdale was more than ready to go; but Diem's several messages to Washington asking for him went unanswered because of opposition to the unorthodox general variously reported at the Pentagon and the State Department.

John Kennedy had been jolted to read Lansdale's memorandum on his Vietnam trip; Eisenhower had spoken to him of Laos but had said nothing about Vietnam. "This is the worst one we've got, isn't it?" the young president said.

In May 1961, Vice-President Lyndon B. Johnson arrived in Saigon to demonstrate American support for the Southern regime. The Americans had decided to increase their aid to the Vietnamese, to pay the expenses of another 20,000 men in the army who would be trained in guerrilla warfare, and to add 100 American advisers to the 685 men in the U.S. Military Assistance Advisory Group (MAAG).

Lyndon Johnson got on well with Diem; with Nolting, Kennedy's ambassador, too. Nolting remarked on the immediate rapport between the outgoing Texan and the mandarin from Hue, surprising in two such different men: the democratic politician sensitive to public opinion and eager for popular approval, and the other, paternalistic, reserved, seeking respect rather than popularity.

In his report to Kennedy, Johnson described Diem as a complex figure beset by many problems, with "admirable qualities but . . . remote from the people . . . [and] surrounded by persons less admirable and capable than he." Johnson toasted Diem in warm champagne as "the Winston Churchill of Asia."

The letter Secretary Thuan brought to Washington requesting stepped-up American aid was a reply to a message from President Kennedy delivered by Lyndon Johnson. Kennedy had inquired about the sort of help South Vietnam needed from the United States. After the Bay of Pigs and the about-face in policy on Laos, he feared his administration might project an image of weakness to the Soviet Union that would threaten American interests in other parts of the world. "We just can't have another defeat this year in Vietnam," he said.

Ever since May, the planners in Washington had been discussing proposals for sending American combat troops to bolster South Vietnam. When the president met with the National Security Council on October 11, one plan placed before him called for 11,000 ground combat SEATO (mainly American) forces as a start to be sent into the central highlands, where they would fight against the Viet Cong supported by 11,800 air, naval, and other forces. Another plan involved fewer men with a more limited mission: small military forces at Da Nang and another port in the South to establish an "American presence." Four hundred Special Forces were already serving in Vietnam; they had been dispatched by Kennedy in May.

Now, on October 11, he directed the sending of an air force unit, a detachment of bombers equipped for counterinsurgency warfare, to serve under MAAG on a training mission. A few weeks later, Secretary of Defense Robert McNamara authorized the participation of these planes in combat operations if at least one Vietnamese crew member were aboard.

At this same meeting of the National Security Council, Kennedy decided on the dispatch of an interdepartmental mission headed by his personal military adviser, General Maxwell Taylor, to look into the question of how the United States could be most effective in Vietnam.

Taylor was instructed by the president to "bear in mind that the initial responsibility for the effective maintenance of the independence of South Vietnam rests with the people and government of that country. . . . While the military part of the problem is of great importance in South Vietnam, its political, social and economic elements are equally significant, and I shall expect your appraisal and your recommendations to take full account of them."

The Taylor mission reached Saigon to find Vietnamese morale in some quarters badly shaken by the growing boldness of the Viet Cong. It also found the Americans serving in Vietnam sharply divided. At MAAG, which had been training and supplying the Vietnamese army for a Korea-type war, the Viet Cong was seen, unsurprisingly, as a military problem to be dealt with as such. Other Americans, civilians at the embassy and elsewhere, argued that increased military aid to the Diem government would be useless without political reforms to enlist popular support.

General Taylor had talked with Diem about sending a military task force—ostensibly to deal with the devastation caused by a flood in the Mekong Delta, which happened to be a center of Viet Cong strength—logistic troops mostly, to participate in flood relief, but prepared to engage in combat operations where necessary. Taylor had in mind a force of perhaps about eight thousand men.

Diem seemed ready to accept these troops, which was unlike him; as out of character as his recent requests to the Americans for combat forces. He had even asked for a treaty with the United States to commit the Washington government to the support of South Vietnam. Secretary Thuan and other highly placed officials would have welcomed American ground forces, but Diem was known to believe the South ought to rely on its own people to defend itself; Thuan had had a hard time persuading him to request even limited help from the Americans.

In Washington that November, Kennedy, given the choice of sending a force to assist in flood relief—now set at eight to ten thousand men—or twenty-five to forty thousand men to engage in military operations, ruled against both. He decided to put off to a later date the decision to send combat troops to Vietnam.

Other recommendations of the Taylor mission were accepted by the American president, and Diem learned from Ambassador Nolting that the United States "was prepared to join in a sharply increased joint effort to avoid a further deterioration in the situation."

Taylor had identified these weaknesses on the Vietnamese government side: inadequate intelligence, the army's lack of initiative and its defensive posture, as well as poor command and control, the inadequacies of governmental administrative procedures. The Americans envisaged a multifaceted counterinsurgency program to deal with these and other problems. Although they saw no reason to help Diem build up his own forces as much as he wished, they were ready to provide an increased airlift flown by Americans for Vietnamese troops, small craft operated by Americans to control the inland waterways and coastal waters, and other specialized personnel and equipment notably in the field of intelligence.

And advisers—military men, and civilian administrators to participate in the machinery of government, and "joint survey personnel" to go into each of the provinces and "assess social, political, intelligence and military factors bearing on . . . counterinsurgency program." Nolting was instructed to tell Diem that the Americans envisaged "a much closer relationship than the present one of acting in an advisory capacity only. We would expect to share in the decision making process in the political, economic and military fields as they affected the security situation."

Diem listened with mixed emotions; he had not anticipated anything like this. "Vietnam does not want to be a protectorate," he protested.

There was more: the Americans expected him not only to mobilize the nation and overhaul the military and command structure, but to bring non-Communist opposition elements into the government. They wanted changes "that will be recognized as having real substance and meaning . . . real administrative, political and social reforms and a real effort to widen its base that will give maximum confidence to the American people, as well as to world opinion that our efforts are not directed toward the support of an unpopular or ineffective regime."

But it was hardly realistic to expect Diem to rewrite the history of the past six or seven years and at such a time. Vice-President Tho, who would join the conspiracy that overthrew Diem in 1963, spoke years later with some sympathy of the late president and of the impossible choice imposed on Diem by the "crushing and contradictory demands of the Americans that he win the war and at the same time turn South Vietnam into an American-style democracy."

At first, Diem balked at the American demands. In November 1961, Nolting reported to Washington that Secretary Thuan had told him Diem wondered whether the United States were getting ready to back out on Vietnam, "as, he suggested, we had done in Laos."

Once before, when the Americans were pressing Diem for changes in his conduct of the war and of the government, Nolting's predecessor had observed, "Should he not do so, we may well be forced, in [the] not too distant future, to undertake [the] difficult task of identifying and supporting alternate leadership."

Now the State Department, not for the first time, began to look around for a more docile ally to replace the South Vietnamese president.

But the Americans finally agreed to compromise, and on December 4, Nolting cabled Washington that Diem had accepted: it was understood that "the fundamental responsibility of the government of Vietnam for the conduct of the war will not be impaired." But there was to be "a closer and more effective relationship" between the two governments, a "partnership." For the first time, American uniformed personnel would participate in operational missions with the South Vietnamese; and American advisers were going to be consulted more closely "in planning the conduct of the security effort."

The first consignment of helicopters with pilots and ground crews disembarked from the aircraft ferry *Core* in December: more than thirty helicopters and some four hundred men. In January 1962, the first American air combat support mission was flown in support of a Vietnamese unit under attack.

General Paul D. Harkins was named to a newly created post: commander, United States Military Assistance Command–Vietnam (MACV). On all military questions, he reported through military channels directly to the Joint Chiefs of Staff and the secretary of defense.

More American military and intelligence advisers arrived in the spring and "began to produce measurable if undramatic results," Taylor wrote. "The new military equipment, particularly the helicopters and armored personnel carriers, . . . had some effect." When he made a return visit to Vietnam in September, Taylor noted that progress had been uneven; and least evident in the political, administrative, and social fields. Diem was still "difficult," acutely sensitive to encroachments on Vietnamese sovereignty, and "increasingly a target of criticism for the resident members of the American press who had never liked him."

"The debate in the Kennedy administration over Vietnam policy . . . revolved around rival analyses about the nature of guerrilla warfare and predictions about the effects of alternative ways of dealing with it," according to Roger Hilsman. Once a guerrilla fighter himself against the Japanese in Burma during World War II, Hilsman was director of the Bureau of Intelligence and Research at the State Department until 1963, when he was appointed assistant secretary of state for the Far East, replacing Harriman, who became under secretary of state.

Hilsman was an articulate proponent of what he described as a "political approach" that emphasized "political, economic and social action into which very carefully calibrated military measures were interwoven": "protect the people, don't chase the Viet Cong, just use the troops to protect the people. Then behind the screen you have social and political reform—education, everything." And the sea of people in which Mao said the guerrillas swim like fish would dry up.

Hilsman had endorsed the strategic hamlet program proposed by the British Advisory Mission, which had arrived in Vietnam at Diem's invitation in September 1961. "Perhaps the highest ratio of talent to numbers seen in Vietnam previously or since," observed William Colby, then CIA station chief, of this team of retired British civil servants who had fought with success against another Communist insurgency in Malaya.

The strategic hamlet program had been launched with fanfare by Ngo Dinh Nhu, the president's brother, in 1962. Peasants were being regrouped in villages that were then fortified, as they had been regrouped in Malaya during the Communist insurgency there, to secure them from guerrilla attack and to prevent the insurgents from levying recruits and supplies.

The Saigon regime was trying to extend its control outside the cities of the South to the villages where most Vietnamese still lived. Composed of several hamlets and closed off from the outside world, often surrounded by a hedge of bamboo or some other protective foliage, the village was the basic administrative unit of Vietnam. Nhu had tried to increase the influence of the government in the villages when the Republican Youth movement was founded in 1961. But by that time the Viet Cong had already infiltrated wide areas and systematically assassinated many local officials, including some of the best in the South.

More than half the hamlets in the country had been transformed into strategic hamlets by spring 1963, some of them better placed and organized to resist attack than others. Nhu was determined to have all the hamlets of South Vietnam surrounded by stockades or barbed wire in record time. The Americans supported the program as a strategy to defeat the Viet Cong. Nhu saw it as that and more. He talked of a social and economic revolution in the villages, a way out of underdevelopment without sacrificing freedom and democracy. Both Diem and Nhu embraced the strategic hamlet program as an opportunity to build a new political base among the peasants, to bypass the unhelpful critics of the government in the urban middle class, and to offset the bloated political power of the army.

Nhu speeded up the pace of the program as relations with the Americans worsened. To curry favor with the president's brother, local officials reported strategic hamlets even where they did not exist. Yet, "hundreds of thousands of peasants . . . slept every night with newfound peace behind their hamlet fences and dutifully gave thanks to the patriarchy of Ngo Dinh Diem for it, as the Republican

Youth told them to." These words were written by Dennis Duncanson, a member of the British Advisory Mission.

In Hanoi, in July 1963, the Communist general Nguyen Chi Thanh called the idea of establishing strategic hamlets in order to isolate the Viet Cong "a relatively clearheaded conclusion. . . . Unfortunately for them [the Americans], they are beginning to be assailed by serious misgivings about the correctness of the plan."

The Americans were concerned that the plan was overextended, and they were impatient with the leadership of Diem and Nhu. Hilsman would say later, "The point is that we were all grossly misinformed about the convolutions, the thickness, the obstacles that Vietnamese culture represents . . . nobody in the world . . . really had the knowledge that would permit the kind of social engineering we were undertaking . . ."

But that spring of 1963, no such doubts assailed the newly appointed assistant secretary of state for Far Eastern Affairs. Hilsman was confident the Americans knew all they needed to know to defeat the Viet Cong, provided Diem and Nhu did not stand in their way.

3.
Why Can't a Puppet Act Like a Puppet?

JANUARY 1963

The young reporters were bitter and angry. Only a few American newsmen were stationed in Saigon at this time; among the best and the brightest of them were the bureau chiefs of the wire services, Malcolm Browne of Associated Press and Neil Sheehan of United Press International, and David Halberstam, who worked for *The New York Times*. In January 1963, they could have summed up their feelings in two words: *Ap Bac*. This was the place at the edge of the Plain of Reeds where an outnumbered insurgent battalion had stood its ground and fought, instead of melting away as guerrillas usually did when confronted with American helicopters and the massed force of the Vietnamese army. The commander of the government troops had refused to order additional men into the battle even when called on to do so by the American officer who was his military adviser, and by his own Vietnamese superior. Eventually these troops did engage the enemy but disregarded the Americans supposed to advise them; three Americans were killed, one helicopter was destroyed, and five others were forced down by enemy fire. Government casualties were high.

John Paul Vann, a lieutenant colonel, the senior military adviser for the region and one of the favorite sources for the American reporters, told them it had been a miserable performance, "like it always is." Another officer who was respected by the young journalists, Lieutenant Colonel Fred Ladd, would say later that strained personal relations between certain of the American advisers and their Vietnamese opposite numbers had contributed to the outcome at Ap Bac. He, like others, believed the battle was singled out for more attention than it deserved. But the angry newsmen blamed Ngo Dinh Diem for everything that had gone wrong: it was the fault of Diem that his officers did not know how to fight Communists; the truth was that he did not really want to fight them.

The reporters were indignant when high-ranking American officers saw fit to present the Ap Bac operation in a favorable light. Admiral Harry D. Felt, United States commander in the Pacific, flew into Saigon for a joint press conference with General Paul D. Harkins, head of the American military assistance command in Vietnam. The two men denied that Ap Bac had been a defeat for the Saigon government, and Felt scolded reporters for being so critical and told them to "get on the team." Harkins said, "I consider it a victory. We took the objective." He seemed unconcerned that the enemy had departed the day before the Saigon forces took back the hamlet.

The most knowledgeable members of the Vietnamese community, men with the greatest reason to fear a Communist victory, treated the encounter at Ap Bac calmly; for them it was only a single episode in a struggle that would be punctuated by defeats as well as victories, with battles on shifting fronts, some political, others military. But the newsmen had little interest and less faith in such long-term perspectives.

Roger Hilsman and Michael Forrestal, a member of the White House National Security staff, paid a brief visit to Saigon at about this time. Later in the year they would play a part in the events leading to the overthrow of Ngo Dinh Diem. But when they returned to Washington that winter Forrestal reported to the president: "The American press representatives are bitter and will seize on anything that goes wrong and blow it up as much as possible. The My Tho operation [at Ap Bac], for example, contained some mistakes but it was not nearly the botched up disaster the press made it appear to be."

David Halberstam, *The New York Times* correspondent, had come to Vietnam to cover a war in a country that he believed to be "perhaps one of only five or six nations in the world that is truly vital to U.S. interests"—not, of course, because this land south of the Seventeenth Parallel happened to be Vietnamese but because it bordered a Communist state and had spawned Communist-led guerrilla forces on its own territory. Washington and Saigon seemed to Halberstam and his colleagues to share a common enemy; it did not occur to any of them to question the necessity of an American role in the struggle against the Viet Cong. In this, they shared the outlook of their sources. John Paul Vann and other Americans serving as military advisers or working for the CIA station in Saigon were highly motivated professionals who were certain of their patriotic duty to help fight this war and were imbued with a sense of urgency about winning it.

All these Americans seemed to be far more committed to pursuing the war than were most Vietnamese, which might have given the young newsmen pause. But in their irritation with the Vietnamese system they had found a scapegoat—the president of the Republic of Vietnam, Ngo Dinh Diem.

They seized the chance to air their pent-up resentment of the Saigon government. Diem seemed to have lost his popularity and turned his back on democracy. His regime was authoritarian and incompetent—not even "a strong and dictatorial government which can guide its population," Halberstam later wrote, but only "this aloof inefficient self-defeating dictatorship"—and Halberstam, Sheehan, and Browne were determined to get that story to the American public.

"Whether they intended it or not their articles reflected their bitter hatred for the Diem government and their avowed purpose (stated to a number of reporters in Saigon) to bring down the Diem government." The person who wrote these words in his Kennedy memoir was Pierre Salinger, the press secretary of President Kennedy. Salinger added: "It is a deep question of reportorial ethics whether the destruction of a government is within the legitimate framework of journalistic enterprise."

Diem would be peculiarly vulnerable to criticism by these few young American journalists as this year of 1963 unfolded—not because he had ceased to be popular among his own people, as many of his American critics claimed, but because he had never been popular, except in the United States.

A handful of Americans had created a myth about the "miracle" Diem had wrought in South Vietnam. They had sold and oversold him to the American government and press, giving rise to inflated and unreal expectations in the United States for which Diem (and Vietnam) was now going to pay dearly.

Supreme Court Justice William O. Douglas had never dreamed anything like that could happen when he introduced Ngo Dinh Diem to John F. Kennedy ten years before.

The host of the luncheon at the Supreme Court that day in May 1953 was one of the most eminent jurists in the United States, a well-known liberal who refused to believe the American government could find nothing better to do in Vietnam than prop up an unpopular government in a losing war. There had to be another way out of this Asian dilemma, and William O. Douglas thought he had found one.

Justice Douglas had recently visited the remote region stretching from the Chinese frontier to the South China Sea where few Americans had ever set foot. He returned frustrated by the American support for the French colonial war in Indochina against Ho Chi Minh's Viet Minh. The policy of the Eisenhower administration did not flow from any knowledge of the area. It was driven by the impulses of the Republican administration's cold warriors, just as the fateful decisions of the Democratic Kennedy administration would be a decade later. Since the time of President Harry S Truman, Washington policy-makers had agreed that the national interest required Americans to intervene abroad to prevent the spread of international communism. But did that condemn the Eisenhower administration to support a colonial war, as this certainly was, despite the cold war rhetoric belatedly invoked by the French to justify it, a war that they seemed unable to win?

In the French-occupied cities of Vietnam, Justice Douglas had been approached by men who introduced themselves to the visiting American as members of a nationalist underground movement. They explained that they were patriots opposed to French rule, opposed also to Ho Chi Minh and the Communists even though the Viet Minh were the only Vietnamese actually fighting the French.

Douglas had been impressed by these people who accepted French protection against the Viet Minh because they could not have survived without it, yet dreamed of a free Vietnam. Their fellow countrymen called them *tram chan,* people who hide under a blanket; the French, exasperated by their refusal to join in the struggle against the Communist-led enemy, labeled them *attentistes,* fence-sitters. They would have nothing to do with the Vietnamese government headed by Emperor Bao Dai who ruled the territory under French control because they did not trust Bao Dai to wrest independence from France.

But Douglas was told of another man who had left the country before he arrived: a man who, unlike Bao Dai, was, he wrote, "revered by the Vietnamese because he is honest and independent and stood firm against French influence—a hero in Central and North Vietnam, with a considerable following in the South too"— Ngo Dinh Diem.

Diem had been forced to leave his homeland hastily in 1950 when the Viet Minh pronounced a death sentence against him, and the French authorities who disliked his stubborn nationalism told him they could not guarantee his safety. He had gone to the United States and was staying with the Maryknoll Fathers when Douglas persuaded him to go to Washington.

"I wanted some important people to meet Ngo Dinh Diem . . . I invited Mike Mansfield and Jack from the Senate . . . and there

were two or three from the State Department that I invited."
Young Kennedy had visited Vietnam himself in 1951 and angered
the French military commander, General de Lattre de Tassigny, by
questioning how Vietnamese could be expected to fight the Viet
Minh if they had nothing better to fight for than to keep their
country a part of France.

Kennedy had never met Diem, "and I wanted them to meet,"
Douglas recalled, "because he was one of the senators who was
traveling and observing, and who was critical of American foreign
policy." He joined Senator Mansfield at the Supreme Court lunch
that day in "examining Diem and questioning him closely."

They were impressed by the confidence and the depth of feeling revealed by this normally shy man when he spoke of his country
and his self-appointed mission to win freedom for Vietnam. He
wanted no part of the French empire (the French Union, they called
it then) but was realist enough to accept the need for French troops
to hold off the Viet Minh. Ho Chi Minh would take over if the
French withdrew, Diem admitted. But he had come to tell the
Americans they were wrong if they thought their French allies
could ever win this war. Only the Vietnamese could do that, and
they would do nothing against the Communists until they were
granted independence.

In Paris years earlier, the French scholar Paul Mus, who had
grown up in Vietnam, had talked about Diem to an American. Mus
had served as an official French emissary to Ho Chi Minh early in
the war and was once spoken of as a candidate for the office of high
commissioner, the highest French official in Vietnam, Laos, and
Cambodia after World War II. He had said then, in 1948, "Only
one man could ever hope to challenge Ho Chi Minh for leadership
—Ngo Dinh Diem. Because he alone has the same reputation for
virtue and austerity as Ho. Vietnamese will only follow a man who
is known to be virtuous and who leads an austere life."

Americans, however, had different standards for their leaders,
and when Diem stopped over in Paris on his way home to head the
government in 1954, diplomats at the American Embassy did not
know what to make of him.

His roots were in Confucian Asia and the Kingdom of Vietnam, independent for centuries before it fell to the French in the 1880s. He was a Catholic as well as a Confucian, in a country where Catholics were a minority and had been massacred within living memory because many had sided with the French at the time of the conquest.

With his inner-directed certainties, his obvious sense of mission, Diem was unlike any of the superficially frenchified Vietnamese politicians usually encountered by American diplomats in Paris. This was not necessarily a handicap, because those politicians seemed more at home in the French capital than in Saigon. Diem, too, could express himself well in the French language and he had access to influential foreigners through his friends in the Catholic Church. Nevertheless he had no Western veneer at all; he was the product of a Vietnamese culture unknown to the American foreign service. The Paris embassy cabled Washington its approval of "the seemingly ridiculous prospect that this yogi-like mystic could assume the charge he is apparently about to undertake only because the standard set by his predecessors is so low."

Other people took Diem more seriously during his stay in the United States in the early 1950s. One day he had received a visit from a fellow Vietnamese, a native of Hue like Diem himself, who had been a close friend of his brother Nhu when they were students in Paris.

Buu-Hoi was in the United States because the president of the American Chemical Society (ACS) had asked a colleague to resume contact with French science after World War II by calling on the three men he regarded as outstanding chemists in France. One of the three had proved to be this young Vietnamese who directed research in organic chemistry at the Radium Institute in Paris. He had accepted the invitation of the ACS to deliver a series of lectures in the United States.

In Paris, Buu-Hoi had not limited his activities to the laboratory. A member of the Vietnamese royal family, he had been ready to fight for Vietnamese independence, as Bao Dai was not. He had worked with the Ho Chi Minh government from the time it was founded—until the fateful year of 1950, when the Communists imposed a dictatorship on the resistance movement and many nationalists broke away from the Viet Minh. In the fall of 1951 Buu-Hoi sought out Diem in his retreat with the Maryknoll Fathers in Lakewood, New Jersey, to offer him support.

This meeting was the start of a relationship that would be interrupted by political differences but would last until the death of Diem. Fourteen years separated the two men—the brilliant scientist who had studied in the West and was already internationally known for his discoveries, and the older man steeped in Asian traditions who had matured in the mandarin bureaucracy that had survived in central Vietnam under the French. Buu-Hoi was a secular-minded Buddhist. He was a great-great-grandson of Emperor Minh Mang, whose fame as an administrator was equaled only by his reputation for implacable hostility to the intrusion of Catholic missionaries from the West into the closed Confucian world of Vietnam. Diem was a deeply religious Catholic, the brother of a bishop and the descendant of generations of Catholics, a member of a tightly knit minority that had suffered sporadic persecution until the French succeeded in imposing their rule. The teachings of Confucius permeated the Catholic community, and both these men from Hue were profoundly Confucian, raised in the tradition of duty to the family and service to the nation. In 1963, when the sycophants and opportunists surrounding Diem would abandon him, Buu-Hoi would mount a last-ditch attempt to save the first Republic of (South) Vietnam—a futile effort to preserve for Vietnamese the right to dispose of themselves without foreign interference.

In the early 1950s all that was in the future, and Diem had come to the United States with his elder brother, Bishop Ngo Dinh Thuc, in search of support for Vietnamese independence. Their arrival coincided with the height of the cold war and the witch hunt led by Senator Joseph McCarthy against Communists, real and imaginary, in the American government. It was a time when anti-Communist credentials were needed for an aspiring Asian politician, and Diem's fervent Catholicism opened many doors. Only some liberals wondered how effective a Catholic leader could be on the continent of Asia, especially one who seemed to have no political and social program beyond independence and anticommunism. They were disturbed when he suggested the United States should

49

bomb Communist China and not particularly reassured when he said he would establish rotary clubs in Vietnam.

Politics, after all, was the art of the possible and there seemed to be no other nationalist candidate as widely respected in his own country as Diem, as likely to rally non-Communist elements of the population who did not wish to live under the Ho Chi Minh government. Diem had not held public office since 1933, but he had earned a reputation for integrity and industry and had been named minister of the interior (the equivalent of prime minister) at the court of Hue in 1932. Nothing he ever did became him better than his decision to resign from that post. He acted in protest against the refusal of the French colonial authorities to grant the Vietnamese a greater voice in their own government. The French stripped him of his medals, and Emperor Bao Dai, who had just returned from school in France, did not intervene on his behalf.

Diem had remained a monarchist even after that experience, but he would have preferred a monarch more worthy than Bao Dai. The father of Diem, Ngo Dinh Kha, had served as court chamberlain to another emperor, Thanh Thai, early in the century until the French had decided to remove Thanh Thai and replace him with his young son, who, they thought, mistakenly, would be more docile. Instead, the boy grew up to lead a revolt against them and in his turn was sent into exile. During the lifetime of Ngo Dinh Diem three Vietnamese emperors who had challenged the colonial authorities were alive in exile. Diem had inherited from his father a loyalty to another member of the royal family, Prince Cuong De, who had fled the country with the approval of Emperor Thanh Thai long before World War I to join the revolutionary leader Phan Boi Chau in Japan.

As a young man, Diem had witnessed the upsurge of emotion that swept the country on the occasion of the death in 1926 of the patriot Phan Chau Trinh, who had hoped to free Vietnam by peaceful reform and been saved from a French prison by the intervention of the French League for the Rights of Man and returned home to die. From Saigon to Hanoi, students in European dress wore black mourning bands and men in the traditional tunic donned white turbans, the traditional sign of mourning. In 1925 the revolutionary Phan Boi Chau was betrayed to the French police in Shanghai. He was condemned to life imprisonment, but Vietnamese popular feeling was so strong that his sentence was commuted to forced residence in Hue where Diem's younger brother Can came to know him. For a time during the 1930s Diem and Chau lived in retirement in the same city, the old scholar contemplating a past that had been rich in incident and danger, the young man left to himself, his career ended before it had really begun.

Other men, nationalists, Communists, risked their lives in conspiracies to oust the French, died at the hands of the colonial authorities, suffered in French penitentiaries and on the prison island of Poulo Condore. But Diem had never been a revolutionary. He chose to act according to the Confucian tradition that a scholar during a difficult period of history should retire to a tranquil spot and wait for better times in which he might be useful. But he kept in touch with nationalists in the country and abroad. A lifelong bachelor, he was teased by other mandarins about stories that he had taken a vow of celibacy and was a religious mystic, that he would have preferred to be a priest rather than a politician; he protested that this was not so, that he had wished to marry the daughter of the leading Catholic mandarin in Hue but she became a nun.

When the Japanese ousted the French administration during World War II, the report spread that Diem had rejected a chance to return as prime minister under Bao Dai. (To this writer, he denied that the Japanese had ever passed on Bao Dai's offer.) He rebuffed overtures from Ho Chi Minh, who wanted Catholic support in forming a national front government before the outbreak of the war with France. In the late 1940s he refused to become prime minister under Bao Dai, who was making plans in Hong Kong to return as chief of state under French protection. Instead, Diem issued a declaration calling on the French to grant Vietnam independence (he asked for dominion status). He headed a nationalist Catholic party that opposed both the French and the Viet Minh. His standing among his own people as a political leader was grounded on a stubborn refusal to compromise his principles and on an unswerving attachment to the cause of Vietnamese independence. The Americans who admired him had no idea that these same qualities one day would lead him into conflict with the Washington government.

When Diem was forced to leave Vietnam in 1950, he had gone first to Japan, where he called on the elderly Prince Cuong De shortly before his death. Cuong De had become a symbol of the past even though some Vietnamese, like the pope of the Cao Dai religious sect, remained loyal to him. Diem had also encountered the future in Japan, in the unlikely person of an American professor, Wesley Fishel, who was soon to join the faculty of Michigan State University. Fishel had encouraged Diem to leave Japan and come to the United States, where Fishel was helpful in making contacts for him. When Diem finally returned to Vietnam, Fishel would follow him to assume the role of adviser and keep American officials in close touch with the new prime minister. Unfortunately, Fishel also helped to insulate him from Vietnamese of other political tendencies among whom he might more profitably have sought advice.

By 1953 Diem had come to like Americans; he was impressed by them although he never understood the country very well, either the people or their government. He had met many Americans in influential positions and acquired supporters ranging from the cold war conservative Francis Cardinal Spellman to the New Deal liberal Justice Douglas. Americans were naturally responsive when he spoke against French colonialism and about the need to oppose Ho Chi Minh with democracy and freedom. It did not occur to his listeners that his view of the world was Confucian—he believed in the immutability of the social and political order, the incarnation of political and moral authority in the ruler, the subordination of rights to duties. Not Western political democracy with the right of the minority to become a majority, and majority rule, but the traditional practice of self-government in the villages and the moral precepts of Confucius: ethical equations that had once supposedly regulated the behavior of the ruler and that of the governing elite.

Months before Diem died, when Americans condemned him for his aloof and stubborn ways and "persecution" of Buddhists, he would send an American journalist a quotation from the teachings of Buddha himself:

> The Wise Man who fares strenuously apart,
> Who is unshaken in the midst of praise or blame . . .
> A leader of others, and not by others led. . . .

A handwritten note from Gia Long Palace said: "President Diem thought you would be interested in the fact that an *Oriental* like Buddha had ideas about the nature of a wise leader that are not unlike his own."

Diem left the United States for Europe in 1953. He stayed in Paris for a while, went to Bruges, Belgium, and then returned to Paris. The Eisenhower administration was not yet ready to intervene directly in Vietnamese politics. When nationalists in Paris asked an American correspondent to arrange a meeting between Diem and Secretary of State John Foster Dulles, who was visiting the French capital, Dulles refused to see him.

In Vietnam, the war dragged on. The regime established by the French under the former emperor Bao Dai was still in place. It was the old colonial system updated, to which the French, in a vain attempt to undercut the nationalist appeal of the Viet Minh, had doled out one after the other of the formal attributes of a national state, except the only one that really mattered: independence.

Bao Dai had gone to live in France, at his château on the outskirts of Cannes, an absentee chief of state. He had often disappointed French officials, not quite permitting them to manipulate him like the puppet foreigners believed him to be, but he had alienated his own people by his bland indifference to the interests of the Vietnamese nation. Frenchmen and Vietnamese alike had been frustrated by the inertia of this disillusioned and embittered man and by his aloofness from all that did not concern his material welfare.

The expatriate former emperor kept his hand in Saigon intrigues through various cronies, and key posts in the Saigon administration were filled by those whom Bao Dai had selected. Only he could appoint a new prime minister, and in 1953 he was in no hurry to offer that post to Diem.

Friends encouraged Diem to keep his distance from the Saigon government until the French evacuated the country and it became truly free. But Diem, who had waited so long to assume office in an independent Vietnam, who had earlier rejected overtures from Bao Dai and even from Ho Chi Minh, could bring himself to wait no longer.

Under French and American pressure for change, Bao Dai finally turned to Diem in 1954. The French army was still fighting in Vietnam and the outcome of the Geneva Conference was in doubt. Even so, Diem accepted immediately that June, and Bao Dai delegated the powers of government to him.

On June 25, 1954, at Tan Son Nhut airport on the outskirts of Saigon, an unfamiliar figure stepped out of a plane into the oppressive afternoon heat. He was of average height for a Vietnamese (although Americans would persist in describing him as short) and sturdily built. He looked with curiosity at the thicknesses of barbed wire the French had laid out to protect their planes from guerrilla attack. Then, diffidently, he went over to the crowd of people waiting to greet him. The newly appointed prime minister, Ngo Dinh Diem, had come home.

For Bao Dai the appointment of Ngo Dinh Diem was the beginning of the end; for Diem it was a badly timed beginning. The new prime minister, who over twenty years had built a reputation as an uncompromising nationalist, found himself on the defensive from the start as compromise after compromise was forced on him. The French war against the Viet Minh that Diem himself had once acknowledged to be a colonial war would in its last weeks become his war. The loss of the northern half of the territory of Vietnam to Ho Chi Minh would not only be a disaster for the French army and the French colonial authorities; it would also be a defeat for Diem's "State of Vietnam," reduced to half its original territory.

Saigon was still the headquarters of the French war effort. Viet Minh successes had forced the French to be more responsive to the claims of the nationalists they were trying to win over to their side, and they had finally conceded that Vietnam was one country; they had removed the administrative barriers imposed during their piecemeal conquest during the nineteenth century, which had divided the central provinces from the north and kept the southern provinces separate from the others. The "State of Vietnam" under Bao Dai claimed authority over north, south, and center, from the Chinese frontier to the southernmost tip of the Nam Bo, the Ca Mau Peninsula. But it had only the power the French allowed it to have, and only in regions that had not been taken over by the Viet Minh.

In French-controlled Saigon, Vietnamese had grown cynical as they watched this war without end in which most of them were spectators and some were profiteers; and the Bao Dai government that festered with intrigue and corruption was isolated from the population and impotent.

But the city was alive with rumors of impending change. From his secret headquarters in the northern jungle, Ho Chi Minh had dispatched a high-level delegation to Switzerland, where the great powers had called a conference to try to make peace in Indochina. The State of Vietnam had also sent a delegation to Geneva. And now Ngo Dinh Diem was back, not a creature of Bao Dai but one of his most severe critics, a patriot whose arrival marked the start of a new era. Or so his brother Ngo Dinh Nhu had insisted in a propaganda campaign that had grown in intensity as the month of June progressed.

Nhu had already organized a congress that had demanded unconditional independence from France; he was one of the founders of a new nationalist political party based on workers and peasants as well as middle-class elements. Nhu had been lining up support for his brother, who needed all the help he could get. In Paris, one of Diem's earliest supporters, his host in the French capital, had tried to form a shadow cabinet for him and had failed because the Vietnamese he approached wanted more of a political program than simply opposition to the Communists under a new leader.

Despite the efforts of Nhu, Diem was greeted with indifference in Saigon. Only some five hundred people had turned up to welcome him at the airport, and no more than twice that number gathered to hear the speech he delivered before Gia Long Palace. His supporters did their best to put a good face on this poor showing and managed to convince some Western reporters that he had been acclaimed on his arrival. In private, however, they admitted their disappointment.

An American watched Diem drive past that day and noted disapprovingly that his car was a fast-moving closed limousine, which did not permit people in the street to get a good look at him. It was the business of Edward G. Lansdale to notice such details. He was the director of the secret operations unit called the Saigon Military Mission (SMM), and he had been working out of Saigon for the past month.

Lansdale had arrived in Vietnam fresh from the Philippines, where this sometime advertising man from San Francisco operating under military cover had achieved a triumph for the Central Intelligence Agency by helping to put down a Communist insurgency.

The newly independent Philippines had been in a wretched state after World War II, its politicians inept, its peasants dissatisfied, the Communist Huk movement threatening the established order. Lansdale had recognized that the guerrillas were strong because the government was out of touch with the people; military force alone could not defeat them. He had gone to work to win over the local population and organized the campaign that transformed Ramón Magsaysay, a relative unknown, into a popular national figure. President Eisenhower had congratulated the CIA station in Manila when Magsaysay was elected president of the republic in 1953. An Indian diplomat told the press that a certain American colonel should change his name to Colonel Lanslide.

Lansdale had been sent to Vietnam to try to stop the spread of a far more powerful Communist movement than the Filipino Huks —and from what he had seen, Diem was in need of help. The day after his arrival Lansdale went to the palace to find him and give him some ideas about how the government could be made, in Lansdale's words, "more responsive to the people, about agrarian economics and reforms, about encouraging the institution of public forums around the countryside, about veteran care, about public health, about making the government more effective in the provinces, and about the personal behavior of a prime minister who could generate willing support by the majority toward accomplishing these ends.''

Lansdale was convinced that ''when the right cause is identified and used correctly, the anti-Communist cause becomes a pro-people fight.'' His ideas were quintessentially American, and in later years a succession of Americans less colorful than he would also try to convince Diem of the necessity for political democracy, good public relations, and effective administration.

But Vietnam was quite unlike the Philippines, a country that had long-standing ties to the West, a Spanish colony for three hundred years before it became an American colony, its people 85 percent Catholic. American principles and practices may have had some meaning in Manila, but analogies from the American experience were neither meaningful nor relevant in Confucian Asia. Americans, however ingenious, could not fill the political vacuum in which Diem found himself.

He needed to consult other Vietnamese who represented the spectrum of opinion among his own countrymen. Instead, he met almost daily with the American colonel from the SMM. Lansdale had a team of young Americans with him and brought in Filipino veterans of his successful campaign in their country. They used the mix of paramilitary, psychological warfare, and political techniques that had worked so well in the Philippines. All these well-meaning foreigners were pursuing a myth, the myth that another Magsaysay could be created in Vietnam, a popular, democratic leader, an outgoing man, a good campaigner who could appeal to crowds, although Diem was none of these things.

On July 7, 1954, Ngo Dinh Diem was officially installed as prime minister of Vietnam. Bao Dai, the chief of state who had delegated his power to Diem, remained in France.

Two weeks later the French signed a cease-fire accord with the Ho Chi Minh government in Geneva.

Diem had miscalculated badly in thinking the Americans could dissuade the French from abandoning at the conference table the northern and north-central provinces they had already lost on the battlefield. Even Catholic areas in the north that the new prime minister particularly cherished were going to be surrendered to the Communists.

And so there was peace at last for the war-weary population of the South. But Diem saw no reason for rejoicing. He declared July 20 a Day of Infamy, and flags were ordered flown at half-mast on all official buildings throughout the country because the French forces were about to evacuate the North; and when the French left, the Bao Dai administration—now headed by Diem—would have to leave with them.

It had been stated at Geneva that the political future of Vietnam would not be decided until a general election was held in July 1956. In the interim, the Seventeenth Parallel became the frontier between the North and the South. Only the southern half of the country was left to the State of Vietnam after Geneva, and it was there in South Vietnam that Diem would have to prove himself.

Wide areas of the South had already escaped the control of his government. His authority did not appear to extend much beyond the city of Saigon. The problem for Diem was not democracy for his government or popularity for himself, neither of which was likely for any regime created out of the seething heterogeneity of South Vietnam, a piece of a French colony suddenly called upon to turn itself into an independent state.

The problem for Diem was to find a people over whom to rule.

When Senator Mike Mansfield came to Saigon that summer of 1954 he found his old acquaintance Ngo Dinh Diem a virtual prisoner in his residence. He did not control the Vietnamese army, which was threatening to revolt. Police and security in the Saigon-Cholon area were in the hands of a sect of gangsters called the Binh Xuyen, who also controlled organized vice in the city. Two important southern politico-religious sects would agree to join the government, but their support was fragile and short-lived. Diem had a following in the central provinces, his own part of the country, but few friends in the Nam Bo other than refugees from the North.

Diem had been little more than a refugee himself when Mansfield had met him in Washington. Now, the senator from Montana went to the palace to call on the prime minister of an independent state.

Mansfield was at a loss to understand why the population did not close ranks behind Diem. Surely they realized they did not have much time left. In two years they would have to face nationwide elections. Yet they seemed oblivious to "the overhanging shadow of the Viet Minh." A "crisis of inertia" seemed to have gripped the South. He decided it was the fault of French officials and Vietnamese factions and "an incredible campaign of subversion by intrigue [that] has gone on in the city of Saigon."

Mansfield had stopped over in Vietnam when he went to Asia to join Secretary of State Dulles in signing the treaty that established the Southeast Asia Treaty Organization (SEATO), in Manila on September 8, 1954. This new pact, which included no Southeast Asian nations as full members other than the Philippines and Thailand, was meant to signal to the Chinese that no further Communist victories would be permitted in Southeast Asia, specifically in Indochina.

The SEATO pact was further evidence of American support for Diem, but it did not make him any more popular at home. American policymakers, even the best-informed of them, took for granted an identity of interests between the United States and the South Vietnamese. It did not seem to occur to Senator Mansfield that there could be many people in South Vietnam who had no wish to live under a regime like that in the North, and yet did not want any part of an American military alliance directed against the Communists.

Mike Mansfield was a man of liberal sentiments and internationalist outlook who had supported the efforts of two presidents to prevent the Communists from taking over Indochina. On a previous visit to Vietnam he had noted, accurately, that "the current of nationalism runs strong . . . it is the basic political reality . . . a desire for independence from foreign control that is deep-seated and widespread."

Yet Mansfield had never expected nationalism in the South to speak with so many voices, to be so chaotic and so negative. Diem at least was a man of integrity and principle, worthy of American support. But what of all these other groups and individuals who also claimed to be patriots and yet failed to rally to the new prime minister? Diem and his advisers dismissed them as variously corrupt, pro-Communist, or pro-French. There seemed to be many such people.

True, Diem, hard worker though he was, had little time to spare for politics as he grappled with the aftermath of the cease-fire accord that had been signed in Geneva. It had set off a vast movement of population that threatened to overwhelm the new regime. The treasury was empty; Diem had found barely enough money to pay government employees for a month. When his spokesmen had urged people to come south, he had never imagined that so many Northerners would decide to leave. The French army and the American navy provided transport and care for tens of thousands, and the United States supplied funds. Cardinal Spellman arrived from New York in a blaze of publicity to present a check from American Catholic charities for the refugees who, as Diem's American supporters liked to point out, had voted with their feet. Some 860,000 people would flee the North before the exodus was over, the majority of them Catholics.

The Geneva Accords authorized the movement of refugees between North and South Vietnam for a strictly limited period. This had been arranged for humanitarian motives. But the French authorities were in a vengeful mood, and the Saigon government was fearful of being outnumbered by the more populous North. An American CIA team belonging to Lansdale's SMM was in the North on a sabotage mission. They were led by Lucien Conein, an OSS veteran, who had operated against the Japanese in 1945. He and his team, for reasons they took for granted and that no one else had the knowledge, or the sense, to question, acted as if the United States were at war with the Ho Chi Minh regime. To all of these several groups, the northern population were pawns in a propaganda struggle; the aim of each group was to persuade as many Vietnamese as possible to leave for South Vietnam.

Some Vietnamese had no choice but to go, for reasons of class, religion, politics, or affiliation with the French and the Bao Dai administration. To professionals and technicians who had worked with the Viet Minh all these years, the end of the war was meaningless from this point of view: They remained where they were. But such people who had not joined the Viet Minh, by staying in the French-controlled cities, had already made their choice. They naturally went south, confident that they remained in the nation, but outside a Communist regime.

The refugees had to apply for permission to go south before the French completed their withdrawal from North Vietnam. Having evacuated Hanoi, the French retreated to their assembly areas at the port of Haiphong and in north-central Vietnam. By May 1955 they had transferred all that was left of their civil authority to Viet Minh administrators. The last French ship in the north left Haiphong for Do Son and the island of Cat Ba in Ha Long Bay. On May 16 all French authority had disappeared north of the Seventeenth Parallel, the line of demarcation between North and South.

Northerners were still begging to leave for the South, however, and Hanoi agreed to extend the deadline for their departure by two additional months. During that period 4,700 people left the North and 1,700 arrived from South Vietnam.

On July 20, 1955, the free movement of population (that the Northern government had never permitted to be entirely free but that was still freer than it would ever be again while Vietnam was divided) had ended. The International Control and Supervisory Commission was left helpless, with sacks of written requests for permission to depart, mostly for political reasons, and no authority to take any action on them. As ICC staff members traveled around North Vietnam, they encountered many people who implored their assistance in leaving for the South, but it was too late.

When Senator Mansfield called on Ngo Dinh Diem in 1954, Diem did not yet have a government of his own, neither national assembly nor popular organization; he had inherited a large, unwieldy bureaucracy of appointed officials with few direct links to the population they professed to rule. Thousands more of these officials were pouring in from the north and the central provinces north of the Seventeenth Parallel, in search of new assignments that would keep them out of the power of the Viet Minh, and were promptly reinstated in their rank and privileges.

Some Vietnamese bureaucrats were thin, hollow-cheeked men, in no way different in appearance from the popular idea of the dedicated Viet Minh cadre; others, sleek, well-fed individuals, looked as if they bore the physical stamp of a privileged caste. But the appearance of diversity was misleading—the great majority of these men who assumed the positions of authority vacated by Frenchmen in the government ministries of Saigon and throughout the southern and south-central provinces had spent their entire careers in subordinate posts at the orders of Frenchmen, and there had learned that passivity was the easiest way to self-preservation. They had never served in any grass-roots movement that might have given them practical experience of government or administration. They knew a great deal more about the prerogatives of power than they did about its responsibilities.

So few of these mandarins had ever identified themselves with the people that the early period of the war with the French had been marked by systematic Viet Minh attacks on mandarins because of popular resentment against their traditional exactions. Some, like Governor Ngo Dinh Khoi, Diem's elder brother, were murdered; others fled to the cities for French protection. A rare exception was Prince Ung Uy, a former governor of Thanh Hoa and Nghe An provinces, who was actually invited back to show himself publicly in regions he had once governed, so that the Viet Minh could benefit from the popularity he enjoyed in central Vietnam, where he was revered for his incorruptibility and his long service in rural development.

In the Nam Bo itself, where Frenchmen had exercised direct administration at every level for nearly a century, Vietnamese had been relegated merely to servants of the administrative and police apparatus through which the colonial regime controlled the people. Many of them were detested by the local population. A notorious example was the *doc phu,* or provincial governor, Nguyen Van

Tam, who in 1940, when the local branch of the Communist Party organized a rising that was joined by many other southerners as it spread through several provinces, distinguished himself by the cruelty with which he repressed the rebels. His countrymen called him "the tiger of Cai Lay" because he directed the mass killing of political prisoners in that district by particularly brutal methods, such as stringing them together like sausages on a rope that was pulled through holes pierced in their hands, and then tossing them into the river to be drowned.

Although some Vietnamese officials who served the French in the Nam Bo later joined the Viet Minh, the majority had identified themselves so completely with the French colonial system that the title *doc phu*—the highest rank held by Vietnamese who worked for the French in the Nam Bo—became a pejorative term used by Vietnamese nationalists to stigmatize former servants of the colonial regime.

It was to this largely discredited Vietnamese bureaucracy that the French turned over their authority after the Geneva Conference: the mandarins, the southern functionaries, the very people who had collaborated with them for so long. Even this, they did grudgingly and piecemeal so that the Diem regime—already handicapped by the public image of the Bao Dai government as an instrument of French policy—was denied even the political benefit of a clear-cut assertion of independence.

Outside Saigon, news that the war was over penetrated slowly throughout the Southern hinterland, where the French defeat on a remote Northern battlefield seemed unreal to many.

Some regions of the South, where the traditional apparatus of village government had broken down, had lost all touch with Saigon and become political vacuums. Other areas gave a token recognition to the State of Vietnam but were ruled in semifeudal autonomy by two politico-religious sects: the Cao Dai, an eclectic religion whose adherents worshiped God in the form of an eye; and the Hoa Hao, a religious group that practiced neo-Buddhist rites. Still other sections of the Nam Bo and a part of the central panhandle rejected the authority of Saigon as they had that of France; they acknowledged only Ho Chi Minh as their leader.

Nowhere was this new peace more confusing than in the U Minh Forest and the mosquito-ridden reaches of the Ca Mau Peninsula in the far south, where the waterlogged land seemed barely to rise from the sea, and in the sterile alum-tainted marshlands of the Plain of Reeds that stretched to the Cambodian frontier; in sections of the rich rice-growing provinces of the western Mekong Delta and the older southern provinces along the South China Sea, where revolutionary traditions were strong; and in the region extending southward from Quang Ngai to Nha Trang along the central coast and into the highlands.

All these areas had lived under Viet Minh control for years, their inhabitants integrated into the system established by the Viet Minh in support of the revolution and the war, whether they were eight years old or eighty. The summer of 1954 brought the news that the Viet Minh had in one stroke both won and lost the long war—for those who had faithfully served the Ho Chi Minh regime so many years now learned that Hanoi was going to abandon its supporters south of the Seventeenth Parallel to the Saigon government of Ngo Dinh Diem.

The independence of the governments of Hanoi and Saigon had been recognized at the Geneva Conference. But the tragic struggle to determine which Vietnamese would rule over the South had only just begun.

In the palace Diem sat alone except for his American advisers and a handful of trusted Vietnamese. The war may have ended, but the French Expeditionary Corps had regrouped in the South and order was still maintained by French forces that seemed determined to remain in South Vietnam indefinitely. French naval units were moored alongside the quay from which could be seen French marines guarding the official residence and private quarters of the admiral in command of the still substantial French naval forces in the Far East. Huge French barracks and military depots sprawled on the outskirts of Saigon. The most powerful man in the capital was not the new prime minister but General Paul Ely, the representative of the French government, who had accepted a temporary mission as combined high commissioner and commander of the French forces in Indochina.

General Ely was on good terms with Diem and got on well with the American ambassador. But other Frenchmen with little interest in Vietnamese independence and no liking for the United States resented American criticism of the way they had ruled their former colony of Indochina and of how they had waged the war and lost it. These Frenchmen were bitter, unforgiving, and they were much closer than Diem to the Vietnamese military forces that opposed the Viet Minh in the South—the national army and the sects.

The Vietnamese army that had served under French command was national only in name, an army without a cause. Its leaders were restless, in search of a political role, seeking a strong regime that Diem seemed unable to establish. They were receptive when French officers encouraged them to reject the man who had become the friend of the Americans, Ngo Dinh Diem.

At the same time French agents plotted against the Americans and stirred up the sects. Lansdale was engaged in an undercover struggle with the French, and several American journalists met with him and his team from time to time "at their own request as U.S. citizens" to help in this secret war of intrigue and propaganda. They were correspondents of *The New York Times,* the *Herald Tribune,* Associated Press, and *Time.* John Mecklin of *Time* and *Life* would be public-affairs officer at the embassy in Saigon in 1963.

The sects were bizarre, exotic, to many Westerners, and their power was bloated by subsidies their troops had received from the French during the war years. But the French had not created the sects. They were an integral part of the diversity of the Nam Bo.

In the steaming heat of the southern plains, politics, religion, and superstition blended and took on original forms. The initial shock of the encounter with the West had been brutal and many sought refuge in the old beliefs: in spirits and in Buddha. In the Mekong Delta some holy men spent their lives in trees, contemplating the wonders of the universe. The humid air of the delta was heavy with phantoms and spirits of the dead, believed still to share in the daily life of the living, influencing their actions and determining their fate.

New sects emerged. Most numerous were the Cao Dai, who included people of all classes, from old southern peasant sects to leading members of the urban community. Many patriots, frustrated by their inability to expel the French, had consoled themselves with the multiplicity of spirits and the ceremonies punctuated by prophecies of future liberation that were features of Cao Daism. And what could a member of the French political police have done when he followed the trail of a man suspected of forbidden nationalist activities and found him sitting around a Ouija board with a group of friends, solemnly invoking the spirit of Victor Hugo or some other member of the Cao Dai international pantheon? The sect was divided into subsects, the most important of them centered on a baroque multicolored temple in Tay Ninh, northwest of Saigon where it supported a religious hierarchy headed by a pope. The Cao Dai maintained a sophisticated system of social welfare. The group successfully defended small landowners and tenants against exploitation by the rich and powerful, and their network of contacts stretched throughout the Nam Bo.

The Cao Dai sect had spread rapidly in the Nam Bo during the last years of French rule even though restrictions were imposed on all religious groups except the Roman Catholic Church. After 1954 the Buddhist community would regard itself as the main sufferer from these government regulations that Diem failed to change. In the colonial era, when the institutions of Vietnamese Buddhism had fallen into decadence, it was the Cao Dai who suffered most from French religious controls.

In 1954, some two million people worshiped Cao Dai in temples scattered throughout the Nam Bo. In the southwest, another million faithful practiced the neo-Buddhist rites of the Hoa Hao, a sect of the poor. The Hoa Hao had been founded in the 1930s by Huynh Phu So, who preached a reformed and simplified Buddhism and invoked old prophecies that promised deliverance from foreign rule and spoke of social and political revolution.

The Cao Daists, the Hoa Hao, and a third sect, the Binh Xuyen, had allied themselves with the Communists to fight the

French after World War II. This uneasy alliance ended when the Communists, unwilling to tolerate any challenge to their leadership of the southern resistance movement, murdered the Hoa Hao bonze Huynh Phu So and tried to murder other sect leaders. The three sects retaliated by changing sides and joining the French in the war against the Viet Minh. The rejection by the sects of the Viet Minh southern leadership did not diminish their own nationalist yearnings. Their alliance with the French had been at best partial and sporadic.

In 1954, the sects ruled their own semifeudal domains unchallenged, and where the sects operated the Viet Minh had been unable to penetrate either as a political or a military force. The Cao Dai and the Hoa Hao had some thirty-five thousand men under arms, men who had fought as auxiliaries of the French army (the Hoa Hao troops were said to be among the best in the South), and they expected to play their part in any independent government and to share in the spoils of peace as they had in the spoils of war.

But Ngo Dinh Diem disapproved of the sects despite their nationalism. He was ready to allow sect soldiers to join the national army but only if they disbanded their separate units and enlisted as individuals. He wanted the sects to turn over the regions they ruled to officials of the central government.

Lansdale also believed it was necessary to integrate the sect armies. In far-off Washington even John Foster Dulles thought so. To a degree these Americans could never understand, the feudalism of the sects was a fact of life in the Nam Bo, and they balked at giving up their privileges.

The American ambassador met with sect leaders to urge them to support Diem. They had not refused money from the French and saw no reason to refuse when it was offered by Americans, and Lansdale eventually succeeded in buying their nominal support. That September Diem was persuaded to broaden his narrowly based government, and several representatives of the sects agreed to join it. But Lansdale could not buy the loyalty of the sects any more than the French could.

The third sect, the Binh Xuyen, unlike the others, had no religious purpose and scant social usefulness; the wealth it derived from the brothels and gambling halls of Cholon did not improve its image. But this battle-hardened band—its members had once paraded under the banner "Binh Xuyen pirates"—had fought for Vietnamese independence alongside the other sects at the beginning of the war. Its tough leader, Bay Vien, was luckier (or less trusting) than the Hoa Hao bonze Huynh Phu So and had escaped a Communist trap to kill him. After breaking with the Communists, Bay Vien and his men wiped out Viet Minh assassination squads operating in the Saigon area and the French made him a general. The Binh Xuyen battened on the thriving Chinese quarter, Cholon, and controlled the main road linking Saigon-Cholon to the sea.

Even Lansdale recognized that Bay Vien was a patriot in his own fashion—and one who commanded several thousand well-armed southern troops and controlled the Saigon police force that the former emperor Bao Dai had turned over to men from the Binh Xuyen during the war. Lansdale tried to work out an understanding with Bay Vien, but Diem was adamant against any deal with the Binh Xuyen chief: "The man's a scoundrel," he said.

In August 1954, Prince Buu-Hoi, who had tried to help Diem during his years of exile, arrived in Saigon to find the authority of the prime minister flouted in his own capital by rebellious army leaders and the Binh Xuyen. A political vacuum had opened around Diem that his supporters among the refugees and his American friends were helpless to fill. Reports came from the countryside that the Viet Minh was tightening its grip on the Southern population, and the central government in Saigon could do nothing to stop it.

Nineteen years had passed since Buu-Hoi had left colonial Vietnam, and in those years the young student had become a famous scientist internationally known for his work in biochemistry and his research on cancer and leprosy. Young people flocked to hear him speak, and local newspapers reported that he was greeted as a national hero. People turned to him as a respected national figure, a professor who was above politics, at a time when the South was floundering in a political morass, at the mercy of forces that seemed beyond its control.

The professor went to call on the Cao Dai pope and other Cao

Dai dignitaries at Tay Ninh and was taken to a secret meeting with the Cao Dai general The at his headquarters on Nui Ba Den (Black Lady Mountain) outside the city. He visited the Hoa Hao at Can Tho in the southwest and was received with ceremony by the Binh Xuyen in Cholon. He talked with labor groups, army leaders, professional men; and that fall, when the Saigon press was heavily censored and partly closed down, he outlined a program of action in an article for the Paris magazine, *L'Express,* whose editors were close to the French premier, Pierre Mendès-France.

Buu-Hoi called for a new "government of national solidarity" in Saigon that would include the sects, to bring about the reconciliation widely desired in the Nam Bo between the non-Communist majority that had sympathized with the anti-French resistance and their countrymen who had served in the Bao Dai regime and the colonial administration. He opposed a military buildup in the South, arguing that the best defense lay in fostering popular participation in economic and administrative institutions and in encouraging political life within the sects. In foreign affairs Buu-Hoi favored neutrality. South Vietnam ought to stay on good terms with the United States and France; but the colonial era was over and it was time for Vietnam to assume its natural place in Asia, to join India and other newly independent countries in following a policy of nonalignment with any of the great powers. Thus the South might hold its own in peaceful competition with the North, and one day the two Vietnams might both be admitted to the United Nations.

These proposals were rejected by Diem and his American advisers, who seemed to nourish the illusion that they could somehow transform the disparate elements in the South, this war-weary segment of a nation where political evolution had been arrested and distorted by decades of colonial rule, and make it over into a militantly anti-Communist state.

They thought they could count on Mike Mansfield for support. The senator's report on his fact-finding mission to Vietnam had been released in the American capital on October 15, 1954. His conclusions had been communicated by the State Department to the Paris government beforehand, to discourage the French from trying to make any changes in Saigon. The influential Democrat from Montana, who had become the Senate authority on Indochina, could conceive of no other leader for South Vietnam than Ngo Dinh Diem. If the Diem government were to fall, Mansfield wrote, "I believe that the United States should consider an immediate suspension of all aid to Vietnam and the French Union forces there, except that of a humanitarian nature, preliminary to a complete reappraisal of our present policies in Free Vietnam."

Buu-Hoi's article appeared in *L'Express* early in November 1954 and was circulated in Vietnam, where support for him and his ideas was voiced in the sects, the army, and labor groups. In Paris, on November 11, a diplomat from the American Embassy arrived at the offices of Mendès-France with a message from Washington. The French premier was to leave shortly on an official visit to the United States, and the State Department wanted to warn him that the American government would have to reconsider its entire policy toward Vietnam if Buu-Hoi (believed to be the candidate of Mendès-France at this time), or anyone of his "political ideologies," were chosen to replace Diem.

In South Vietnam, leaders of the sects and the army refused to support Diem. They turned as a last resort to their self-exiled chief of state, Bao Dai, who was still in France, exactly where American and French officials wanted him, removed from the temptations of the Saigon political arena. None of his subjects professed to be more faithful to the former emperor than the flamboyant chief of staff of the Vietnamese army, General Nguyen Van Hinh.

For weeks the general had been threatening to mount a coup d'état in Saigon. In October a coup had once seemed so close that General Ely had offered Diem the protection of French troops, which he refused. Working behind the scenes, Colonel Lansdale, Professor Fishel, and Ambassador Donald Heath had done what they could to stop General Hinh; and Bao Dai under pressure from Washington summoned the outspoken general to France. Hinh was in no hurry to obey. He did not leave Vietnam until November when finally the Americans convinced him that the United States would cut off its aid to the Vietnamese army if he tried to overthrow the regime.

The Washington government had openly declared its support

for Ngo Dinh Diem. He had received a letter from President Eisenhower, dated October 23. The letter spoke of the need for reforms in the Vietnamese government, but that did not lessen the impact of this message from the White House: the American government had decided to assist Diem "in developing and maintaining a strong, viable state. . . ." In November, General J. Lawton Collins arrived in Saigon as special U.S. representative with the rank of ambassador, replacing Heath. Collins announced that the United States would give "every possible aid to the government of Diem and to his government only."

Dulles had warned the new envoy that the chances of saving a non-Communist regime in the South were slim, no better than one in ten, he said. But Collins was unprepared for this Confucian Catholic patriot who accepted help from Washington yet resisted American advice when it ran counter to his own strong convictions. A few months later, Collins had reached the end of his rope and had come around to General Ely's position that Diem was impossible. A replacement had to be found. Yet Collins and other American officials could think of no better qualified leader than Dr. Phan Huy Quat, a Dai Viet politician from the North. Dr. Quat had been born in north-central Vietnam and in his youth had been a student leader in Hanoi. He had served several prime ministers as minister of defense in the Bao Dai regime under the French during the war. Americans believed Quat was a strong man, "able, forceful, resourceful" although with "only slight political following."

The loyalty of the national army was still in doubt when the rebellious sects openly challenged Diem early in March 1955. By that time Bao Dai, too, had had enough of Diem and wished to replace him—with none other than the colorful freebooter who headed the Binh Xuyen, Bay Vien himself!

Fighting erupted in Saigon between the Binh Xuyen and troops faithful to Diem. The French army interceded and imposed a truce on the rival groups.

A Hoa Hao leader, Ba Cut, clashed with an army battalion in the countryside. The Hoa Hao and the Binh Xuyen set up a blockade of Saigon. From Indonesia where the Afro-Asian countries were holding a conference at Bandung, the head of the South Vietnamese delegation, one of the few able ministers in Diem's cabinet, announced his resignation and called for a new provisional government to prepare general elections for a national assembly.

The Diem regime seemed to be crumbling under attack from all sides, and the capital lived in fear of a new explosion of violence. Collins was about to leave for consultations in Washington. He called on Diem on April 17 and found him adamant against trying to appease the sects; it was intolerable, he told the American envoy, that his police force should remain in the hands of his enemies.

True, Ngo Dinh Diem was both a suspicious and a naïve man, unworldly and full of prejudice, so that it was often hard for him to grasp facts and understand people. But he believed deeply in the rightness of his cause, and he was not without courage.

He told Collins that his government had to fight communism, feudalism, and colonialism all at once and had no time to waste. He did not want civil war, but the feudalists (he meant the sects) were unscrupulous. Compromise had been useless during the war with the Viet Minh, and he did not intend to compromise now. Collins could not understand such intransigence. He wired Washington, "I see no repeat no alternative to the early replacement of Diem."

The day after General Collins reached the American capital he went to lunch with General Eisenhower. State Department officials were still sympathetic to Diem, but Collins apparently convinced the president that Diem had to go. Collins wanted to replace him with Dr. Quat, the Dai Viet Northerner who had served in the Bao Dai government under the French.

Barely six months after Eisenhower's statement of support, telegrams were dispatched from Washington to the American embassies in Saigon and Paris that called for changing the Vietnamese regime while pretending not to do so. The official line was that the Americans supported Diem and would continue to support him— but only "unless and until Vietnamese leaders" found someone else whom Bao Dai would agree to appoint in place of Diem.

The object was to make it look as if Vietnamese in Saigon had chosen the new man, but "Collins and Ely will probably have to be in practice the catalysts . . . to recommend a name for Bao Dai to designate to form a new government." If Diem refused to serve in a lesser post and to support the new government, "the program should nevertheless be carried out anyway." So much for "Free Vietnam"!

As it happened, this interesting exercise in colonialism was never put to the test; the telegrams were overtaken by events. For on that same day, April 27, Diem appointed a new chief of police in Saigon. The Binh Xuyen began military action against the government the next day. And the face of Saigon changed overnight.

General Ely had been right to fear an outbreak of fighting in the city. More than eight hundred civilians were killed or wounded, and more than twenty thousand houses were destroyed in the vicinity of the Petrus Ky lycée and the Y bridge, where Bay Vien had his headquarters. (This devastation would be grist to the Viet Minh propaganda mill.)

But Diem and his brother Nhu had their own contacts in the army and the sects, and Lansdale had been working to organize resistance to the Binh Xuyen. Diem had counted on his troops' holding firm against Bay Vien's men, who were hopelessly outnumbered, and they did hold. Contrary to the dismal predictions of the French, Diem seemed to be winning. Lansdale and others cabled the news to Washington: "any change in leadership or command at this time could result in chaos."

Senator Mansfield called for ending American aid to the Saigon regime if Diem were forced out of office. Other senators and members of the House Foreign Affairs Committee rallied to Diem's support.

The battle against the Binh Xuyen raged in Saigon during the first days of May. Bay Vien and his men were driven out of the city and fled to their old hideouts in the great Rung Sat swamp that stretched between Saigon-Cholon and the South China Sea.

From his château near Cannes Bao Dai tried to gain control over events in the Vietnamese capital, but it was too late for that. Diem ignored his summons to Cannes to discuss a political solution of the crisis. Officers loyal to Diem frustrated an attempt by one of Bao Dai's generals to assert the power of the former emperor over the army.

In the city of Saigon, pro-Diem groups had seized the political initiative. Diem's brother Nhu helped to organize a new "revolutionary congress" with delegates from the provinces, the trade unions, and other elements who declared their support for the prime minister. Nhu reportedly had CIA backing. Other nationalists proclaimed themselves a Revolutionary Committee and called on Diem to remove Bao Dai, reestablish law and order, and expel the French from Vietnam.

The month of May 1955 marked the beginning of the end of the military resistance of the sects. Army units tracked down the Binh Xuyen in the marshes; and Bay Vien fled the country with French help in November and did not return. A young Hoa Hao leader, Ba Cut, held out for months until he was captured and condemned to death. Despite appeals for mercy from many quarters, Ba Cut was guillotined at Can Tho in 1956. Ngo Dinh Nhu said a reprieve was not possible because the army was against it. Particularly adamant against it, he said, was the heavyset southern officer, now a general, who had led the offensive against the sects and been decorated by Diem. Americans would later dub him "Big Minh." In Saigon that year, some people spoke with sympathy of Ba Cut. ("He came from our Wild West," one doctor told this writer.) They said that he was an authentic southerner and that he had died well; the government had been wrong to execute him.

The Cao Dai pope still refused to make his peace with the regime. One of the Cao Dai generals who had joined Diem went to Tay Ninh and placed the pope under house arrest, an action that was widely condemned in Cao Dai circles. In 1956, Pham Cong Tac, the pope who had once been sent into exile by the French colonial authorities because of his nationalist activities, left Vietnam again, this time to escape a Vietnamese government.

He fled across the border with some of his followers and took up residence in Cambodia. From time to time he met with representatives of the Hanoi government in Phnom Penh and worked for a peaceful settlement with the Communists until his death some two years later. When his followers asked permission to bring the body of their pope back to Tay Ninh for burial, Diem refused.

The battle against the sects was over and hailed as a great victory by supporters of the Diem government. But it was a hollow victory that had made more enemies for Diem. When the Viet Minh began to reorganize its forces in the South (forces that the government labeled "Viet Cong" or "Vietnamese Communist"), it recruited many of its troops from the sects; the military commander of the Binh Xuyen was appointed to the Central Committee of the National Liberation Front in 1962.

There was no place left for Bao Dai in the South after the defeat of the sects. He had counted on the French authorities he knew so well for help against Diem, but they, too, had lost in the struggle for power in Saigon. The stay of French troops on Vietnamese soil was coming to an end sooner than most people had expected.

In October 1955, Bao Dai was deposed in a referendum that gave Diem the unlikely majority of 98.2 percent of the popular vote and proclaimed him the first president of the Republic of Vietnam.

At Diem's request, the last French troops were evacuated from Vietnam, in April 1956.

The Saigon regime had unleashed a press campaign against the French. The Diem government still resented the French for their involvement with Bao Dai and the sects; feared them, too, because they maintained a diplomatic link with the Communist North. And the Saigon regime in those days was eager to oblige the Americans who seemed so anxious to replace French influence in Saigon with their own. At a price: the anti-French political stance of the government helped to alienate many members of the educated middle class who sent their children to French schools, as did the president's brother Nhu. Having learned to know the West through French culture, they had imbibed many French attitudes and prejudices—including a belief in the innate superiority of French civilization over that of the upstart Americans.

Ngo Dinh Diem had few friends abroad and had only one ally, the United States, by the end of 1955. But the atmosphere of crisis had disappeared from Saigon. A professional diplomat replaced General Collins as ambassador. President Diem was on excellent terms with his American advisers, and American writers and politicians began celebrating the "miracle" that Diem had accomplished in Vietnam.

It did not seem to occur to any of these Americans that Diem's major victories had been achieved against non-Communist groups and individuals who should have been incorporated into the government of the South, that he was almost completely isolated in his own country.

SPRING 1963

Eight years had passed since those tumultuous spring days when Diem had tested his strength against the sects and won. Diem was no longer just one politician among others, different only in that he had managed to make powerful foreign friends as they had not. In 1963, he was the chief of state of a functioning regime that had a visible presence in the cities and the countryside of the South. There was now a national government in South Vietnam, and that government was wholly identified with the personality of Ngo Dinh Diem.

The regime was authoritarian; the country was governed by an appointive bureaucracy. David Halberstam wrote, "There were elections though no opposition candidates were permitted; there was a legislature but it was the rubber stamp kind." Halberstam would call it "a government that had no parallel." Diem said indignantly to a visiting American journalist, Marguerite Higgins, "Show me a single Afro-Asian country that has at this moment adopted the kind of democratic regime that is advocated by the liberal Occidentals."

American officials had tried in vain to persuade him to allow an effective anti-Communist political opposition. In April 1960, at a meeting in the Hotel Caravelle, then the newest and most luxurious hotel in Saigon, eighteen Vietnamese had issued a declaration accusing the government of arbitrary arrests and dictatorial methods; of using the official political parties to control the population and divide the army. They had called for liberty and democracy, for reforms in the army and the administration and in economic and social policy. Among the Caravellistes, as they came to be known, was Dr. Quat, whom some Americans had wanted to make prime minister in 1955. The manifesto was a sweeping indictment of the regime, but the Ngos were unimpressed. They might have found the Caravellistes more convincing if most of the eighteen had not been out-of-office politicians who during their government service had shown little understanding of the difficulties besetting the South and no disposition to deal with them. Diem and Nhu, in any case, had come to believe that the real problems of the country were in the rural areas where these urban middle-class politicians had no roots, where the battle had to be fought against the Communist-led insurgents and against underdevelopment.

A Western ambassador watched Diem drive through the streets of Saigon as Lansdale had once watched him drive past years earlier. When the ambassador asked why he paid no attention to people in the street, Diem replied, "They are just spoiled middle class, always complaining, not worth anything."

Nhu for his part did not bother to hide his contempt for his urban middle-class critics. His intellectual brilliance had made him arrogant; and these politicians hated him in return.

Only after the murder of Diem and Nhu were the opposition politicians able to play an active part in Saigon political life. Most would reveal themselves then as weaklings without political following or national purpose. They would justify the low opinion in which they had been held by Nhu and Diem—but not the lack of subtlety shown by the two brothers in dealing with them.

Dr. Quat finally would become prime minister in February 1965, when Diem was dead. Quat held the post only until June of that same year, when he chose to turn over political power to the Vietnamese army.

In 1963, Diem was as reluctant as ever to delegate authority, except to the handful of people he trusted. Above all, he relied on members of his family—an unsurprising tendency in this country where the family more than the individual was the basic unit of society and obligations to the family by Vietnamese tradition overrode those to the state. Diem's brothers had stood by him from the beginning, even in the worst days of 1955, when it seemed that nearly everyone else had abandoned him.

There had been six brothers once. Khoi, the eldest, a mandarin like Diem, had achieved the rank of provincial governor before he was killed by the Viet Minh after World War II: they had buried him alive with his eldest son.

Next in line was Monsignor Thuc, a Roman Catholic prelate. Strong-minded and self-righteous, he was the product of a Vietnamese Catholic tradition, unfortunate in this land where Catholics were a minority, that had never recognized the separation of church and state. Diem deferred to his elder brother, in obedience to Confucian doctrine, treating him with much the same unquestioning respect he would have showed his father had he lived.

Their youngest brother, Luyen, had been sent abroad to serve as ambassador to the Court of Saint James's. But Can, the second youngest, was still in Hue, where he shunned the limelight and held no official position in the government. His modest title was that of adviser on political parties and groups. But it was well known that Ngo Dinh Can for years had directed the political and military affairs of the regime in the central provinces and that he could be ruthless.

Can operated out of the family residence in Phu Cam, the Catholic quarter of Hue. He was a pragmatic, down-to-earth man with few intellectual pretensions, an ultranationalist with an instinct for practical politics and an understanding of the uses of power. When his brothers fought the sects in the Nam Bo, he had battled against other non-Communist opposition groups in the central provinces, the Dai Viet and the VNQDD. Highly structured, conspiratorial societies bound by secret oaths, these two groups were among those Ho Chi Minh had outmaneuvered in Nationalist China during World War II. Later, Ho had brought them into his government when he wanted their support before the war with France, and then had tried to destroy them both when he no longer needed them. Many VNQDD members had escaped to China, although some stayed with the Viet Minh. But most surviving members of the Dai Viet had remained behind and cooperated with the French. Opportunistic, authoritarian—faction ridden even then —they had carved out a substantial fief for themselves in the north, in the administration, army, and police established by the French under Bao Dai. But when the French left, the Dai Viet had to leave, too.

A group calling itself the Revolutionary Dai Viet, and the VNQDD, tried to establish new bases south of the Seventeenth Parallel, in the central provinces, where they already had branches. But Ngo Dinh Can would brook no challenge to the authority of the Diem regime. He set about uprooting their networks, and in 1955 the Revolutionary Dai Viet and the VNQDD rose in separate revolts against the government in the central provinces. Their resistance was broken by the army, and their leaders were imprisoned.

This setback did not cause the two parties to lose either their political drive or their ambition for power. There were several Dai Viet factions in Diemist Vietnam. Some operated secretly, others openly, in the army, the administration, and the political life of the South, biding their time.

They could do nothing in the central provinces as long as Ngo Dinh Can was in control, though the region remained a VNQDD stronghold. Can had his own political networks and his intelligence service (and the reports of his agents did not always tally with information received in Saigon by his brother Nhu). Even so, the entourage of Can was not so competent as he believed, and it had been infiltrated by the CIA.

In Saigon, Nhu, next in age to Diem, lived with his wife and children in a wing of the presidential palace. He was Diem's closest adviser and had become a controversial political figure in his own right, as had his pretty, sharp-tongued wife.

Once, General Collins had complained about Diem's lack of original ideas; that was one reproach no one could address to Nhu. Unlike the president, who had been trained as an administrator and sometimes seemed preoccupied by detail, Nhu was an intensely political man. He was more at ease with ideas than people, was fascinated by theory and concerned with broad questions of policy, foreign and domestic. Nhu always deferred to Diem, but the president respected the intelligence of the younger man and had come to rely on his judgment.

In the mid-1930s Nhu had been one of the leaders of the Vietnamese students in Paris. A liberal Catholic and an anticlerical, he had helped to organize his fellow students to demonstrate in favor of the French Popular Front headed by the Socialist Léon Blum. These students were the precursors of the Vietnamese organization that received Ho Chi Minh with ceremony and pride when he visited Paris as president of the Democratic Republic of Vietnam in 1946.

Nhu had returned to colonial Vietnam before the outbreak of World War II to serve as an archivist at the Central Library in Hanoi. He became active in the Vietnamese labor movement and toward the end of the Viet Minh war against France began to work with the CIA to prepare the way for an independent nationalist regime in Saigon—Diem's regime.

Nhu was still in regular touch with the CIA. Lansdale had departed from Vietnam in 1956, leaving as Diem's closest American contacts Professor Fishel and another American adviser, Wolf Ladejinsky, an expert on agrarian reform. In the post-Lansdale years, the CIA station chief met weekly with Ngo Dinh Nhu, and William Colby, who held that post until he was replaced by John Richardson in 1962, admired the political intelligence of the president's brother, though Colby, who one day would be Director of Central Intelligence, did not appreciate Nhu's excessive interest in intrigue and conspiracy.

By 1963, Diem, and Nhu in particular, recognized that the regime could not survive without a political base and had established one of their own. It was not what Diem's American advisers either expected or approved, but the problems confronting the Ngos were urgent, and distinctively Vietnamese. The brothers had found no answers in the republican constitution that had been adopted in October 1956. The South needed representative government—but it needed effective government even more. The country was in desperate need of strong leadership, some form of popular organization that could enable the state to defend itself against anarchy and subversion, and a discipline that could unite the members of this demoralized Confucian society.

Diem recognized these needs, but he lacked a doctrine with broad popular appeal. Nor did he have a competent and independent civil service at his disposal. And so Diem identified the welfare of the Republic of Vietnam with the fate of his own regime, and the administrative apparatus was paralleled by semiofficial organizations whose purpose was to strengthen the hold of the Diem government on the country.

Drawing their inspiration in part from the Vietnamese experience in the North, the Ngos had created an apparatus of participation and control that extended over the South. The members of the Can Lao (the Labor and Personalism Party), a secret party, acted as agents of the government and honeycombed the ranks of the army and the bureaucracy. They wielded political influence but never were so effective or so powerful as the Communist Lao Dong Party in the North. The Movement for National Revolution, which had been intended to control its numerous members and rally them in support of the regime, had deteriorated into a weak group of opportunistic government officials. The government counted far more on the Republican Youth, a paramilitary organization of blue-uniformed young men and women who were active in the cities and the villages of the South. The Republican Youth claimed well over a million members and were led by the brother of the president, Nhu, himself. Madame Nhu, his wife, headed a Women's Solidarity Movement.

The Vietnamese army, trained and supplied by the Americans, was also, of course, a mass organization. Judging by what had happened at Ap Bac, it was not functioning very well, and Americans blamed that on Diem and Nhu.

The population of the South had no wish to live under communism as it was practiced in the North. But they had had enough of war. Few people in or out of the army were eager for more fighting, this time against the Communist-led insurgents, except for some Northerners and Catholics and, of course, the Ngo family. Americans, however, chose to attribute these lukewarm attitudes also to the failures of the regime.

In March 1963, Chester Cooper, a CIA analyst, came to Saigon on a mission to explore whether "we could win with Diem." He stayed in Vietnam for six or seven weeks and was received by Diem and his brother Nhu. Nhu seemed to him to make sense, but Cooper was disconcerted by Diem, whom he found "highly nervous, terribly repetitive, not altogether relevant." Cooper, who had never met Diem before, "didn't know if he was ill or whether he was sane or losing his mind." However, Cooper recommended staying with Diem.

Months earlier, Senator Mike Mansfield had found Diem "very withdrawn, very secluded. He was not the Diem I knew. So the only conclusion I could come to—it was at best a guess, an estimate—was that he had fallen under the influence of his brother and his wife and they were taking control. . . . I think he was gradually being cut off from reality."

Yet, when Roger Hilsman and Michael Forrestal of the White House staff had called on Diem in January, only a few weeks after Mansfield's visit, Hilsman had a very different impression of the president. He thought Diem much improved from the previous January, when he had seemed distraught, disorganized, and cut off from his own people. In January 1963, Hilsman reported Diem "calmer, more self-possessed, and more statesmanlike. He still talked compulsively and interminably—but what he said was more to the point and showed a deep concern for the welfare and future of all his people." He made Hilsman squirm with his "devastatingly correct and completely fair critique of the mistake in siting weapons, in cutting fields of fire, and so on" by the West Point commander of an American Special Forces camp that had been overrun by the Viet Cong a few days earlier.

On their return to Washington, Hilsman and Forrestal reported to President Kennedy that the Southern forces were winning, though more slowly than had been hoped. But more vigorous leverage was needed to get Diem to do what we wanted, to overcome his general resistance to advice. There were already American military advisers, not just at the lower levels of the army but with every province chief, and steps were being taken to put Agency for International Development (AID) advisers in at least twenty of the forty-one provinces. "An effort should be made to increase this influence at the local level even more by putting additional U.S. AID people with province chiefs and . . . even at selected places further down the civilian hierarchy."

Of all Diem's visitors in these months, Mike Mansfield, who was supposed to be his friend, was the most pessimistic. In his report to the president, the senator wrote, "We are once again at the beginning of the beginning." He questioned the capacity of the Saigon government to carry out the "immense job of social engineering" called for by the new American approach and expressed doubts about Diem's leadership now that he was older and the problems were more complex.

In Saigon, reports of what Senator Mansfield had written set off rumors of a pending coup d'état. The Vietnamese president was shocked by press accounts of the senator's report and could not believe them. Ambassador Nolting called the Mansfield report "the first nails in Diem's coffin."

In the cities that spring, most Vietnamese paid little attention to the efforts of Americans working to defeat a peasant-based insurgency that did not seem to touch their own lives. When this writer visited Hue in April and asked a local doctor for the latest news, he did not speak of war but of peace. "Something important," he said. "The Buddhist Youth are organizing."

In Ceylon, the international journal *World Buddhism* had reported from Vietnam "a great deal of Buddhist activity and signs of a revival of Buddhism."

The movement to restore the old religion from the decadence into which it had fallen had begun in the 1920s but had taken on new life when the country became independent. In the South, young people, deprived of political freedom, turned in increasing numbers to Buddhism. And a new generation of Buddhist monks was in touch with the world Buddhist movement. Impressed by the primacy enjoyed by Buddhism in other newly independent nations like Ceylon, Cambodia, and Burma, some Vietnamese bonzes dreamed of official recognition of the faith as the national religion in their country, too.

During the first days of March 1963, more than twenty-five thousand people—Buddhist monks, nuns, laymen—converged on the Southern port of Vung Tau. The town, hardly changed since colonial days, could not accommodate them, and many spent the night on white sand beaches bordering the South China Sea. Cars and buses arrived carrying sacred relics for the inauguration of a giant image of Buddha and a temple that had been constructed overlooking the sea. The money to build them had been raised by popular subscription.

The Venerable Narada, a Singhalese monk who had made other visits to Vietnam, had brought the sacred relics from Ceylon. He spoke at the dedication ceremony and apostrophized, "O merciful Buddha, the Supreme Teacher of the majority of the citizens of Vietnam!"

What this upsurge of interest in Buddhism might portend did not interest American reporters that spring. They were in Vietnam to cover a war, and their articles reported complaints of American officers that the Vietnamese did not want to fight or fought badly, that Diem and Nhu disagreed with the Americans on how the war ought to be fought.

The newsmen received little help or sympathy from Ambassador Nolting and other high-ranking Americans at the embassy and the Military Assistance Command, who were now themselves involved in the counterinsurgency effort, working closely with the Saigon government. They tried to present the Vietnamese military effort in the best light, to maintain the goodwill of the Diem regime and at the same time to disarm American critics of President Kennedy's Vietnam policy at home. The relations of the Nolting embassy with the resident American press were strained, antagonistic. The reporters challenged official optimism—American and Vietnamese—that the war was going well.

For David Halberstam, it was "great and unreal fun." On his birthday in April, he was up in a helicopter with picked troops chasing the Viet Cong in the Ca Mau Peninsula: "a particularly successful day and we had made several strikes, capturing about 15 Viet Cong and killing about 10 others . . . in those days a reporter's Vietnam was a marvelous and rare combination of constant excitement, some danger, the exhilaration that comes from being around brave men, beautiful countryside, good food and lovely women . . . and recurrent fights with American officialdom. . . ."

4.
A Checkered History, a Fragile Balance

One spring day in 1963, cars drew up before a fortified hamlet in the south-central highlands. Among the people who got out were three men, unlikely traveling companions for a sightseeing trip that was not part of their official duties: Gordon Cox, Canadian, unassuming, well informed, agreeable; Ramchundur Goburdhun, Indian, exuberant, and assertive; and Mieczyslaw Maneli, their colleague, a sometime professor at the University of Warsaw, the new delegate of Communist Poland on the International Control and Supervisory Commission.

Maneli walked over to the fence of pointed stakes that circled the hamlet and extended his hand to try its strength. Not very solid, he said with a laugh; even his young son in Warsaw could have pushed it down. Did the government really expect to keep out guerrillas with that?

After nine years, the ICC was taken for granted in Saigon; the bitterness forgotten of the traumatic period after the Geneva Conference when most of the infractions of the cease-fire accord reported by the International Commission had been in the South and a government-inspired mob had attacked the hotel of the commission in the Southern capital. The ICC was not only there to oversee the armistice. It had been entrusted with another assignment: to supervise general elections in 1956, which would pave the way for a political settlement between North and South and the unification of Vietnam.

Those elections whose imminence had once worried Senator Mansfield had not been held. And the ICC, its mission unfulfilled, had reduced its personnel to cut down on costs and stayed on.

The commissioners kept their headquarters in Saigon but they visited Hanoi from time to time; and teams composed of Indians, Poles, and Canadians were stationed at specified entry points in the North and the South.

They went through the motions of investigating the introduction into the country of fresh troops, military personnel, arms and munitions; and the establishment of foreign military bases—all forbidden by the armistice accord—as the ICC had been directed to do years earlier by the great powers at Geneva in 1954. The commission was powerless to do any more than observe, its right of investigation was strictly limited by both Vietnams; and it addressed reports at intervals to the governments of Great Britain and the Soviet Union, co-chairmen of the Geneva Conference.

These ICC reports had chronicled the growing American military presence in the South in violation of the Geneva cease-fire accord. Embarrassed by this unwelcome publicity, the Washington government hid increases in American military personnel and American military aid when it could and played them down if they could not be hidden.

Yet the ICC had acknowledged that the Diem regime might have good reason to seek American help. On June 2, 1962, the

International Control Commission had formally charged the government of Hanoi with covert aggression and subversion aimed at the armed overthrow of the Saigon government.

This ICC Special Report had not been unanimous. The Poles refused to endorse the views of their Indian and Canadian colleagues. Saigon officials had not expected anything else. They regarded the Poles as agents of the enemy, who reported to Hanoi what they learned in the course of their service in the South, and the Poles were ostracized by government officials when their presence was not required by protocol.

Now, suddenly, without explanation or publicity, this policy had changed; on that spring day in 1963, Maneli, the new Polish commissioner, was traveling as an honored guest of the Southern government.

The three diplomats from the ICC were escorted by Prince Buu-Hoi, who had made his peace with Diem years earlier; at the request of the president, the professor had been working with a group of diplomats since 1958 to end the isolation of South Vietnam in the world community. Their greatest successes had been in the Afro-Asian countries, and though Buu-Hoi continued his scientific work in the West, he himself had become ambassador-at-large to various countries and several United Nations bodies. He was also director of the Vietnam atomic energy center that was being constructed in the red earth of the central highlands outside the resort town of Dalat. The three ICC commissioners stopped off in Dalat during the trip that took them to this fortified hamlet. They arrived as tourists in this pleasant town where well-to-do Vietnamese came to enjoy the cool air, a respite from the debilitating lowland heat.

Seventeen years earlier other visitors with a mandate to unify Vietnam by peaceful means had come to Dalat, during a different spring. Those earlier visitors had been Vietnamese patriots seeking freedom from colonial rule in 1946 when the Ho Chi Minh government had still been the broad national front movement it claimed to be and the only Vietnamese government in the country. Ho had just signed an accord in which the French had conceded that the Democratic Republic of Vietnam was "a free state within the Indochinese Federation and the French Union." The Vietnamese had agreed in exchange to accept French troops on their territory. This "free" state extended southward only to the Sixteenth Parallel below Da Nang in central Vietnam. The French had refused to recognize the Vietnamese claim to the lands farther south; they promised only that the future of the Nam Bo would be decided by referendum at a later date. They did agree to further talks with the Ho Chi Minh government and a meeting was arranged at Dalat.

The conference had opened on March 13 at the Lang Bian Palace Hotel, an old-fashioned, sprawling colonial structure overlooking a lake. French military operations were still going on in the Nam Bo, and the Viet Minh military commander in the south had launched an offensive to strengthen the bargaining position of the Vietnamese delegation, isolated and without allies at Dalat.

Later, in Diem's day, when the great powers recognized the partition of Vietnam under two independent regimes, Ho Chi Minh and his followers would be forced to keep up the fiction that revolutionary warfare in the south was not directed by the Hanoi government and was beyond its control. But in 1946 only one independent Vietnamese government existed, and had its capital in Hanoi, and there was no need for pretense that March at Dalat.

A delegate from the Nam Bo demanded the liberation of all those who had been arrested in the south by French troops "for having been in the ranks of the resistance, for having tried to work for the unity of the Vietnamese nation."

Then General Vo Nguyen Giap spoke with emotion: "They will tell us that these are really military operations [in the Nam Bo] but that these operations have been directed against bands of 'malefactors' or against 'irregular troops.' What a delicate and bold distinction between irregular troops and regular troops . . . you will recognize with me that these armed elements of the Nam Bo, who obey our orders and are in liaison with our headquarters are indeed Vietnamese soldiers, of the army of Vietnam.

"They will tell us that it is understood that hostilities should stop, our troops should lay down their arms, the Tonkinese [northern] soldiers should be repatriated. As if there were a surrender and not an armistice, as if the Tonkinese soldiers were not in Cochinchina [the Nam Bo], in their own country, Vietnam."

Twenty-nine years later in May 1975, another meeting was held at the Lang Bian Palace Hotel. Saigon had fallen to a conquering army from the North. After a celebration in front of Independence Palace that had become the headquarters of the victors and a ceremony marking the birth of Ho Chi Minh, the triumphant military leaders adjourned to the same hotel in Dalat to sum up their successful campaign. General Van Tien Dung, their commander, recalled the other conference held there in 1946 when the Vietnamese had asked for "independence and unity" and been rebuffed. Giap had wept when it was over.

Weeks after that earlier Dalat Conference, another Vietnamese delegation had arrived in France to put forward the same demands during more extended but equally unsuccessful negotiations at Fontainebleau.

"We signed a convention on March 6, that makes four months already, and we have not yet built anything constructive," said Pham Van Dong. "Why? Because the question of Cochinchina [the Nam Bo] has not been settled."

"As long as Cochinchina remains detached from Vietnam, no understanding will be possible between France and Vietnam," said a Communist delegate from the Nam Bo.

That October, Ho Chi Minh told his countrymen: "I can affirm categorically that sooner or later Vietnam will be independent, north, center and south reunified. Compatriots of the Nam Bo and the southern part of the Trung Bo [the center], north, south and center are integral parts of Vietnam. We descend from the same ancestors, we are blood brothers. . . ."

The French had created a separate state in the south. They occupied all the towns and were trying to "pacify" the countryside. Popular resistance was directed by the Viet Minh through the Committee of the Nam Bo. The young secretary-general of that committee, Tran Buu Khiem, would be one of the founding members of the National Liberation Front in 1960.

In 1946 the French had moved to consolidate their foothold

in the north. They shelled the city of Haiphong to teach the Vietnamese a lesson on the occasion of a minor customs incident. Six thousand people were killed in that one day, according to an official French estimate.

They had meant to intimidate the Vietnamese. They succeeded only in convincing them they had no choice left but war.

On December 19, 1946, the Vietnamese struck. They attacked French garrisons in Hanoi and other key points. The fighting was fierce, and the Vietnamese forces were driven out of their capital.

The French were carrying on a brutal "pacification" of Hanoi that took a heavy toll of civilians when Ho Chi Minh issued a declaration on December 21, 1946: "Countrymen! Our resistance will be long and difficult. Whatever the sacrifices, whatever the length of the resistance, we will fight until the end, until the day when Vietnam is completely independent and reunified."

Early in 1953, a Vietnamese traveler presented himself at the office maintained by the Viet Minh in Rangoon, Burma. Isolated by mountain and jungle in their Thai Nguyen headquarters, the Viet Minh leaders had seen their few remaining links with the countries outside China erode as each successive year of war bound them closer to their powerful northern neighbor. But west of the rugged highlands of Laos, they still maintained a window on the non-Communist world in the Burmese capital.

It was the obvious place for anyone arriving from Europe to make direct contact with the Viet Minh, avoiding Chinese intermediaries—especially a man who was seeking a way to end a war that Peking wished to continue. That was the mission of Buu-Hoi.

The professor was a high official of the Diem government when he visited Dalat with the diplomats of the International Control and Supervisory Commission in 1963, but he had gone to Rangoon as a private citizen ten years earlier. His patriotic credentials had been impeccable and certainly enough to assure him a hearing even though he, like many other nationalists, had broken with the Ho Chi Minh government when the Viet Minh imposed an openly Communist dictatorship on the resistance in 1950. Once the elected president of the twenty-five thousand Vietnamese workers and soldiers stranded in France after World War II, he had been a delegate to the conference at Fontainebleau whose collapse was a prelude to war in 1946. A further recommendation to the Viet Minh was that he had never been a professional politician but was a scientist with an international reputation.

Buu-Hoi came from Paris accompanied by Jacques Raphael-Leygues, a Radical Socialist politician, after an interview with Vincent Auriol, president of France. He had been authorized by the French president to propose to the Ho Chi Minh government the opening of direct negotiations with France.

In the letter he left in Rangoon to be communicated to the Viet Minh leaders, the professor pointed out prophetically that this was their last hope of dealing with their French adversaries face to face without foreign interference. The next time, he warned, they would be confronted by the United States, backed by force far beyond anything the Vietnamese had ever known.

The French government did nothing to follow up this overture. The Viet Minh, for its part, eventually delivered a negative answer through its supporters in Paris.

Years afterward, Frenchmen blamed domestic political feuds for the lack of support the mission had received from certain members of the French government. Hanoi officials claimed that the difficulties encountered in forwarding the message to their inaccessible headquarters had prevented the Viet Minh from replying in time. Both sides felt the need to fall back on such embarrassed explanations long after the event, apparently because they realized, too late, that the Buu-Hoi mission had offered an opportunity that would not come again.

A last chance of preserving Vietnamese unity had been thrown away almost casually in 1953, perhaps inadvertently, and the two adversaries by their inability to make peace between themselves had condemned Vietnam to partition.

When the Ho Chi Minh government agreed to negotiate many months later, the Vietnamese people were placed at the mercy of the conflicting ambitions of the great powers: not another Dalat or Fontainebleau this time, but a full-scale international conference that opened in Geneva in May 1954, to end the war in Vietnam—

and in Laos and Cambodia, because fighting had long since spread to their territory as well.

The only documents actually signed at Geneva were cease-fire accords, the only signatories of the Vietnamese armistice agreement a French brigadier general and the Viet Minh vice minister of defense. It laid the groundwork for partition: "pending general elections which will bring about the unification of Vietnam, the conduct of civil administration in each regrouping zone shall be in the hands of the forces who are to be regrouped there"—those of the Ho Chi Minh government to the North, those of the Bao Dai government and the French in the South.

True, the Final Declaration of the conference stated that any political settlement in Vietnam should be based on the principles of independence, unity, and territorial integrity, and that the regrouping of the opposing forces under the cease-fire agreement was not to be interpreted as establishing a political or territorial boundary. In July 1956, general elections were going to be held; talks between North and South to arrange those elections would start in a year.

But this Final Declaration was little more than a pious statement of intention, approved by neither the United States nor the State of Vietnam and unsigned by any of the nations represented at Geneva. The prospect of elections to decide the future of the South was unacceptable to the Diem government because of the weakness of the new nationalist regime in Saigon and its belief that any election allowed by the Hanoi government would not be free.

The Vietnamese revolutionaries were frustrated in their hope that they could profit from the Geneva Conference to unify the country under Ho Chi Minh even though they had not yet succeeded in taking over the South by force of arms. (Only in 1975 would they be strong enough to seize Saigon as the Chinese Communist forces had seized Peking in 1949.) Privately, Viet Minh leaders blamed their Chinese Communist allies for this disappointment.

The Chinese had used the war to win an invitation to the international conference table. They had been out to convince other nations of their own moderation at Geneva, if necessary at the expense of the Vietnamese. Viet Minh resentment at what Foreign Minister Chou En-lai had done in Geneva, and what he had failed to do, would simmer for a quarter of a century before it became public when the Hanoi government listed its many grievances against China in a white paper, in 1979.

It was bad enough that Chou had joined the Russians and the British in proposing a cease-fire that split the country in two. Even worse, Chou had not insisted on a political settlement. The armistice agreement became a blueprint for partition, and the Ho Chi Minh government had been given no choice but acceptance.

The Hanoi regime would reproach the Chinese with not wanting a strong, unified Vietnam on their southern border—although no Chinese government had ever wanted that. In addition, Chou had refused to back Viet Minh ambitions in Laos and Cambodia, and Pham Van Dong had been forced to abandon his attempt to have the Viet Minh–sponsored resistance movements in both states represented at Geneva.

In their white paper of 1979, the Hanoi government accused the Chinese of welcoming the partition of Vietnam. The Russians proposed the admission of both Vietnams to the United Nations in 1957; their proposal, which would have perpetuated the division of the country, was rejected. But the white paper claimed that the Chinese on July 22, 1954, had suggested to Diem's brother Luyen that the Saigon government open a legation in Peking. If this offer was indeed made, then the Diem government was shortsighted in failing to take advantage of it.

On August 11, 1954, the armistice, already in effect in the northern and central provinces, was extended to the Nam Bo. The Viet Minh claimed the Geneva Conference had been a triumph for Hanoi, soon to be sealed by nationwide elections. That was the official line, to galvanize Viet Minh militants and sympathizers in the south-central provinces and the Nam Bo, to rally them against the Saigon government. But high-level Communist cadres spoke a different language, as did the Viet Minh leaders who were not naïve men.

True, the French were committed to carrying out the Geneva Accords in their entirety but the French were in the process of liquidating a policy that had led them to defeat and forced them to grant the Vietnamese their independence. No government in Paris was going to impose elections on the Vietnamese against the wishes of the Diem regime and its American ally. Pham Van Dong never had any illusions on that score. At Geneva, he had said to a Vietnamese visitor, "Those elections will never be held."

That summer of 1954 the desire for peace and normality had been strong throughout the South. In Saigon, men gathered in small groups to talk of the new perspectives opened by the Viet Minh victory in the North. Most Southerners did not know Diem and what they heard of him made some people think he had been imposed on them by the United States and Cardinal Spellman and that John Foster Dulles meant to use the South as a pawn against the Communists and risk a new war.

Such Western-educated Southern intellectuals and professional men saw Vietnam as one country and, rightly or wrongly, were confident they could establish a neutralist government that could make its peace with Hanoi. They looked forward to a lasting settlement with the North and eventual unity and had begun to organize peace committees even before the war ended. They were the obvious target of Viet Minh agents whose tactic was to draw them into support of the objectives of the Ho Chi Minh government. The North lost the goodwill of some of these well-disposed Southerners when it mistakenly used a Communist, the chief of the Vietnamese Communists in Paris, as its emissary to them. If Hanoi blundered, Diem did, too.

He allowed himself to be persuaded by his American advisers that these were simply Communist-front groups. He was already suspicious of liberal Southerners, of liberal non-Communist personalities who might have contributed to a broadly based nationalist government. The members of the Saigon-Cholon peace committee were eventually arrested. Some later emerged from political obscurity in 1960 as founding members of the National Liberation Front, the political arm of the Viet Cong.

By 1955 it was no longer prudent to talk openly in Saigon

about coexistence between North and South, unification, even democratic liberties or free elections, because these had become the slogans of the Communists in their drive to ensure the holding of elections in 1956. Newspapers that wrote of such matters were suspended; some newspaper offices were sacked by angry refugees.

Although the American government had sent a delegation to the Geneva Conference, it had not wanted this peace any more than Diem himself. The Americans had tried in vain to persuade the French to continue the war against Ho Chi Minh, and Mansfield and other Democrats had joined the Republicans in opposing the holding of the Geneva Conference and had deplored its outcome. But at least, after Geneva, the French were in no position to refuse to the regime in Saigon its full independence so often promised and so long deferred.

Diem had acted with American support when he rejected overtures from Hanoi for talks to prepare the way for elections. Other members of the international community treated the failure to unify Vietnam with indifference; the Chinese and the Russians showed little more concern than any of the other powers that had been represented at Geneva.

A fragile balance had been attained in Vietnam. Hanoi, having recognized the fact of partition, assumed that each side would act against the other, but within certain limits. The relative restraint of the Communist leaders was predicated on the assumption that the Americans would not increase their military presence in the South.

In South Vietnam, a Communist-directed campaign of assassination had begun in the villages—against officials, teachers, health workers, police—to undermine the authority of the Saigon regime and further isolate the villages from the central government. The official line of the party decreed by the leaders in Hanoi called for Southern members to limit themselves to political action against the Saigon regime, but political action did not seem to exclude political terror.

This "political" line was obeyed despite sharp disagreements in party councils, at a time when the Saigon government was trying to wipe out the party organization. General Tran Van Tra commanded the Viet Cong "Zone B2," which covered the Nam Bo and extended to the foot of the central highlands. When Tra published his memoir, *Concluding the Thirty Years War,* in Saigon (now Ho Chi Minh City) in 1982, he revealed his bitterness at the heavy losses inflicted on the Southern revolutionaries because of the "naïve" policies of 1954–59 when beleaguered militants "died with guns in their hands not daring to use them," having been ordered not to by the party.

"The period 1956–59 was a political fight," said Pham Van Dong when he was prime minister on 1967. "It saw the mutual assistance pact between the United States and Saigon and the introduction of U.S. staffs. This led to the formation of the National Liberation Front."

"If [Ngo Dinh] Nhu had only been willing to leave open a channel to the North, the National Liberation Front would never have developed." The speaker was Nguyen Van Chi, long the unofficial representative of the Hanoi regime in Paris.

In 1959, Lao Dong Party leaders decided that armed action was needed to support the political struggle against the Diem government. The Chinese Communists had tried to hold back their Vietnamese comrades, but the Chinese finally agreed that the party would be destroyed as a force in the South if it did not fight, even at the risk of exposing its secret organization to government attack.

The new line was adopted at a meeting of the Central Committee in January. This Hanoi directive was passed down from one level to the next in the pyramid of committees in which the party was organized until it reached the villages of the South.

The campaign of assassination and terror intensified in the countryside, and armed guerrilla bands emerged. Some were elite units that had never disbanded or surrendered their weapons despite the Geneva Accords and had been hiding in the jungle. Other guerrillas collected arms from caches where they had been stored since the armistice. They attacked isolated army posts to get military supplies.

The Hanoi government had begun to send arms to the South along a network of trails through Laos and by sea. Native Southerners evacuated to the North after the Geneva cease-fire agreement were infiltrated back to participate in the insurgency.

Now the enemy was an independent Vietnamese government, not the French colonial regime, and the Seventeenth Parallel had become an international boundary; Hanoi was obliged to hide its intervention and insist on the local origins of the spreading violence in the South.

First, the Resistance Veterans Association had called for armed action to overthrow the regime and set up a new government of national union to open talks with the North and arrange the peaceful unification of the country. This declaration purported to be a spontaneous initiative of Southerners driven by Diem's repression to appeal to the North for help and was publicized abroad by Western liberals. They might have been less sympathetic if they had realized the veterans had acted by order of the party; its aim, to win Southern support for the decision made in Hanoi for armed action against the Diem government. In September, a party congress in Hanoi endorsed the new policy and called for a national front in the South.

The National Liberation Front emerged three months later, on December 20, 1960, at a meeting in a hamlet in the jungle close to the Cambodian frontier. In attendance, representatives of groups and individuals opposed to Diem: members of the sects, dissidents, and revolutionaries who had been hiding out in the jungle; others who had slipped away from Saigon where they had carried on ordinary pursuits as a cover while conspiring against the regime. A group of French-educated middle-class Southerners in the capital had secretly organized what they called a mobilization committee to prepare for this moment; four of its seven members, unknown to the others, seem to have been members of the Communist Party. Together, these disparate elements founded the National Liberation Front, an exact copy of the Viet Minh front organized by Ho Chi Minh during World War II. At the first congress of the front, February–March 1962, a permanent committee was formed and a president elected, a French-trained Saigon lawyer who had once been active in the Saigon-Cholon peace movement.

The Hanoi radio proclaimed the new front and diffused its manifesto and its program. The Viet Cong now had a political arm and a declared political goal: to overthrow the Diem regime and in time unify the country by peaceful means. During a transitional period of unspecified length, the State of South Vietnam would be sovereign and independent under the leadership of the front and might join Cambodia and Laos in a zone of neutrality and peace.

One non-Communist conspirator from Saigon who claimed to have been a founding member of the front in 1960 emerged as minister of justice in a provisional government proclaimed by the front in 1969, years after Diem was dead. Truong Nhu Tang liked to think of himself as a Southern nationalist, yet he had found it normal that neither the program nor the manifesto of the National Liberation Front was written in the South. They were skillfully drafted in Hanoi to appeal to different elements in the South—intellectuals, students, middle class, peasants, workers—and Tang had been so impressed when he read the two documents that "I suspected I was seeing in them the delicate fingerprints of Ho Chi Minh."

When Tang wrote these words in the 1980s, he was a defector from Communist Vietnam. He was one of the boat people who fled after Hanoi took over the country and imposed its rule on the South. Yet even then, when the autonomous regime established by the front after the fall of Saigon had been absorbed by the North, this former Viet Cong minister professed not to understand why Ho Chi Minh's "fingerprints" ought to have aroused suspicion and anxiety among non-Communist Southern nationalists who chose to join the National Liberation Front while Ngo Dinh Diem was president and South Vietnam was still independent.

In 1963, many Americans dismissed the National Liberation Front as merely an instrument of North Vietnamese imperialism, even though the front's adherents were native Southerners, some of whom had never accepted the Diem regime, while others had real grievances against the government in Saigon that had managed to alienate them without any help from Hanoi.

To other Americans, the rebels were just what they said they were, Southern patriots forced into revolt by Diem's brutal misrule, who had seized the initiative in disregard of the wishes of the regime in Hanoi and called on the Ho Chi Minh government to support armed action against Diem.

All these Americans—whether critics or supporters of Washington policy in Vietnam—made the same mistake, unaware that they were doing what many Frenchmen had done before them: underestimating the Ho Chi Minh government and its followers in the North and the South, refusing to credit them with the ability to formulate a nationwide revolutionary strategy and the patience to carry it out over a period of many years.

After the battle of Ap Bac, clashes intensified between government troops and the Viet Cong during the first months of 1963.

The insurgents were fighting to overthrow Diem and the government they labeled "My Diem." *My* means United States. The National Liberation Front now had official representatives in Hanoi and sent emissaries abroad as if it really were independent, as many of its adherents claimed and some perhaps believed. But Hanoi leaders saw no upsurge of political support for their Southern satellite, no prospect that it could dislodge the Americans from the South.

"We would even accept a bourgeois government in Saigon," a North Vietnamese diplomat had told a French journalist in Geneva, in August 1962. "All we ask is that it follow a policy of neutrality, national independence and good relations with the North. Let it receive aid from France; we don't mind. We would prefer to see French advisers and French capital in Saigon than American advisers and American capital."

Both Hanoi and Saigon had sent delegations to another Geneva Conference because of the breakdown of peace in neighboring Laos. The Communist Pathet Lao, the wartime ally of the Viet Minh, had threatened to overwhelm American-supported rightist elements and take control of Laos. But a coalition government had finally been established in that country.

The North Vietnamese foreign minister, in Geneva for the occasion, approached an opponent of Diem, a former prime minister of Bao Dai, who was living in exile in France, to sound him out about heading a South Vietnamese government on the Laotian model. Tran Van Huu was no friend of the Viet Cong or of the

Hanoi regime. But he was known to favor a neutral and independent South and the opening of normal economic and cultural relations with the North.

They met at the Perle du Lac restaurant on the bank of Lake Léman. The lunch was elaborate, the conversation friendly (both the guest of honor and the host were natives of the Nam Bo), but Huu and the delegation from Hanoi did not reach an understanding that day or any other day.

Although the secretary general of the National Liberation Front happened to be traveling in Europe at the time, he was not invited to this meeting at the Perle du Lac. A strong and active Viet Cong was still indispensable to the political strategy of the men in Hanoi, but they had their own priorities, and different times required different tactics.

In earlier years, the Ho Chi Minh government had approached the Saigon regime directly to propose opening normal relations between North and South and had been rebuffed, not once but several times. Diem in those days had lacked confidence in the ability of his regime to hold its own in competition with the North and had placed his trust unquestioningly in his American allies.

But that spring of 1963, the strains in the American alliance were beginning to tell, and Diem's policy in Afro-Asian countries was directed at winning support for South Vietnam's entrance into the United Nations in the hope of lessening its dependence on the United States. He had been warned by King Mohammed V of Morocco and other Third World leaders of the danger of depending too much on a single ally. Ngo Dinh Nhu paid an official visit to Morocco after the king's death as the guest of his son, Hassan II, in 1961. Nhu also received an invitation from Gamal Abdel Nasser to visit Egypt. In Burma, Diem had authorized his minister plenipotentiary to dine with the representative of Ho Chi Minh, both guests of the neutralist Buddhist prime minister, U Nu, in 1960.

Kennedy's attempt to neutralize Laos impressed on Diem and Nhu the urgency of the need for a more independent foreign policy. In September 1962, Diem rejected the proposal of Prince Norodom Sihanouk for another international conference, this time to neutralize Cambodia and safeguard its territory (against the South Vietnamese). Diem's reply, written in the unmistakable style of his brother Nhu, noted that Vietnam did not follow the fashion of neutrality, which seemed to have gained the favor of the free world (an acid reference to Laos), because Vietnam had been attacked by international communism and communism was not neutral. However, the letter went on to insist on the excellent relations of South Vietnam with the neutral countries of the Third World and on Vietnamese respect for their freedom to choose their national and international "options."

Diem and Nhu had given serious thought to their own options by the time Maneli, the new Polish commissioner, went sightseeing with his ICC colleagues in the south-central highlands. Diem was confident of the strength of the Republic of Vietnam that spring of 1963. He had no inkling of the crisis that was brewing in his native city of Hue.

5.
Incident
in
Hue

MAY 1963

There was no mistaking the identity of the man in clerical dress
whose car approached the outskirts of Hue that morning early in
May. His features were heavier than those of his brothers in Saigon,
far removed from the lean good looks of Nhu, and his manner was
poised and confident, whereas Diem by contrast often seemed self-
effacing. This was Monsignor Ngo Dinh Thuc, his air of authority
a reminder that he was a prelate of the Roman Catholic Church,
archbishop of Hue, the dean of the Vietnamese Catholic hierarchy
who was treated with deference even by the president.

He was on his way back from a visit to the shrine of La Vang
near Quang Tri City in the northern part of his diocese, a shrine
that had prospered under his patronage. On the whole it had been
a gratifying week for Monsignor Thuc. A Catholic, his own

brother, Ngo Dinh Diem, had ruled the first Republic of South Vietnam for eight years, and now Thuc himself was in the middle of a countrywide celebration of the twenty-fifth anniversary of his consecration as bishop. Services in his honor had already been held in Saigon and Dalat during the first days of May. There had even been services in Hue, although formal celebration of the jubilee in that city was not scheduled to take place until the end of June. But on this seventh day of May 1963, it was obvious to those who knew him that Archbishop Ngo Dinh Thuc was frustrated and angry.

The archbishop was oblivious to the irritation caused by the scale and ostentation of the preparations for his silver anniversary. He had never understood that his conspicuous activities in the name of the church could seem threatening to Vietnamese who were not Catholic; not that their sentiments, had he realized them, would have weighed much with him. Ngo Dinh Thuc had little respect for the popular amalgam of Buddhism, Confucianism, and Taoism by which most Vietnamese lived; little awareness that Buddhism, however superficial its practice by many, could awaken feelings and beliefs as deep-rooted as those inspired by his own church. The people as he saw them were passive, acquiescent, potential subjects for conversion. He did not pause to wonder at their silence or what lay beneath it or how long it would last.

Even some Catholics thought Monsignor Thuc had lavished excessive attention on La Vang, the shrine from which he returned that morning. It was said that the Virgin Mary had appeared there in the nineteenth century. This was during one of the sporadic persecutions of Catholics that had been a feature of life in another independent Vietnam when the emperor still ruled in Hue. Catholics had suffered then because they collaborated with the French conquerors, and La Vang had become a place of pilgrimage. But Monsignor Thuc had not been content to leave it at that. He had transformed La Vang into a center for the cult of the Virgin, with financial donations made often for motives far removed from religious fervor, many by government officials from Vice-President Tho down who were not Catholics but thought it politically expedient to support the archbishop's projects.

Now the population was asked by a national committee composed of people of different faiths to give money for his jubilee. In Hue, where Buddhist officials complained they were obliged to contribute a month's salary, Father Cao Van Luan, the rector of the university and himself a Catholic priest, heard students and faculty criticizing the exaggerated scale of the preparations for the jubilee. He went to see the president's younger brother, who was the principal authority in Hue. Ngo Dinh Can may not have been a highly educated or a sophisticated man, and he was certainly no democrat, but in his way he was close to the people, more so than any of his brothers. Can deplored the archbishop's imprudent confusion of church and state. "But my hands are tied," he told the rector. "My brother the archbishop doesn't listen to me anymore. You had better go to Saigon and tell President Diem."

For Ngo Dinh Nhu, the President's closest adviser, when appealed to in Saigon, political logic dictated the same conclusion that Can had reached by instinct in Hue. Nhu saw no reason to give national importance to a religious event even if the religion in question happened to be his own. But in President Diem's eyes, it seemed, his elder brother could do no wrong.

The archbishop had not always been so indifferent to popular feeling. During the war for independence, when he was a much younger man and merely bishop of Vinh Long, in the south, he had taken a strongly nationalistic political stand as did his brother Diem. Many other Vietnamese Catholics in those days identified their security and prosperity with France, as they had done ever since the previous century when the persecution of Catholics had served as a pretext for the French conquest of Vietnam. Two Vietnamese bishops had actually collaborated with the French against the Viet Minh. Ngo Dinh Thuc had rejected any such collaboration and made it a policy to keep in touch with Catholic priests who joined the popular resistance and with members of southern Catholic families fighting in the ranks of the Viet Minh. One of these was Pham Ngoc Thao, a protégé of Monsignor Thuc who later rallied to the administration of Ngo Dinh Diem. (This was one political convert the archbishop would have cause to regret. By May 1963 Thao was already engaged in plotting against the Diem government.)

It was only after the war with France that Ngo Dinh Thuc's

attitude had changed. Whereas many of his Southern countrymen were content to enjoy the fruits of independence in peace, Thuc saw this new state headed by his brother as a place of challenge and opportunity. It was a heady period for this ambitious man, with the number of Catholics south of the Seventeenth Parallel swollen by the exodus from the North so that one in ten citizens of the new state of Vietnam was Catholic. Never had the dream of converting all Vietnam to Christianity seemed more attainable, or his own dream of advancement to still higher rank within the church more possible.

Catholics seemed more numerous than they actually were as their religious processions crowded the streets and roads on every conceivable occasion. The frequent Catholic holidays were publicly celebrated by the devout president, and priests were in evidence at official events. Villages of refugees were settled along the roads, transplanted bodily from the North. The steeples of their new churches rose above the flat rice lands, and churchbells rang out over the countryside, proclaiming their presence. To one visiting Catholic, they were like early Christian communities in the fullness of the faith, ruled by their own priests who had brought them to the South. But they were medieval in their religious beliefs, unwilling and unable to adapt to the surrounding population.

His headquarters at Vinh Long was close enough to Saigon for Ngo Dinh Thuc to make regular visits to the capital, where a veritable court gathered around him in the late 1950s. The people he received were no longer patriots risking their lives for a national ideal, but officeholders and office seekers attracted by the political influence he did not scruple to exercise in secular as well as religious affairs. But all his considerable influence in Saigon could not win the office he coveted for himself. That required a decision from Rome, and the Vatican moved with slow deliberation.

Even though Vietnamese had been ordained priests as early as the seventeenth century, two centuries before the French seized control of Vietnam, the Vatican had allowed only Europeans to be bishops there until 1933. When Ngo Dinh Thuc was named bishop of Vinh Long in 1938 he was the youngest bishop in the country and his prospects for further advancement looked bright. But the years passed, war came, the French were defeated and expelled, and still he was marooned in Vinh Long. When the French bishop of Saigon retired in 1955, Vatican officials were at last ready to accept a Vietnamese as the highest-ranking prelate in the capital, but they did not want Ngo Dinh Thuc in that key position. Ignoring Diem's open displeasure, they chose a man more aware of the need to keep the church separate from politics than was the president's elder brother.

Monsignor Thuc spent twenty-three years as bishop of Vinh Long before the word so long awaited finally came from Rome. He was to be archbishop of Hue. Thuc would have to take up residence in the old imperial capital, and Ngo Dinh Nhu, for one, was relieved to be free of his brother's continual interference with the affairs of government. The Vatican had evidently judged it advisable to send Ngo Dinh Thuc away from Saigon, where Nguyen Van Binh, a moderate man who was careful not to identify either the church or his own person too closely with the Diem regime, became archbishop.

In their satisfaction at seeing Thuc settled far from the capital since 1961, neither church officials in Rome nor Nhu in Saigon seemed to realize that Hue was not after all very remote from Saigon, nor did they understand that the onetime capital of the Nguyen emperors was singularly ill-adapted to receive this strong-minded ecclesiastic whose ambition was still unsated. They had no idea, any more than he did himself, of the disruptive effect of his presence in Hue.

To the outsider, the city of Hue seemed somnolent in 1963, a political backwater insulated between mountain and lagoon from the currents of change. The deserted palace within the walled Citadel, like the tombs of the Nguyen emperors that blended into the outlying countryside, made clear that if the history of Vietnam had once been made from this place, that time was long past. The city of Hue and the surrounding area were poor, the land yielded little, and industry was nonexistent. The sole resource of Hue was its gifted people. Men from Hue were important in the governmental and cultural life of independent Vietnam, both North and South.

It seemed therefore only natural that the first chief of state of South Vietnam should have come from this city, for the old imperial capital had long been a breeding ground for administrators and intellectuals. In the village of Vi Da on the Perfumed River, just across the canal that borders Hue, elderly members of the imperial family lived with the simplicity decreed by the Confucian tradition. In the city itself scholars were compiling a dictionary in Chinese, Vietnamese, and French; studying the archives for works of family history; translating French classics into Vietnamese; annotating still another edition of the national poem, *Kim Van Kieu*. These citizens of Hue with a family custom of public service, who had known the Ngo family all their lives, expected that these men, too, would devote themselves to serving their country as their ancestors had done.

Ngo Dinh Can was the only one of the brothers who had never left the city. He liked to be known simply as "Uncle Can." But in fact, though not in name, he controlled Hue and the central provinces from the family residence where he lived with his bedridden mother. His rule was authoritarian, paternalistic, sometimes brutal. The old Confucian traditions were still strong in Hue, and life was austere and little affected by the Western influences that had left their imprint on Saigon.

Can governed through a shrewd combination of patronage, efficient administration (headed by Ho Dac Khuong, the delegate of the central government), and a monopoly of power. He jealously guarded his autonomy from Saigon and allowed no voice to political criticism, no place to political opposition, in particular the Dai Viet and the VNQDD, whose networks he had smashed in 1955. His clandestine operations seemed remarkably successful in countering Viet Cong activity, even in provinces like Quang Ngai where the Viet Minh had been entrenched. This writer was able to drive unchallenged through the night across these long disputed central provinces on the road to Saigon and even stopped in one village to await the ferry that replaced a nonexistent bridge. The authorities in Hue anticipated no difficulty, and none arose.

Ngo Dinh Can relied on his personal relations with traditional elements in Vietnamese society to govern, and one of these was the

Buddhist community. When Catholics came to complain that he was giving financial help to the Buddhists, Can retorted, "It is about time they got some help. Under the French the Catholics got everything. Now it is the turn of the Buddhists."

So Can had ruled unchallenged until the arrival of his brother, Monsignor Thuc, in Hue in 1961. Thuc attacked his new post with vigor. As he had during the years at Vinh Long, he founded religious and community institutions, encouraged economic development, proselytized unceasingly, and intervened in affairs of government wherever he saw fit. Even people who were not particularly devout Buddhists felt themselves on the defensive. And Can saw his position steadily eroded as his energetic elder brother encroached on his authority.

At the same time the government in Saigon undertook to reassert administrative control over Hue and the central coastal provinces. Early in 1963 Ngo Dinh Nhu sent a trusted Catholic layman to see Can and suggest he leave the country. He ought to pay a visit to Japan, Nhu instructed the emissary to tell his brother.

Ngo Dinh Can had lost much of his power by May 1963. Freedom in Hue was no more real than it had ever been, but the precarious balance he had established was threatened. If organized opposition emerged in Hue, Monsignor Thuc had unwittingly ensured by his arrogant and ill-considered behavior that it would be Buddhist.

Perhaps Can in his desire to show he was still the only bridge the government possessed to the Buddhist community had deliberately encouraged Buddhist leaders to make their presence felt that May, as Diem and some others later believed. It is possible that these leaders would have acted as they did regardless of Ngo Dinh Can. Certainly the archbishop had no inkling of the rising Buddhist bitterness as he drove back to Hue on May 7. In any case, he was too concerned with his own frustrations to think of theirs. For in the midst of this festive period of his anniversary celebrations he had once again been reminded of his own unfulfilled hopes. It was no secret that Ngo Dinh Thuc dreamed of a cardinal's hat. Just a few days earlier he had gone to honor the new bishop of Da Nang. Thuc did not hide his resentment at the popularity of the new bishop and was heard to say, repeatedly, "Why are there Vatican flags?" It seemed to Thuc that yellow and white Vatican flags were flying everywhere in Da Nang, in disregard of an unenforced government regulation that only the national flag could be flown in public places and that religious flags were restricted to religious institutions. Thuc's displeasure at the enthusiastic reception given the new bishop made him acutely sensitive to the entire question of religious flags.

Immediately thereafter, on May 6, a circular recalling the terms of the order on the display of flags was dispatched from Saigon. It reached Hue when the city was already festooned with Buddhist flags for the forthcoming celebration planned for the anniversary of the birth of Buddha. These were the flags that Monsignor Thuc saw prominently displayed when he drove back to Hue from La Vang on May 7. No sooner had he arrived than he summoned Ho Dac Khuong, the government delegate who represented the Saigon government in the central provinces, to order the flags removed. In vain, Khuong protested that it was too late. Such action at this time, with the flags already in place, would deeply offend the Buddhist community.

Khuong was an unassuming man, Confucian in upbringing. His father and grandfather had been ministers at the imperial court, and he himself had once served in the Viet Minh administration. His aunts were dedicated Buddhist nuns. Rather than bow to the archbishop's demand, Khuong appealed to Saigon for instructions. The reply was immediate. The flags had to come down.

The minister of the interior, who happened to be in Hue at this time, later told a United Nations mission investigating these events that he had taken it on himself to suspend the order and had gone to the pagoda to reassure the bonzes that their flags could stay. But at least some of these flags were taken down by the police. Later, in Saigon, Ngo Dinh Nhu would tear at his hair, saying, "Why did my brother insist on sending such a stupid order about the flags? Who cares what flags they hang out?"

To Archbishop Thuc it had mattered. And it mattered even more to certain Buddhist monks in Hue who had been awaiting just such an opportunity.

Their resentment had been building for a long time. They complained about the preferential treatment accorded Catholic refugees in Saigon, at the access accorded Catholic priests to government facilities and government funds, at overzealous officials in several neighboring provinces who had actively harassed worshipers of Buddha, at Archbishop Thuc's relentless drive to increase his own influence and that of the Catholic Church. When whole villages could convert en masse to Catholicism, as they did, it was natural to see this as acquiescence to outside pressure. (Some of these villages were found to have been under Viet Cong control from the start so that even their ostensible conversion was an act of political expediency, not religious faith.)

The militantly anti-Communist government of Diem was more receptive to the anti-Communist Northern refugees both Catholic and non-Catholic than to Buddhists, who seemed to lack the equivalent anti-Communist credentials. Even more important, and it had taken Hue Buddhist leaders a while to realize this, it was their disorganization that had made it impossible for them to compete with the Catholics. Organization had been the strength of the Catholic communities even in colonial days and had enabled many of them to flee the North to resettle south of the Seventeenth Parallel with support from the government and from abroad. Hue Buddhist priests had complained for years to visiting Buddhist laymen about their inability to change conditions in their favor. For example, they were still subject to a regulation dating from French colonial times (when there was no central Buddhist hierarchy, Buddhist pagodas were isolated units, and many of them had fallen into decay) that recognized them only as "associations" and, unlike the powerful religious institution that was the Roman Catholic Church, were subject to government controls and restrictions. This was just one of the many outdated regulations still around in Diemist Vietnam that no one had thought about changing.

HUE, MAY 8, 1963

The Buddhist Youth were out in force on May 8 to join in the festivities commemorating the birth of Buddha. On that morning the faithful gathered early. Five hundred strong they crossed the bridge over the Perfumed River to bring religious emblems to Tu Dam pagoda and carried with them signs attacking the government. At the pagoda, the bonze Thich Tri Quang came forward to address the crowd. He read the signs aloud and in an incendiary speech accused the government of religious oppression and called for equal treatment of all religions. The crowd applauded. In the audience were Ho Dac Khuong and General Le Van Nghiem, the commanding general of the region, and the province chief. They did not react to his challenging speech, and the ceremony ended quietly.

When word of Tri Quang's speech was brought to him, Ngo Dinh Can was surprised but not alarmed. "Why does he attack me?" Can asked. He had thought the material aid he had given the Buddhists on various occasions and the personal relations he had maintained with leading bonzes would have been enough to satisfy Tri Quang. After all, several members of Can's entourage were in regular touch with the Buddhists and so Can was reassured when one of them reported everything to be under control. He was promised that what had transpired that morning would not be repeated.

But Can had underestimated Tri Quang. This brooding inner-directed bonze would prove to be charismatic as no member of the Ngo family had ever been. Yet Tri Quang and Can, who both professed to know no other language than Vietnamese and never appeared in Western dress, were each in his fashion authentic nationalists deeply rooted in the Vietnamese soil. Can as a young man used to call on the great patriot Phan Boi Chau, who spent his last years in Hue, bringing gifts of food to the sampan on the Perfumed River where Chau passed his days, and learning political lessons at his feet. Tri Quang drew his inspiration from the ancestral religion that was reemerging from centuries of neglect as the country reemerged from almost a century of colonial rule. Can was trying to preserve a status quo that was stagnant and perhaps doomed. Tri Quang derived from another Vietnamese tradition, that of politically ambitious priests who played on popular beliefs and superstition. Throughout Vietnamese history such men had always been eventually eliminated by the government in power.

On May 8 Tri Quang stepped out of the obscurity of the pagoda onto the political stage. Fireworks had been planned for the evening as in past years, but he took it on himself to turn the crowd away from Tu Dam pagoda. He directed people to assemble instead at the Hotel Morin and from there to move on the local radio station.

The religious program approved by the local government authorities was already on tape and about to be broadcast. But bonzes and Buddhist laymen called on the station director to broadcast the speech of Tri Quang instead. The director protested that the speech had not been authorized. As the crowd grew larger and more impatient, he telephoned for help to Major Dang Sy, the deputy province chief who was in charge of public security and commander of the Hue garrison.

Dang Sy went to look for the province chief who was his direct superior and found him at the house of Ngo Dinh Can. Despite the province chief's assurances that he personally had seen Tri Quang earlier and there would be no riot, the report came that the crowd was getting out of hand and the radio station was in danger. Dang Sy tried without success to phone his division commander for instructions, then consulted with General Le Van Nghiem, commander of the first military corps. He was told to take his orders from the province chief because the affair was a civil and not a military problem.

Major Dang Sy arrived at the radio station two hours after the first report of the riot reached his headquarters. He had a company of men with him in rubber-tired armored cars. Because they had no tear gas at hand they were equipped with MK III grenades. They were still in their cars about fifty meters from the building when the night was ripped by two explosions. In the darkness, with the crowd shocked and scattering, Dang Sy feared the explosions meant a Viet Cong attack like the recent one on a police station. He fired three warning shots into the air. This was the signal for his men to use their grenades. At least fifteen were thrown. The crowd fled, leaving seven dead and one child dying. The victims were mutilated, some decapitated. There were mangled shreds of flesh and bone and torn bodies with no trace of any lethal projectile.

It was a strange and terrible night. None of the Vietnamese present had ever witnessed explosions of such exceptional force. They corresponded to nothing in the arsenal at the disposal of Dang Sy's men. Officials thought Viet Cong plastic must have been used even though the Buddhist doctor who examined the bodies said he had never seen such injuries and did not believe they could have been caused either by plastic or by grenades. In later years, men who had served with the Viet Cong at that time denied they had any plastic that could have produced such destruction.

On the night of May 8 word of the deaths swept through the city and, with it, outrage. It did not help when Monsignor Thuc pointed out that two of the dead were Catholic or that eight were killed and not the nine reported by the foreign press. Officials insisted the Viet Cong was responsible. Diem ordered an investigation and was informed the deaths had been caused by plastic charges. He was convinced: his government was not at fault. Having made up his mind, he was not going to change it because people in Hue refused to hold the Viet Cong responsible for what had happened and because American diplomats echoed their disbelief. Insulated by his inner circle at the palace and, in any case, hearing only what he wanted to hear, Diem did not understand the depths of the anger in Hue or appreciate how easily that anger could be turned against his regime.

In time a trial would be held to determine responsibility for the deaths in Hue—but not until a year later when Diem was dead. Major Dang Sy was tried by another regime, one headed by General Nguyen Khanh, who was courting Buddhist support. Dang Sy was tried alone for the eight deaths because he was the only Catholic in the chain of command that had brought him to the Hue radio station that spring evening in 1963.

Some people had accused Dang Sy's men of firing on the crowd and crushing the victims with their armored cars. Others had blamed the deaths on the grenades thrown at Dang Sy's orders, and this was the accusation against him at his trial. At the trial it was brought out that the American concussion grenades they had used were described in the United States Department of the Army Field Manual on "Grenades and Pyrotechnics" and could never have been lethal because "the maximum capabilities of the MK III grenades are concussion, burst eardrums and shock." Pressure was put on Dang Sy to testify in 1964 that Archbishop Thuc, who by that time was living in exile, had personally given him the order to fire on the crowd. But he refused to implicate Monsignor Thuc.

Dang Sy was condemned to life imprisonment at hard labor and ordered to compensate the victims' families. His lawyer had insisted on the fact that Mrs. Dang Sy came of a Buddhist family and that her husband had acted under orders. When the trial was over, the lawyer for the defense pointed out that the court had failed to establish either the nature or the source of the lethal explosions. A member of the tribunal had argued that the evidence did not justify so harsh a sentence. General Khiem, then minister of national defense, later said that Dang Sy had to be condemned to appease Tri Quang. "It was a price Nguyen Khanh felt he had to pay in order to win Tri Quang's favor."

The London *Economist* would call the sentence an "outrage . . . at a cynically rigged trial. He [Dang Sy] took his orders from the proper authorities and carefully used percussion grenades only on the fringes of the mob that had been whipped up by Tri Quang. He was then accused of responsibility for the still unexplained deaths of eight demonstrators in plastic bomb explosions."

George A. Carver, who became a high-level CIA official, wrote in 1965 that "the spark which lighted the powder was struck in Hue on May 8, 1963, under circumstances whose details will probably always remain matters of controversy. . . ." As a young officer working undercover in 1960 Saigon, Carver had learned to dislike the Diem regime and had been forced to leave the country after he was compromised by his contacts with leaders of the abortive coup that took place that year. He would later become special assistant for Vietnamese affairs to the Director of Central Intelligence.

In 1970, the Catholic newspaper *Hoa Binh* tried to reconstruct the events of May 8, 1963. It described how Ngo Dinh Can had been roused from bed that night to be told of the bloodshed. He promptly summoned local officials to a meeting. If the *Hoa Binh* is to be believed, these men did not hold Dang Sy responsible for what had happened and did not think the Viet Cong had anything to do with it. They decided that the real culprit was not Vietnamese at all but American. The Saigon regime was on such bad terms with the Kennedy administration that Ngo Dinh Can was convinced the explosions had to be the work of an American agent who wanted to make trouble for Diem.

The account in the *Hoa Binh* went further. It spoke of a Captain Scott who arrived in Hue from Da Nang the day before the anniversary of the birth of Buddha in 1963. Several years later Scott was a military adviser in the Mekong Delta and they quoted him as saying at that time, "Dang Sy is totally innocent and has no reason to be in jail right now. Major Sy is only a victim. I can't see how people could think it was Viet Cong plastic or a Viet Cong grenade." And then, according to the *Hoa Binh* article, Scott described an explosive that was still secret and known only to certain people in the Central Intelligence Agency, a charge no larger than a matchbox with a timing device. Later, in another conversation, he was reported to have admitted that the agent who had set the explosive was he.

This writer has been unable to prove or disprove the truth of this account.

Whatever the circumstances, eight people were dead, most of them children, and at least fifteen others injured. Urgent action was required from Saigon to appease the anger of the inhabitants of Hue. Unfortunately, the Vietnamese government had rarely been known to take urgent action even on occasions much less difficult than this one. The archbishop would try to justify himself and the regime. Ngo Dinh Can, apparently the only one of the brothers to grasp the political importance of the moment, asked immediate compensation for the families of the victims.

Angry Buddhists demonstrated in Hue on May 10. Arrests were made and further demonstrations forbidden. That same day the

Buddhist clergy issued a manifesto demanding that the government rescind the order against the flying of Buddhist flags in public places, give Buddhists legal equality with Catholics, stop the arbitrary arrests and the intimidation of Buddhists, indemnify the families of the victims of May 8, and punish the officials responsible.

A delegation of six monks and two laymen submitted these five demands to President Diem in Saigon on May 15. Afterward they held a press conference at Xa Loi, the most important pagoda in the city. It was the first of the press conferences that the bonzes were to develop to a fine art in attracting foreign support for their cause.

At this first encounter between Diem and Buddhist leaders there was no hint of the gathering storm. Diem explained that the national flag had to be given preference over all religious flags, and that the order relegating Buddhists to the level of an "association" was an administrative error he was happy to have reported to him. His reminder that freedom of worship was guaranteed in the constitution did not persuade the delegation. When the secretaries of the interior and civic affairs who were also present at the meeting said that only troublemakers, not monks, were being arrested in Hue, the delegates protested the use of such a word to describe Buddhists. Diem and the secretary of the interior both insisted on the fact that Catholics and others who did not practice Buddhism had been among the victims on May 8. It was important to make the point that people had not been killed in Hue simply because they were Buddhists.

The very next day the office of Monsignor Nguyen Van Binh, archbishop of Saigon, issued a communiqué reminding Catholics the Vatican flag should be flown only inside churches or other buildings belonging to the church, never outside. The Vatican flag had recently been seen in front of churches, in streets, before private houses, and even on cars during important holidays or processions, according to the communiqué. It called this a misuse of the flag and belatedly ordered that the practice stop.

On May 18, Ambassador Nolting met with Diem on instructions from Washington to urge him to redress Buddhist grievances and try to win back public confidence. The only way to do that, in the opinion of the State Department, was for Diem to admit government responsibility for the incident in Hue, compensate the families of the victims (as he had already told the Buddhist delegation he intended to do), and reaffirm religious equality in the country.

But neither then nor ever was Diem willing to bow to political expediency and accept responsibility for acts of which he believed his government innocent.

Nolting, having delivered this message, was ready for a long planned holiday. There was not yet an atmosphere of crisis in Saigon that would have justified postponing his departure. Confident that Diem had the situation well in hand, Nolting turned over the embassy to a chargé d'affaires and left Vietnam on May 23.

In Saigon, Buddhist leaders kept the issue of the Hue dead before the public. A memorial service was held at An Quang pagoda, at which the secretary general of the Buddhist Sangha Association delivered the funeral oration. Then hundreds of yellow-robed monks and nuns formed a procession to take the memorial tablets through the streets of the city to Xa Loi pagoda.

A week after the departure of Ambassador Nolting more than three hundred Buddhist priests and nuns appeared outside the National Assembly carrying banners that called on the government to satisfy their five-point demands. They sat there for four hours before disbanding at the behest of the General Association of Buddhists to return to their pagodas and join other monks and nuns in Saigon and in other parts of the country for a forty-eight-hour fast. This was only the beginning, spokesmen at Xa Loi promised to anyone who would listen as they passed out leaflets proclaiming the intention of Buddhist leaders to continue the "struggle" for the five points.

In Hue, where it had all begun, tension remained high. Two messengers from Ngo Dinh Can, both representatives of Hue in the National Assembly, arrived in Saigon with instructions to warn President Diem that all was far from well in the town of his birth. They were told to remind the president of the time when the electricity had failed in Hue during one of his visits and the crowd was ready to lynch the Frenchman they held responsible. Now, Can had them tell his brother that if Diem came to Hue, not even a cat would turn out to see him.

Can usually shunned Secretary of the Presidency Nguyen Dinh Thuan when he visited Hue, because he regarded him as too close to the Americans to be loyal to Diem. But when Thuan came to Hue that summer Can received him. "Tell my brother Diem the situation is very bad, much worse than the other two times," he said.

By this time Diem was less concerned about the reported behavior of the Buddhists than he was about the real intentions of the Americans. When Thuan passed on Can's message about conditions in Hue, Diem only laughed and said, "My brother has lost his courage."

6.
Attempted Coups and Rumors of Coups

SPRING 1963

It seemed to be only an argument over money, a simple matter of the Vietnamese withholding piastres they had promised as their share of a counterinsurgency fund. The American Embassy knew better: the Vietnamese were approaching "repudiation of concept of expanded and deepened U.S. advisory effort, civil and military" —the "fundamental element [of] our agreement with [the Vietnamese government] in December 1961 on greatly stepped up U.S. assistance effort." Nolting cabled Washington that it might be necessary to threaten Diem with withholding American aid from other military projects "to convince Diem that we mean business."

The real problem troubling the Vietnamese president was not money but men—the American advisers who seemed to be everywhere, too numerous, too deeply involved in Vietnamese affairs.

And now the Americans wanted still more influence for their officers serving with Vietnamese fighting units and intended to bring
in many more military advisers. Worst of all, they insisted on
bypassing the central government to deliver supplies directly to the
provincial authorities, allowing the American advisers on duty in
the provinces to control the distribution of aid to the hamlets. The
Americans would run the new rural economic development plan
(and run it more efficiently than the Vietnamese government, they
would say). For Diem, this amounted to direct administration by
foreigners, a new colonialism that he could not tolerate. The Saigon
government requested that the Americans withdraw most of the
two thousand advisers they had in the provinces.

To the French ambassador, Diem complained about the influx
of American military men. "All these soldiers I never asked to come
here. They don't even have passports." Lalouette advised Diem to
ask "gently" that some of the Americans leave. The normally astute
ambassador misread the mood of the Americans, who were not
ready to entertain any such suggestions however gently put. The
fact that Diem and Nhu wanted the provincial advisers removed
had set off warning bells in the offices of Washington policymakers.
Lalouette himself would one day trace the decision to abandon
Diem that was made in Washington later that year back to this
attempt to have the provincial advisers recalled in April.

Said one knowledgeable Vietnamese: "Everyone close to Ngo
Dinh Diem knew that for him the question of Vietnamese sovereignty was primordial; no question of foreign aid could supersede
that." The same source quoted Nhu as saying, "If we don't seek a
way to make peace and the war goes on, it will be a danger to the
regime."

Diem said privately that the Americans had been asking for the
right to establish an air and naval base at Cam Ranh Bay or Da
Nang, manned by a permanent military establishment, and that
they had become more pressing since 1961. In July 1962, during
an inspection at Cam Ranh Bay, he had pointed to a mountain close
by, saying to his aides, "The Americans want a base there but I shall
never accept that." As late as August 1963, he told the French
ambassador he would never comply with such demands. Some

members of his Can Lao party considered this refusal one of the main reasons for the overthrow of Diem.

After his death, his successors readily granted the Americans the bases that had been refused to them by Diem.

On May 10, 1963, Ngo Dinh Nhu received Warren Unna, a visiting correspondent from *The Washington Post.* The anniversary of the birth of Buddha had been celebrated two days earlier and tragic events had occurred in Hue, as both Nhu and Unna must have known. But the events were so recent that they apparently did not feature among the questions put to the brother of the president.

Several Americans had recently been killed in action, and American criticism of the Vietnamese conduct of military operations had sharpened. This clearly was on Nhu's mind when he informed Unna that one-half of the American military personnel stationed in Vietnam could be withdrawn. Their presence made it look like an American war, and many of the American casualties had been cases of "soldiers who exposed themselves too readily. At least 50 percent of the American troops are not absolutely necessary in the field." Withdrawing them would be something spectacular to show how successful Kennedy's policy had been. He did not wish to seem anti-American or xenophobic. (Unna would describe him as known to be rabidly anti-American.) "American public opinion is very impatient but this is a war of patience . . . a long and difficult war."

To Unna's question about when there could be a general offensive and massive extermination of the enemy, he replied that would be after we have finished the strategic hamlet program. Consistent with the doctrine behind that program, he preferred to concentrate on denying food and supplies to the enemy rather than on military confrontation. "Military people like to have big operations," he said, "but we prefer to use local [paramilitary] forces for small actions and keep the regular army as a striking force for strategic reasons later on." This analysis did not conform to the thinking of the American military, and Unna told Nhu that his desire to restrict military action to small encounters could be seen by Americans as an attempt to preserve the army to protect the regime from a rearguard civil uprising.

In Washington, officials read the account of this interview with "strong irritation" and the influential *Washington Post* reacted with outrage. Nhu had said, "half the Americans in Vietnam should leave and the other half should not expose themselves to enemy fire. And after nearly a decade of hostilities the time to take up the offensive had not come yet." "What were the Americans to make of these fantastic statements?" "How much longer must the United States help President Diem to lose his war and waste its money?"

A few days later a joint communiqué was released in Saigon announcing that the two governments had reached agreement at last and the Saigon government was going to pay its share of the funds needed for counterinsurgency and economic development projects, particularly those supporting the strategic hamlet program during 1963. "Counterinsurgency projects will continue to be initiated and developed by the Vietnamese authorities." There would be "full" and close coordination between the Vietnamese and Americans. "The execution of the projects will continue to be closely coordinated between the Vietnamese authorities and American experts in the provinces." The communiqué included a statement endorsing "the present level of the advisory and support effort."

It would take much more than a sentence in a communiqué to expunge the effect of Nhu's words asking that the American military presence be halved. "In any case," Hilsman cabled Nolting, "slate would not really be wiped clean here . . . this incident [is] likely to leave lasting bad impression."

Nolting was preparing to depart on home leave. He called on Nhu and found him regretful of the problems caused by his interview with *The Washington Post*. Nolting reported him sincere and cordial and suggested that the president's brother, who was a thin-skinned man, might have reacted emotionally, as he sometimes did, to Unna's questions. Nhu had agreed that the time was not ripe for lessening the American adviser support role but said he intended to work toward that end, which was desirable for both countries. He told Nolting that Vietnam had to strive for self-sufficiency in all fields if it were to endure as a free nation. Foreign assistance could not be expected to continue in its present dimensions for a long

period, and it was up to the Vietnamese people to make it unneces-
sary. All this seemed entirely consistent with American objectives,
Nolting reported to Washington.

The ambassador also spoke to Vice-President Tho, who did
not like Nhu and rarely agreed with him.

Tho was "more bullish than I have ever seen him. . . . He
thought things were going well internally in struggle against the
Viet Cong, emphasizing particularly economic improvements in
rural area. He was most outspoken in appreciation of U.S. support.
. . . With regard to U.S. advisors Tho said that it is true that the
presence of U.S. advisors, especially civilian, in remote country
areas caused the Vietnamese people to wonder who was running
the government. . . ."

In Washington, President Kennedy was asked at a press conference about the interview Nhu had given to *The Washington Post.*
He said: "We would withdraw troops, any number of troops, any
time the government of South Vietnam would suggest it. The day
after it were suggested we would have some troops on their way
home. That is No. 1. No. 2 is that we are hopeful that the situation
in South Vietnam would permit some withdrawal in any case by the
end of the year. . . ."

Kennedy had given the only possible response. But of course
the Americans were not in Vietnam to oblige Diem; they were
there to serve the interests of the United States and to demonstrate
American credibility to the Soviets and the Chinese Communists in
other parts of the world.

If the Ngos did not allow them the freedom of action they
wanted, they could always find other Vietnamese more amenable
to American wishes.

Major General Duong Van Minh was known to visiting Americans
for his size—hence the sobriquet "Big Minh"—his tennis game
(excellent) and his rank. The titular senior general in the Vietnamese army, he was second only to the elderly and ailing chief of
the Joint General Staff of the armed forces, General Ty. Like other
Vietnamese generals, Minh had begun his military career in the
French army and had fought against his own people in the war the

French had lost, the war that had won independence for Vietnam while condemning it to partition. Unlike General Don, also a major general and a native of the Nam Bo as he was, Minh had never been a French citizen, nor had he been accused of close ties with French intelligence as had General Le Van Kim, Don's brother-in-law and intimate friend. Minh was a professional soldier, not a policeman like General Mai Huu Xuan, for example, who had served in the colonial administration under the notorious *doc phu* Tam.

The French had reluctantly established a Vietnamese army during the war of 1945–54 though, as Bao Dai, then chief of state, had protested in 1954, "Vietnamese soldiers who are incorporated as auxiliary units of the French army do not constitute a Vietnamese army." From among these auxiliaries had come the leaders of Diem's new army, and they accepted the advice of American officers as readily as they had once accepted the orders of the French. Minh had won the favorable attention of the president when he defeated the Binh Xuyen and the Hoa Hao sects, native southerners and non-Communists like him. But he had since fallen into disfavor at the presidential palace and for years had freely expressed his aversion to Nhu and his wife and complained to Vietnamese and Americans about Diem's attempts to divide and downgrade the army. General Don, who retained the favor of the palace, found it "a little strange that he [Minh] survived as well as he did."

General Tran Van Don seemed to get on well with everyone. A personable man, the son of a doctor who became an ambassador under Diem, Don had studied in France and dealt easily with Westerners. In 1954, he had been chief of staff to the rebellious General Hinh. Hinh had slipped back into the country to join the sects in their unsuccessful revolt and, seeing the hopelessness of their cause, had left Vietnam as secretly as he had come, to return to France and serve as a general in the French army. But Don became Diem's army chief of staff and presided over the ceremony in Saigon at which Vietnamese burned the military insignia they had adopted from the French to replace them with American insignia. He became commander of the First Corps that operated in five central provinces (the northern provinces of South Vietnam), one of the military regions into which the American advisers had divided the country. His troops were on duty to maintain security in the countryside and stand ready to repel any invasion from the North. Don chafed under the control exercised by the president's brother Can over military operations in the central provinces and exchanged complaints with General Minh about incompetents in the army and the administration.

When the Taylor mission visited Saigon in 1961, they found that General Minh, though commander of the Army Field Command, had no right to issue orders directly to the troops. That was the responsibility of the chief of staff of the Joint Chiefs of Staff, an energetic young general named Nguyen Khanh, and relations had been tense between Khanh and Minh.

The Americans wanted President Diem to give General Minh active command of the Vietnamese armed forces. Lansdale, who was then working in the office of the secretary of defense, had to point out in December 1961, "We know that Big Minh has been outspoken about a coup. Diem certainly knows about the way Big Minh has been talking, also. Now we ask Diem to give practical control of his military force to a man who talked about a coup. What realistic assurances can we give Diem that the action he fears won't take place?"

A year later, Minh was assigned to a new post in Saigon, that of military adviser to the president. But Diem was not interested in the advice of Duong Van Minh. The new post brought him neither power nor responsibility, and the resentful general was left with ample time to look after his orchids and his collection of Japanese dolls. He also had time for many conversations with General Don and other people about the need to replace the Diem administration by men better able to confront the threat from the Viet Cong. Don also was based in Saigon in 1963. He had been named commander of the army, a newly created post that entitled him to a headquarters but not as yet to actual command of the army or any unit in it.

Minh was still the army's senior general, and in the summer of 1962 it had been natural for William Colby, the CIA station chief, to consider him when he drafted his final report from Vietnam. Colby wanted to recommend someone who could take over the presidency if Diem were suddenly removed from the political scene as Magsaysay had been when he was killed in a plane crash in the Philippines.

After a tour of duty in Vietnam that had lasted three and a half years, Colby was going home to become head of the Far Eastern Department at CIA headquarters. He noted with satisfaction that the CIA now had "contacts and influence throughout Vietnam, from the front and rear door of the Palace, to the rural communities, among the civilian opponents of the regime and the commanders of all the key military units."

One of Colby's agents was Lucien Conein, whose career spanned the nearly two decades in which American intelligence agents had been active in Vietnamese affairs. Conein had fought against the Japanese for the Office of Strategic Services (when other OSS agents were working with Ho Chi Minh), then run secret operations against Ho for Lansdale's Saigon Military Mission. Now a lieutenant colonel, he was back in Vietnam working with the cover of adviser on military affairs to the Ministry of Interior, a post that allowed him easy access to old friends he had first known in the French army who had become Vietnamese generals, in particular Tran Van Don. These connections would unexpectedly thrust Conein into a key role in implementing a decision made in Washington to embark on a policy so delicate, and so dangerous, that it could not be entrusted to diplomats.

All that was in the future when William Colby went to pay farewell visits to several generals, to Don and to Ton That Dinh, a dashing young officer from Hue, the youngest general in the army and a favorite of the Ngo brothers. They had given Dinh early advancement and many favors, and took his loyalty for granted. Because of this trust in the handsome and spirited protégé, Dinh had been given command of the Third Corps in the region north of Saigon and controlled the forces around the capital.

Colby also went to say good-bye to General Nguyen Khanh, the chief of staff who had practically edged General Minh out of the chain of military command. Nguyen Khanh was an odd-looking moon-faced man with a driving ambition and few scruples. He was a man to be reckoned with, distrusted perhaps by certain of his colleagues but a fighting general with a fine military record who was respected by some of the middle- and low-ranking officers who regarded Minh, Don, and their friends as lightweights, parlor generals.

William Colby believed only a military man could replace Diem because the civilian politicians represented only themselves or a small faction and had no political base, and Nhu and his wife were too unpopular for the president's brother to succeed him. Robert Thompson of the British Advisory Mission shared Colby's view of the irrelevance of politicians; he dismissed efforts to encourage Diem to broaden his political base as "meaningless when in reality political power was in the army not the people."

But Colby decided against "Big Minh" because of his "lack of political force and strength of personality." And Colby did not want Don. Instead, the man from the CIA preferred Nguyen Khanh, whom he found "bright, aggressive and with a political sense." The Vietnamese president thought highly of this dynamic young southerner, too. Diem did not know that Khanh had been engaged in plotting coups against the regime with various factions since 1961.

Khanh would later boast of being the first general to approach the CIA about organizing a coup against Diem. He was less forthcoming about another role he might have played in 1963. At the time he was in command of the Second Corps in Pleiku in the central highlands. Being in direct command of troops—as other leading plotters were not—and being based far from the capital, he was well placed to offer a haven to people on the run. He would tell his fellow generals they could find a refuge at his headquarters if their coup failed and they had to flee; and it is not impossible, as will be seen, that he may have had a similar understanding with Diem and Nhu.

When the American Military Assistance Advisory Group (MAAG) had organized this conventional army in divisions under a corps headquarters and a general headquarters, they had built up a force that could easily be coordinated with American forces if ever the North Vietnamese decided to launch an open invasion across the frontier as the Koreans had done. This sort of organization was taken for granted in the United States where the aloofness of the army from politics was also taken for granted, so it did not occur to the American military advisers that when transplanted to Vietnam it would create what Thompson called "a warlord outlook in the senior commanders and fire[d] their ambitions. On their own, they lacked the experience or ability to command much more than a regiment, let alone a country. They also lacked the modesty to comprehend this."

Diem, having no direct military experience himself, deferred too much to his generals and in the end paid with his life for his weakness toward them. Yet, paradoxically, he had no respect for the generals. He had little faith in the ability of his conventional army to fight a guerrilla war and, with good reason, doubted its loyalty.

In the years since 1954, the national army had become a kind of occupation force in its own country. It was top heavy with high-ranking officers who had time on their hands; the men were ill paid and denied leave. They held static defense positions, engaging from time to time in large sweeps of open country while waiting for an invasion force from the North that did not come. This was still a guerrilla war of surprise attacks by small units, and the brunt of the fighting fell on the ill-equipped paramilitary civil guard. But army doctors were forbidden to treat casualties in the civil guard and the local village militia or to care for civilians.

Unlike the Viet Cong, which in the Viet Minh tradition had been trained to identify with the civilian population on whom it depended for survival, the army owed nothing to the rural population among whom it was stationed. It behaved accordingly; it demanded food from the peasants, stole chickens, attacked villages rather than troubling to look for the Viet Cong suspects who might have sought refuge there—if troops bothered to come at all when the presence of the Viet Cong was signaled to them. Piastres generated by the sale of American commodities under the American Commodity Import Program paid the army, and the Americans provided it with supplies and equipment. In the North, the highly indoctrinated People's Army that had defeated the French was a pillar of the Ho Chi Minh regime. In contrast, the Southern army had no national tradition and operated in a political vacuum where conspiracy thrived, leaving it open to manipulation by factions and outsiders.

Diem treated the army like a sect that had defeated the other sects because it was better led and benefited from American aid. General Hinh had once used the army to threaten the regime and Diem did not intend that to happen again. He kept other military forces under separate command. The elite Special Forces, counter-guerrilla units who received most of their funds from the CIA, were independent of the army. Their commander, Colonel Tung, reported directly to the presidential palace, where he consulted with Nhu but received his orders from Diem. The paramilitary civil guard attached to each province chief was controlled by the palace through the Ministry of Interior. Local village militia operated under independent commands and were encouraged to compete with each other to improve their performance.

When Nhu came to recognize the growing political danger of a large conventional army, he looked to the strategic hamlet program as a counterbalance to restore the primacy of the civil authorities.

"President Diem," noted Robert Thompson, "was forced to devote much of his time and energy to manipulating the army commands in order to retain control and maintain his position."

Unable to provide the army with a national ideology, Diem had come to identify loyalty to the state with loyalty to his government. He undercut the authority of commanders by dealing directly with their subordinates and used the government Can Lao Party to control the army and to neutralize potential dissidents, in particular the Dai Viet and VNQDD officers, who had never really accepted the Diem regime.

A number of these officers were graduates of the military school the Dai Viet and the VNQDD had established at Yen Bay in the North after World War II, when Chinese Nationalist troops arrived in Vietnam to disarm the defeated Japanese. At that time the Vietnam Nationalist Party (VNQDD) and the Dai Viet had controlled wide areas of the northern countryside near the Chinese frontier, in defiance of the Ho Chi Minh government in Hanoi.

Since Ngo Dinh Can had crushed the attempt of the two parties to establish similar bases—and another school—in the central provinces, many VNQDD and Dai Viet officers had joined the army, professing a loyalty to the regime they did not feel. They seemed to have no future in an army where promotions were made on the basis of political allegiance rather than military competence; the political manipulation of appointments angered those who were passed over or saw no hope of advancement and sharpened their resentment against Diem. This was one cause of the coup d'état that had been attempted on November 11, 1960.

They had begun before dawn. Paratroop battalions under their commander, Colonel Nguyen Chanh Thi, seized the headquarters of the Joint General Staff, police headquarters, and Tan Son Nhut airport and moved against the palace. Colonel Thi issued an order of the day declaring the rebels against communism and in favor of true liberty, true democracy. A Revolutionary Committee declared its existence. Civilian politicians with Dr. Phan Quang Dan, an old opponent of the regime at their head, rallied to the support of the rebels.

The CIA was in touch with both the palace and the rebels. American ambassador Elbridge Durbrow pressed Diem to negotiate, as CIA agents were under orders to do with the rebels. This embassy policy was endorsed by a strong cable from Washington: "we consider it overriding importance to Vietnam and Free World that agreement be reached soonest in order avoid continued division, further bloodshed with resultant fatal weakening Vietnam's ability [to] resist Communists."

From the palace, Diem declared his readiness to talk to the rebels, and they stayed their attack as the negotiations went on through the afternoon and into the night. Diem refused to resign but seemed willing to agree to a provisional military government.

All this was not exactly as it seemed. The two rebels most in view, Colonel Thi and Dr. Dan, had joined the coup at the last minute, and most of the rebel soldiers had been told they were going to attack the palace in order to save Diem from the presidential guard that had mutinied against him. Only one or two officers in each of the rebel units knew what was going on, and they counted on the discipline of their men to follow them.

The real leaders of the coup were Lieutenant Colonel Vuong Van Dong; his brother-in-law, Lieutenant Colonel Nguyen Trieu Hong, who was killed in the attack on the police station; and Hong's uncle, Hoang Co Thuy, a lawyer. The coup was organized by a group of VNQDD and Dai Viet party members, some of them middle- and low-ranking officers, others civilians.

Diem deliberately dragged out the negotiations in order to give loyal forces in the Mekong Delta time to come to his aid. He was in radio contact with them almost from the start. General Khanh had to climb over the palace wall to reach the president. Khanh won the reputation that day of having helped to save Diem, though some people were suspicious of his contacts with the rebels during the coup. He had been intrigued by their plan to install a military government and had remained on good terms with the rebels until he was sure that Diem was going to carry the day. The deputy chief of the civil guard had also joined Diem at the palace. No other generals appeared on the scene.

At 9:00 A.M., thirty-six hours after the coup began, the infantry and armor of Colonel Tran Thien Khiem, commander of the Fifth Military Region, arrived from the delta to liberate the president, and the coup was over. Thi, Dong, and other rebel officers fled to the airport and boarded a plane for Cambodia, where Prince Norodom Sihanouk granted them asylum. A key civilian conspirator, presumably Hoang Co Thuy, was secretly removed from the country by the CIA and sent to a refuge in Europe.

When the palace was under siege, Diem had promised to make much-needed changes in his administration. He did not feel obliged to keep these promises made under duress; the measures announced afterward, like regrouping government departments under several "superministers," disappointed many Vietnamese who had hoped for real reform.

To Diem and Nhu, the lesson of the coup was that they needed to tighten their control over the government and the army. They also had to deal with the sobering realization that they had lost the unequivocal support of the United States. "The least you can say," Nhu remarked in May 1963, "is that the State Department was neutral between a friendly government and rebels who tried to put that government down . . . the official attitude of the Americans during the coup was not at all the attitude the President would have expected."

That spring of 1963, the generals were restive. Khiem, the southern Catholic loyalist who had saved Diem in 1960, had been made a general by the grateful president. Khiem had succeeded Nguyen Khanh as chief of staff and was in a position to command troop operations, as Minh and Don who outranked him were not. Khiem, who had been a protégé of Diem, was now very close to the Americans, and it seemed that he himself was not adverse to a coup d'état in Saigon.

The generals were more dependent than ever on the Americans as the military struggle with the Viet Cong intensified. Their stake in the war and the American largesse it assured was greater than it had ever been. Unlike Diem and Nhu, they had no inconvenient political ideas that might disturb the Americans. They had no political ideas at all—other than the desire for power. But they would not move against Diem unless they were sure that was what the Americans wanted them to do.

7.
From
Hue to
Saigon

JUNE 1963

A day in June, scarcely a month after the disastrous affair at the Hue radio station. Still another hot, humid Saigon morning, and Buddhist monks and nuns with their demonstrations in the streets of the capital seemed to have fallen into a pattern as repetitive and monotonous as the weather. Xa Loi pagoda had become the headquarters of the Buddhist drive, a crowded bustling place where laymen and bonzes came and went freely and activists courted the foreign press. The inhabitants of Saigon attended to their own affairs, unperturbed. Until this day. After June 11 the world as they knew it would never be quite the same again.

Ironically, as it would seem in retrospect, the news from Hue had been encouraging, better than in past weeks. But it was too little and too late—in the unlikely event any of the Buddhist leaders might have had second thoughts—for them to revise the scenario they had decided upon for June 11.

The dispute that had set Hue Buddhists against the local authorities should have been settled weeks earlier, there on the banks of the Perfumed River where it had begun. Buu-Hoi, for one, had written to Nhu to urge that Diem move swiftly to reassure the Hue Buddhists by establishing a Ministry of Religious Affairs. Even if Diem and Nhu had been willing to consider the idea, the name of Le Khac Quyen suggested by Buu-Hoi to head such a ministry might have been enough to turn them against it. Quyen was a respected Buddhist layman, but he also happened to be the doctor called on to examine the bodies of the victims at the radio station who had refused to support the official claim that Viet Cong plastic had killed them; before the end of the summer he would be jailed as an opponent of the regime.

Diem had seen no good reason to appease the Hue Buddhists at that time, and he turned a deaf ear when his brother Can urged appeasement on him. True, he did dismiss the government delegate, the province chief, and Major Dang Sy, but only because of their failure to maintain order in the city. Ngo Dinh Can still resided in the family house with his mother (he never did make that trip to Japan suggested by his brother Nhu), but he too was in disgrace, accused of stirring up the Buddhists at the start.

All the reports from Hue that Diem chose to believe had favored a hard line. The new delegate of the central government, the highest official in Hue, told Archbishop Ngo Dinh Thuc, "Don't coddle the bonzes. Take a strong stand and they will come crawling on all fours." This was language that the archbishop understood; it was the policy he himself had preached from the beginning. As for the commander of the armed forces in the city, Colonel (later General) Do Cao Tri, he interpreted his mission quite simply as one of repressing the militant Buddhists. Ngo Dinh Can, who knew the Hue Buddhists as these men did not, was obliged to watch the worsening situation from the sidelines. Lucid and aware but helpless to intervene, Can was reduced to sending warnings to the president through third parties, messages that were ignored in Saigon.

On June 3, Hue erupted into action when a crowd defied the order forbidding public demonstrations and assembled near Ben Ngu bridge at one o'clock in the afternoon. The demonstrators were dispersed, not by the police force that was untrained in riot control, but by the army. The crowd formed again and then again, six times in all, until the troops carrying tear gas grenades finally broke it up early in the evening. No one was killed, but some sixty-seven young people were sent to the hospital with burns not usually associated with tear gas. The Diem government, it had seemed, could do no right in Hue. The American consul who went to inquire about the injured concluded that this time the soldiers must have used blister gas against the demonstrators.

His report sent the American chargé d'affaires William Trueheart to see an incredulous Secretary Thuan in Saigon with an angry protest and the threat of a public condemnation by Washington of its Vietnamese ally. Thuan's remarkable command of the English language did not include the word *blister,* and Trueheart had to explain it to him. Mustard gas or any sort of poison gas could not possibly have been used, Thuan responded spiritedly. And investigation proved him right. Tear gas grenades had indeed been used but ones so old they dated back to French times; and the acid used to activate the grenades had broken through. This belated explanation failed to expunge the report widely believed in Vietnam and spread abroad by the American press that an act of deliberate brutality had been perpetrated by the Diem regime in Hue on June 3.

The dilatory tactics of the government had persuaded no one. They had only led the Buddhists to crystallize their dissatisfaction and improve their organization, and to carry their struggle from Hue to the streets of Saigon. Talks with the government were at an impasse until June 4, when Diem finally appointed a high-level Interministerial Committee to deal with Buddhist grievances, headed by Vice-President Tho and including Secretary of the Presidency Thuan and Secretary of the Interior Luong. The committee was named in time to receive a militant bonze from Hue, Thich Thien Minh, known to be close to Tri Quang, who arrived in

Saigon that same day with full powers to negotiate on behalf of the beleaguered Buddhists in the old imperial capital.

Some forty monks had gathered in Tu Dam, the famous Hue pagoda where once, in 1951, delegates had come from all parts of Vietnam, north, south, and center. They had founded the General Association of Buddhists at Tu Dam and named the esteemed bonze Thich Tinh Khiet its highest dignitary. Khiet was still at the pagoda that first week in June twelve years later, a frail old man of eighty, and with him were Tri Quang and other leading bonzes. They had been joined by a number of Buddhist laymen, and together they fasted inside the pagoda as troops and gendarmes cordoned it off: traffic in the city was paralyzed by road blocks and barbed wire.

The emissary of the bonzes, Thich Thien Minh, returned to the pagoda in Hue on June 5 with reassurances from Saigon and more, a preliminary accord on the five points. After this promising beginning, President Diem himself broadcast a conciliatory address to his fellow townsmen in Hue the following evening and went so far as to admit that what he called errors had been committed. But the next day, June 7, government aircraft dropped leaflets over Hue attacking Tri Quang and demanding that the Venerable Khiet declare who was really in charge. This propaganda attack was unsettling news to Buddhists in Hue and to Trueheart at the American Embassy in Saigon, who had been pressing the government to come to terms.

The Saigon authorities, however, insisted that they stood by the agreement with Thich Thien Minh; that it was the activist monks in the capital who were guilty of bad faith, that at Xa Loi pagoda they had already broken the truce negotiated with Minh by distributing tracts that called on the population to demonstrate against the government, and that they had even presumed to appeal to the International Red Cross to intervene on behalf of their fellow Buddhists who were fasting at the pagoda in Hue.

The city of Hue still festered like an open sore, but the Buddhist struggle assumed new dimensions in Saigon, close to the seat of government and with easy access to foreigners, mainly Americans both official and unofficial. Few people quite realized it yet, but the stakes had grown and altered as forces were set in motion that could shatter the brittle structure of this makeshift state.

For Buddhist leaders meeting in secret council it was clear that Saigon had to be the stage for the event they planned for June 11. Not a word of their deliberations filtered out; they maintained silence to the end. It was the government that seemed determined to seize center stage by attempting to drown Buddhist activism in a sea of official rhetoric.

The regime had begun in May with a well-publicized drive among southern Buddhists who had not followed the lead of the Hue bonzes. Priests and laymen in small groups and large throughout the south were called on to make known their allegiance to President Diem, and day after day local newspapers reported their declarations of support.

This did not reassure the activists at Xa Loi pagoda, nor was it meant to do so. American officials and writers of the time, at a loss to make sense out of Diem's behavior, resorted to a facile epithet—that he was still, as always, the mandarin he once had been and as a mandarin was bound to reject concessions out of hand as an unacceptable sign of weakness. But what of Ngo Dinh Nhu, whom these same Americans were inclined to blame for what they disliked most in Diem? Nhu had never been a mandarin and he despised the failings of the breed as much as the Communists did. Yet he too treated the Buddhists with open suspicion. Both men read political danger in the new militancy of the Buddhists. And in the eyes of the Ngos the attitude of their American allies served only to heighten the danger.

Once, the French colonial authorities had encouraged a Buddhist revival, in a fruitless attempt to weaken the revolutionary nationalists who challenged their rule. In 1963, certain Americans, such as Assistant Secretary of State Roger Hilsman, seeking a justification for abandoning Diem, discovered overnight that Vietnamese nationalism was incarnated in Buddhism. The Confucianism that had formed Diem, and left an indelible imprint on Vietnamese life, was Chinese and therefore foreign. Diem's Catholicism was foreign, too. Buddhism, on the other hand, although it had come to Vietnam from India and China, gradually adapted itself to Vietnamese culture and traditions. It followed as the night the day that the Americans ought to break with Diem and support the militant bonzes who spoke with the authentic voice of Vietnamese nationalism. After the death of Ngo Dinh Diem, when Tri Quang, having exploited American friendship to serve his own purposes, would turn his batteries against the United States, other American officials would find shorter and less flattering words to describe this charismatic bonze.

A former teacher of history with better reason than Hilsman for desiring the Americans to turn against Diem watched the unusual activity in the pagodas of Saigon and Hue with cool skepticism. He was General Vo Nguyen Giap, who had long since abandoned his classroom to become the architect of the victory over France and minister of defense in the Ho Chi Minh government. Buddhism, Giap noted, exercised an influence in Vietnam that was not particularly deep, even though it extended over a relatively large number of people.

In June 1963 few American officials and newsmen were concerned about a realistic appraisal of the religious forces in South Vietnam. Uncurious about the complex reality but certain at least of their dislike for Diem, they had already made up their minds. With the president's Catholicism shared by only one-tenth of the population, the vast majority of Vietnamese had to be Buddhists, and their natural spokesmen were not in the presidential palace but behind the walls of Xa Loi pagoda.

In vain did the Saigon government respond by turning against them the figures put forward by the Buddhist activists themselves. At least until the incident at the Hue radio station Buddhist spokesmen had been frank to disdain all those who observed only vestiges of the old religion, mixing them in a traditional amalgam with popular Taoism and Confucianism. How many adherents had they then claimed for modern reform Buddhism? No more than four million in this country of perhaps fourteen million. They were most numerous, homogenous, and best organized in the central provinces, where Tri Quang represented an activist element in the movement. Farther south, Buddhists were divided into a variety of sects under their own leaders and lived alongside other local sects and such highly organized communities as the Cao Dai and the Catholics.

Both Diem and Nhu feared that if the government were to give way on some Buddhist demands it would only be confronted with others. They had been traumatized by the struggles of 1954–55, when the politico-religious sects and General Hinh, working hand in glove with the French in the Nam Bo, had threatened the survival of the regime and the Dai Viet and the VNQDD had challenged its authority farther north. These Buddhists seemed to be another sect, one based in the central provinces. The Buddhist activists still represented only a numerical minority in the country, and in this state so recently formed and still lacking in cohesion, concessions to one particular group would encourage other groups and minorities, both religious and political, to put forward their own claims. There could be only one outcome: a further weakening of the national government that was already fighting for its life against the Communists.

The Ngos regarded Buddhist activists with particular suspicion because of the miasma about them of neutralism, and the menace of foreign interference in Vietnamese affairs. Diem had no good reason to believe that Buddhist leaders shared the militant opposition of his regime to the Communists; he was convinced that they did not. Although the bonzes seemed to have no problem about seeking confrontation with the Saigon regime, when put to the test in Hanoi they had followed a more traditional Buddhist line of accommodation with the government in power, passively accepting Communist rule.

It was no secret that Buddhists had already found encouragement and support in Cambodia and Ceylon, two countries whose leaders were not admired in Saigon government circles. Adherents of the Hinayana form of Buddhism that prevailed across the border in Cambodia were also to be found in the Vietnamese Buddhist movement in the South. Their presence raised the specter for the Ngos that Norodom Sihanouk might encourage Vietnamese Buddhist activists to try to impose on Vietnam the neutral stance he held in his own country, where he steered a middle course between the

Communists and the West. Diem's policy of courting the Third World was a strategy for diplomacy in areas safely removed from the borders of Vietnam. Closer to home, the Ngos remained firmly anti-Communist. They had sponsored plots against Sihanouk in the past, with the Americans and on their own, and they did not trust him now.

Sihanouk had never hidden his distaste for the Saigon government. Hanoi, he had said often enough, was bound to be victorious, and the sooner the National Liberation Front took over the sooner the region would be at peace. As long ago as November 1961 a delegation from South Vietnam had attended the Seventh World Buddhist Congress held in Phnom Penh. The Vietnamese delegates had not only used the occasion to strengthen their ties with their Khmer coreligionists; in the Cambodian capital they had also encountered important Buddhist delegations from both North Vietnam and Communist China that were present with the sanction of their respective governments.

The best-known foreign connection of the renascent Buddhist movement was with Ceylon and had been ever since the First World Congress of Buddhism met in Colombo in 1950. That city was the seat of the World Buddhist Association, to which the newly formed Vietnamese General Association of Buddhists had adhered after the meeting at Tu Dam pagoda in 1951. The Saigon government had treated as normal the outpouring of religious fervor that had greeted the inauguration of the temple at Vung Tau in March 1963. But now some bonzes were talking of inviting a mission from Ceylon to come to their assistance, and the Ngos discerned behind the Venerable Narada and the great statue of Buddha overlooking forest and sea the outlines of another Asian government that was no friend of their regime. Ceylon, like Cambodia, had been one of the founders of the movement of nonaligned states that persisted in proclaiming their neutrality in the struggle between the Communist powers and the West.

And so it was that when the monks at Xa Loi and Tu Dam pagodas complained of the reluctance of the Saigon government to accede to their claims on religious questions, and American observers echoed their charges of religious persecution, the Ngos heard only political demands on which they could not conceivably give way. It was a dialogue of the deaf.

The Ngos moved not to satisfy the Buddhist activists but to counterbalance them and succeeded only in goading them to more drastic action. Two mass movements headed, respectively, by Ngo Dinh Nhu and his wife were brought into play. First, the National Revolutionary Movement issued a call for the unity of the population behind President Diem. Its declaration, innocuous enough in a political vacuum, was incendiary in the charged atmosphere of Saigon that first week of June. It declared that the national flag should have precedence over all others, that freedom of religion was guaranteed in the constitution and had indeed been respected, that all citizens had a duty to honor the law and fight communism, divisiveness, and underdevelopment.

All of this was unexceptionable—except that Buddhist activists wanted new and separate treatment for their own religion and had no alternative to "divisiveness." Opposition plotters whispered to Americans among whom they were seeking support that the Buddhists preferred even the Communists to the Ngos—which was not true. It was only that their immediate adversary was the government; in Saigon the Communist threat was remote, unreal, and, in any case, others could be counted on to deal with the Viet Cong.

On June 7, a few days after the declaration issued by the regime's National Revolutionary Movement, it was the turn of Madame Nhu's Women's Solidarity Movement. Their resolution, made public the following day, was sharp and shrill. Not only did it link Buddhism to neutralism—an insult in Saigon if not many other capitals—but it questioned the motives of the activist monks, declaring that a robe did not necessarily make a bonze and that Vietnamese Buddhists risked being mistaken for a small antinational branch of a dubious international association exploited and controlled by communism and oriented toward the sowing of disorder or neutralism. The women's resolution included in passing a sideswipe at "those inclined to take Vietnam for a satellite of a foreign power," for which American officials read, as they were meant to, the United States.

This resolution was a strident hodgepodge of invective that

recalled Madame Nhu's pronouncements at their worst and was unconscionable in its identification of Buddhist activism with communism. At the very least, it was a violation of the truce agreed to with Thich Thien Minh and threatened to sabotage that accord even before it could take effect. Trueheart, the American chargé d'affaires, hurried to protest directly to President Diem and brought with him a French translation of this extraordinary document. The president, who appeared not to have seen it before, read it carefully in the presence of the American diplomat. Later, Diem directed that it not be publicized by press or radio, but his order did not come in time to stop the English-language *Times of Vietnam* from printing it.

At this interview with the president on June 8, Trueheart told Diem that if he did not disavow the women's resolution and it resulted in further repression by the government, the United States would consider that the Diem regime was at fault and would "dissociate" itself from the government's actions. It had already publicly denied that American planes had been used to carry troops to Hue.

Nolting was still on holiday, and Diem's only high-level contact with Washington was with the chargé d'affaires seated in his office at Gia Long Palace, offering not understanding but threats. Such harsh language could only intensify Diem's doubts about the American alliance and sharpen his awareness of his own isolation; whatever its intended effect, it would not soften his stand on the Buddhists.

Secretary Thuan had told Trueheart during one of their frequent meetings that what happened next would depend on Hue. The two men remained in daily touch during this period. Thuan was convinced that Tri Quang and his associates in Tu Dam pagoda still controlled the activist movement; even now, they had only to give the signal and the bonzes at Xa Loi pagoda would bow to their decision and halt the agitation in Saigon.

On June 10, word finally came from Hue that the Buddhist laymen at Tu Dam pagoda had ended their long vigil and were departing voluntarily. The police had withdrawn their cordon from around the pagoda. There was surface normality in Hue at last. But never had normality been more deceptive.

The activist bonzes were ready to move. In Saigon, they had demonstrated their mastery of Western propaganda techniques—press conferences, leaflets, demonstrations. They had learned they could count on friends among the foreign newsmen who disliked Ngo Dinh Diem. They now turned to another weapon, one that was distinctively their own, that allowed them the only violence permitted by the Vietnamese Buddhist tradition.

The morning of June 11 various foreign reporters were alerted by telephone of an impending event.

False alarms were common, however, and only one journalist bothered to reply to this summons, Malcolm Browne of Associated Press. A few days earlier Browne had accompanied a bonze brought in for questioning to a Saigon police station—and had himself been held there for an hour with several of his colleagues. Now, Browne set off for the busy intersection at Phan Dinh Phung and Le Van Duyet where he had been told to wait and took a camera with him.

It was a little after midday when an elderly Buddhist monk dressed in a saffron robe and accompanied by two other monks arrived in an old sedan. Later, his identity would be revealed: he was Thich Quang Duc, a monk who had spent his life in the service of Buddha and now at the age of seventy-three was ready for his final act of devotion. With calm dignity he seated himself in the lotus position while his companions poured a can of gasoline over him. He lit the match himself and sat motionless in the classic Buddhist attitude of prayer as the flames consumed him. There was the smell of burning flesh as a crowd gathered. In three or four minutes it was all over and the blackened lifeless figure toppled over on the pavement.

People had watched passively, no one had raised a finger to intervene, while a Vietnamese bonze holding a microphone repeated—not in Vietnamese but in English: "A Buddhist priest burns himself to death. A Buddhist priest becomes a martyr."

Never had the European aspect of Saigon seemed more superficial or more deceptive. This was a sacrifice out of another era and another world. To foreigners knowing little of Vietnam the death of this old monk evoked dark images of persecution and horror corresponding to a profoundly Asian reality that passed the understanding of Westerners. It inspired awe and dispelled any lingering doubts they might have had about the sufferings of Buddhists under Diem. Malcolm Browne had not forgotten to use his camera, and his pictures were flashed around the world, providing apparently irrefutable proof of the desperate condition of Buddhists in South Vietnam.

Yet, objectively, no single act of the Saigon government seemed to have justified the sacrifice of Thich Quang Duc. Madame Nhu could not keep silent. She had wanted to put the suicide into perspective, she would explain months later when it was too late for explanations. The shocking word she found to describe what had happened was one her young daughter had heard American photographers at the American commissary in Saigon use about the prospect of further self-immolations—they had called them *barbecues.*

Even Madame Nhu with her unfailing instinct for the wrong word at the wrong time had never achieved an epithet more devastating than this one. There were now two terrible facts to be laid at the door of the Saigon government—the suicide itself and the fact that the sister-in-law of the president had dismissed it as a barbecue. An intolerable image of the Diem regime was set in word and picture, never to be expunged.

The activist bonzes found they had a weapon of choice that had captured the horrified imagination of people in many places throughout the world. They would use that weapon time and again in their struggle with the Diem government. In Washington, no less a personage than Senator Frank Church, a member of the Senate Foreign Relations Committee, would say in September, "Such grisly scenes have not been witnessed since the Christian martyrs marched hand in hand into the Roman arenas."

Senator Church was wrong, for Vietnam alone had seen many self-immolations over the years—although, to do the senator justice, no one could have gleaned that information from the American press. Throughout that summer of 1963 reporters would turn out reams of copy about the Buddhists and their trial of strength with the Diem regime. The American public had the right to know, as they liked to say. But never in all that time did these reporters who were so dedicated to the truth stop to inquire whether such deaths by fire had ever before occurred in Vietnam. Yet there was no secret about it: they had only to talk with knowledgeable people, Vietnamese and others, and consult old books and newspapers.

The practice of Vietnamese bonzes' burning themselves to death to honor Buddha could be traced back for centuries. As late as 1950 such a case had occurred in North Vietnam. The French authorities had tried to stamp out the practice in colonial days but were not always successful. They did keep one monk who was intent on suicide away from the flames in Hue, but he finally succeeded in starving himself to death. During the 1920s and 1930s, Saigon newspapers from time to time matter-of-factly recorded the death of a bonze who had burned himself alive.

In 1948 in the Chinese city of Harbin, one bonze had resorted to self-immolation as a form of protest, seating himself in the lotus position on a pile of sawdust that he had soaked in soybean oil and set afire, apparently to protest the treatment of Buddhists by the Chinese Communists. He died alone, and only the next day when his neighbors saw the smoke did they come over to inquire what had happened. They found his heart untouched just as the Saigon faithful found the heart of Thich Quang Duc in 1963. This Chinese suicide was little known because it did not take place on a public square; and Peking, of course, did not permit foreign correspondents the freedom they enjoyed in Saigon.

But no such details about the practice of these and other forms of suicide in Vietnam and China appeared in the American press. The self-immolation the Buddhist activists had organized in Saigon on June 11 was new and alien to Western experience and generated shock waves that were all they could have wished, demonstrating that they had planned well and judged their audience accurately.

American chargé d'affaires Trueheart called on President Diem to inform him of the horror of the American government at the death of Thich Quang Duc. Out of all that Trueheart had to say, Diem heard one statement loud and clear: Once again, Washington had threatened to dissociate itself from his regime.

On the evening of June 11, President Diem told the nation

that he was profoundly troubled by the death of Thich Quang Duc. He declared in a radio address that Buddhism was protected by the constitution and he personally was its guardian. He appealed for serenity and patriotism and announced that negotiations would resume with the Buddhists.

The army responded immediately to this appeal. It was a time to tighten ranks behind the government and isolate any and all divisive elements in the country. Thirty high-ranking officers headed by their commander, General Le Van Ty, declared their resolve to carry out all missions entrusted to the army for the defense of the constitution and the Republic.

Their declaration was an impressive display of support for Diem from the senior officers of South Vietnam. But in this, as in so many other happenings at that time, appearances were misleading. Among the thirty officers who put their names to this document, some were already engaged in plots against the regime, and one would be personally involved in the murder of Diem. Two prominent generals had been spared the charade of professing a fidelity they did not feel. Duong Van Minh, military adviser to the president, and Tran Van Don, commander of the ground forces, both happened to be on a mission abroad.

The government, however, had made its point for the benefit of its unsympathetic American ally and for Vietnamese public opinion—no group of activists, Buddhists or otherwise, could dictate to the nation. Diem was now ready for an accord with the Buddhists.

The patriarch Thich Tinh Khiet, chairman of the General Association of Buddhists, had arrived from Hue after the suicide of Duc. But he was exhausted by the plane trip and the fast at Tu Dam pagoda that had preceded it and was unable to meet with government officials. Tri Quang also remained in seclusion behind the scenes. Talks opened in Saigon on June 14 between a delegation of Buddhist monks and the Interministerial Committee, and three days of discussion were needed before they could reach agreement on the five points. On June 16, they presented to the press a document that would be known henceforth as the *Joint Communiqué.*

The flying of the Buddhist flag was regulated at last and in detail. On religious holidays it could be flown outside the pagoda on condition that a larger national flag was displayed at the same time. The Buddhist flag might be flown alone only inside the pagoda. No religious flags would be permitted on national holidays.

A new bill was to be drafted and presented to the National Assembly that would place relations between government officials and the religious authorities on a more equitable footing. In the interim, the Interministerial Committee would order a lax application of the contested regulation—Du 10—that dated back to the time of Bao Dai.

The government agreed to appoint a committee to study any case in which Buddhists were reported detained. Clemency was promised for all who had supported the five points, and public officials were to be reminded of the order forbidding religious discrimination. Normal religious activities within the bounds of a pagoda or at the headquarters of the General Association of Buddhists would not require government permission. And the authorities would be lenient in censoring Buddhist literature and prayer books and granting permits for the construction of such buildings as pagodas, schools, and charitable institutions.

The Joint Communiqué assigned no responsibility for that most controversial question, the May 8 incident at the Hue radio station. It simply stipulated that government officials responsible for the incident would be severely punished if proved guilty. Compensation had already been paid to the bereaved families, and they might receive more according to the individual case.

The Joint Communiqué was solemnly signed by the three men who comprised the Interministerial Committee—Vice-President Tho, Secretary Thuan, and Secretary Luong—and by the members of the Buddhist delegation, who were joined on this occasion by the elderly Thich Tinh Khiet.

When the document was sent to Gia Long Palace for the signature of the president, Diem added a few words of his own: "The points put down in this joint communiqué were approved in principle by me from the very beginning." And so they had been. The problem was, and remained, how to translate principle into practice.

Thich Tinh Khiet sent a letter of thanks to Diem and called on

Buddhists to return to their normal lives and pray for the serious implementation of the Joint Communiqué, to respect national laws, and follow the instructions of the General Association of Buddhists. He formally declared the end of the movement that had begun the previous month in the city of Hue.

A date was announced for the funeral of Thich Quang Duc, and four thousand people gathered at the pagoda to honor the memory of the self-martyred bonze. At the last minute the ceremony was postponed. Several days later, in the early morning of June 19 under a clouded sky, the remains of Duc were finally carried out of Xa Loi pagoda. Attendance had been limited by agreement between Buddhist leaders and the police, and only some four hundred monks and the executive members of Buddhist organizations drove in a procession of cars to the cemetery some ten miles south of the city.

For the government the crisis was over, or should have been. But the Joint Communiqué was no more than a statement of intention, meaningful only if the signatories chose to give it meaning. Khiet had called it the start of a new era, and it could have been that—if the central government had moved rapidly to deal with Buddhist complaints as they arose (although it had never moved rapidly before); if inefficient local officials mired in old policies would conscientiously carry out new instructions from Saigon; if the atmosphere were not envenomed by charges and counter-charges. And, above all, if the bonzes would be content to return to their prayers and their pagodas.

Instead, the Joint Communiqué had only sharpened the appetite of Buddhist activists for politics. They were suspicious of government intentions and in no mood to be conciliatory. They had felt their strength and were riding a wave of success, confident after the signing of the Joint Communiqué that the government would not resort to drastic measures against them whatever the provocation.

At Xa Loi pagoda, they maintained frequent contacts with foreign newsmen, among whom one articulate monk fluent in the English language was in particular demand. The monks stepped up the production of leaflets attacking the government and distributed articles from Western newspapers critical of the regime. They continued to organize demonstrations, and the faithful who crowded into the pagoda were inflamed by accusations that the government was not going to allow Buddhists to worship freely; by stories of Buddhists persecuted and arrested. Tri Quang himself was now established in Saigon at Xa Loi pagoda at the heart of the action, and the movement spread from the pagodas of Saigon and Hue to pagodas in other cities.

The Buddhist movement had become increasingly hostile to the regime and intensely political, and it was no longer clear what the monks really expected of the government or even whether they knew themselves.

But the Americans did know what they expected. At the American Embassy the Ngos alone were blamed for the unrest. Trueheart repeated his threat that the United States would have to dissociate itself from the regime if it failed to appease the Buddhists. Diem, who was already raw from his clashes with the Americans over control of the struggle against the Viet Cong, remembered other American threats and steeled himself for still more demands from Washington. He did try to circumvent the diplomacy of ultimatums practiced by Trueheart. He sent a message to the absent American ambassador asking him to return to Saigon, and when there was no reply he sent a second message later that month.

Ambassador Nolting, who was vacationing with his family in Europe, did not receive either message even though both the embassy in Saigon and the State Department might have reached him had they desired. When eventually he learned of Diem's futile appeals, Nolting thought he knew what had gone wrong: that the people who wanted Diem to hang himself did not want him back in Saigon.

Nolting's absence had not only deprived Diem of wise counsel; it had also cut him off from Washington at a time when public criticism of his government had sharpened in the United States. Diem's isolation was even more complete than he knew because his own ambassador in Washington had turned against him.

Tran Van Chuong had been Diem's ambassador in the American capital since 1954; his wife was the South Vietnamese observer at the United Nations. The Chuongs were the estranged parents of

Madame Ngo Dinh Nhu. They were an adaptable couple, having collaborated with the French when Vietnam had been a colony of France, and later with the Japanese when they had occupied the country during World War II. In Washington, they had played a passive role, basking in Diem's apparent success during the good years, silent and self-effacing when the regime required defenders. Chuong had objected to the policy of courting diplomatic support for the Saigon government in the Third World. He had argued that the only support that could possibly matter in Saigon was that provided by Washington. Now, he recognized that American opinion had turned against Diem and the future was uncertain. It did not occur to either of the Chuongs to resign. Instead, they quietly began to intrigue against the government they were supposed to represent.

Late in May, Chuong had made a trip to the airport to meet a visitor from Hue whose position in Vietnam would not normally have entitled him to this personal attention from the ambassador. But the political connections of Father Luan, rector of the University of Hue, were of interest to the Chuongs, who both had political ambitions of their own. Chuong took the rector to meet American politicians and officials from whom he heard strong criticism of Diem. By the time Father Luan left Washington he had become an ally of Chuong and would soon break with the regime himself. But when he went back to Saigon in June he called at Gia Long Palace to report on his visit to Washington and was received by the president.

The date was June 24. The Buddhist affair still dominated news reports from Saigon, and Diem spoke to the rector from Hue with a frankness he did not permit himself before Americans. "If we make a concession now, the United States will ask for more," he said. "How many concessions do we have to make to satisfy them? . . . I wish to increase the army; the United States refuses to supply weapons and other means. The United States wants only to send troops to Vietnam."

A few days later Diem finally had news of Nolting—but not what he had hoped. On June 27, President Kennedy named Henry Cabot Lodge as the next ambassador to South Vietnam. Nolting himself only learned of his imminent replacement when he happened to listen to the radio while on his ill-timed holiday.

He may not have intended to stay on much longer in Saigon, but he had not expected to be informed in this summary fashion that his term of office was about to end. Nolting went back to Washington to defend a cause that was already lost. He had carried out Kennedy's instructions to achieve a friendly working relationship with Diem, of a kind that had eluded his predecessors at the American Embassy in Saigon. Now this conciliatory policy was discredited in Washington and so, it seemed, was the ambassador. More than Nolting's own career was at stake, for the prospect of abandoning Diem was no longer considered unthinkable in the American capital. Nolting found himself engaged in a lonely battle on behalf of the beleaguered leader in Saigon he had learned to esteem. Men like Robert McNamara at Defense and John McCone at the Central Intelligence Agency still saw no alternative to Diem. But at the State Department Under Secretary of State George Ball, Averell Harriman, and Roger Hilsman were simply fed up with the Vietnamese president. Ball later called him "a weak, third-rate bigot."

JULY 1963

In Saigon, a memorial service had just been held for the repose of the soul of Thich Quang Duc. It had been attended by emotional crowds, and Khiet had appeared in his yellow robe wearing a peach-colored hood embroidered with dragons. The following day he addressed a letter to President Diem, to complain that the Joint Communiqué was not being observed and that the condition of Buddhists in Vietnam had deteriorated in the past two weeks. Vice-President Tho, himself a Buddhist, replied in writing to deny this allegation.

Ngo Dinh Nhu decided to intervene. He told a reporter, "If anyone is oppressed in this affair, it is the government which has been constantly attacked and whose mouth has been shut with Scotch tape." The Republican Youth movement that Nhu headed released a so-called Study Document No. 3 under his signature that criticized the Joint Communiqué. "Our duty is to call on the population to resist the indirections [sic] of superstition and fanaticism." There was also the now-customary jab at the United States, a reference to "the lack of composure and realism on the part of our friends." Another release signed by Nhu called for "vigilance against political speculators and Communists who may abuse the Joint Communiqué and take it out of the religious context which is its *only* domain."

That first week of July, at a State Department briefing for the president, Kennedy and his advisers discussed rumors from Saigon that the government did not intend to live up to the Joint Communiqué, and for the first time there was serious discussion at the highest levels of the American government of the possibility of removing the Nhus from power. It was agreed that this was not possible under the circumstances. However, there were certain to be coup attempts in the months ahead. Diem might even be killed. Hilsman was optimistic that a coup would not lead to chaos; it was an encouraging sign that there had been no noticeable letup in the war against the Viet Cong during the Buddhist crisis.

At this same meeting, Hilsman reported that a Buddhist activist element favored increasing their demands as well as charging that the government was dragging its feet, so Diem was not wrong in thinking that they might push so far as to make his fall inevitable. But why had Trueheart's threats not convinced Diem to appease the Buddhists?

Nolting did his best to give Under Secretary of State Ball some insight into the complex figure who was president of South Vietnam. He said that when Diem gave his word he had always followed through and was certain to do so again, in his own way. But there was no point in pressuring Diem because the more he was prodded the slower he went. His regime would fall if Washington repudiated him. But Nolting did not doubt that Diem meant to live up to the Joint Communiqué unless, of course, he came to believe that he was dealing with an attempt to overthrow his government.

Henry Cabot Lodge was scheduled to report to Washington no

later than July 15 for briefings to prepare for his new post. In the meantime, it was decided that Nolting should go back to see what he could accomplish during a few last weeks in Saigon.

The South Vietnamese government chose this time to hold a trial of nineteen former officers involved in the coup that had failed in November 1960. The population would see what happened to plotters who dared to rise against the government. Thirty-four civilians accused of complicity in that coup were also called to appear before the Special Military Court.

The Americans received an unsubtle warning not to interfere. The official prosecutor declared that he had the documents to prove that a foreign country had been behind the abortive revolt but was not free to identify that country in public. It was later revealed that in secret session he had narrowed his charges to two Americans—George Carver, known afterward as an officer of the Central Intelligence Agency but then identified only as an employee of the United States economic mission (called USOM, for U.S. Operations Mission), and Howard C. Elting, described as having been deputy chief of the American mission in Saigon.

One of the politicians summoned to appear before the military court was the well-known novelist who wrote under the pen name of Nhat Linh. He was the Dai Viet leader Nguyen Tuong Tam, who had been Ho Chi Minh's minister of foreign affairs in 1946 when he fled the country rather than head the delegation to Fontainebleau and make concessions to the French. Both the Dai Viet and the VNQDD had later fought the Diem regime in 1955 and been defeated. But Tam, like the VNQDD leader Vu Hong Khanh, who had also once served under Ho Chi Minh, had been able to live quietly in the South Vietnam of Ngo Dinh Diem. They may not have liked the regime that excluded them from power, any more than did other members of the VNQDD and the Dai Viet, but they had had no choice short of exile—until November 1960, when the plotters had tried unsuccessfully to alter the balance of power in the country.

The authorities had never taken the charge of conspiracy against Tam seriously enough to arrest him, and he was at home when he learned of the pending trial. This time it was too late to leave the country had he wished to do so; he was older, too, and perhaps tired of political scheming. He did not attempt to defend himself but took cyanide and died in the hospital hours before the trial opened.

In the testament he left behind, Tam identified his death with that of Thich Quang Duc. He wrote, "I also will kill myself as a warning to those people who are trampling on all freedom." But many people in Saigon did not accept the suicide of Tam as uncritically as they had the fiery death of the old monk, even though this latest suicide was also in the Vietnamese tradition. "It was a question of his honor," an elderly gentleman said. "Why shouldn't he kill himself if he wanted to?" Vietnamese leaders had always chosen death rather than humiliation. But a young engineer disagreed: "The Viet Minh don't kill themselves. They suffer and fight," he said. Many members of Tam's own party also condemned his suicide as romantic and sentimental.

The trial that opened on July 8 was brief. The seven officers and two civilians who had fled the country when the coup failed in November 1960 were found guilty in absentia and condemned to death. Five servicemen were acquitted; the others were sentenced to prison terms ranging from five to ten years. The old comrade of the dead Tam, the VNQDD leader Vu Hong Khanh, was given six years in prison. Phan Khac Suu, the agricultural engineer who had served in Diem's first government and later joined Diem's opponents in the Caravelle group, received eight years. And Dr. Phan Quang Dan, who had been elected to the National Assembly in 1959 and not permitted to take his seat, was sentenced to seven years even though he had only joined the conspirators at the last minute. Fourteen of the civilian defendants were acquitted, among them the late Nguyen Tuong Tam.

The trial was over, and the talk in Saigon was no longer of the coup that had failed but of other coups that might succeed. Members of the Dai Viet had approached American CIA agents at the start of the Buddhist crisis to ask for support in a plot against Diem. The Dai Viet and other politicians were already in touch with Buddhist activists. But it was in the army that both the Dai Viet and the VNQDD were particularly influential, especially among young officers who saw no future for themselves in the armed forces of Ngo Dinh Diem.

These officers found an outlet in the American press. "Ambitious young anti-Communist officers" became a favorite source of David Halberstam for his articles in *The New York Times.* On June 22, he reported their conclusion that "the last six weeks have damaged the war effort irreparably." On July 3, in a front-page article, he wrote what amounted to a call for the United States to support a coup against the government. "Some American officials" were reported to favor a new Vietnamese government in place of the one headed by Diem, and "some young military officers" were ready to oust him "but they give the impression that they would like the Americans to make a public statement calling for a change. It is widely believed here that any statement from Washington critical of Ngo Dinh Diem for his handling of the Buddhist crisis would touch off an internal military strike at the government."

When the Ngos had first claimed that Americans were active behind the scenes in the agitation spreading in Saigon, they had sounded *paranoid*—a favorite word among Americans for Diem and Nhu that summer. But who could disbelieve Halberstam, with his excellent sources in the Central Intelligence Agency, when he reported that the CIA had been openly sending its agents into the pagodas and making daily contact with Buddhist priests and "other participants in this crisis"? These agents were acting under orders —and they did not go to the pagodas to discuss the finer points of Buddhism.

The CIA was in touch with members of the military, with opposition politicians, and with leading monks including Tri Quang himself; and if such people chose to interpret this American interest as tacit encouragement of their dissatisfaction with the government, the agents by all accounts had no instructions to persuade them otherwise.

As they grew more suspicious, the Saigon officials increasingly directed their frustration not at the U.S. government, but at the American newsmen who had been so frank in expressing their distaste for the regime.

The Diem government, like the governments of the great majority of countries in the Third World, had never appreciated the power of the American press and failed to understand why American reporters claimed the right to act in Vietnam with a freedom that was not permitted their Vietnamese counterparts. The long hostility between authorities and newsmen flared up on July 7 when several reporters trying to cover a Buddhist ceremony were attacked at the entrance of a pagoda by plainclothes police. One of the newsmen was knocked down and kicked; others were hustled; rocks were thrown at them. Several of their cameras were damaged and one was taken from them. Halberstam, Sheehan, Browne, and Peter Kalischer of CBS protested in a letter to President Kennedy that the government of South Vietnam "has begun a campaign of open physical intimidation to prevent the covering of news which we feel Americans have a right to know."

July 7 was Double Seven Day, the seventh day of the seventh month, and the anniversary of the accession of Diem to power. On the eve of this holiday, thirteen high-ranking officers were decorated. Generals Don and Minh, who had returned from Thailand late in June, were among the large audience at the award ceremony.

In a proclamation on the occasion of Double Seven Day, Diem reiterated that the "problems raised by the General Association of Buddhists have just been settled." But he spoke of the "underground intervention of international red agents and Communist fellow travelers who in collusion with fascist ideologues disguised as democrats were surreptitiously seeking to revive and rekindle disunity at home while arousing public opinion against us abroad." These "ideologues" presumably belonged to the Dai Viet, which was more like a brotherhood than a party, with a predilection for conspiratorial action and authoritarian government that had led other people, not just Diem, to accuse them of fascism. Only some Americans were receptive to Dai Viet claims to be "true nationalists" and revolutionaries and were naïve enough to be impressed by one Dai Viet politician who declared his unlikely attachment to that singularly un-Vietnamese concept, "the revolutionary spirits of 1776."

Diem was hurt by Buddhist attacks on him, indignant at what

he regarded as slanders and falsehoods in Vietnam and overseas. He was exhausted, tense, and deeply mistrustful of American intentions. He was in a martyr's mood himself, Nolting reported.

The two men spent seven hours together during the first two days after Nolting's return on July 11. The ambassador strongly deplored Trueheart's resort to threats as a substitute for diplomacy. In a cable to Washington Nolting advised against trying to blueprint Diem's course of action and called for an end to talk of dissociation. It would be much more effective to explain to Diem the rising anger among the American public about the reported treatment of Buddhists in South Vietnam.

As far as Nolting could tell, the Buddhist affair was limited mostly to the larger cities and the central coastal region and had not spread to the southern provinces of the Mekong Delta. He assured Washington that there was still a reasonably good chance of establishing a base for a continued American presence in South Vietnam.

Ambassador Nolting, General Harkins, the American commander in South Vietnam, and John Richardson, the CIA station chief, all believed that Diem even then could provide such a base, but this opinion was not shared by many of the younger men who served under them. At the embassy, in the aid mission, in the United States Information Service, among military advisers and intelligence agents, there was little confidence that this authoritarian and inefficient regime could ever lead its people to defeat the Communists. Whether the problems and conditions they complained of in Vietnam were comparable to or worse than those in many other countries recently emerged from colonial status throughout Asia and Africa was almost beside the point. The Americans were here, their country was taking a stand, and Vietnam would be held to a higher standard. The Americans in Saigon were not prepared to see any connection between the tortured history of Vietnam and the autocratic regime, the ineffectual and unwieldy bureaucracy, the problem-ridden army that now existed in the South. Most Americans in Saigon looked no further than the controversial personalities of Diem and Nhu and blamed the Ngo government for everything that seemed to be going wrong in the country.

This was the simplistic view, reflected in the press, that had gained currency in the State Department and at the White House. Diem's apparent inability to seize the initiative from Buddhist activists was simply the last straw.

A month had passed since the self-immolation of Thich Quang Duc, and the government and the Buddhists were no closer to an understanding. Buddhist demonstrations in the streets, Buddhist agitation at the pagoda, went on unchecked. The government seemed to have no policy. It was passive, apparently unable to appease the Buddhists, yet unwilling to interfere with them—until July 17, when the police broke up a demonstration in Saigon and arrested many monks and provided Buddhists with a new grievance against Diem.

His advisers told him he could not continue to ignore what was going on. Even Ngo Dinh Nhu agreed with Ambassador Nolting that the president had to take the lead in seeking a solution to the continuing crisis. At last Diem was persuaded to broadcast an address in which he declared all military and civilian authorities were working to implement the government's "utmost desire for conciliation in settling the Buddhist problem." He called for a mixed commission with representatives of the official Interministerial Committee headed by Vice-President Tho and the Buddhist Intersect Committee working together, to make on-the-spot investigations whenever there were complaints about violations of the Joint Communiqué.

But emotions were running high, the Buddhist movement was stronger and more confident than ever, and activists saw no advantage in relaxing their pressure on the government. They refused to cooperate in any joint investigation before all Buddhists arrested since May 8 were released and again demanded punishment of those responsible for the bloodshed in Hue.

Diem could not, would not, assign blame for the Hue tragedy to his own officials when he believed them innocent. He was impervious to the need to convince Buddhists that justice had been done in Hue, by holding a new investigation, a trial if necessary.

The monks were carrying on a war of nerves against the regime, and it was announced that the mother of Buu-Hoi, who had been a Buddhist nun for many years, had left Hue for Saigon to burn herself to death for Buddha. The threat of this impending suicide by the mother of the prominent scientist never materialized, but it contributed to sustaining the atmosphere of tension and was used by the monks for weeks as a propaganda ploy. The highlight was a press conference at Xa Loi pagoda at which the woman was produced to repeat her suicide threat. Outside, a "spontaneous" demonstration of war veterans, many of them maimed, used government sound trucks in a protest against the behavior of the Buddhists. This clumsy attempt at counterpropaganda backfired because the sorry demonstration on the street had obviously been organized by the authorities.

On July 31, the police did not intervene when mass demonstrations were held by the Buddhists in Saigon, Dalat, Nha Trang, Qui Nhon, and Hue.

Supporters of the regime had come to Nhu to warn him that the Buddhists could prove dangerous, and he had brushed aside their warnings. Without a party of their own the Buddhists could not have any power, he had said. They still had no party, and they were not nearly so representative of the varied Vietnamese community as they claimed. But they had become a focal point for opposition elements, providing an outlet for popular discontent with the controls that were the response of the government to the Viet Cong threat.

In the Vietnamese capital, this threat from the Viet Cong still seemed unreal to members of the articulate middle class, a problem perhaps but only for other people, inhabitants of the remote countryside, not themselves. It had never entered the heads of such Saigon middle-class elements that they should make sacrifices for any government, certainly not fight for this one or any other. As they had once accepted French protection even while they complained loudly about the colonial regime, so they had tolerated Diem. But now the strained political climate opened the regime to attack from all sides and played into the hands of its enemies in Saigon and Washington.

Saigon. A view of the National Assembly on Tu Do (Freedom) Street,
formerly Rue Catinat.

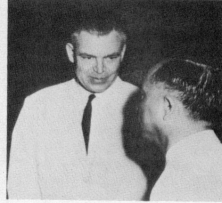

OPPOSITE TOP LEFT: President Ngo Dinh Diem.

OPPOSITE TOP RIGHT: Ambassador Nolting liked and admired President Diem.

OPPOSITE BOTTOM: Lyndon Johnson got on well with Ngo Dinh Diem.

LEFT: June 1961. Secretary Nguyen Dinh Thuan brings a message from President Diem to President Kennedy.

BELOW: General Maxwell Taylor and Defense Secretary Robert McNamara with the president at the White House.

ABOVE LEFT: The Vietnamese president and his family. His aged mother is seated. (*Left to right*) Ngo Dinh Nhu, President Diem, Archbishop Thuc; Madame Nhu stands fifth from the left; to the right of her are Ngo Dinh Can and his brother Luyen.

ABOVE RIGHT: The author, with Vietnamese friends.

OPPOSITE BOTTOM: Geneva, July 1962. The international conference that neutralized Laos on paper, although it was never neutralized in practice.

INSET: President Diem receives Laotian Prime Minister Souvanna Phouma in Saigon in 1956.

LEFT: Buu-Hoi, scientist and diplomat.

ABOVE: The tomb of Emperor Minh Mang on the outskirts of Hue.

RIGHT: The Buddhist patriarch Tich Tinh Khiet.

OPPOSITE: Saigon, July 1963. Hundreds of Buddhists leave Xa Loi pagoda peacefully after a rally there.

OPPOSITE: **November 4, 1963. Thich Tri Quang (*left*) and two companions leave the U.S. Embassy in Saigon two months after they were given political asylum there.**

BELOW: **Henry Cabot Lodge and the president, who appointed him ambassador to South Vietnam in the midst of the Buddhist crisis.**

TOP: Three conspirators. (*Left to right in foreground*) Generals Duong Van Minh, Le Van Kim, and Tran Van Don, in July 1963.

OPPOSITE BOTTOM: Washington, D.C. The Executive Committee of the National Security Council of the Kennedy administration.

BELOW MIDDLE: President Kennedy at Hyannis Port with Under Secretary of State W. Averell Harriman (*left*) and Secretary of State Dean Rusk (*right*).

BELOW RIGHT: October 1, 1963. Buu-Hoi pays a visit to the State Department on behalf of the South Vietnamese government. Here he is signing the nuclear test-ban treaty. Assistant Secretary of State Roger Hilsman stands behind him next to Tran Van Dinh, Vietnamese chargé d'affaires.

ABOVE LEFT: Ngo Dinh Nhu, the Vietnamese president's brother and inseparable adviser, in his office at Gia Long Palace, September 1963.

ABOVE RIGHT: Robert F. Kennedy, the American president's brother and alter ego.

RIGHT: Dalat, October 28, 1963. President Diem and Ambassador Lodge said nothing of importance to each other at the inauguration of the Atomic Energy Center four days before the coup d'état.

AUGUST 1963

On August 14, Nolting called on Diem to bid him farewell for the last time. The previous weeks had been difficult for the American ambassador. He had worked hard for conciliation, but despite his efforts Buddhist opposition to the government had gathered momentum.

The leaders at Xa Loi were unappeased, and the atmosphere at the pagoda that this writer visited at the time was highly charged. The place was filled with people, and the constant chanting, the intermittent clanging of a gong, the heavy incense—all this in the half-light—sustained an atmosphere of near-hysteria.

On August 3, a second monk had burned himself to death at Phan Thiet. On August 13, a third, near Hue.

Ngo Dinh Nhu complained to foreign newsmen that the government showed weakness in dealing with the Buddhists and speculated about a coup d'état that would also be directed against them. His wife returned to the politics of vituperation and accused the monks of barbarism and burlesque, of subversion and worse. They responded to her attack with a refusal to cooperate with the committee of investigation that was about to leave for the central provinces to look into complaints that Buddhists had suffered repression and discrimination.

In a series of letters to Diem, the bonzes demanded the release of everyone held by the government who claimed to be Buddhist. They warned against any attack on Xa Loi pagoda, accused the government of maneuvers to wreck its professed Buddhist policy, and said there were plans afoot to exterminate the Buddhist religion.

Vice-President Tho replied on behalf of the government that Madame Nhu spoke only for herself, and that military action against the Buddhists was unthinkable. Incidents had occurred that needed to be investigated. But he called in vain on the Buddhist Intersect Committee to participate in a joint commission of inquiry to Hue and Hoi An.

Nolting had urged Diem to act and break the stalemate. Even Nhu, who regarded the Buddhist activists as subversive, promised to be conciliatory, and on August 13 Nolting at last had been able to report to Washington that Diem consented to make a statement, to satisfy world opinion. He also agreed that Madame Nhu ought to leave the country and said he would arrange that himself.

By the next day Diem was no longer sure he wanted to make these concessions after all. He was angered by an article in *The New York Times* that said his Buddhist policy was adversely affecting the war effort, and outraged at the sight of Buddhist banners in Saigon that attacked him personally.

When Nolting called at Gia Long Palace at 11:00 A.M. to make his formal farewell, he had to go over the same ground once again. Diem objected that both the American press and the American government were ignorant of the true dimensions and complexities of the Buddhist affair. They had no understanding of the Ngo family and of their individual contributions to the country. He spoke in particular of the selflessness of his brother Nhu. Ambassador Nolting was unable to accept this as a reply. He told President Diem frankly that the United States could not continue its "present relationship" with him unless Diem made a declaration to show who was running the country, to undo some of the damage caused by Madame Nhu and restore faith in the intentions of the government. Diem finally allowed himself to be persuaded and said he would try to have a statement ready before Nolting's departure the following day.

Then it was time to say good-bye. The relationship between the two men had not always been untroubled. Once, the clash over security policy had brought the two governments almost to the breaking point, and there had been other differences even on this last day. But Ngo Dinh Diem, who was slow to give his trust, had come to appreciate the quality of the American and wished to tell him so. He said that Nolting's tenure in Saigon had been one of the best experiences of his life and that exchanges like the one they had just had would in no way mar their friendship. "I heartily reciprocated his sentiments," Nolting reported to Washington.

Diem had put one searching question to Nolting before he left Vietnam: "Does your departure mean that the American government has changed its policy from what you and I agreed two and one half years ago?"

"No, Mr. President, it does not," Nolting had replied.

But Diem had been skeptical, and Nolting wired Washington to reassure him. He received a reply signed "Rusk" that instructed him to tell Diem on "highest authority"—the president—that no change was contemplated.

Nolting showed the telegram to Diem, who looked at it for a long time. Then he said, "Mr. Ambassador, I believe you, but I don't believe the telegram that you have received."

The time had come for Buddhist leaders themselves to worry about the hysteria they had whipped up in the countryside. Messages were dispatched under the signature of the patriarch Khiet ordering that there be no more suicides "unless necessary." On August 15, a middle-aged nun burned herself to death in the town of Ninh Hoa near Nha Trang, and it was not sure that her death had been authorized by the activist hierarchy. A few days earlier, an eighteen-year-old girl had tried to chop off her left hand for Buddha. But on August 16, a "necessary" suicide was staged in Hue in the courtyard of Tu Dam pagoda, where police watched as an elderly monk, the father of a Buddhist scholar studying in Japan, set himself on fire.

Tempers were high among the Buddhist population of Hue, even though the government in Saigon had ordered an end to the martial law imposed on the city by the local authorities, even after the lifting of the blockade of Xa Loi pagoda. In Hue, there was repression—General Tri used both the army and the police against the Buddhists, and tensions were exacerbated by the unabashed proselytism of Archbishop Thuc.

The overbearing and self-righteous conduct of the president's elder brother had become a matter of concern to the Vatican. After the self-immolation of Thich Quang Duc in June, the pope appealed to the South Vietnamese government to show tolerance toward Buddhists, and his message was echoed in a pastoral letter addressed to his fellow Catholics by the archbishop of Saigon, Monsignor Nguyen Van Binh. In August the pope again urged moderation on the government through diplomatic channels and Monsignor Binh, who was about to leave for an Ecumenical Congress in Rome, wrote in another pastoral letter, "Let us not confuse the spread of the faith with the development of political influence or social prestige." He asked for an effort of understanding, moderation, and kindness. But these words were lost on Monsignor Thuc, who had been planning a major speech at the Rex Cinema in Saigon and was persuaded to call it off only after the suicide of the nun at Ninh Hoa.

Even Ngo Dinh Nhu, who usually was well informed, had no idea of the unrest among students and faculty at the University of Hue. His brother the archbishop chose to blame the rector, Father Luan, now known even to American officials as an opponent of the regime, and convinced Diem to dismiss him on August 15. Members of the faculty resigned en masse to protest the failure of the government to resolve the Buddhist affair.

The fear and the hate were palpable in Hue when this writer visited the old imperial capital that August. Leading citizens believed that Archbishop Thuc intended to convert the entire city to Catholicism, by force if necessary. These Buddhist gentry had been deeply offended by the attacks of Madame Nhu, which sounded even more crude in the original Vietnamese than in translation— she talked like a fishwife, they said. Determined young men gathered at the pagoda, where they stood guard against a surprise attack, and one elderly man who joined them said he was ready to fight to the death with the others if the government sent in troops.

In Saigon, on Sunday August 18, some fifteen to twenty thousand people collected at Xa Loi pagoda. Their numbers had tripled since the previous Sunday. Tri Quang had told an American official in Hue he would not end his campaign until the government was overthrown. To certain visitors, if not to U.S. officials, at Xa Loi pagoda, he spoke frankly of his goal, which was even more ambitious than a Buddhist-dominated Vietnam or the fall of Diem—he wanted a neutralist regime in Saigon. For the time being, he found it expedient to collaborate with anti-Communist opposition groups even though they hoped to dislodge Diem only in order to replace him and pursue the war against the Communists with renewed vigor and American help.

The Ngos may not have been wrong in their belief that the Viet Cong had infiltrated the Buddhists and encouraged popular demonstrations against the regime, even though the Communist leaders respected discipline too much to feel anything but distaste for the irrational and uncontrollable elements of the Buddhist movement. The Communist leaders also knew as well as Diem and the readers of *The New York Times* that the CIA was in touch with the Buddhists. Subversive politicians were already working with the Buddhist activists—but they were associated with the Dai Viet.

On August 18, the crowd assembled at Xa Loi pagoda heard the monks attack Madame Nhu. They went further. In banners prominently displayed and in harangues to the crowd, they called for the overthrow of the government, and the faithful responded with enthusiasm.

Diem had procrastinated too long; the dispute with the militant Buddhists should never have been permitted to come to this. The failure of the government to act in time had played into the hands of ambitious men—some bonzes, others secular politicians—who had transformed an issue of religion into a test of political force and threatened the survival of the government itself.

Since the beginning of August Polish ambassador Maneli, who was strategically placed in the South Vietnamese capital to report to his Communist friends, had been sending cables and reports to Warsaw, the Hanoi government, and the Soviet ambassador in Hanoi, saying that Diem and Nhu had only one choice left: They would either have to leave the country or else decisively crush the Buddhist movement.

Vietnamese army leaders did not see the issue in these stark terms. The generals realized that the government could not sit by passively while its authority was flouted daily, but they had their own interests and their own objectives that were no longer, if they ever had been, the same as those of Diem. They welcomed this opportunity for the army to move to the forefront of the political stage.

The evening of August 18 ten senior generals met to discuss the situation and decided that martial law was required. They agreed that all bonzes who came from places other than Saigon had to be returned to their provinces and their own pagodas. This could not have been accomplished without the use of force because men would be breaking into pagodas where they would not be welcome, removing bonzes who did not wish to leave, and taking them back to pagodas where they did not wish to go.

AUGUST 20–21, 1963

Seven of the generals summoned to the palace on August 20 by Nhu for consultations presented their plans to the president's brother and discussed at length how the subversive militants among the bonzes would be taken into custody and the pagodas changed back into religious institutions. Nhu sent the generals to see Diem.

The president listened as they set forth their arguments. This group of generals was headed by Don and included the two men who had intervened during the abortive coup in 1960, Khiem and Khanh. Also present were the ebullient Ton That Dinh, still a favorite of the Ngo family; Tri, who ruled Hue with an iron hand; and Don's brother-in-law, Le Van Kim. Only one of the seven, Huynh Van Cao, was not engaged in plotting against the government.

Don spoke of Communist infiltration at Xa Loi pagoda and warned that troop morale was deteriorating because of the demagogic appeals of the militant bonzes. If the monks summoned a large crowd to march on Gia Long Palace, the army might not intervene to stop it.

On the recommendation of the generals, Diem ordered that martial law be declared the next day throughout the country. Troops were to be brought in to occupy strategic points in Saigon. General Don was appointed acting commander of the armed forces to replace General Ty, then under medical treatment in the United States, and General Ton That Dinh became military governor of Saigon under the direct orders of the office of the president.

Diem said the pagodas had to be handled with special care,

that he did not want any of the monks hurt. General Don was sufficiently impressed by the president's concern for the welfare of the bonzes that he remarked on it when telling CIA officer Lucien Conein about this meeting.

But Diem had given the generals no hint that his solicitude had been aroused by the prospect of an operation against the pagodas that very night. Don told Conein of his surprise on discovering the action was under way in the early hours of August 21.

With Diem's approval, Nhu had profited from the declaration of martial law to order armed men into the pagodas that had been taken over by Buddhist activist monks. For Diem and Nhu, this was 1954 and 1955 again writ large and they had had no other choice; the regime was under attack and fighting for survival; the army and the pagodas seething with revolt, opposition politicians conspiring behind the scenes with the military and the Buddhists. And behind them all, foreigners—not Frenchmen this time, but Americans.

Nhu deliberately chose a time when the American Embassy was leaderless; Nolting's successor had not yet arrived in Saigon. Bypassing the army high command, which worked closely with the Americans, he sent against the pagodas the combat police and the Special Forces under Colonel Tung, the shock troops of the regime, who received orders directly from the office of the president.

Some of these men were in army uniform; Nhu tried to pass off the pagoda raids as an action of the regular army. His motive: to shift to the military the onus of an operation that was bound to distress many of his countrymen and anger his American allies and to discredit the plotters in the army who were looking for American support against him. In the past, Nhu's Machiavellian tactics, manipulating the generals and playing one off against the other, had kept conspirators off balance and thwarted plots against the regime. This time, he would soon discover he had overreached himself in faking army involvement in the pagoda raids and had played into the hands of his enemies.

The combat police and the Special Forces seized twenty to thirty key pagodas throughout South Vietnam. They forced their way in, broke down doors barricaded against them, and were not gentle with the bonzes, many of whom resisted. Monks and nuns were rounded up and taken away. At Xa Loi alone, some said, four hundred people were arrested—others put the figure at six hundred —and nine monks were sent to the hospital for treatment of their injuries. Similar scenes of violence occurred in other pagodas. In one pagoda in Hue, monks and nuns held out against the attackers for eight hours, and crowds of sympathizers rioted in the city.

Stories of murdered bonzes circulated rapidly through Saigon and Hue and appeared in the foreign press. The CIA reported the Buddhist leaders were either dead or being held for trial. The number of the alleged Buddhist dead had shrunk to four by the time a fact-finding mission dispatched by the United Nations to investigate the situation arrived in Saigon on October 24 with the names of the monks believed killed during the raids—two in Saigon and two in Hue—and found all four alive.

When the government seized Xa Loi pagoda, the aged Thich Tinh Khiet, whom the activist monks had made into a figurehead, was taken to a military hospital on the outskirts of Saigon. Two monks had managed to escape over the wall into the United States economic mission next door during the attack. There was no sign of Tri Quang, who seemed to have disappeared.

The new American ambassador, Henry Cabot Lodge, was in Honolulu for last-minute briefings with Nolting and other officials when news came of the pagoda raids. In Washington, the State Department denounced this "direct violation by the Vietnamese government of assurances that it was pursuing a policy of reconciliation with the Buddhists."

Lodge went on to Tokyo, where he received instructions to leave immediately for Saigon. It was half an hour past the 9:00 P.M. curfew on August 22 when his plane reached the Vietnamese capital. Lodge shook hands with General Harkins and Trueheart, who had come to meet him at the airport. Then he looked about and asked, "Where are the gentlemen of the press?"

8.
Washington Decides for a Coup

Henry Cabot Lodge had not been the first choice of President Kennedy to replace Nolting as ambassador to South Vietnam. Secretary of State Dean Rusk had persuaded him to offer the post to his old adversary from Massachusetts who lost his Senate seat to Kennedy in 1952 and had been Richard Nixon's running mate, the vice-presidential candidate on the Republican ticket that Kennedy had defeated in 1960. The president joked that the idea of getting Lodge mixed up in such a hopeless mess as Vietnam was irresistible. Of course it made good political sense to enlist a leading Republican politician to carry out the unpopular policy of a Democratic president, and a man experienced in public life would know how to handle the press, which had been such a problem for Nolting.

When Hilsman and Forrestal had made their recommendations for Nolting's eventual successor, after their mission to Vietnam in January, they had asked for someone who could show more vigor in getting Diem to do what the United States wanted; if not a general, a public figure with the character and the reputation to dominate American officialdom. Lodge was all of that, and known for his propensity for independent action. Madame Nhu complained that Kennedy was sending a proconsul to Vietnam. Many Americans in Saigon would be delighted at Lodge's highhanded methods of dealing with the Vietnamese government that summer and fall. We have our own mandarin now, such people would say with satisfaction as Lodge proceeded to demonstrate that he was a diplomat who did not believe in diplomacy. But only a few weeks after the new ambassador took over in Saigon Robert Kennedy reminded the president of his warning that he would have a lot of difficulties with Lodge. John Kennedy replied—in his brother's words—"it was terrible about me 'cause I always could remember when I was right." By that time Kennedy was so dissatisfied with the behavior of his ambassador that he was seriously considering how to replace him.

Yet in August Lodge had seemed to many people an excellent choice. He was fluent in the French language—a necessity in Vietnam for diplomats who could not speak Vietnamese—and reputed for his diplomatic experience. Unfortunately, this experience had been limited to his tenure as American ambassador to the United Nations, where he had distinguished himself by his indifference to the problems of the Third World and his inability to make friends among its representatives.

In addition, Lodge had excellent relations with the American military. He was a major general in the reserves and had been acquainted with General Harkins since they had served together at Fort Bliss in the 1920s; some members of the White House staff had opposed his appointment in the belief that he would naturally take the side of the Pentagon and of Ngo Dinh Diem. There was no doubt that the Joint Chiefs of Staff were pleased that Lodge was to be the new ambassador. He was invited to a lunch at the Pentagon, where they spoke to him about what they regarded as tendentious reporting on Vietnam and explained that Diem had to be supported for lack of an acceptable alternative; Lodge had listened and allowed them to think he shared their opinions. He gave no sign that he was about to set forth on a very different course as soon as he arrived in Saigon.

Before that final conference in Honolulu there had been other briefings in Washington, where cables from Saigon and Hue detailed the story of American anger and frustration with Diem. Lodge had also talked with Madame Tran Van Chuong, still the official representative of Diem at the United Nations and the wife of his ambassador to Washington, who recounted to him tales of horror about what was supposed to be taking place in South Vietnam. She spoke of mass executions and a reign of terror and told him that if Diem and the Nhus did not leave the country they would be killed. As things turned out, it would require a plot activated and nurtured by Lodge himself to realize this prophecy for Diem and his brother.

Lodge was no friend of the Ngos by the time he reached Saigon. Nolting was convinced he had gone to Vietnam with orders to break with Diem as soon as possible. According to Arthur Schlesinger, the instructions Lodge had received from the president were loose, allowing him a certain latitude and reflecting Kennedy's own uncertainties about his Vietnamese policy.

AUGUST 23, 1963

The new ambassador lost no time in making American sympathies known. On that Friday, his first day in Saigon, he called on the two monks who had taken refuge at the USOM building next door to Xa Loi pagoda during the raid and arranged for suitable vegetarian meals to be prepared for them. It made a good story in Saigon and in Washington, good propaganda too, showing the friendship of the American government for the persecuted Buddhists. Nine days later, however, on advice from their superiors in the Buddhist hierarchy, the two bonzes decided to leave the American mission and retire to An Quang pagoda. They got into a taxi and drove off.

American officials and newsmen were disconcerted by these monks, who acted as if they did not need the United States to protect them against their own government. But rather than try to find out why the two men had not been afraid to go back to the pagoda, which might have required revising some of their own preconceived ideas about the situation in Saigon, the Americans preferred to dismiss the entire episode.

Lodge by that time was involved in a complicated plan to translate his own preconceptions into action. He had arrived in Saigon to find a cable from Hilsman that called for an immediate reply. What was the situation since the night of August 20/21? Had there been a military takeover or was Diem still in control and stronger than ever, with the cooperation of the military? Or could it be that Nhu was now calling the shots?

Even if the military were not yet in the saddle, Hilsman wrote in his cable, they might still be able to use martial law to their advantage. If there were any chance of that, the American government ought not to press to have martial law canceled too quickly. What did Lodge think?

SAIGON, AUGUST 23–25, 1963

Secretary of the Presidency Thuan awaited the arrival of the American with impatience on the morning of Saturday, August 24. Rufus Phillips was a friend and a professional contact. Phillips's contacts with Vietnamese were extensive, dating back to the time he had served under Lansdale in the Saigon Military Mission. He had been "one of Ed's people" in that CIA team working to bolster the new Diem regime when Thuan made his acquaintance in 1955. Phillips later served in the CIA in Laos, and in 1962 he had returned to Vietnam, where he now directed American economic assistance to the strategic hamlet program. Ngo Dinh Nhu had told Warren Unna of *The Washington Post* that the American public might not know "that you have many CIAs in the American system. The White House, the Army, the Navy, the Air Force, every American organization or agency has its own intelligence and all those agencies spread out on a limited place are of course ever conflicting among themselves. . . ." In an Associated Press dispatch, Malcolm Browne would list three American intelligence agencies operating in Vietnam: the 704th Military Intelligence Detachment, the embassy's security office, and the aid mission's Rural Affairs Agency headed by Rufus Phillips, described as a former CIA agent.

Thuan had been eager to talk to Phillips ever since the attack on the pagodas and had finally reached him the previous evening to invite him to breakfast.

Thuan was distressed, outraged, anxious about the future. The policy of conciliating the Buddhists, with which he had been associated from the start, was in shreds. Public feeling against the government's clumsy handling of the Buddhists, compounded by simmering resentment over government controls that had grown more onerous as the struggle with the Viet Cong intensified, had reached the boiling point. Vu Van Mau, the northerner who had served as foreign affairs secretary since 1954, appeared with his head shaved like a Buddhist monk and submitted his resignation to the president on the grounds of ill health. The Voice of America gave wide publicity to the condemnation by the United States of the pagoda raids. It also broadcast the information from Washington that Ambassador Chuong had resigned in protest. This was denied in Saigon, where it was revealed that Chuong's last telegram had been so critical of the regime that it had been regarded as "inadmissible in form and substance" and Diem, after years of complaining privately about his ambassador, had finally dismissed him a day or two before he announced his resignation.

Diem had also moved to silence Chuong's daughter, Madame Nhu. He had written her a formal letter forbidding her to make public statements or give press conferences and had ordered that no statement she made be printed.

At midnight on August 22, Generals Don, Dinh, and Khiem had gone to tell Nhu they had learned that student demonstrations were planned for the next three days and recommended that all Saigon schools be closed, and Nhu agreed. But when he accompanied the generals to ask permission of the president, Diem refused to close the schools. "The young people must have some means of expressing themselves," he said. And express themselves they did. On August 23 there were well-organized demonstrations against the government at the University of Saigon. They were followed by mass arrests that fueled other student protests, and the movement spread to the high schools.

The pagoda raids had frightened Diem's private secretary, Vo Van Hai, who feared his life was in danger and when he spoke to a State Department official in Saigon implored him to keep his name secret. More than twenty years later, when the State Department released a copy of Paul Kattenberg's report of this interview in response to a request under the Freedom of Information Act, someone took Hai's request for secrecy seriously enough, long after it could possibly matter, to clip out his name where it appeared, in every place but one.

In this interview, Hai confirmed that the Special Forces, and not the army as people in Washington had believed, had been used for the raid on the pagodas. He claimed that the entire Buddhist affair had been stage-managed by Ngo Dinh Nhu, who definitely had never believed in conciliation. Hai thought the president had genuinely desired a settlement with the Buddhists, as Diem may well have done. And certainly his brother and his brother's wife had not made his task any easier. But Diem had never understood that time was not on his side; his failure to defuse the crisis weeks earlier had discredited the traditional, apolitical leaders among the monks, allowing younger, politically ambitious activists to take over the movement, men far more interested in confrontation than in compromise.

To the president's private secretary, Hai, the high point for South Vietnam had been the late 1950s—when the Viet Cong had seemed weak and the Americans unchallenged. Ever since that time the country had gone downhill, and it was the fault of Nhu, to whom Hai had lost all influence over Diem (a reason, Kattenberg pointed out, to take what he had to say with a certain skepticism). Nhu had to be removed before the government lost all support, Hai said. The generals would move against him if given the word to do so. "It would not be difficult."

When Rufus Phillips arrived at the home of Secretary Thuan the following day, August 24, there was more talk of generals and this time from one of the most highly placed men in the Diem administration. Thuan had worked patiently on behalf of the government for years and had served as a middleman between the Americans and the presidency. He was a moderate, reasonable man with great confidence in the Americans as reasonable people with whom he shared a common goal. He had come to look on Nhu much as they did—as unpredictable and dangerous, a man of visions and arrogance. And now he thought Nhu was disturbingly triumphant because he had tricked the army and the Americans by using the Special Forces against the pagodas under cover of martial law.

Thuan had decided not to resign, out of loyalty to Diem, he told Phillips on Saturday morning. To the Nhus, too, Phillips reported him saying, but his loyalty to Nhu could no longer have been very strong, judging by what else he had to say to Phillips that morning. He added there was another reason he did not resign: concern for the safety of his family.

For Thuan there was still no alternative to Diem as president. There never had been, no one else was so respected and so widely acceptable in Vietnam. But the same could not be said of the Nhus. "Under no circumstances should the Americans acquiesce in what the Nhus had done," he said. If they did, the only results would be chaos and disaster. It was up to the United States to act, to be very firm and to exercise leadership. If the Americans withheld their support from Diem as long as his government included the Nhus, then the army could be counted on to expel Nhu. He had no doubt that the army would turn against the president's brother once it was convinced that the United States would not tolerate a government "with the Nhus in control." As assistant secretary of defense was one of Thuan's titles he spoke with a certain authority.

Thuan had embarked on a game dangerous for an official whose career had been lived in the shadow of Diem and whose future depended on the president's continuing in power. Perhaps this highly intelligent man had been misled by the warm personal relationships he had developed with many Americans over the years. He expected too much of the Americans. He overestimated their ability to fine-tune their encouragement to the generals so they would force out the Nhus and yet keep Diem as president. And Thuan had made the cardinal error of assuming that Washington policymakers still cared to see Diem in power. He could not know that his own words would be used against Diem in Washington, where his condemnation of Nhu was given great weight, coming as it did from one of the senior and best-liked members of the Vietnamese government. American officials who did not share Thuan's appreciation of Diem read Phillips's report of their interview as confirming their own strong feelings that Nhu had to go and that the army should be the means of removing him. And if the entire Diem regime were brought down at the same time, few Americans would regret it.

At least two generals had already approached Americans in Saigon to talk of plots since the pagoda raids. General Don, the acting commander of the armed forces, told CIA agent Conein that the Voice of America ought to correct its report that the army, and not the police and the Special Forces, had been responsible for the attacks on the pagodas. The military would benefit if the Voice of America absolved it of blame for this unpopular action.

In a conversation covering many subjects ranging from his ideas about Diem's sex life or lack of one to the fact that the generals and not the Ngos had taken the initiative in proposing martial law, Don spoke vaguely of a larger plan in which the declaration of martial law was only the first step, "and the secret of what is going to happen is not mine to give." It was unclear whether the later stages of this plan would be controlled by members of the military or civilians or even Ngo Dinh Nhu himself. Don personally believed it was practically impossible to separate Diem from the Nhus, but he said things could not go back to what they had been before martial law; some ministers had to be changed.

All this was provocative but vague, in contrast to the interview that Secretary Thuan's friend Rufus Phillips had the same day, August 23, with the man who was Don's deputy, his brother-in-law and closest friend, Brigadier General Le Van Kim.

Kim also demanded that the Voice of America retract its statements that the army was responsible for the pagoda raids. The population had to be told the truth. Otherwise, it would turn against the army, which would be seriously handicapped in its fight against the Viet Cong.

Whereas Don had simply allowed as how he preferred Diem to Nhu, Kim bitterly attacked Nhu, claiming he had tricked the army into establishing martial law. Kim asserted that Nhu was now in control in Saigon. Kim and seven other generals had signed an oath of loyalty to Diem even though they did not approve of the action against the Buddhists. They had to sign "or expose themselves to individual elimination by Counselor Nhu."

Kim said that if the United States took a clear stand against the Nhus and in favor of the army ousting them from the government, the army would act to remove them.

Roger Hilsman in his memoir of the period would write that the generals were afraid Diem was planning to have them executed. Could they really have believed they were going to be killed? Even allowing for the shock of the pagoda raids and the paranoia endemic in Saigon (and perhaps deliberately fostered among the generals by Nhu), it is hard to take this statement at face value—especially since General Don had expressed no such fears for himself.

According to Hilsman, the generals also believed Nhu might try to make a deal with Hanoi and sell out the whole country to the Communists. General Khanh would tell that to his CIA contact in Saigon on Sunday, August 25. This was an argument of weight for the Vietnamese military as for the Americans. President Kennedy had seen nothing untoward in authorizing Averell Harriman to sound out the Hanoi delegation about negotiations, in Geneva the year before, and to do so behind the back of the South Vietnamese. There seemed to be a double standard in these matters: that the Diem government might approach the Northern regime on its own was inadmissible, a betrayal of the national interest, American and Vietnamese.

WASHINGTON, AUGUST 24, 1963

If the generals were to move against the regime, the key question was, as Kim had told Phillips, what would be the position of the United States? The telegram reporting this interview was received in Washington at 9:30 A.M. on Saturday, August 24.

A handful of men in the State Department and the White House had been awaiting an opportunity to encourage the Vietnamese army to move against the government. They intended to exploit the latest crisis in Saigon to the full. "Averell [Harriman] and Roger [Hilsman] now agree that we must move before the situation in Saigon freezes," Michael Forrestal of the White House staff wrote in a memorandum to President Kennedy.

The three men had decided to act by the time Lodge's reply to Hilsman's telegram inquiring about the new balance of power in Saigon reached Washington at 2:05 P.M.

The word *coup* had not appeared in Hilsman's telegram, but it was clear that his real question was, should the United States support military action against the Diem government at this time?

Lodge advised against it, not because of any doubts about the propriety of supporting a coup against the president of South Vietnam but for the eminently practical reason that Diem and Nhu probably still had the "strings of power in their hands." Military power in Saigon was divided among three commanders, Generals Don and Dinh and Colonel Tung of the Special Forces, and none of the three was disaffected with the president or with Nhu.

Given the evidence at the disposal of the embassy, this was a fair reading of the situation. Don was a cautious man and evidently not ready to turn against the government; he had made that clear to Conein. His intimate friend, General Kim, spoke a different language, but even Kim had said the army would not move against the Nhus unless the Americans told them to go ahead.

Lodge added that there was no sign the military had agreed among themselves on a leader. "Action at this time would be a shot in the dark."

Lodge's cable was already out of date by the time it reached Washington. "Harriman, Hilsman and I favor taking . . . action now," Forrestal informed the president. Kennedy was at his Hyannis Port residence in Massachusetts for the weekend. The three men had drafted a cable of their own to Lodge. The substance, according to Forrestal, had been generally agreed to by Admiral Felt. "Clearances [are] being obtained from [Acting Secretary of State] Ball and [the Department of] Defense. . . . Will advise you reactions Ball and Defense, but suggest you let me know if you wish comment or hold-up action." A copy of their draft was dispatched to the president.

This would become Department of State telegram No. 243.

It stated that the American government could not tolerate a situation in which power lay in Nhu's hands. Military leaders were to be informed that the United States would find it impossible to continue military and economic support to the government unless prompt dramatic actions were taken by Diem to redress Buddhist grievances and remove the Nhus from the scene. Diem should have a reasonable opportunity to remove the Nhus, but if he were to remain obdurate, "then we are prepared to accept the obvious implication that we can no longer support Diem. You may also tell appropriate military commanders we will give them direct support in any interim period of breakdown central government mechanism . . .

"Ambassador and country team should urgently examine all possible alternative leadership and make detailed plans as to how we might bring about Diem's replacement if this should become necessary."

It was the time of year in Washington when the climate in the American capital and that of Saigon are not dissimilar, and it would seem to General Taylor that some of the conspiracy-laden atmosphere of Saigon had found its way back to Washington. Harriman and Hilsman were determined to send their cable that very day. They found Acting Secretary of State Ball on the golf course, and he telephoned the president in Hyannis Port. Kennedy made no difficulty about giving his approval, assuming that the appropriate officials agreed.

After the call to Kennedy the rest was simple. Ball telephoned Rusk in New York and told him the president had already agreed, and Rusk gave his own unenthusiastic endorsement. When Roswell Gilpatric (McNamara's deputy at Defense) was called at home by Forrestal, he too was told that Kennedy had cleared the telegram and he was assured that Rusk had seen it. Gilpatric reluctantly gave the clearance of the Department of Defense but was concerned enough about the substance of the cable and the way it had been handled to alert General Taylor, chairman of the Joint Chiefs of Staff. Taylor sent for a copy of the cable. When he read it, his first reaction was that the anti-Diemists in the State Department had taken advantage of the absence of the principal officials to get out instructions that would never have been approved as written under ordinary circumstances. John McCone also was out of town, and rather than try to locate him Harriman had reached Richard Helms, who provided the clearance of the Central Intelligence Agency.

With the president's approval State Department telegram 243 was dispatched to Saigon at 9:36 P.M. on August 24.

John Kennedy would regard this as a major mistake on his part, according to his brother Robert. "He had passed it off too quickly over the weekend at the Cape—he had thought it was cleared by McNamara and Taylor and everyone in State. In fact, it was Harriman, Hilsman and Mike Forrestal at the White House and they were all the ones who were strongly for a coup. Harriman was particularly strong for a coup. . . ."

The next day Hilsman gave UPI a story about the pagoda raids that exonerated the army, and he arranged for Voice of America to broadcast it.

He had made the first moves to encourage the generals to rise against Diem. Now it was Lodge's turn.

SAIGON, AUGUST 25–27, 1963

Henry Cabot Lodge would later describe his feelings when he received that cable on Sunday, August 25. He was thunderstruck. There had been no hint of any such plan when he had left Hilsman and the others in Honolulu. And now "they were asking me to overthrow a government I hadn't even presented my credentials to." He would say, years afterward, that he thought the cable was ill-advised, reprehensible, insane. But that was not what he said about the cable at the time. Four days after he received it he informed Rusk, "I am personally in full agreement with the policy which I was instructed to carry out by last Sunday's telegram."

Evidently Lodge had no qualms about encouraging a group of generals to overthrow their own government and doing so without knowing what leaders they had, if any, and how they intended to go about it. He might reasonably have asked Hilsman to explain how he could be expected to serve an ultimatum on Diem and, before the Vietnamese president had any chance to respond, go straight to the generals to conspire against him. But Lodge saw no contradiction here. "I can read English," he would say when questioned about it.

He did see an inconvenience in his instructions. Why go to Diem at all with our demands for "prompt dramatic actions" to appease the Buddhists, when the chances he would accept them were virtually nil and when Nhu would use the opportunity to forestall or block action by the military? He proposed to Washington that he say nothing to Diem about U.S. demands but go straight to the generals and tell them that the Americans were prepared to have Diem without the Nhus but it was up to the generals to decide. Lodge was authorized to tell the generals—which generals or what they wanted or how capable they were no one knew, but "our" generals whoever they turned out to be—that they could rely on American economic and military support whether or not they decided to keep Diem as president of South Vietnam.

That Monday in Saigon, Lodge called a meeting to consider how to organize a coup. He decided the "American official hand" should not show. The CIA station, which had been instructed to take its orders on policy from the ambassador, was put in charge of the operation.

On that same morning Lodge came face to face with the man he was plotting to overthrow when he presented his credentials to President Diem.

The day had begun inauspiciously for Lodge with the 8:00 A.M. broadcast of Voice of America. As he had expected, it removed the taint of the pagoda raids from the army:

"High American officials blame police, headed by President Diem's brother, Ngo Dinh Nhu, for anti-Buddhist activities in the Vietnam Republic. The officials say Vietnam military leaders are not, repeat not, responsible for last week's attacks against pagodas and the mass arrests of monks and students.

"Washington officials say Vietnam secret police carried out the raids and arrests, and that some of them were disguised as army troops or members of the youth corps. . . ."

But Lodge had not anticipated the broadcast would go on to state, "The officials indicate the U.S. may sharply reduce its aid to Vietnam unless President Diem gets rid of secret police officials responsible for the attacks."

Instructions had been mislaid at the offices of Voice of America. Lodge was furious when he read the transcript of the broadcast. It ended any chance of the generals' effort achieving surprise, he wired Harriman. "The United States must not appear publicly in the matter, thus giving the 'kiss of death' to its friends."

He was worried about his own personal security. Diem and Nhu must have learned about the broadcast, and he believed them to be capable of a violent and irrational response. General Harkins and John Mecklin, the public affairs officer for the embassy, had come to his residence with other officers of the American mission to escort him to the ceremony. As eleven o'clock approached Lodge turned to Harkins and said, "Paul, perhaps you had better not come. If they try any funny business, it might be better if one of us were on the outside."

Harkins left alone to go back to his office. Lodge and the others got into their cars and drove to the palace.

Diem received them with his usual courtesy. Tea was served and there was small talk, nothing of any consequence, and at five that afternoon Lodge returned for a private conversation with Diem.

After the trepidation with which the new ambassador had brought his credentials to the Vietnamese president, this second untroubled encounter that day must have seemed an anticlimax to Lodge. He spoke to Diem about the importance of public opinion in the United States in winning the support of Congress, which was necessary to get funds. Americans had been shocked by Madame Nhu's attacks on the bonzes and by the idea that the government was persecuting Buddhists. He said nothing about the hostility to

Nhu in Washington, made no comments about the role of the president's brother. He did suggest that a dramatic gesture like liberating Buddhist prisoners would favorably impress American opinion.

But most of them had already been freed, Diem told him. Diem also presented him with a book published at Xa Loi pagoda, which stated that the General Association of Buddhists counted at most a little over four million adherents. This book Lodge sent under diplomatic pouch to Washington, where it might have proved instructive reading.

Diem spent the next two hours talking about his own family and the underdevelopment of Vietnam, the lack of educated and responsible people at his disposal. He told Lodge of how agitators had taken over a small Buddhist sect, and of a plan to create unrest around the country that would have pulled troops out of Saigon, leaving the city defenseless. For this reason he had been compelled to declare martial law.

At the end, Diem said he hoped there would be "discipline, particularly as regards the United States' activities in Saigon," and that there would be an end to reports of interference by American agencies in Vietnamese affairs.

Lodge had attended a meeting that morning to discuss the messages two CIA agents were to take to General Khiem and General Khanh. They were to tell both men that the Nhus had to go and that the question of retaining Diem was entirely up to them and the other generals. Now, Lodge looked Diem in the face and said blandly that he had just arrived in Vietnam and naturally could not know everything that was going on, but he would look into it.

It was early evening when Lodge drove away from Gia Long Palace for the second time on August 26. No one at the embassy in Saigon or the State Department in Washington seemed shaken by the events of the day. Yet it had been a frightening day: frightening in that not one of the officials gathered at his residence that morning had found strange or unjustified Lodge's fears of "funny business" at the palace; frightening that no one had questioned the need for General Harkins to stand by on the outside. These people, the ones who were expected to make cool and fair judgments on

which to base American policy in the days ahead, had totally misjudged the reactions of Ngo Dinh Diem. There had indeed been
paranoia in Saigon that Monday, but at the embassy, not the palace.

The next day Lodge called on Ngo Dinh Nhu at the request
of the president's brother and met the man he had been led to
believe was Diem's evil genius, whose removal had become the
immediate objective of American Vietnamese policy. Nhu's once
handsome features were gaunt and strained—the tensions of the
past weeks had left their mark—but he spoke with his usual ease and
authority, and Lodge was impressed. He found, like other Americans before him, that Ngo Dinh Nhu was actually "a highly intelligent and effective man, and would be so considered in any country." Lest these words appear too favorable, Lodge added in his
report to Washington based on the brief half hour he spent with
Nhu, "My guess is that he is ruthless, not wholly rational by our
standards and that he is interested above all in survival of himself
and [his] family."

Nhu naturally could not let the episode of the Voice of America broadcast go by in silence. Such broadcasts had to stop, he told
Lodge, because they hurt the standing of Vietnam with other foreign countries. In any case, he said, it was unjustified because the
generals had specifically demanded the action against the pagodas.

When Lodge again tried to explain that foreign policy could
not be made in Washington without the support of Congress and
public opinion, Nhu spoke of the overheated atmosphere that had
existed inside the pagodas, the pressures that Westerners did not
understand. He had wanted to clear the air before the arrival of
Lodge. He repeated what Diem had said, that the Buddhist prisoners had been and were being released. However, he wished the
release to proceed quietly, with the bonzes in each region handling
it by themselves. He particularly did not want to make a dramatic
gesture of it because this would be ill-advised in the Vietnamese
context, however useful it might be to public relations in the United
States.

As he conducted Lodge to the door, Nhu said he hoped there
would be no more statements out of Washington; Lodge responded

that he hoped there would be no more inflammatory speeches out of Vietnam.

WASHINGTON, AUGUST 26–27, 1963

Noon in Washington came a half day later than noon in Saigon and Lodge's first Monday in Vietnam was already over when President Kennedy met with members of the National Security Council on August 26 to discuss the cable that had ordered the American ambassador to overthrow the Saigon government.

In the cool halls of the White House the hectic plotting of the weekend took on an air of unreality. Robert Kennedy had talked with Taylor and McNamara and discovered that "nobody was behind it, nobody knew what we were going to do, nobody knew what our policy was; it hadn't been discussed, as everything else had been discussed since the Bay of Pigs in full detail before we did anything—nothing like that had been done before the decision made on Diem, and so by Tuesday we were trying to pull away from that policy. . . ."

President Kennedy belatedly realized that no one had spelled out to him the ramifications of the policy he had approved so lightly. He was irritated at the disagreement among his advisers. Taylor, McNamara, and McCone all were critical of the attempt to run a coup in Saigon. Even Rusk seemed to have second thoughts. "The government split in two," Robert Kennedy recalled. "It was the only time really in three years, the government was broken in two in a very disturbing way."

Ball tried to defend the dispatch of the telegram with the argument that the Nhus were an evil influence on Diem. He had decided they were out to destroy the government to increase their own power—not that he personally had any problems about overthrowing Diem, who in his eyes had no legitimacy and was simply a creature of the United States. But to other men at the conference table many questions had been left unanswered by the cable Ball had signed at the behest of Harriman, Hilsman, and Forrestal.

Hilsman undertook to answer one such question, about the

direct support Lodge had been instructed to offer the generals. He explained that logistical support of the South Vietnamese forces through some other port than Saigon was intended, to keep supplies out of the hands of the Diem government. This was news to McNamara and Taylor, as the American military had been given no notice of any such operation, had never considered one, and would need time to work out plans.

But should a group of generals be called on to choose a head of state? Who would it be? And how exactly was Lodge to carry out the various instructions he had received?

The reluctance of the military and civilian representatives of the Defense Department to abandon the civilian regime in Saigon doubtless reflected their preference for dealing with established authority and ignoring local political problems. Yet these spokesmen of the American military establishment were properly sensitive to one political problem confronting American policymakers that August: namely, was the United States capable of installing the kind of regime it desired in Saigon? Inexplicably, this had never even seemed a problem to the impatient men in the State Department. It is true that some members of the American military had an advantage over most State Department officials—they had firsthand knowledge of the mediocrity of the Vietnamese generals who were expected to supply the leader to replace Ngo Dinh Diem.

The National Security Council began daily meetings to thrash out a Vietnamese policy. Former ambassador Nolting, who had returned to Washington, was invited to attend over the objections of Harriman.

The argument was made that Nolting's views were colored—Hilsman would later say he suffered from "localitus"—but this argument was overruled by President Kennedy, who felt that Nolting's views might in fact be properly colored. And so on August 27 it was given to Nolting to make another, futile attempt to explain and defend the man in Saigon he would never again see.

Once removed from the daily tensions of the drama unfolding in Vietnam, Nolting himself had at first been caught up in the wave of anger and indignation that had swept American officials when they learned of the pagoda raids during the meeting with Lodge in

Honolulu. The raids had seemed a repudiation of all Nolting had worked for in Saigon, discrediting not only Diem but also the ambassador who had become his friend.

In his emotion, Nolting had sent a personal message to the Vietnamese president: "This is the first time you have ever gone back on your word to me." He already regretted having sent this message and after the murder of Diem would find consolation when told that the Vietnamese president on reading it had only shaken his head and said, "He doesn't know what provocation we were under."

In Washington, at the meeting of the National Security Council, Nolting insisted that Diem had indeed kept his word, was not a liar but a man of integrity. He had promised Nolting to make a conciliatory statement about the Buddhists and he had done just that, to the well-known journalist Marguerite Higgins of the *Herald Tribune.* He had also asked the government of Australia to invite his sister-in-law Madame Nhu to pay that country a visit. Nolting had decided that the Ngo brothers must have changed their minds about making peace with the Buddhists after his departure. He speculated that this was probably because the Buddhists, provoked by Madame Nhu, had continued in their intransigence.

It was clear that martial law had been declared at the request of the generals. The Special Forces may have been jumpy and resorted to greater force than anticipated, but Nolting saw no reason to believe they had been ordered to use brutal methods in the pagodas. Politics in Vietnam was messy and would remain so for a long time, he said prophetically. Some fourteen hundred Buddhists had been reported arrested as well as perhaps one hundred students, but Nhu had already assured Lodge that the monks were being released and returned to their pagodas.

Then Nolting spoke of Nhu and pointed out what others at the table either did not know or were unwilling to admit, that Ngo Dinh Nhu was a man of ability who was responsible for the successes achieved under the strategic hamlet program (as Nhu had made a point of informing Lodge during their first meeting that same day). Nhu was feared by the people and by Vice-President Tho, but he did know how to command. Nolting tried to explain

that Nhu even then was not anti-American but simply and profoundly Vietnamese. The ambassador seemed unaware of the distaste Nhu had developed for Americans, perhaps because Nhu
made a rare exception for Ambassador and Mrs. Nolting (and for
members of the military services) when he dismissed most of the
Americans he met as arrogant, intellectually mediocre, and lacking
in understanding of the country in which they operated—the very
faults some Americans professed to find in Nhu himself.

In Washington, Nolting told the National Security Council
that the generals did not have the guts of Diem and Nhu. They
were badly split and had no real leadership.

There had been rumors in Saigon that Nhu was planning his
own coup against Diem, but both brothers had assured Nolting
they were on excellent terms. In the course of time the younger
man might one day replace the elder. But now Nhu should not be
given any more power than he already had. The only way Diem
would ever separate himself from his brother would be by sending
him abroad. Nolting drew a smile from Kennedy when he recalled
that his predecessor, Ambassador Durbrow, who had been so unpopular at the presidential palace, had tried in his time to persuade
Diem that Nhu had to go, but in the end it was Durbrow who left.
And again Nolting said, as he had on previous occasions, that Diem
would not respond if pushed, but he could be convinced by Lodge
that the situation had to improve if Vietnam were to continue to
receive American aid.

Rusk remarked that Lodge had not yet come to grips with the
real problem in his talks with either of the brothers. But perhaps
Lodge was waiting to see what the generals were going to do.

Lodge was not the only person who was waiting. The highest
officials of the American government sat in suspense, waiting on
reports from CIA officers engaged in what William Colby called
"frantic efforts" to find the Vietnamese generals willing to undertake a coup against President Diem.

SAIGON, AUGUST 24–30, 1963

American interest in finding a replacement for Ngo Dinh Diem was not new, and undercover contacts mainly through the CIA had left certain generals in no doubt that they were being encouraged "to take some hand in the matter" well before the pagoda raids. But until August 24, official American policy had dictated support for Diem. Now, overnight, this was no longer the case. Colby, who as CIA station chief in Saigon had worked to shore up the Diem regime, was head of the Far Eastern Department of the Central Intelligence Agency in Washington, and it was he who received the first reports from the Vietnamese capital as his successor, John Richardson, set about reversing that policy. The preparatory work had already been accomplished, but time was needed to translate it into an actual conspiracy, especially, Colby pointed out, against a regime accustomed to mistrusting the loyalty of its subordinates. The events of this last week in August would prove the regime had good reason for its suspicions.

The CIA turned first to the man in whom they had particular confidence, who happened to be one of the few generals Diem did trust—none other than Brigadier General Khiem, the man to whom Diem owed the survival of his regime in 1960. The CIA knew him to have become disaffected with the government since his being named chief of staff of the Joint Chiefs of Staff late in 1961. Khiem was close to American intelligence (so close that General Don would speculate that he had become a special CIA agent himself). He told Conein of the CIA that General Minh had held a meeting of generals to discuss action against the regime and there would be a military coup in Saigon within the week. Khiem was immediately given assurances that the United States would take all possible steps to assist the families of the generals in case the coup failed.

General Khiem had agreed the CIA ought to see General Nguyen Khanh in his Pleiku headquarters in the central highlands. Khanh had already approached a CIA officer the previous day in Saigon to talk about a coup, saying the generals feared the Ngos were seeking an accommodation with Hanoi and if this proved true the generals would act. He had asked what the Americans would do in the event of a coup, and a note from the State Department had been sent to Lodge on Sunday, August 25, praising Khanh as one of the best of the generals, both courageous and sophisticated. "His analysis seems to confirm other evidence indicating need for speed in making U.S. position clear to generals." But on Monday, August 26, in Pleiku, Khanh told his CIA contact, when he came to offer American support for a coup, that the general and his friends were unsure about Nhu's intentions in regard to Hanoi and were not ready to move after all.

But what of General Minh? Even a civilian group of plotters that included the labor leader Tran Quoc Buu had put forward the name of Duong Van Minh as their candidate to replace Ngo Dinh Diem as chief of state. Minh was an obvious choice; with General Ty ailing and out of the country, he was the senior general in the Vietnamese army and for years had made no secret of his desire to see a coup in Saigon.

On Thursday, August 29, the ubiquitous General Khiem arranged a meeting between Conein and Minh. The general was cautious, unwilling to go into details, suspicious that the Americans might betray the conspirators to Ngo Dinh Nhu. What would he consider a sign that the American government did indeed intend to support the generals? Conein asked. Minh replied, echoing the message broadcast inadvertently by the Voice of America on Monday: Let the United States suspend economic aid to the Diem government. The message that Harriman, Hilsman, and Forrestal had sent from Washington had been understood by the generals for whom it was intended.

This interview seemed inconclusive to American officials—they appeared no closer to a coup than before. But for the generals it marked an important step forward. Rufus Phillips, the old friend of General Lansdale and Secretary Thuan, received a visit from General Kim, the man whose fear of preemptive action by Nhu and whose talk of a coup had provided one excuse for the cable of August 24. General Kim was accompanied by a Dai Viet politician. They wished to know whether the new ambassador had authorized Conein's approach to General Minh. Phillips reported this query to

Lodge and was instructed to say that Conein had indeed acted with Lodge's approval.

Still, there was no coup, and uncertainty was growing in the National Security Council.

President Kennedy had been disturbed to learn that the senior American military officer in Vietnam did not seem to share the optimism of Lodge. General Harkins had seen no reason to hurry ahead with a coup; he doubted the plotters commanded enough troops to give them a clear-cut advantage over the forces still loyal to the government. Harkins favored a direct approach to Diem to try to persuade him to separate himself from his brother Nhu. Separate and contradictory cables from the ambassador and the general revealed that Lodge had not bothered to inform Harkins that he had no intention of allowing Diem this last chance to avoid a coup.

In the American capital, Lodge's enthusiastic cables reporting what proponents of a coup wished to hear overrode the reservations of General Harkins. Lodge was caught up in the excitement of conspiracy, unwilling to consider suggestions for a delay. The prospects for a coup were fine, and he had great confidence in the generals expected to lead it—especially Minh, Khanh, and Kim. "The game had started," he noted on Thursday, August 29, in language that was pure Rudyard Kipling. "We are launched on a course from which there is no respectable turning back: the overthrow of the Diem government."

He had no illusions about the American role in the plot. "The chance of bringing off a generals' coup depends on them to some extent but it depends at least as much on us—we should proceed to make all efforts to get the generals to move promptly." At Lodge's request, General Harkins was instructed to encourage the generals by repeating to them the messages previously passed on by CIA officers. In exchange, Harkins was to ask for information about the plans of the conspirators.

The United States was now irreversibly committed to the generals, Lodge had told Washington. At this point Kennedy objected. The wounds inflicted by the disaster at the Bay of Pigs were still too fresh for him not to insist on the right he had failed to exercise in regard to Cuba, the right to turn back at any time. "I know from experience that failure is more destructive than an appearance of indecision."

But in practice Secretary of State Rusk and the other members of the National Security Council abdicated policy-making to the ambassador in Saigon, whom they authorized to suspend American aid to the Diem regime at his discretion. When Rusk suggested that perhaps Lodge might bring himself to talk to Diem even now and try to separate him from Nhu, Lodge's reply that Thursday was peremptory: The prime objective is to get the Nhus out. "The best chance of doing it is the generals taking over the government lock, stock and barrel." He coolly informed Rusk: "I am contemplating no further talks with Diem at this time."

WASHINGTON AND SAIGON, AUGUST 29–30, 1963

Roger Hilsman sat at his desk in Washington composing possible scenarios about how Diem and Nhu might react to these maneuvers and how the United States ought to respond. Supposing they declared Lodge and other important American officials persona non grata, the important point was not to remove them from the territory of Vietnam but to stall until a coup could be brought off. If the Ngos tried for any sort of understanding with the Communists that would lead to neutralizing South Vietnam or establishing a coalition government in Saigon, again a coup was the only answer, to bring to power a government ready to carry on the war.

Once a coup did begin it was essential that it not be a replay of November 11, 1960, when the government had used negotiations to win time while rallying loyal forces to its aid. This the United States had to prevent at all costs: the entire Ngo family had to be brought under the control of the coup leaders and the United States should warn the coup group not to stop to negotiate but to press their military advantage to the logical conclusion. The United States should spare no effort to influence Diem's supporters to abandon him and join his enemies. The Americans themselves ought to be ready to use military measures to prevent loyal forces from rallying to Diem's support or encourage the coup group to do so. They should also encourage the coup group to capture and remove promptly from Vietnam any members of the Ngo family outside Saigon including Can and Thuc who were normally in Hue.

Even after all these years, Hilsman's several scenarios read with a startling immediacy. And what if hostilities continued in Saigon? Then the United States should offer full use of American equipment available in Vietnam to assist the coup group and if necessary bring in American combat forces to help them achieve victory. Hilsman envisaged the possibility of what he called a Götterdämmerung in the palace. If necessary, the coup group should be encouraged to fight to the end and destroy the palace. The Ngo family had to surrender unconditionally lest they seek to outmaneuver both the coup forces and the Americans. If the family were taken alive, the Nhus ought to be banished. But Diem should be treated as the generals wished.

In Saigon, as the month of August came to an end, Henry Cabot Lodge found he could not be a Kipling hero if the generals refused to play the parts assigned to them. He complained of their inertia and said he felt he was pushing a piece of spaghetti. "The days come and go and nothing happens. It is of course natural for the generals to want assurances and the United States government has certainly been prompt in its reactions. But here it is Friday and, while much has been done, there is not yet enough to show for the hours which we have all put in."

The National Security Council did not like to hear about inertia. They were sobered and uneasy at "the absence of bone and muscle" among the plotters. Lodge was informed that "the highest levels" were giving almost full-time attention to his problem.

In Saigon, the highest levels of the South Vietnamese government could do no less. The coming and goings of American agents and their wide contacts among likely opposition elements in and out of the army had not escaped the attention of the authorities.

During this conspiratorial week Paul Kattenberg, the head of the Vietnam desk at the State Department, was received at Gia Long Palace. The previous Saturday he had talked with the frightened private secretary of the president and reported on their gloomy conversation to Washington. Now, Thursday, as Kattenberg's visit to Saigon drew to a close, he called on President Diem and stayed with him for three hours. It was a long, unsatisfactory meeting between these two men who were old acquaintances.

Diem as usual spoke most of the time. He justified his policies at length and insisted that Communists had infiltrated the Buddhist movement. He passionately defended his brothers against attacks by the American press and spoke of the total integrity of the archbishop and the pure intellectual and philosopher Nhu who had never sought a single favor for himself. "I wish the Americans could provide me with another like him," Diem said.

Even Madame Nhu, whom he had chided for her behavior, had been mightily provoked by the American press. He credited the Nhus and their Republican Youth movement of both sexes with bringing a new vital democratic generation out of the vacuum in which he had found Vietnam on his return in 1954. His youngest brother, Ngo Dinh Luyen, had tried to explain what was really going on in Vietnam, in London where he was ambassador, unlike the former ambassador in Washington, the father of Madame Nhu, who had never forgiven the Diem regime for having taken away some of his rice lands under the land reform program in the 1950s.

Diem had no way of knowing that Thursday in Saigon that the Chuongs, Madame Nhu's parents, had been busier politicking against him that very same week than they had ever been in the years they represented his government. The whiff of Saigon conspiracies had been strong in Washington the evening of August 27 when they had invited to their home General Lansdale, whose exploits on behalf of the Central Intelligence Agency had made him a colorful figure in the early years of the Diem regime. They had told Lansdale it was too late for Diem to reform his government or liberate Buddhists and students. Diem was finished and had better leave the country while he still could and take the Nhus with him. (Chuong apparently did not discuss with Lansdale what Secretary Thuan would recall with mild astonishment years afterward, his proposal to Diem that he invite Mrs. Chuong to return to Vietnam as prime minister so she could resolve the Buddhist crisis.)

Chuong had heard that the Americans wanted to see Prince Buu-Hoi prime minister in Saigon. There seems to have been no truth in this story, but the former ambassador warned Lansdale it would be a dangerous choice. Buu-Hoi, with his old ties to the Viet Minh, would be another Souvanna Phouma, he said; and like the Laotian prince, he would try to make peace by reaching an understanding with the Communists, whom the Chuongs feared as much as did the American government in 1963.

At Gia Long Palace in Saigon two days later, Diem told Paul Kattenberg he had dispatched a new ambassador, Do Van Ly, to replace Chuong in Washington. Criticism of Vietnam's treatment of its Buddhists was already widespread at the United Nations, and if the General Assembly held a debate on the subject, Prince Buu-Hoi would represent the Saigon government. Diem said Buu-Hoi had become ill when he saw the condition to which the bonzes had reduced his mother; he realized the insane atmosphere that the younger bonzes had created in the pagodas and the Buddhist community.

According to Diem, the Buddhist issue was now solved, the young agitators were out of the way, and the country could get back to winning the war and building democracy through the strategic hamlet program. He blamed the American press for irresponsible misstatements and dangerous misunderstandings and insisted that the generals had indeed requested martial law on the eve of the pagoda raids.

Kattenberg reported to Washington: "More than on earlier occasions (1955, 1958) he talked largely to himself. While there [is] no doubt he is in full possession [of] his faculties, impression of growing neurosis cannot be escaped. . . . I was unable to break in more than once or twice, but did manage [to] convey to him, I think . . . that his image abroad, and I thought in Vietnam too, had deteriorated considerably. I asked whether he intended [to] convoke [the] national assembly [to] explain government actions and whether and when he would hold new elections. He responded he was studying possibility [of] meeting [the] assembly, failed to respond to question on elections."

In a rare moment of naked emotion Diem burst out to Kattenberg, "I am ready to die, at once, if the sweat and blood of the last nine years is now to be sacrificed to a small group of agitators in

Buddhist disguise. . . ." "Try to help us," he said as Kattenberg prepared to leave. "Help us to help you," the American replied.

Meanwhile news of the conspiracy directed against Ngo Dinh Nhu had reached the French Embassy, which still had a network of informants among Vietnamese who had served France in the old days and maintained connections with French intelligence. Ambassador Lalouette sent a warning to Nhu through a Vietnamese who had been a friend of the president's brother since their student days in Paris.

Nhu chose to bluff it out with the generals. He singled out Khiem and others to tell them he was now doing just what the Americans wanted and assured them he was on excellent terms with President Kennedy. But when he spoke to two Italian diplomats, the ambassador d'Orlandi and the papal delegate Asta, he dropped the pretense that all was well and under control. According to d'Orlandi, Nhu pleaded with them for papal intervention to save the regime and for their personal intercession with Lodge.

It turned out that neither was needed, at that particular time. Nhu had underestimated the indecision among the generals—just as the Americans had done.

SAIGON AND WASHINGTON, AUGUST 31, 1963

By Saturday, a week after the dispatch of the cable of August 24, a series of telegrams to Washington announced that Lodge in Saigon, like Harriman, Hilsman, and Forrestal in the American capital, had misjudged the readiness of the Vietnamese generals for a coup. It was not that the leaders had any scruples about doing what the Americans had expected of them, but that Harkins had been right—they did not yet control the forces necessary to move against the regime. And they were still not entirely convinced of the good faith of the Americans.

This coup is finished, Richardson wired Colby at the Central Intelligence Agency. Generals Khiem and Khanh had decided to do nothing for the present. Khiem told Harkins that General Minh had called off his plans. General Kim also reported failure to his American contact, Rufus Phillips.

The restless Catholic revolutionary Colonel Pham Ngoc Thao had also been plotting his own coup, but he had little following, was suspected by many of the generals because of his brother in the Hanoi government and his own past in the Viet Minh, and was talked out of attempting a rising against the government at this time by CIA officer Conein and General Khiem.

Officially, the American plot to overthrow Ngo Dinh Diem was over by August 31. That was obvious to Ambassador Lodge, to Under Secretary Ball as well. Henry Cabot Lodge would later find it politically expedient to dissociate himself from the ultimate consequences of the policy he had launched on his arrival in Vietnam in August and would disclaim any responsibility for the deaths of Diem and Nhu. He had the proof, a telegram from Rusk at the end of August saying the coup was canceled. To George Ball, a lawyer by profession, that same cable was all the evidence needed; anything that happened afterward was "an indigenous affair."

The Vietnamese generals, however, were neither politicians nor lawyers, and for them the week of signals and contacts, the talk of pressures against the government and promises to the military could not be expunged by a piece of paper as though all of it had never happened. Leading generals had been told that the American government was at last ready to support them against the regime, and they had joined in what had turned out to be, not a rehearsal —their plans were not advanced enough for that—but soundings, for the coup that was soon to come.

A decision to withhold aid from the Diem regime was the signal the generals would look for, to be assured the Americans meant what they said about favoring a coup against the government; and no argument would prove more persuasive in rallying others to their cause than fear of losing the aid on which the Americans had taught them to depend for survival.

The game had only just started, and Robert Kennedy, the brother and alter ego of the president, knew enough of the real world not to be taken in by the legal fiction that the part played by

Americans in organizing a coup in Saigon had ended in August. "The result [of the cable of August 24] is we started down a road from which we never really recovered. . . . Harkins was against it and Lodge wasn't talking to Harkins. So Henry Cabot Lodge started down one direction, the State Department was rather in the middle, and they suddenly called off the coup. Then the next five or six weeks we were all concerned about whether they were going to have a coup, who was going to win the coup, who was going to replace the government. Nobody ever really had any of the answers to any of these things . . . the President was trying to get rid of Henry Cabot Lodge. . . . The policy he [Lodge] was following was based on that original policy that had been made and then rescinded . . . that Averell Harriman was responsible for. . . ."

In Saigon, Lodge received a cable from Hilsman dated August 31 assuring him the Americans would support a coup with good prospects of success but would not actually mount one. Hilsman said, "When the spaghetti was pushed, it curled; now we must try pulling."

Lodge spoke with surprising frankness to the French ambassador. "The generals are not willing," he said to Lalouette. "We will have to go after the colonels."

SEPTEMBER 1963

On September 2, the American television network CBS celebrated the extension of its news program from fifteen minutes to half an hour by interviewing President Kennedy, in his backyard at Hyannis Port, mostly about Vietnam. "We are prepared to continue to assist them, but I don't think the war can be won unless the people support the effort," he said, "and in my opinion, in the last two months the government has gotten out of touch with the people."

Do you think this government has time to regain the support of the people? he was asked (by Walter Cronkite).

"I do. With changes of policy and perhaps with personnel, I

think it can. If it doesn't make those changes, I would think that the chances of winning it would not be very good."

Appropriately, it was a media event in the United States that marked the next scene in the unfolding drama of the decline and fall of the Diem regime; and unsurprisingly, accounts differed about that too, this time in regard to what the president had really meant to say. Hilsman reported that Kennedy had rejected more innocuous language prepared by his staff in order to make a strong statement, which in Vietnam was read as a virtual ultimatum. But if ultimatum it was, this was accidental, according to Pierre Salinger. The president's press secretary called the CBS broadcast a partial distortion, a disservice to Kennedy's overall views about President Diem. It had come about because the half-hour filmed interview in which John Kennedy had shown respect and sympathy for Diem's problems had been cut to twelve minutes to meet the needs of CBS. The television network had not cleared the cuts with the White House; CBS was not in the habit of clearing interviews with its sources and had no qualms about tailoring an official policy statement by the president of the United States to the requirements of commercial television.

The result was headline news, incendiary in the tinderbox of Saigon intrigue. General Don, asked years later how he had interpreted Kennedy's words, said, "That he would support any change, any change."

When the National Security Council met the following day, Kennedy himself suggested that Lodge be instructed to make plain that the broadcast had not been meant as a personal attack on President Diem, and it was agreed to send a transcript of the complete interview to the ambassador. Kennedy had not yet taken Lodge's measure if he expected him to make any move that could soften the impact of the American president's words.

To another Cronkite question about Vietnam, Kennedy said, "I don't agree with those who say we should withdraw. That would be a great mistake."

Kennedy had been absent two days earlier when Paul Kattenberg had made the case for withdrawal before the National Security Council. The State Department official had returned to Washington disheartened and pessimistic, the frustrating interview with Diem at Gia Long Palace still fresh in his mind. He saw no future for the Diem government, no hope that the war could be won with Diem or without him. The American position in South Vietnam had been eroded beyond repair, he argued, and there was only one course left to the United States, to leave honorably before the inevitable time in six months, perhaps a year, when the Vietnamese people would turn against their government and throw the Americans out.

But Kattenberg's had been a lone voice at the National Security Council. The pressures on Kennedy were for escalation, not withdrawal; he had to contend with members of the American military who favored increasing the commitment of the United States to the war and wished to reassure them that he had no intention of abandoning the struggle against the Viet Cong.

Predictably, the question of the Buddhists was also raised during the CBS interview and the president responded, "The repressions against the Buddhists we felt were very unwise . . . we don't think this is the way to win."

In Saigon, the previous evening, three monks had walked past the American Embassy and then suddenly started to run toward the chancery, calling "Let me in! Help me!" Two of the three were student monks. One, a former employee of USOM who spoke some English, had been a monk only since April; the other, a monk for four years, had not realized they were bound for the American Embassy. They had come along to find refuge for the third man, whose distinctive features were his own introduction to the Americans: Tri Quang had surfaced as unexpectedly as he had disappeared almost two weeks earlier.

Once secure within the embassy walls, Tri Quang asked for asylum. He explained that he had been arrested as an ordinary monk under another name and had been released that afternoon after twelve days' detention. The important monks knew that he planned to appeal for help to the Americans, he told them. He wanted to go secretly to the United States, Thailand, or India, he would write in a letter addressed to Ambassador Lodge, but perhaps not India after all, he added, with belated caution, because it was a neutralist country and that did not appeal to him. (This was hardly the time to alienate his hosts by revealing his own neutralist sentiments.)

The Americans issued a statement saying they were "delighted that of all the embassies in the city he chose ours." Lodge rejected a request from the Vietnamese government that the fugitive bonze be turned over to the authorities and Tri Quang took up residence at the American Embassy. An American official compared the situation of their robed, shaven-headed guest in Diemist Saigon to that of Cardinal Mindszenty, who had been granted sanctuary in the American Embassy in Communist Budapest.

On August 31, when Rusk had proposed a postmortem to members of the National Security Council, to consider the motives that had led them to support a coup in Saigon, they had made much of "the great pressures of American public opinion, the state of American and world opinion"—in other words, the popular image of South Vietnam as a land of grievous religious persecution. The second highest official in the State Department, Under Secretary of State Ball, actually seems to have believed that the Diem regime "was destroying Vietnamese society by its murderous suppression of the Buddhists." But Assistant Secretary of State Hilsman, for one, had few illusions about what had been happening in South Vietnam.

In another contingency plan, a memorandum drawn up at the request of the National Security Council and dated September 16, Hilsman considered whether the United States ought to choose a policy of reconciliation with a "rehabilitated" Saigon regime or resort to a variety of pressures to force the regime to do as the Americans wanted. In either case, he suggested that the Buddhist question might be put to good use.

If the Washington government elected to follow the "reconciliation track," it could make a start in New York at the United Nations, by urging the Afro-Asian bloc to tone down the resolution then being drawn up to condemn South Vietnam for violation of human rights in its treatment of the Buddhists. The Vietnamese were dealing with a political struggle in which opposition groups had tried to overthrow the government, and Americans had only to point to many other cases where Afro-Asian countries had found it necessary for their political survival to arrest opposition leaders, outlaw political parties, muzzle the press. Hilsman gave one timely example: the government of Burma had recently arrested the president of the World Federation of Buddhists for political activities hostile to the government.

The State Department could place the facts in perspective, Hilsman wrote, by issuing a memorandum that noted the "essentially political and nonreligious character" of what had occurred— "that only a small number of pagodas were actually occupied with force and violence . . . practice of the Buddhist religion had never been seriously interrupted as far as the vast majority of the Vietnamese are concerned."

Initially, this point of view might have been presented to key members of the Senate and the House at a White House breakfast, before being circulated privately to the rest of Congress and then issued as a white paper to defend a country with which the United States was closely associated in repelling Communist aggression.

All this the American government might have done had it wished to follow the "reconciliation track," but it did not choose to do so, nor did Hilsman advise that it should. Instead, the National Security Council adopted his "pressures track plan" against Diem. This called for accepting inscription of the question of Vietnamese violation of human rights on the agenda of the forthcoming meeting of the United Nations General Assembly, with the implied threat of bringing down on Diem's head the opprobrium of the international community.

But if the Buddhist issue did not have the overriding importance in the quarrel between Washington and Saigon that the general public had been led to believe, why had American officials summoned a coup into existence in August, only to find the Vietnamese generals not nearly so ready for it as the American government? Why did the Americans still hope for a coup in Saigon?

During the postmortem at the National Security Council on August 31 it was agreed that Ngo Dinh Nhu had emerged as a major obstacle to American plans for carrying on the war against the Communists. He and his wife were blamed for having alienated broad and influential segments of the Vietnamese population during the Buddhist crisis. But other quite separate objections to Nhu were also advanced, and these had nothing to do with Buddhists. Nhu was dangerous, it was said, because he had tried to get the Americans to withdraw their people who were acting as advisers to the Vietnamese at the provincial level. To make matters worse, a message had been intercepted by the Americans, indicating that Nhu was talking privately to the French, presumably about trying to reach an understanding with North Vietnam.

Nhu was dangerous because he was working for independence for Vietnam—even from the American ally who had given the Vietnamese so much. But Nhu was not alone in this. Behind him stood another person who shared his conviction that the invasive Americans had to be resisted, who had fought their encroachments on Vietnamese sovereignty long before most Americans knew there were any Buddhists in Vietnam, who objected strenuously to American soldiers entering the country at will and operating in it as if it were their own—Ngo Dinh Diem himself.

It was significant that the exact number of American military in Vietnam had been kept secret from the Vietnamese president. Diem had reluctantly agreed to accept as many as 12,000 men. Now reports from Washington spoke of 13,000 or perhaps 14,000. One of the most prominent of the Vietnamese generals sought out a Catholic layman from Hue who was known to be in Diem's confidence. "You have to tell the president," he said. "[Secretary] Thuan has kept it from him. There are now 16,000 Americans in the country and he doesn't know it. Tell the president."

On September 9, two weeks to the day from his first encounter with Ngo Dinh Diem, Henry Cabot Lodge returned to Gia Long Palace. He went reluctantly, although not with any sense of awkwardness about exchanging polite greetings with the Vietnamese president who would no longer be chief of state if Lodge had had his way. The governments of Saigon and Washington needed to resume their dialogue if the war against the Viet Cong were to proceed as the Americans wished. But Lodge did not see why he should make overtures to Ngo Dinh Diem. Lodge had not intended to go to see Diem, had done so only because his instructions from Washington to call on the president had become so pressing that he could not disregard them.

Now they were face to face, and Lodge began to talk about what the Americans expected from Diem. The Vietnamese government may not have had all the details of the August plot, but few informed Americans doubted they knew what had been going on. Yet Lodge seemed to be baffled by Diem's behavior. Confronted with the man who had invited the generals to do whatever they liked with their president, Diem, not surprisingly, fought back: justifying himself and attacking his enemies. Lodge decided this posture revealed Diem's medieval view of life.

Lodge informed Diem of the concern in Washington about the activities of certain of his relatives. There was no need to discuss the archbishop, who had already left the country. The papal delegate in Saigon, having done his best to curb the verbal excesses of Monsignor Thuc, had finally persuaded him to make an extended visit to Rome, and he had departed on September 7 with the new bishop of Da Nang, to attend the Ecumenical Conference.

Madame Nhu boarded a plane for Europe the same day Lodge made his call on Diem. She was bound for a meeting of the Interparliamentary Union in Belgrade, and it was rumored in Saigon, and feared in Washington, that she planned to continue on to the United States. President Kennedy emphatically did not want her in the country, and there was relief among Washington officials when they learned Diem had told Lodge that she was not going to present the case of South Vietnam to the United Nations. Diem had been surprised anyone would think his sharp-tongued sister-in-law could have been entrusted with a diplomatic mission of such importance. Ngo Dinh Nhu remained in Saigon. Lodge warned Diem that his government ran the risk of condemnation at the United Nations, while in Washington congressional opinion had turned against the Diem regime, and the American aid program was in jeopardy. There was only one way to stave off disaster. Lodge repeated Kennedy's statement on CBS: a change in personnel and in policies was necessary.

Lodge had already approached Nhu directly on this subject, with the help of the Italian ambassador and the papal delegate.

Since there had been no coup, Lodge had thought it unrealistic to insist that Nhu leave the country, but he could be asked to limit his activities to the strategic hamlet program. Nhu had declared he was ready to resign from the government and retire to Dalat. Lodge proposed that a prime minister be named under Diem. (Like a number of Americans and certain Vietnamese, he thought Secretary Thuan might properly fill that post.) Nhu agreed that the appointment of a prime minister would be a useful public relations gesture. He also accepted suggestions from Lodge for easing tensions by such conciliatory measures as liberating imprisoned Buddhists and students and repealing the order that relegated Buddhists to the status of "associations."

Nhu had told Lodge he would leave government service for good once martial law was lifted. He preferred to go only after certain American agents who were still promoting a coup against the government ("the family," Lodge wrote in his report of this interview) had also left. "Everybody knows who they are," Nhu said. He asked that the American radio in Vietnam stop its attacks on the government and insisted as his brother the president might have done that American troops coming to Vietnam be required to have Vietnamese visas.

Nhu had also spoken with feeling on another subject, his contacts with the Viet Cong, saying the insurgents were not only discouraged but felt used and let down by Hanoi and were ready to give up. "I am highly useful to Vietnam because I am now the intermediary accepted by the Viet Cong for their dialogue. However, and in order to underline the act of folly you are committing, I am ready to depart, if we can reach agreement."

A week had passed since this interview. When the two Italian diplomats had pressed Nhu about it, he flew into a rage and told them they were trying to force him to commit political suicide. They decided he meant them to tell Lodge that he had asked too much of Nhu. The Italians thought the scheduled departure of Madame Nhu ought to be enough to appease the Americans.

Nhu had lashed out to the press against Vietnamese abroad who might engage in coups against the government: "What they really want is a protectorate. They want America to fight in their place, that America fights all the war on their behalf." He spoke again of reducing the number of American advisers in the country and outraged many Americans who believed they had the right and the duty to remain in Vietnam and increase the number of advisers as they saw fit. These Americans regarded Nhu not only as unappreciative but as hostile when he talked of pulling back Americans in the field to training and logistic support "on a progressive basis, starting now." Only because there had been a considerable improvement in the situation, he said. But they believed the real reason was to limit the number of American military men in Vietnam, and they were not wrong.

An American reporter had asked about persistent stories that Diem had lost control of the government to Nhu, which both brothers denied. "The president is very authoritarian," Nhu said. "He asks the advice of everyone, even Americans, but it is he who decides and he who accepts the consequences of the decisions he makes." Diem said, "I make the decisions and before history I, not my advisers, must accept responsibility for the decisions."

In Washington, on September 6, the National Security Council considered what to do next in Vietnam. Robert Kennedy raised the question of whether it was possible to win the war with Diem and Nhu. "We have to be tough," he said. "We have to tell Diem that he must do the things we demand or we will have to cut down our effort as forced by the U.S. public." If we thought we were going to lose with Diem, why not grasp the nettle now?

Secretary of State Rusk said, if we decided to pull out of Vietnam, "we might tell Diem that we wish him well." It was not inconceivable that Diem could win the war without us, but Rusk believed that unlikely.

What did Secretary Thuan think now? McNamara suggested that General Harkins see Thuan and find out. Perhaps he had changed his mind and was no longer saying that Nhu had to go. McGeorge Bundy, the president's national security adviser, agreed that Thuan ought to be consulted. Since it had been his views that had triggered recent American activities in Vietnam, according to Bundy, they must find out whether he still believed the war could not be won with Nhu. The question may well have been put to

Thuan; this writer has seen no report of his reply. Bundy thought they could accept Nhu in Saigon, provided his wife remained abroad. But Nolting felt Nhu would have to go for the sake of American public opinion, although it would be a real loss for Vietnam.

On September 9 at Gia Long Palace, Lodge told Diem that his brother should go away at least until the end of December, when the appropriations bill was due to be voted on in Washington. It was the first time Lodge had broached the subject of Nhu's departure to the president, and Diem was shocked. "Why, it would be out of the question for him to go away when he could do so much for the strategic hamlets." He defended his brother against the distorted picture Americans had been given of Nhu, his adviser on so many issues of foreign and domestic policy, "the only man in the cabinet who is neither a technician nor a lawyer nor a bureaucrat." Diem did not sound like a man who had lost control of the situation. "If American opinion is in the state you describe then it is up to you, Ambassador Lodge, to disintoxicate American opinion."

Diem inquired why the American government had not yet given its agreement to the appointment of the new ambassador he had named to replace Chuong in Washington. Lodge was unable to reply. Weeks later, Diem would raise the same question with Tran Van Dinh, his loyal chargé d'affaires in the American capital who was visiting Saigon. By that time the answer was obvious. The State Department wanted to show its displeasure with Diem; while in Saigon, Lodge had renounced all attempts at direct diplomacy and waited like a minor potentate for the president of Vietnam to make the first move toward him.

Yet there was one American Lodge would not only have permitted but encouraged to reopen talks with Diem—General Lansdale. On September 10, when Rufus Phillips joined in the deliberations of the National Security Council, he told them that he and Lodge had agreed that Lansdale should return to Vietnam, to use his friendship with Diem to counteract the influence of Nhu. Hilsman included this suggestion in his memorandum but only if the government decided to follow the "reconciliation track," which was rejected. Conceivably, Lansdale might have been helpful in

Saigon, enabling Diem to keep open a channel to the Americans at this crucial time, but the appointment was blocked in Washington, and Diem was left with no American adviser to breach his isolation.

Phillips was only one of several American officials who had returned from Vietnam to give their reading of the situation to the National Security Council on September 10. A two-man mission of inquiry had come back with divided views. The representative of the State Department, a foreign service officer with many contacts among Vietnamese urban elements, did not believe the war could be won with Diem. The representative of the Defense Department, a military man who had gone out into the countryside, was equally sure that the war could still be won even under the present regime, and former ambassador Nolting agreed. Rufus Phillips, the protégé of Lansdale who was directly involved with rural affairs through the strategic hamlet program, said the military war was not going well in the delta, and the political war was being lost. The Buddhist crisis had not reached the delta, but some fifty strategic hamlets had been overrun there. The program was overextended, and Nhu had alienated the army and the civil service. (Yet Phillips would say years afterward, "There were some things going wrong with Diem that we could have changed by persuasion. Instead, we chose a forceful way of change. The Diem coup was a horrible mistake with a war going on.") In September 1963, Phillips favored the gradual withdrawal of American aid to put pressure on the regime for changes, and an end to the financial support provided by the Americans to the Special Forces that had carried out the pagoda raids.

John Mecklin, the former journalist who had become public affairs officer at the embassy, had also been called to Washington for consultations. He had given up on Diem. If the United States could not quickly produce a "spontaneous" coup by economic pressures against the regime, the Americans ought to plan a coup. It would be time for a coup if cutting off all aid failed to unseat the regime; and were the coup to prove unsuccessful in whole or in part, American troops should be brought in. They could rely on the new regime to invite them to stay.

Under Secretary of State Harriman remained an inflexible

enemy of Ngo Dinh Diem, convinced that the United States would never achieve its objectives with Diem in control. But Defense Secretary McNamara still disagreed. And CIA director McCone said his people believed that the Vietnamese military would be willing to work with Nhu. The CIA did not see the situation as ominous. He urged that another direct approach be made by the Americans to Nhu and suggested that Lodge had not been there very long and ought to get out of Saigon and see the country.

But Henry Cabot Lodge had made up his mind in August and was not about to change it now. Two days after his interview with Diem he sent a cable to Washington headed "eyes only for Rusk": ". . . the time has arrived for the United States to use what effective sanctions it has to bring about the fall of the existing government and the installation of another . . . if there are effective sanctions which we can apply, we should apply them in order to force a drastic change in government. . . . The only sanction which I can see is the suspension of aid.

"Renewed efforts should be made to activate by whatever positive inducements we can offer the man who would take over the government—[General] Big Minh *or whoever we would suggest* [italics added]. We do not want to substitute a Castro for a Batista.

"We should at the same time start evacuation of all dependents, both in order to avoid the dangers to dependents which would inevitably ensue, but also for the startling effect which this might have."

The activists in Washington did not quarrel with the unabashed colonialism of the ambassador but were not yet ready to break with Diem. Messages were sent to Lodge urging him to resume talks with the Vietnamese president. It might be difficult to inspire confidence in Diem, who "had on several occasions over the past several years undoubtedly gotten the impression that we were trying to unhorse him." But: "We continue to believe that discussions with him are at a minimum an important source of intelligence and may conceivably be a means of exerting some persuasive effect even in his present frame of mind. If you believe that full control of American assistance provides you with means of resuming dialogue, we hope you will do so. We ourselves can see much virtue to reasoning even with an unreasonable man when he is on a collision course. We repeat, however, that this is a matter for your judgment." Once again, the final decision was left to Lodge.

It was hardly surprising that Washington policymakers failed to persuade Diem to make concessions; they could not even persuade Lodge, who was waiting for Diem to come to him.

On September 18, the Indian ambassador, Goburdhun, brought Lodge and Nhu together at a dinner in his home. The American used the occasion to expound on the importance of public opinion in the United States. If only Nhu would stay away until after Christmas it might help to get the appropriations bill through Congress. Now, there was the danger of Senator Church's resolution to suspend aid to South Vietnam. The Ngo family had to do something to convince the Americans there had been real improvement. A symbolic act showing Diem "atoning" to the Buddhists would be desirable and "would hopefully provide some material for a photograph."

Lodge congratulated himself that it was not he who had arranged this encounter in the house of the Indian ambassador. He thought it "made for a time most favorable to me and put me in a much stronger position than if I had sought an audience." His policy of silence toward Diem was paying off. "I believe that for me to press Diem . . . would be a little shrill and would make us look weak, particularly in view of my talk with Nhu last night at dinner. . . . I would rather let [Diem] sweat for a while. . . ."

Lodge had enthusiastically endorsed the use of economic pressures against Diem to persuade him to reform the government during this "interim period"; he was intrigued by the problem of using the withholding of aid as a sanction that would affect the Ngo brothers and yet do no harm to the economy or the war effort. Lodge's idea was that "whatever sanctions we may discover should be directly tied to a promising coup d'état. . . . In this connection I believe that we should pursue contact with Big Minh and and urge him along if he looks like acting." He added, "I particularly think that the idea of supporting a Vietnamese army independent of the government should be energetically studied"—a Vietnamese army without a political base or a political direction, fighting the Viet Cong at the behest of foreigners!

Once, Americans had talked of helping the Vietnamese to build their country and introducing modern techniques to this gifted and courageous people whose development had been stultified by colonial rule. The desire to halt the spread of communism in Asia explained the nature of the regime the United States had supported in the South since the mid-1950s, and America's ideological commitment had been compatible with a form of Vietnamese nationalism. But the policymakers of the Kennedy era, priding themselves on their tough-mindedness, were impatient with high-sounding protestations of respect for the independence of South Vietnam as an ally and sovereign nation. In the name of the struggle against the Viet Cong, they claimed the right to intervene in Vietnamese affairs as they chose.

When President Kennedy was asked about his policy toward the Diem government, on September 12, he said bluntly: "What helps to win the war, we support; what interferes with the war effort, we oppose."

Tennis at the Saigon officers' club: on the court, two men who had played together in other years, General Maxwell Taylor, chairman of the American Joint Chiefs of Staff, and the tall thickset Vietnamese general whom Americans liked to call Big Minh. On the sidelines, a most unlikely spectator, Robert McNamara, secretary of defense and one of the most powerful men in the American government.

McNamara's schedule for the brief time he was to spend in Saigon had not called for waiting out a tennis game in the heavy tropical heat. But he and Taylor, soon after their arrival in the Vietnamese capital on September 24, had been summoned to this particular game by an American who informed them General Minh had something of importance he wished to talk about privately. So many other people in Saigon and Washington seemed to lose their sense of proportion during these tense months that it was not surprising two of the most highly placed members of the American military establishment should have agreed to come to this obscure place, to hang on the words of this unimpressive man who did not command any troops, but happened to hold the rank of senior general in the South Vietnamese army.

General Minh was accustomed to collaborating with foreigners. After having served in the French army during the Vietnamese war for independence, he had worked with many Americans over the years. But that day in September he was in no hurry to share any secrets with the visitors, and McNamara watched impatiently as the tennis match went on.

On previous visits to Vietnam, Taylor, like other Americans, had found General Minh "friendly and congenial, with the additional credit point of being a formidable tennis player." Minh had complained bitterly two years earlier about the inadequacies of President Diem, and Taylor had been startled by "his willingness to criticize the President to a foreigner like me. I had not yet acquired experience with the Vietnamese bent for running down their closest associates to the casual passer-by."

General Taylor had accompanied McNamara to Saigon that September 1963, on yet another mission of inquiry, to see how military operations were proceeding and to decide how the United States ought to handle the Diem government. Their time was too limited and the trappings of the mission much too official for McNamara and Taylor to discover facts or hear opinions not already reported to Washington by other Americans. But Kennedy did not look to this mission for new insights on Vietnam. What he needed from the Department of Defense was confirmation of conclusions already reached by others, at the State Department and the White House; to persuade the Secretary of Defense and the chairman of the Joint Chiefs of Staff of the necessity for the strategy of pressure and conspiracy that had been devised in Washington to deal with the problem that would not go away—the problem presented by the recalcitrant president of South Vietnam, Ngo Dinh Diem.

On September 17, the National Security Council had already endorsed the principle of using escalating pressures against the Saigon regime, as proposed by Roger Hilsman, to force Diem to make improvements in the regime during this "interim period" when a coup did not yet seem to be in the offing.

Senator Church had received White House approval to introduce his resolution, which he had done on September 12. It called for condemnation by the United States Senate of Diem's repressive handling of the Buddhist problem and an end to American aid unless he changed his policies. Five days later, Lodge was again authorized to use aid as a bargaining weapon and to work for a wide range of specific actions by the Saigon government. Some were directly related to the Buddhist affair, like freeing imprisoned Buddhists and students, rehabilitating pagodas, and establishing a Ministry of Religious Affairs. Others—a free press, free elections, an end to the secrecy in which the official government Can Lao party operated—were a prescription for instant political democracy and a regime never known in either North or South Vietnam. Lodge was also told to work for changes in the cabinet. And as Diem was not ready to separate himself from his brother, Lodge could at least try to reduce the visible influence of both Nhu and his wife.

Whether Lodge would actually work for all or any of these objectives once again was left for him to decide. President Kennedy may well have complained privately to his brother Robert about his ambassador in Saigon. But Kennedy was uncertain enough of his own policy to leave Henry Cabot Lodge remarkable latitude. The president "particularly emphasized" that these latest instructions were fully open to the ambassador's criticism and amendment and assured him that even when Defense Secretary McNamara and General Taylor reached Vietnam the following week they would in no way encroach on Lodge's preeminence in making political decisions about American policy in Saigon.

Officially, the policy of the United States toward the Diem regime, after the failure to stimulate a coup in August, was in suspension during September and would remain so until October when McNamara and Taylor returned to Washington. Meanwhile Saigon was rife with speculation that American aid would be reduced, perhaps ended, and American personnel withdrawn. Lodge was informed that $18.5 million of the Commodity Import Program had been frozen in Washington, and it was soon public knowledge that no import licenses for goods subsidized by American economic aid had been signed since September 15. By the end of the month the French Embassy was receiving daily calls from government officials inquiring about the relatively small French loans then awaiting approval.

Roger Hilsman would later say that this freezing of the Commodity Import Program could not have had a significant impact on events because the effect would not have been felt for three months. But in the streets and cafés of Saigon people wondered aloud how long the Diem government could survive if American support flagged, and opponents of the regime took heart in seeing that the Americans were not after all so wedded to Ngo Dinh Diem as they had feared.

Martial law was lifted in mid-September and national elections, originally scheduled for August 31 and postponed because of the crisis, were announced for September 27. But the crackdown against Buddhist and student activists had left the atmosphere of Saigon oppressive with rumors of impending coups and unease about what was going to happen next.

Within hours of Lodge's dinner with Ngo Dinh Nhu at the house of the Indian ambassador, General Minh and Secretary Thuan separately unburdened themselves in pessimistic language that was promptly relayed to Washington. Lodge reported that on September 18 Minh had said that the Viet Cong was growing stronger and more students were joining the insurgents; there was great graft and corruption among Vietnamese administering American aid; and the heart of the army was not in the war. This last item of intelligence was hardly surprising—the heart of the army had never been in the war; only newcomers to Vietnam could have expected enthusiasm for this fratricidal struggle that seemed to go on without end.

Secretary Thuan made his own confidences to a foreign ambassador who, by Lodge's account, reported him as saying the war was going badly, and everything was deteriorating. The generals were not willing to move, and he would be glad to leave the country. The diplomat who hurried to recount this interview to his American colleague had actually offered Thuan political asylum and talked of six or seven other ministers who might be persuaded to resign with Thuan at their head and perhaps topple the government.

"So we now have the secretary of defense and the number one general on record—not just the Saigon rumor mill," Lodge wired Washington.

All was not quite as it seemed. For a start, the secretary did not agree with everything the general had said. Thuan was personally in charge of administering the American aid program. He was outraged when he learned afterward of General Minh's comments about corruption and denied there was any truth in them. As for the views attributed to him, Thuan repudiated those only a day or two after Lodge had cabled them to Washington. Thuan told General Harkins it was not true that he wanted to resign and leave the country. He called the story a fantastic rumor that could endanger his life if repeated. He had simply been feeling discouraged. His health was not very good, and he had thought he might like an ambassadorial post. He asked Harkins to squelch the rumor that he wanted to resign and that he could get anyone else to go with him.

Secretary Thuan was on hand as usual to greet Taylor and McNamara when they arrived in Saigon on September 24. They brought with them representatives of other departments of the American government. Michael Forrestal came from the White House, and William Sullivan, Harriman's right-hand man, from the State Department. William Colby represented the Central Intelligence Agency.

Colby welcomed the chance for a frank discussion with Ngo Dinh Nhu, whom he had not seen in over a year. The president's brother was in sore need of conversation with a responsible American who knew him as a dedicated political leader, in contrast to Lodge, who seemed to regard Nhu as a lost creature from another world. (After their encounter at the Goburdhuns', Lodge had written of "his obvious ruthlessness and cruelty" . . . a "lost soul, a haunted man who is caught in vicious circles. The furies are after him.") But for American officials, Saigon was now Lodge's fief and Colby was not free to call on Nhu without permission from the ambassador. Lodge forbade him to renew his contacts at the presidential palace. Colby responded by staying away from other Vietnamese and confined himself to visiting with his CIA colleagues.

McNamara and Taylor found that Lodge, unlike Nolting, was not willing to share his authority with other members of the American team in Saigon, General Harkins in particular. He did not consult on military matters with the senior American commander in Vietnam, but sent his own military reports to Washington and did not bother to show them to Harkins.

And Lodge wanted John Richardson out of the country. The CIA station chief, who was identified with the policies of the Nolting era, had few defenders among his younger officers opposed to the regime. They did not share his appreciation of Diem and Nhu and had been sending to Washington their own reports that contradicted Richardson's dispatches.

At the Saigon officers' club, Secretary McNamara and General Taylor used the break in the tennis game to give broad hints of encouragement to General Minh. But they were unable to draw him out. He never did get around to producing the important information they had been led to expect that day.

The McNamara-Taylor mission was still in Vietnam when a dispatch arrived from Rome, where Madame Nhu was visiting after the meeting in Belgrade. She was quoted as saying, "Young officers of the United States military mission are acting like little soldiers of fortune. They do not know what is going on. With their irresponsible behavior they have forced senior officers into following a confused policy." She could not have chosen a worse moment to attack American soldiers in Vietnam than this period of acute tension between the two countries.

Since the start of the Buddhist affair, Madame Nhu had achieved international notoriety with one outrageous remark after the other. Now, Lodge seized the occasion to answer back. He called her talk of little soldiers of fortune shocking and cruel. *The New York Times* treated her remarks and his reply as front page news, illustrated with a picture of the ambassador who had spoken up to defend his countrymen against the blatant ingratitude of the

Ngo family. In an editorial they hailed his statement as long over-due: "President Diem must decide whether he is fighting for his family or his country. . . ."

Neither Nhu nor Diem ever realized that this woman, who played no part in deciding high-level policy and whose invective, crude and ill-considered though it may have been, was simply an echo of her husband's ideas, had come to epitomize the malevo-lence that foreigners attributed to the Diem regime. In the past, Diem had defended her right to speak out on the grounds that she was a deputy in the National Assembly. But after this interview in Rome, when asked whether she spoke for his government, he replied: "Madame Nhu has herself stated on several occasions that she has nothing to do with my government except that she supports it because she believes it to be relatively better than others, espe-cially in regard to the emancipation of Vietnamese women."

McNamara and Taylor were nearing the end of their mission of inquiry. Predictably, they had not encountered much sympathy for Diem's political problems. The most publicized opponent of the regime, Thich Tri Quang, was still an honored guest at the Ameri-can Embassy.

Finally, on September 29, McNamara and Taylor called on the president. They went to the palace for a three-hour meeting with Diem followed by a formal dinner. Ambassador Lodge accom-panied them. The president's brother Nhu did not appear.

The visitors were disconcerted by Diem's serene self-assur-ance. He dismissed McNamara's concern about the disturbing con-trast between the undoubted progress they had observed in the military situation and the political problems that threatened to un-dermine it. Taylor, more sensitive than Lodge had been on an earlier occasion, realized that Diem would find any conciliatory gesture difficult, since he had to be aware that the Americans were at the least privy to, if not actual accomplices in, the plotting going on around him. Even so, Taylor thought he might have been more accommodating to representatives from the Department of De-fense, whom he had reason to regard as friendly, unlike his enemies in the State Department.

Diem was calmer and more relaxed than he had been in August. But he had not spoken to the American ambassador in almost three weeks, and Lodge's decision to keep his distance during all that time had increased Diem's isolation, leaving him mired in his own positions, more defensive than ever against outside critics.

Now, as he smoked cigarette after cigarette, he defended himself to his important guests from the Pentagon. He said the Buddhist movement had grown too rapidly and was experiencing growing pains. "Some American services" in Saigon were engaged in plotting against the regime. He was preparing a dossier on the subject. As to Madame Nhu and her latest remarks about soldiers of fortune, she was free to speak and had the right to defend herself against unfair attacks by the foreign press.

Taylor stressed the need to respond to the anxiety about events in Vietnam that was widely felt in the United States. Lodge compared Madame Nhu to Madame Chiang Kai-shek, who he said had played a decisive role in losing China to the Communists. McNamara, for his part, held no brief for the American press but spoke of a real crisis of confidence in the United States about supporting the war against the Viet Cong. He singled out three events that had particularly upset the American people: the resignation of Foreign Minister Vu Van Mau after the pagoda raids, "the relief" of Ambassador Chuong in Washington, and the closing of Saigon University.

After this, Lodge was satisfied that Diem could no longer doubt the Defense Department agreed with the State Department in their disapproval of recent happenings in Vietnam. McNamara had been extremely clear about that.

For Taylor, it had been "a depressing evening, the refusal of this stalwart, stubborn patriot to recognize the realities which threatened to overwhelm him, his family, and his country."

But Lodge, who had done nothing to prepare Diem for this meeting, who had not tried to understand Diem's problems or help him understand the American point of view but had simply removed himself from Diem's sight since September 9, found Diem's reactions on September 29 "just about what one might have expected as he does not react on the spot to any initiative that is made to him." He thought Diem seemed much younger and brighter than at their last meeting.

The following day, just before their departure, McNamara and Taylor went with Lodge to call on Vice-President Tho, who told them everything seemed to be going wrong and the Americans ought to do something about it. But any particular action they might take would be useless: protests would be ineffectual, withholding economic aid would accomplish nothing, and introducing American troops or attempting to organize a coup would be "idiotic."

It was a depressing end to a depressing trip. If Diem had friends in the Department of Defense they no longer included McNamara and Taylor, who returned to Washington persuaded now, as they had not been in August, that Diem had either to change his ways or go. And when they made their report, on October 2, it did not occur to either the secretary or the general to question the right—and the duty—of the American government to force the issue.

In Saigon, Diem and Nhu seemed to American observers as inflexible and unaware as ever. The election returns for the National Assembly were announced and to the surprise of no one, Nhu and his wife were reelected with more than 99 percent of the vote from their respective districts.

On October 7, when Diem addressed the first meeting of the new assembly, he offered a Vietnamese perspective. He reviewed the achievements of the past year, new strategic hamlets, military actions against the Communists. The Buddhist affair "reminds us of how underdeveloped we still are," he said. He pointed out with justifiable pride that his government had now established diplomatic relations with more than eighty states—nearly all the states in the non-Communist world. At the American Embassy, it was noted that he had said little about the substantial aid South Vietnam received from the United States, an economy of praise that contrasted with his statements in other years.

9.
The
Last
Weeks

When Mieczyslaw Maneli, the head of the Polish delegation to the International Control and Supervisory Commission (ICC), had returned to Saigon from Hanoi that spring, several Western diplomats had decided that he ought to see Ngo Dinh Nhu. They were looking for a suitable occasion to bring the two men together when the Buddhist affair erupted, forcing them to postpone the meeting, so that Maneli and the brother of the president did not come face to face until the last week in August when Henry Cabot Lodge was trying his hand at organizing a coup d'état in Saigon.

They met at a diplomatic reception, the first held by the new acting foreign minister, Truong Cong Cuu, which was attended by Lodge. The new American ambassador was a center of attention as he chatted with his foreign colleagues, seemingly impervious to the tensions outside the brightly lit room. But other Americans present did not hide their concern. In the provinces, Vietnamese were being arrested simply for listening to Voice of America broadcasts, John Mecklin, the public affairs officer for the embassy, told this writer, who was among the guests.

In another part of the large room, Monsignor Asta, the papal delegate, was talking to Maneli with no indication that there was anything unusual in the presence of the Pole, the first time a diplomat from any Communist country had been invited to a reception in Saigon by a foreign minister of South Vietnam.

Monsignor Asta turned to Ngo Dinh Nhu and introduced Maneli to him. As if on signal, other diplomats moved toward them, apparently engaged in conversation, to give an impromptu air to this encounter they had separately urged on Nhu. They were Lalouette, ambassador of France; Goburdhun, the Indian chairman of the ICC; and d'Orlandi, ambassador of Italy.

"I have already heard a great deal about you from our mutual friends," Nhu said to Maneli.

He continued, "There exists in the Vietnamese people a sensitivity and mistrust not only of the Chinese but of all occupants and colonizers, all." Maneli wondered whether Nhu were speaking of the United States, and he was probably not alone among the listening diplomats to speculate about that.

Then Nhu said: "Now, we are interested in peace and only in peace. I believe the International Commission can and should play an important role in restoring peace to Vietnam."

Maneli replied that he was ready to play "the most active and constructive role possible" in the ICC to restore peace and unity to Vietnam.

"The Vietnamese government wishes to act within the spirit of the Geneva Accords," Nhu said.

Shortly after this encounter Maneli received an invitation to call on Nhu at Gia Long Palace.

The meeting was scheduled for September 2, and Goburdhun and Lalouette, in particular, had high hopes for its success. When Goburdhun had visited Hanoi in his capacity as chairman of the ICC, he had discovered the Northern government did not seem to regard the fighting in South Vietnam as a reason for refusing to consider trade relations with the Saigon regime. Ho Chi Minh had said to Goburdhun that Ngo Dinh Diem was "a patriot in his way." Ho had once remarked with apparent sympathy that Diem with his independent character would have a hard time dealing with the Americans who liked to control everything. To Goburdhun, Ho had said, "Shake hands with him for me if you see him."

The Indian diplomat had returned to ICC headquarters in Saigon much intrigued by what he had heard in the North. He was personally opposed to communism and represented a country that prided itself on its political democracy. Above all he was an Asian and a citizen of the Third World, and he sympathized with the efforts of the Saigon regime to preserve itself from the overpowering embrace of its American ally. He had been impressed by the brilliance of Ngo Dinh Nhu and his readiness to break away from the political stereotypes of the past. Now, Goburdhun saw an opening for personal diplomacy, to help North and South reach an understanding that might bring peace to this divided country. Then the Vietnamese would be able to follow the lead of India and align themselves with other neutralist states.

When Goburdhun told the French ambassador about his visit to Hanoi, Lalouette recognized an opportunity for his own government that might never come again, a chance to mediate an end to the fighting and dislodge the Americans from the South; to free the Vietnamese in North and South from dependence on other foreigners and reestablish the influence of France over this country it had ruled for so long.

The French still maintained a small diplomatic mission in the North. But a more likely emissary to sound out the intentions of the Hanoi government was Maneli, the new representative of Communist Poland, who had served in Hanoi in 1954 and 1955 as legal adviser to the Polish delegation to the ICC.

When Maneli went to Hanoi in the spring of 1963, he found the city sad, Stalinist, and cynical. He passed on Lalouette's message that Diem would be responsive to overtures from the North because he wanted to reduce American pressure on his regime.

Let Diem prove his good faith, was the reply. He could gradually open postal relations with the North and accept Northern coal in exchange for Southern rice. The North was ready to accept a Western-style democracy in the South and would not press for rapid unification. But not until July, when Maneli made another trip to Hanoi, did the Northerners agree to accept Diem as head of this Southern government.

Lalouette, for one, was confident that Diem could have held his own in any arrangement worked out with the North. "He would have had to change the system if he stayed on, but he had the government and administration, and he had good men. All he had to do was move toward a political solution."

Ho Chi Minh called publicly for a cease-fire accord in the South that summer. It was not the first such appeal he had made, to support the National Liberation Front in its struggle against the Diem regime. But unlike the Southerners organized in the front who were fighting to oust Diem from power, the Hanoi leaders, urgently concerned to halt American military intervention in Vietnam, seemed prepared to reach an understanding with Diem to do so.

The Northerners saw advantages in dealing with Ngo Dinh Nhu at this stage. After all, Nhu was certainly capable of thinking logically: he had graduated from the École des Chartes (the school for professional archivists in Paris), Prime Minister Pham Van Dong said. Maneli had asked how he should act if he were invited to meet Nhu. "Go and listen intently. One thing is sure: the Americans have to leave. On this political basis we can negotiate about everything. Everything," Dong said. "We have a sincere desire to end hostilities, to establish peace and unification on a completely realistic basis. We are realists."

Lalouette also regarded himself as a realist. He believed negotiations were feasible because the Northern leaders had come to see that the only way to seize the South was by force and they wanted to avoid an all-out war.

The situation of the North was not an enviable one in 1963. This predominantly agricultural country was suffering the worst drought it had known since the restoration of peace in 1954. There had been bad years before, when perhaps 100,000 hectares of rice paddy had been ravaged by drought, but never a year like this when over twice that area was affected, more than one-tenth of the arable land in North Vietnam. River levels had dropped too low for the water to reach the rice fields and saltwater had poured into the riverbeds along the extended Northern coastline.

North Vietnam had not been able to feed itself in the best of times; deprived of the rice it received from the South before partition, it had been forced to rely on the largesse of the Sino-Soviet bloc, which had supplied food and other necessities, for peace and for war. Now the Northern government was also on the defensive against an overbearing ally. The rift between China and the Soviet Union had left Hanoi at the mercy of their rivalry and vulnerable to unwelcome pressures from the Chinese. Maneli, who reported regularly to the Soviet Embassy in Hanoi as well as to his own government in Warsaw about the prospects for an understanding between North and South Vietnam, noted that the Northern leaders made a point of keeping the talks secret from the Chinese Embassy.

It is possible that contacts between the two sides had started as early as 1962, as the Saigon newspaper *Hoa Binh* reported years afterward. In 1962, relations between Diem and the Americans were already strained, and any visitor to Gia Long Palace would have been identified, so Ngo Dinh Nhu could not have received Viet Cong emissaries there; according to the *Hoa Binh,* he met them during visits to his hometown of Hue. A North Vietnamese ambassador with family in Hue later said his own brother had been Nhu's contact in the old imperial capital in 1963 and their negotiations had been going well. Maneli learned that direct talks had already begun when he returned to Hanoi in July, and Lalouette heard about them from both sides.

The talks were not about a detailed agreement; it was too soon for that. They dealt with parallel actions each side might take, such as lessening guerrilla activities and limiting government military initiatives. To Lalouette, it was evident that these secret talks were the reason the Viet Cong did not seek to profit from Diem's growing difficulties with the Americans by launching a major offensive against the Saigon forces. In certain areas where fighting had petered out, local military understandings between opposing commanders were reported.

The level of Viet Cong military activity was relatively low during the last days of August. This was the time that General Charles de Gaulle decided to intervene personally in Vietnamese affairs.

He had waited until August 29, when American officials were feverishly plotting a coup in Saigon, to issue a declaration to the Vietnamese—Northerners and Southerners alike—inviting them to join in a national effort for independence, peace, and unity. It was a call from the Olympian isolation of the Elysée Palace in Paris, the residence of the French president, to neutralize Vietnam and reunify the country.

Oracular, confined to generalities, the declaration was vintage de Gaulle. The French foreign minister, Maurice Couve de Murville, had warned the American government it was imminent, saying he did not think it would cause any embarrassment to the United States. Just a statement of long-range policy, French spokesmen explained; it was not meant as interference in Vietnamese affairs. But de Gaulle summoned the Vietnamese to be independent at the very moment Americans were trying to replace Diem with a leader more amenable to their bidding, and the general had chosen to speak of peace when the overriding concern in Washington was how best to prosecute the war. An editorialist in *The New York Times* concluded that this French declaration of August 29 was at the least ill timed if not deliberately unfriendly to the United States.

All de Gaulle offered in the unlikely event the Vietnamese acted on his advice was a vague promise of French cooperation. He could not pretend to compete with the substantial economic and military aid programs through which the Americans had entrenched themselves in the South. But his words had weight, real if incalculable, because he appealed to other, older ties that still linked Vietnamese and French.

In Communist Hanoi, which had few relations with the French these days, Prime Minister Pham Van Dong talked to the Polish diplomat Maneli about the special ties that had survived war and revolution. "The relationship between France and Vietnam is based on our having been a colony. France was a mother country. We were influenced by French culture and literature, by the great French democratic and socialist traditions, by the French socialist and communist movement. That is the way it was and will continue to be."

In the South, French cultural influence was still strong and French economic interests were important. The first South Vietnamese parliamentary mission ever to visit the French capital had been officially received in Paris in February, and French business groups were planning to send a goodwill mission to Saigon. Neither Ngo Dinh Diem nor his pro-American regime was popular at the Elysée Palace. But Diem's recent efforts to take a more independent line in his dealings with the United States demonstrated a nationalism that had not gone unnoticed by de Gaulle.

The general had been unlucky in his earlier ventures into Vietnam policy. In 1945, when the country was still part of the French colony of Indochina, he had offered the Vietnamese a new status, liberal for the times, that would have perpetuated the division of Vietnam into three separate parts that their French conquerors had imposed on them. This policy had been overtaken by the Vietnamese revolution and was out of date before anyone could put it into effect.

De Gaulle had then thought of permitting the reunification of the country but under a national leader of his own choice, one more effective than Bao Dai (and less threatening to the French than Ho Chi Minh). He had remembered Duy Tan, the courageous boy emperor of Vietnam, who, at the age of sixteen, in 1916 had led a revolt against French colonial rule and been captured and sent into exile. In December 1945, de Gaulle had received the former emperor in Paris, but Duy Tan was killed in a plane crash soon afterward. There had still been time to grant unity and independence to the Ho Chi Minh government in 1946 and avert years of war, but de Gaulle had used his great influence in and out of the French government to oppose concessions to the Viet Minh leaders.

He had been forced to recognize that the era of empire was

over when he returned as president of France in 1958, four years after the Geneva Conference, and proclaimed himself the champion of decolonization. In this new role he launched a policy of courting influence among the former colonial countries of the Third World and sought to define a new mission for France as a great power outside the two opposing blocs of East and West. Now, in 1963, he feared increasing American involvement in the Vietnamese war would only sharpen the dangerous division of the world between the Communists and the West. Like Lalouette and the other ambassadors in Saigon who shared his views, de Gaulle did not believe a military solution possible in Vietnam. There had to be a political settlement, and the French by helping to achieve an understanding between North and South could return to their former colony in a new role and speed the departure of the Americans who had had the temerity to replace them.

De Gaulle's few sybilline words on August 29 were the first public endorsement by the French government of the policy Ambassador Lalouette had been quietly working at for months. The only response from President Diem was a mild statement that he could not contemplate a neutralist status for the South that would have required a break with his American allies.

When Lalouette got wind of the coup the Americans were trying to bring off in Saigon that same week, he feared all his patient diplomacy had been for nothing. He told Maneli one evening that if Diem were to be overthrown the last, small chance of peace in Vietnam would be lost. Anyone chosen by the Americans to replace him would be more dependent on them; Diem alone had the courage to retain enough independence so that he could perhaps work for peace. Maneli immediately dispatched a report of this conversation to Warsaw and sent copies to the North Vietnamese government and the Soviet ambassador in Hanoi.

Lalouette's worries proved premature; Henry Cabot Lodge was left trying to push a piece of spaghetti in Saigon and Maneli was able to keep his appointment with Ngo Dinh Nhu at Gia Long Palace on September 2. The brother of the president told him he was not against negotiations and cooperation with the North. Vietnamese never forgot who was a Vietnamese and who a foreigner even during their most ferocious battles. If we could begin a direct dialogue we could reach an understanding, Nhu said. And the ICC and Maneli himself could play a positive role. And then Nhu said, "In the near future I do not foresee anything that might lead to direct talks but this may very soon be clarified."

Maneli asked him about the persistent rumors in Saigon and Hanoi that the dialogue had already started.

"Are you falling for these rumors?" Nhu asked as if in jest. Pham Van Dong had replied in similar language when Maneli had first asked him the same question in Hanoi. "Do you believe it, comrade?" he had said.

The French ambassador was sorely disappointed when Maneli told him about his meeting with the brother of the president. It seemed to Lalouette that Nhu was backtracking. He had been very cautious, too cautious. He was still deluding himself that he could reach an understanding with Lodge and did not want to burn his bridges behind him. "If he does not rid himself of these illusions he will be lost. It is a tragic mistake," Lalouette told Maneli.

Nhu himself told Lodge about his meeting with Maneli later that same day, September 2, when he talked to the American ambassador about leaving the government and retiring to Dalat. He said that Maneli had spoken of de Gaulle's declaration and of Ho Chi Minh's recent appeal for a cease-fire and asked what he could tell Prime Minister Pham Van Dong on his next visit to Hanoi. Say nothing to Dong, Nhu said he had replied. "As regards de Gaulle, while he has a right to his opinion those who do not take part in the fight have no right to interfere. Our loyalty to the Americans forbids us to consider either statement. The Americans are the only people on earth who dare to help South Vietnam. Therefore I have no comment."

Then Nhu spoke of his contacts with the other side and told Lodge that the talks whose existence he had denied to Maneli were already under way. The Italian ambassador d'Orlandi, who was present at this meeting, recorded in his diary an account of Nhu's words that was not limited to the generalities Lodge reported to Washington. D'Orlandi, not Lodge, was the source for Nhu's statement, quoted previously, that "I am now the intermediary accepted

228

by the Viet Cong for their dialogue." And d'Orlandi reported Nhu's explanation that the other side had put forward peace proposals not only because of the success of the strategic hamlet program but also because they resented the yoke the Chinese were imposing on Hanoi, and they realized the resumption of trade between North and South would be of advantage to both. According to d'Orlandi, not Lodge, Nhu had said the Communists did not even insist on neutralizing the South because they were satisfied that when the fighting ended the American presence would be less necessary to the Saigon regime.

If Nhu did not choose to discuss with Maneli his contacts with the Viet Cong, he had good reason to insist on their importance to the Americans. He was fighting for his own political survival and for the life of the Diem government.

Ambassador Lalouette tried to persuade the American ambassador that Diem should be left in power and told him about Goburdhun's report that Pham Van Dong was ready to exchange Northern coal for Southern rice. "I urged Lodge not to make the coup," he recalled to this writer years later. By that time he was convinced that nothing he might have said that September would have swayed Lodge: Lalouette had come to believe that the American had been sent to Vietnam with instructions to remove Diem as soon as he could.

On September 10, Lalouette called on Lodge again and inquired what conclusions the American government had reached about Vietnam. Lodge told him that the United States was determined not to withdraw from the country and wanted the Saigon government to make radical changes in personnel and policies. It was hopeless, Lalouette said later. "They had made up their minds to negotiate from a position of force."

He could not carry on his patient diplomacy in secrecy any longer. At this same meeting he protested to Lodge against an article in *The New York Times* that claimed the French ambassador had tried to persuade other Western diplomats to join him in putting pressure on Lodge to soften his position on Diem. *The Times* reported that France was backing Ngo Dinh Nhu as the person to lead a great national movement toward reunification. The story was sensational, inaccurate, and, for Lalouette and the Quai d'Orsay, singularly ill timed. It was officially denied in Paris, and the French government assured the Americans they did not intend to support Ngo Dinh Nhu or any other Vietnamese.

Lalouette told Lodge on September 10 that he had been summoned to Paris for consultations and expected to remain there only five or six days. But weeks passed and he did not return, and the French Embassy was left in the hands of a chargé d'affaires and ceased to be a center of diplomatic activity in Saigon.

Months afterward, when Diem and Nhu were dead, the French foreign minister told the American ambassador in Paris that Lalouette had been recalled because he had taken the French diplomatic representative in Hanoi who was visiting Saigon to meet the South Vietnamese foreign minister without authorization from Paris. That episode and the highly exaggerated publicity in the American press about Lalouette's activities had made his continued stay in Saigon undesirable.

The Quai d'Orsay had evidently been unwilling to support a government as unpopular as Diem's while facing bitter American opposition. But General de Gaulle had not yet given up on the Saigon regime, and during the last days of October he met secretly with the South Vietnamese ambassador at Rambouillet to tell him of his concern about the latest news from Saigon and inquire what immediate help France could offer.

De Gaulle had intervened too late. Diem had been too slow to respond. And Nhu was too clumsy.

The departure of Ambassador Lalouette did not still the rumors in Saigon of a possible rapprochement between North and South. The rumors were more persistent than ever and were actively promoted by Ngo Dinh Nhu himself.

In Washington that September, Nhu's calculated indiscretions were treated variously as loose talk; attempts to blackmail the Americans as their demands became more pressing; efforts to wreck the Saigon government and win more power for Nhu and his wife (George Ball's contribution); and evidence that Nhu was mad. At the CIA, Chester Cooper, who prepared a report on the subject for the director, put the chances at less than 50 percent that the Hanoi regime was seriously interested in any form of rapprochement short of reunification, which he did not believe "Nhu's acute appreciation of Communist tactics and untrustworthiness" would permit him to accept. Cooper had thought that Nhu had made sense when they spent three and a half hours together in March. But now the CIA analyst felt bound to consider the possibility suggested by some American observers that the extraordinary pressures under which Diem and Nhu had been operating that summer had driven both of them mad. In that case, Cooper did not presume to speculate about what either brother might do next.

The story that Nhu had become irrational (Lodge, as has been seen, did not think him wholly rational from the start of their acquaintance) was supported by American reports he had been taking opium and heroin, reports said to have originated with no less a personage than Secretary of the Presidency Thuan. When these weeks had become history and Secretary Thuan was a private citizen living in retirement in Paris, he told visitors that he had never made any such accusation against Nhu. It was not the first time Thuan felt obliged to repudiate confidences attributed to him about matters of political importance. This articulate man, who spoke excellent English and French, seemed singularly prone to misunderstandings (unless, of course, Thuan had his own reasons for making remarks to foreigners that he found expedient to disown afterward). A public denial that Ngo Dinh Nhu had been taking drugs came only years later (from an unexpected quarter that could hardly be accused of partiality), when General Don, one of the leading plotters against the Diem regime, published his memoirs.

The activists in the State Department and the White House operated in symbiosis with Vietnamese who had staked their personal future on the continuing presence of the Americans in the South; those people who were most apprehensive that Ngo Dinh Nhu was venturing on a course that could deprive South Vietnam of American protection. A State Department analyst wrote: "Reports that Nhu is already in contact with Hanoi are so credible and widespread as eventually to undermine morale in the army and bureaucracy regardless of their current accuracy . . . many top level officers seem convinced that he could deal with Hanoi." David

Halberstam reported the fears of high officials, civil servants, and Catholic refugees from the North that Nhu might turn to neutralism.

In Washington, Roger Hilsman in his memorandum of September 16 defined what he believed to be the minimum goal of Nhu: "a sharply reduced American presence in those key positions which have political significance in the provinces and the strategic hamlet program." His maximum goal: "a deal with the North for a truce, complete removal of the U.S. presence and a 'neutralized' or 'Titoist' but still separate South Vietnam." The president's brother had "decided on an adventure," Hilsman concluded, and this was the reason Hilsman gave for rejecting the "reconciliation track"—diplomacy and persuasion in dealing with a "rehabilitated" Diem government—in favor of strong pressures against the regime.

When Ambassador Lalouette looked back on the fateful year of 1963 and his daring attempt to achieve a political solution in Vietnam and how it had failed, it seemed to him that "Nhu's request in April for the withdrawal of American advisers [his minimum goal, according to Hilsman] was the main reason for the American decision to overthrow Diem. That, and the growing pro-French alignment of the Saigon government."

The "pressures track" that Hilsman proposed and the National Security Council adopted, on September 17, became the basis of the report McNamara and Taylor brought back from Saigon at the beginning of October.

The McNamara-Taylor mission had been unable to discover any hard facts about what Ngo Dinh Nhu had been up to. But they had heard enough to write in their report: Nhu's flirtation with the idea of negotiations—whether or not serious at present—suggested a basic incompatibility with U.S. objectives.

OCTOBER 1963

Secretary McNamara and General Taylor came back to Washington to report that the military program in South Vietnam had made such progress that one thousand American military advisers could be withdrawn by the end of the year, and most of the others could be out of the country by 1965 "when the major part of the U.S. military task can be completed."

This optimistic statement issued by the White House on October 2 was greeted with surprise and controversy in Washington because it conflicted with the stream of pessimistic dispatches that American reporters had been filing from Saigon.

General Taylor had not been reassured by the behavior of President Diem. But he deplored the attitude of the American press in the South Vietnamese capital:

"Many of the reporters had long since abandoned any pretence of impartial reporting and had committed their reportorial skills, which were often considerable, to disparaging Diem in the name of religious freedom. . . . The anti-Diemist theme was that oppressive actions of the Chief of State were seriously impeding all progress in Vietnam. Since this kind of reporting was the principal source of public information at home, most of our people pictured the situation as a chaotic mess for which the repressive tactics of a religious fanatic were largely responsible. To me, it was a sobering spectacle of the power of a few relatively young and inexperienced newsmen who, openly committed to 'getting' Diem or 'getting' [General] Harkins, were not satisfied to report the facts of foreign policy but undertook to shape them."

In reality, McNamara and Taylor were not so sanguine about the situation in South Vietnam as they appeared. Bundy at the White House had found the suggestion that the American military could evacuate Vietnam as early as 1965 so unrealistic that he had tried to have it expunged before the White House released the president's statement to the press. He had been overruled because McNamara had agreed with Kennedy that the target date should remain; but neither McNamara nor Taylor was able to explain publicly that it meant rather more, and less, than appeared at first glance. Although the secretary and the general had returned from Saigon not dissatisfied with the progress of the war, they were determined to improve the effectiveness of the South Vietnamese forces. The suggestion that American advisers might be recalled was intended to exert pressure on the Vietnamese for "better performance."

The White House statement of October 2, reflecting opinion at the State Department, went on: "The political situation in South Vietnam remains deeply serious. The United States has made clear its continuing opposition to any repressive actions in South Vietnam. While such actions have not yet significantly affected the military effort, they could do so in the future."

The McNamara-Taylor mission had been impressed by the attitude of the Vietnamese the Americans knew best—intellectuals, civilian officials, and "a high proportion of military people"—whom they regarded as the "urban elite or 'Establishment.' " Their discontent "has reached the point where it is uncertain that Diem can keep or enlist talent to run the war. The loss of such men as Mau [formerly foreign affairs secretary] and Tuyen [former head of the presidential security service], and the deeply disturbed attitude of such a crucial figure as [Secretary of the Presidency] Thuan, are the strongest evidences of the seriousness of the situation."

The McNamara-Taylor Report noted that the lack of enthusiasm of this "urban elite" for Diem and Nhu was not new, like the well-known distrust of the Ngos for them. But since the Buddhist crisis and the student demonstrations, these elements had begun to complain of repression, and their resentment had focused on Nhu. They disliked his apparent fascination with "outright totalitarianism" and his ideas (shared with Diem) of social revolution. "A further disturbing feature of Nhu is his idea of negotiating with North Vietnam, whether or not he is serious in this at present. This deeply disturbs responsible Vietnamese. . . ."

The findings and recommendations of the McNamara-Taylor mission, which were approved by the president but not revealed to the press, called for selective pressures—"leverages"—notably a freeze of the Commodity Import Program, to force the Diem government to change its behavior.

In Vietnam, the network of Americans involved in the aid program was to be enlisted in explaining the full implications of the new policy: "The potential significance of the withholding of commitments for the 1964 military budget should be brought home to top military officers in working level contacts between USOM (the American economic aid mission), MACV (the American Military

Assistance Command in Vietnam) and the Joint General Staff." It was not only the 1964 budget that was in question; the mission looked beyond the immediate future. "There is the implicit leverage embodied in our constantly making it plain to Diem and others that the long term continuation of military aid is conditional upon the Vietnamese government demonstrating a satisfactory level of progress toward defeat of the insurgency." It was recommended that American civilian and military personnel "adopt an attitude of coolness toward their counterparts, making only those contacts and communications which are necessary for the actual conduct of operations in the field."

To sum up: "the recommended actions are designed to indicate to the Diem government our displeasure at its political actions and to create uncertainty in that government *and in key Vietnamese groups* [italics added] as to the future intentions of the United States."

Thus Vietnamese who counted on the maintenance of the status quo under American protection were threatened with the loss of critical aid from the United States against the Viet Cong. And this, American officers and officials were to make clear to the Vietnamese military and other interested parties, had been brought about by President Diem and his refusal to act as the Americans wished. Diem and his brother Nhu in effect were singled out as the sole obstacle to the continuing flow of American aid.

There was more: the Special Forces headed by Colonel Tung that Diem kept in or near Saigon for political reasons must be transferred to field operations under the direct command of the Joint General Staff (and no longer receive their instructions from the presidential palace) or lose their subsidies from the American Military Assistance Program and the CIA. They included airborne ranger, civil guard, and "civilian airborne ranger" companies.

The McNamara-Taylor Report explained why the Special Forces had to be sent away from the capital. It was not only because they (unlike other Special Forces units already in the field) had played a conspicuous part in the pagoda raids, but also because they "are a continuing support for Diem." Their going would also remove a target of American press criticism. And it would be welcomed by high military officers and disaffected groups. This last was an understatement. Such people would be more than pleased; they would be stimulated by the departure of these forces loyal to Diem. As interested American officials well knew, one reason for the failure of the generals to attempt a coup in August had been the presence of Colonel Tung's troops in the Saigon area.

When the order to end American funding of Special Forces units held in or near the capital was transmitted to Saigon, additional instructions called for other CIA-funded paramilitary activities conducted through Colonel Tung to be transferred to General Harkins's command: "This transfer is contributory to the objectives of bringing these operations under Joint General Staff control and reducing Colonel Tung's independent power."

On October 3, Secretary McNamara told the group of high officials considering the Vietnamese question in the Situation Room of the White House that the Kennedy administration could not stay in the middle much longer. He believed Diem would respond to the American "selective pressures" by moving partway toward a policy that would improve the political situation in Vietnam and so improve the military effort. McNamara actually thought there was a chance this economic and psychological offensive against the Saigon regime could lead to a reconciliation with Diem. If it failed to accomplish that, even the secretary of defense recognized that it was bound to precipitate a coup d'état in South Vietnam.

President Kennedy met with his advisers the morning of October 5 to discuss the McNamara-Taylor Report and the new instructions drafted for Lodge. The president asked about the impact of suspending the Commodity Import Program that provided about 40 percent of South Vietnam's imports. The American-funded commodities, which were brought into the country through commercial channels, generated piastres that were used to support the South Vietnamese budget. Half of that budget went to the military effort.

But now the $5 million allotted for the Commodity Import Program in August were to remain frozen, along with $20 to $25 million intended for the next quarter of the fiscal year. "In addition, U.S. working levels (when ambassador approves) should inform Vietnamese military (and also civil budget officials) that commodity import assumptions being used for budget planning purposes must now be considered uncertain. . . .''

The Vietnamese could have the sweetened condensed milk they had been promised, but only if they negotiated for it month by month. Deliveries of other items such as wheat flour, cotton, and tobacco would also have to be discussed as needed. And loans amounting to $14 million for the Saigon waterworks and a Saigon electric power project were suspended.

"Psychologically, a major problem might arise as the decision to suspend [the commodity imports] became more fully known in Saigon official and business circles," noted the official working group that had reviewed the McNamara-Taylor Report in Washington. "Inflation would start to become a substantial danger in 2–4 months, but the situation would require the closest possible scrutiny." And the Saigon government might be obliged to reduce its military forces and its contributions to the strategic hamlet program and other key programs.

Administrator David Bell (who directed AID, the American economic aid agency) replied to Kennedy's question that the suspension would halt the flow of goods into the country. It might not affect the government budget, but if continued would seriously affect the economy.

Director of Central Intelligence McCone foresaw an economic crisis in the Saigon business community, and this "would be more pronounced than the political effects such a suspension might have upon Diem and Nhu."

What of the political impact of the whole package on the generals and the other conspirators, actual or potential? These "leverages" by which Kennedy and his advisers presumed to calibrate decisions in Washington to produce changes in the behavior of Diem in Saigon went much further than a simple cut in aid. In August, General Minh had told CIA agent Conein that a cut in aid to the regime would convince the generals of American support for their coup. These selective pressures did that and more, inciting the military to overthrow Diem precisely because he had incurred the displeasure of the Americans.

In Washington, that morning of October 5, Kennedy directed

that there was to be no official announcement of a change in policy, no use of words like *suspended, held up,* or *stopped.* McNamara, Rusk, and Bell were scheduled to testify before congressional committees. They should say simply that American programs were under continuing review in the light of the president's statement that we supported those things that favored the war effort and would not support those that did not.

Detailed instructions laying out the policy were dispatched to Ambassador Lodge. "He talked to newspapers all the time," Robert Kennedy later complained about Lodge. From the White House, McGeorge Bundy sent a cable to the ambassador on October 5, headed "eyes only," that insisted on the need for secrecy this time. It was of the "greatest importance that, to the very limit of our abilities, we should not open this next stage to the press. . . . Nothing could be more dangerous now than an impression that a set of major acts is being kicked off and a set of requirements imposed on government of Vietnam by the United States. This is of particular importance since some officials and reporters honestly believe in just such a public posture of disapproval and pressure."

The New York Times and not just its reporter in Saigon was up in arms against the Diem government. On October 6, it carried a front-page headline: RUSK CONDEMNS ATTACK ON U.S. NEWSMEN. Reading further, it transpired that Ambassador Lodge had protested the beating of three American correspondents who were watching a Buddhist monk burn himself alive in Saigon on October 5. It was the first such suicide since the government had seized the pagodas.

Senator Mike Mansfield was reported shocked by the beating of the correspondents and called for an apology and compensation. Secretary Rusk announced that Lodge had protested the physical assault by plainclothesmen in the most serious terms. David Halberstam, the correspondent of *The New York Times,* was one of the three men involved in the incident; the other two newsmen worked for the NBC television network.

Foreign news agencies in Saigon had received telephone calls at 11:30 A.M. announcing that something might happen at the central market at noon; six newsmen had gone to see. The bonze arrived in a taxi at 12:30 P.M. He sat down on the street, his legs crossed in the lotus position. He took a can of gasoline out of a bag he carried, poured it over himself, and lit a match, and the flames swept over him.

Halberstam and one of the NBC correspondents tried to protect the other man from NBC when he attempted to get away with films of the suicide. According to the Reuters account published in *The New York Times,* Vietnamese plainclothesmen had made several attempts to seize the camera before they attacked the Americans. The Reuters dispatch pointed out that the Saigon government had repeatedly accused news cameramen of complicity with Buddhist dissidents.

NBC protested the beatings as senseless brutality and declared that those responsible should be brought to trial as in any civilized country. A century earlier, King Mongkuk of Siam had also been concerned about the need for civilized behavior when he threatened to punish anyone who failed to prevent an attempt at religious self-immolation.

Certainly it was senseless and brutal to beat up newsmen; but the Americans did not seem bothered by other, troublesome questions raised by the incident. "The extent to which the often solicited presence of journalists exacerbates any situation in our business is a matter of legitimate and intense concern and debate." These words appeared in a *New York Times* editorial on March 13, 1983, when an American in Jacksonville, Alabama, notified a local television station that he was going to set himself afire in the town square as a protest against unemployment in the United States. "The question of whether that Alabama camera crew was reporting or creating news is easily answered," *The New York Times* editorial concluded. "Two decisions lit the nearly fatal fire: Mr. Andrews's match and the switch that set the cameras whirring."

But that was written twenty years after the bonze's self-immolation. In 1963, American newsmen spurned suggestions that they themselves had become actors in the Byzantine drama they were reporting from Saigon and might have some responsibility for what took place.

It was mid-October and President Kennedy was awaiting a report from Henry Cabot Lodge. In Saigon, the American press had gotten wind of the cuts in the aid program.

Roger Hilsman was working with representatives of the Pentagon, AID, the CIA, and the United States Information Agency. They had been charged with maintaining a "continuous review" of the impact of the new policy, and on October 10, the State Department had asked Lodge for an evaluation of "entire spectrum of results, both favorable and unfavorable. [They] wanted regular reports in consultation with all U.S. elements Saigon."

But Lodge had seemed in no hurry to reply and President Kennedy intervened personally four days later to put specific questions to his ambassador:

"1. Are we gaining or losing on balance and day by day in the contest with the Viet Cong?

"2. Is the government responding at any point to our threefold need for improvement in (a) campaign against VC, (b) internal political developments, and (c) actions affecting relations with American people and Government?

"3. What does the evidence suggest on the strengthening or weakening of effectiveness of GVN [Government of Vietnam] in relation to its own people?

"4. And more specifically, what effect are we getting from our own actions under Deptel 534 [the 'selective pressures'] and what modifications in either direction do you think advisable?"

In Washington, they needed to monitor the gradually increasing effect of the suspension of the Commodity Import Program, to make adjustments as the Saigon government reacted, Kennedy explained. "It takes time to work out each position here, and accordingly it is important to me to have a constant sense of your own evaluation of the situation. I should be glad to have such an evaluation now, in the light of the considerable interlude that has passed since McNamara returned with an up-to-date account of your views."

Lodge acknowledged receipt of the president's cable on October 15: "Will send my best evaluation before country team meeting tomorrow, Wednesday." He promised to send weekly reports thereafter as Kennedy had requested.

Henry Cabot Lodge was now in unchallenged command of American policy-making in Saigon. He had succeeded in having John Richardson removed as chief of the CIA station, thus closing the one remaining channel whereby the Ngos had been able to communicate directly with Washington, bypassing the unfriendly American Embassy. The identity of Richardson had been revealed in the American press, and he left Saigon on October 5.

Local Americans in and out of the CIA who resented Richardson's past support of the Saigon regime and his collaboration with Ngo Dinh Nhu had not been the only people satisfied to see him go. More significantly, Vietnamese conspirators in the army were immensely relieved by the departure of this powerful friend of the Diem government. Now, it seemed that they really could trust the Americans not to warn the palace if they attempted a coup d'état.

The McNamara-Taylor Report had endorsed Lodge's highly personal interpretation of the role of an American ambassador in Saigon. "Your policy of cool correctness in order to make Diem come to you is correct. You should continue it." If it did not work, Lodge might one day have to go to Diem to ensure he understood overall American policy. But, "decision on when this becomes imperative rests with you, in light of your assessment situation."

By adopting the recommendations of the McNamara-Taylor Report, the White House had once again renounced the use of diplomacy in Saigon.

A dissenting voice had come from the Central Intelligence Agency. William Colby, who had revisited South Vietnam with the mission, was singled out in a footnote to its report as alone recommending that "selected and restricted unofficial and personal relationships approved by the ambassador should be maintained with the Ngos where persuasion could be useful." Colby proposed to Director of Central Intelligence McCone that the CIA unofficially suggest to Nhu that he withdraw from the scene in order to end the stalemate and offered to go to see Nhu himself. McCone passed on the proposal to the proper authorities, but it was not accepted.

On October 5, President Kennedy used the special CIA channel to tell Lodge that, as the McNamara-Taylor Report had recommended, he was not to take any initiative to promote a coup openly. However, there should be "urgent covert efforts under broad guidance of ambassador to identify and build contacts with alternative leadership if and when it appears." It was essential that this effort be fully secure and wholly deniable. "To provide plausibility to denial suggest you and no one else in Embassy issue these instructions to [CIA] Acting Station Chief and hold him responsible for making appropriate contacts and reporting to you alone. All reports to Washington should be on this [CIA] channel."

The ambassador was thus authorized to go far, very far, in "surveillance and readiness" for a coup but not to encourage one actively. These were the guidelines laid down in this cable—CAP 63560—that until October 30 General Harkins believed described official American policy in Saigon. But there had been second thoughts in Washington within twenty-four hours, and new instructions had been issued that Lodge read, understandably, as superseding his initial instructions, although he did not bother to explain that to Harkins.

The change had come about when Lodge reported on the CIA channel that General Minh had just spent more than an hour in Saigon that morning with CIA agent Conein, discussing plans to overthrow the government. Lodge had personally authorized Conein to talk with the general. The meeting, on October 5, had been arranged with Conein by General Don in Nha Trang three days earlier after Don had set up an "accidental" encounter with the American agent at the Saigon airport.

General Minh had mentioned familiar names as his coplotters, among them, Generals Don, Kim, and Khiem. (Minh was not entirely sure that he could trust Khiem and asked Conein for copies of papers Khiem professed to have received from the CIA to make sure they were authentic.) General Minh told Conein they were considering several plans of action, one of which called for the assassination of Diem's brothers Can and Nhu. He said they had to work quickly because lower-ranking officers were working on their own coup that could be abortive and lead to catastrophe. He did not expect American support, General Minh said, but the conspirators needed assurances the Americans would not thwart them and wanted a promise that American military and economic aid would continue.

In Washington, Director of Central Intelligence McCone met privately with the president and his brother Robert to recommend a hands-off attitude toward a coup in Saigon. The CIA had analyzed potential leaders and could see no one who could take over and improve the situation. Let the American government "try to bring all the pressure we could on Diem to change his ways," McCone said. "Mr. President, if I was manager of a baseball team, I had one pitcher, I'd keep him in the box whether he was a good pitcher or not." He explained later: "By that I was saying that, if Diem was removed we would have not one coup but we would have a succession of coups and political disorder in Vietnam."

But it would seem that the only reason Lodge had been told not to promote a coup in Saigon was uncertainty about the readiness of the generals to act. American policymakers had been waiting for General Minh to make a move since August, and they did not intend to scare him off now.

On October 6, Lodge received from the CIA channel "additional general thoughts which have been discussed with President." "While we do not wish to stimulate coup, we also do not wish to leave impression the U.S. would thwart a change of government or deny economic and military assistance to a new regime if it appeared capable of increasing effectiveness of military effort, ensuring popular support to win war, and improving working relations with U.S." In other words, Lodge was directed to encourage the conspirators.

In Saigon, Lodge studied the instructions he had received for selective pressures against the regime. His first response, on October 6, had been to hail them as "excellent" and "outlining a course of action which should yield constructive results." But he felt "it hard to see today a good future for the U.S.–GVN [Diem government] relationship. I say this because the only thing which the U.S. really wants [is] the removal of or restriction on the Nhus. . . ." And "we cannot remove the Nhus by non-violent means against their will."

An Italian journalist had just called at the American Embassy to tell Trueheart about an interview he had had with Ngo Dinh Nhu. The brother of the president had said that the Vietnamese could get on without American advisers, who, in any case, were incapable of fighting a guerrilla war. The Americans ought to treat South Vietnam the same way they treated Yugoslavia; the Vietnamese needed helicopters, transport, and economic aid from them, not military personnel. Nhu said that he and Diem had always opposed massive American military intervention, even at "the time of greatest danger, that is, the winter of 1961–1962." The fact was that it was impossible to win the war with the Americans, who were an obstacle to the revolutionary transformation of society that was necessary for victory.

Lodge cabled Washington, October 7, "We cannot assume Diem and Nhu have the same aim as we. Clearly Nhu wants our help without our presence which, in his view, we use as an excuse for interfering in their internal system of government. . . . And Nhu is a strong influence on Diem." They might well request the Americans to leave the country. In Lodge's opinion, if the Americans started to withdraw, that alone might be enough to trigger a coup.

Nhu told various people that the South might have to get on without any American aid at all. He said, "If we have no more cars, no more money, we will have to go back to using bicycles. We will have to work hard and try to run our country without aid."

He had warned army leaders as early as August 15 that they might have to stand alone without the United States if the Kennedy administration decided to appease the Soviet Union and other Communist countries. Ever since Kennedy had accepted the neutrality of Laos in 1962, the Ngos had doubted his will to oppose international communism. And they had not been reassured when he signed a partial nuclear test ban treaty with the Russians. In August, Nhu had given the assembled officers the cheerless news that they had to be aware of the need for economy, that all equipment should be carefully deployed for maximum effectiveness because the Americans might decide to reduce military as well as economic aid. But now it was mid-October and President Kennedy still supported the struggle against the Viet Cong; the army did not have to face the enemy alone. True, there had been cuts in aid, but American officers and officials were there to reassure military leaders that these were not directed against them. Only the Ngos stood in the way of a resumption of aid.

Saigon was tense, and the rumor reached the American Embassy, not for the first time, that the Ngos were planning to assassinate Ambassador Lodge. Presumably, some government official had decided to respond to the interfering Americans by launching a war of nerves against them. If this was the case, it was a mistaken strategy that served only to confirm the ugly image local Americans had of the regime. The rumor was taken quite seriously at the embassy. Although in Lodge's opinion it would have been "unbelievably idiotic" for Diem and Nhu even to think of assassinating him, he informed Rusk and Harriman that his associates considered it a real possibility. "Nhu is apparently pleased with his raids on the Buddhist pagodas last summer and is said to be annoyed with me for having advised him to leave the country for a while. Also he is reported to be smoking opium."

Lodge's associates must indeed have believed Diem and Nhu mad to imagine them ready to assassinate the American ambassador whatever the circumstances. That Nhu could be seriously accused of planning Lodge's murder, and for such motives, revealed the depths of incomprehension that separated the embassy from Gia Long Palace.

A message from the State Department advised that detailed security arrangements be made at the embassy "in view of present critical situation." Escape routes were studied to get Americans out of the chancery if it were attacked; a helicopter would be ready to take off from the roof of the chancery and fly them to safety. And highly classified documents were to be destroyed or evacuated.

Americans did one day have to escape from the chancery, leaving many classified documents behind, but that was in 1975, when Saigon fell to the Communists. In 1963, the United States was dealing with a friendly government in South Vietnam, not an enemy, but many Americans in Saigon and Washington seemed unable to tell the difference.

On October 16, Lodge used the CIA channel to send the first of the weekly reports he had promised President Kennedy. Robert Kennedy said later of Lodge, he "wouldn't communicate. . . . You'd send out a message and ask a lot of questions and he'd send back a message of one line: 'Your message both concerned and amused me. Signed Henry Cabot Lodge.' "

This particular cable to Kennedy was longer than that but not much more informative. Lodge thought the Americans were holding their own in the "long, smoldering struggle." He said that Vietnamese were supposed to be capable of great violence on occasion but could see no sign of that at the present time. Some local businessmen were worried about the withholding of commercial imports, and Thuan had told him that Diem was, too, but he had received no request from Diem.

Two days later, the embassy reported to Washington that Nhu had told an American correspondent that the government would probably draw on its foreign exchange reserves to compensate for the suspension of commercial imports (as the architects of the "selective leverages" had anticipated). The same cable reported without comment the opinion of the correspondent in question that the freeze on these American imports seemed to be creating conditions favorable for a coup; people were losing faith in the government, and majors and lieutenant colonels were complaining about the high cost of living.

The timing of the other "leverage" called for in the McNamara-Taylor Report had been left up to Lodge. On October 17, Major General Richard G. Stilwell went to Gia Long Palace on instructions from the ambassador to see Secretary Thuan. Stilwell told Thuan, who combined the office of deputy secretary of defense with his other functions, that he had been been traveling around the country with General Don. They had been visiting various lesser military headquarters, to make sure that all units were making their contribution to the war effort.

Thuan understood immediately. "You've come to talk about the Special Forces," he said.

Ten Special Forces companies were then stationed in the Saigon area. Seven of these elite units belonged to the Vietnamese army and were supported by the American Military Assistance Program. The other three civilian companies, subsidized by the CIA, had provided the men used in the pagoda raids. It was made clear to Thuan that the civilian companies would lose all support unless they were effectively subordinated to the Joint General Staff and committed to field operations. This applied also to the other seven units. Special Forces already in the field—mountain scouts and border surveillance personnel—would continue to be paid by the Americans, but the funds would no longer pass through the hands of the Special Forces commander, Colonel Tung.

President Diem was informed of these decisions by a letter from General Harkins. Colonel Tung knew nothing of what had happened because he was out of town.

The following day, Secretary Thuan and Lodge met at a reception and Thuan went over to sit with the ambassador. Thuan said that President Diem wished to know whether Washington had reached any decision regarding resumption of commercial imports. "I told him I believed they had not," Thuan said. "Is that right?"

Lodge said that as far as he knew no decision had been reached. He reported to Washington that Thuan gave a broad grin and said, "That's what I thought and told the president. I will tell him that's what you think."

And then Thuan said, "I have faith that all this is going to work out so that your mission will be a great success. I don't know how or when but I think it will be soon."

Secretary Thuan may have thought that President Diem was coming to accept the idea that he would have to separate himself from his brother Nhu. Thuan was absorbed in his parallel relationships with Diem and with the Americans and obsessed by distrust for Nhu. He was not unduly concerned about the effect of the American "selective pressures" on the generals.

The leading generals had agreed among themselves weeks earlier, in mid-September, to mount a coup against the government. But they held off, unwilling to cross the Rubicon.

Senior troop commanders were now committed to the conspiracy. Among them, stationed in the south-central highlands, was

General Nguyen Khanh, highly regarded by officials in Washington but not by General Don or General Minh, who did not trust him but were afraid to exclude him. They had also enlisted General Ton That Dinh, whose adhesion to the plot seemed a prerequisite for success because Dinh controlled the troops around Saigon. President Diem had entrusted the capital to him during the summer when he had named Dinh military governor, but Diem had refused to grant the volatile young general the additional star he coveted, doubtless making him particularly receptive to the blandishments of Don and his friends.

At least one plan was already drawn up for this coup that some Americans counted on to bring popular government to South Vietnam. The strategy had been devised by one of the conspirators who was not himself a general or even a soldier. He was a notorious specialist in intrigue, Dr. Tran Kim Tuyen, who had been dismissed some months earlier from his post as head of the Direction of Political and Social Studies at the presidency, the presidential security service—more precisely, the government "intelligence and dirty tricks outfit," in the words of a CIA analyst well placed to appreciate its activities.

In September, the English-language *Times of Vietnam,* which acted as a mouthpiece of the government, had complained that "foreign adventurers and ex-USOM," Americans, in other words, were trying to whitewash Dr. Tuyen at the expense of Diem and Nhu. Dr. Tuyen was one of two men (the other was former foreign secretary Mau) whose alienation from the regime had so troubled members of the McNamara-Taylor mission that they had singled him out by name in their report of October 2. They had neglected to mention that the wily little doctor was not admired by the "urban elite"; he was so unpopular that in 1960 the American ambassador, the predecessor of Nolting, had tried, unsuccessfully, to persuade Diem to send him abroad, along with Nhu and his wife.

For Tuyen, who yielded to none in his aversion to the Communists, it was leadership that was needed in the South—not liberalization, and certainly not democracy. American intelligence reported that he had created "an extensive and well-compartmented organization," "an amalgam of military, civilian nationalists, Buddhists and student groups."

Years afterward, in 1971, Dr. Tuyen wrote an interminable series of articles to defend the Diem regime and deny American accounts that he shared responsibility for the coup that overthrew it. True, he was not implicated by any of the generals who wrote their own memoirs of the coup and was abroad when it took place. But he provided the plans that were executed by others.

Dr. Tuyen plotted with two men who like himself were practiced at working undercover. One was Colonel Thao. Some Vietnamese officers suspected Thao had never changed his loyalty from the Hanoi regime in which his own brother was a high official, and when the North finally defeated the South in 1975 the victors would claim that Thao had always been one of their agents. By that time he had been dead for many years; the coup against Diem was only the first of several in which this inveterate plotter was involved before he was captured and tortured to death by the police of the generals then ruling in Saigon.

In 1963, Thao's political ideas seemed fuzzy. He professed to agree with Dr. Tuyen on the need for a more effective government to carry on the war. Thao had been named inspector general of the strategic hamlet program, a useful post for making contacts with middle-level commanders, colonels, and captains, his fellow plotters. According to reports reaching the Americans, Thao had moved to take over military leadership of groups organized originally by Dr. Tuyen.

The third man who worked for a coup with Tuyen and Thao was Colonel Do Mau, director of military security, whose complicity was indispensable for any coup d'état. Do Mau had sought out General Don after the pagodas were raided, and Don and his friends had counted on the colonel as a fellow conspirator since September. It was he who accompanied General Minh to receive the formal adhesion of General Nguyen Khanh to the coup, and also that of a certain Colonel Thieu, whom the coup would turn into a general.

But even though Colonel Do Mau had thrown in his lot with

the generals, he remained in touch with younger officers, many of them adherents of the Dai Viet party, others VNQDD members, who felt no allegiance to Diem and had been organizing since August to overthrow him. These junior officers commanded troops, particularly airborne, marine, and armored units, invaluable for the plotters.

Implicated in these several conspiracies—committed to Generals Minh, Don, and Kim; close to Dr. Tuyen and Colonel Thao; and in direct contact with the Dai Viet military plotters—was the officer who had intervened to stop the abortive coup against the regime in 1960, General Khiem, now chief of staff to the Joint Chiefs of Staff. A sometime member of the Dai Viet party, he was the president's godson and one of the few generals Diem really trusted. In the end, it would be Khiem alone of all the generals scheming against the regime who would try to warn Diem about the impending coup, and Diem would refuse to listen.

How many separate factions were organizing for a coup? Perhaps as many as six and possibly more. They included politicians, many affiliated with the Dai Viet and some with the VNQDD. These politicians intrigued with the Buddhists and were active among the students, encouraging demonstrations against the government that provoked the regime to respond in the only way it knew, by large-scale arrests, which heightened the opposition to Diem in Saigon and in Washington. The labor leader Tran Quoc Buu and some of his colleagues had joined forces with the politicians and students working for the overthrow of the government. Buu, who was much admired in American official circles and had highly placed friends in the American labor movement, was regarded with suspicion by some Vietnamese, who believed him in the pay of the Americans; his critics seem to have anticipated his ties to the CIA by several years.

That all these plotters were in touch with Americans in and out of the embassy was not surprising. Ever since the military conflict had sharpened under the Kennedy administration, many American officials had envisaged a change in the Saigon government and made contacts in the Vietnamese army and administration with that in mind; different groups of Americans had different candidates.

But now the decision had been made to act through the generals. The Americans reportedly had used Dr. Tuyen to reach General Khiem. Even though the other generals were suspicious of Khiem's attachment to the regime and wondered whether he had acted as a double agent during the stillborn coup of August, they were encouraged by the news that he was with them; as operations officer at military headquarters he was in direct control of the disposition of troops. General Minh had sounded him out first and then General Don had gone to see him, in September, to find that Khiem was working on a plot of his own for a coup, which had been developed with CIA officers operating out of the embassy. But Khiem had agreed to give up that particular scheme and join Minh, Don, and Kim.

The generals still seemed to think they could make a deal with Diem. Don went with Dinh to Gia Long Palace to deliver a letter asking for a reorganization of the government that would give the military no less than the key cabinet posts of defense, interior, psychological war, and education. They also wanted the Nhus out of the government.

There would be no coup until a reply was received from the president, General Khiem told his CIA contact that September. But he reassured the American that the generals had not given up their plotting. They feared that Nhu might actually succeed in working out a reconciliation with the North. A dangerous prospect, according to Conein, because "what the devil were they fighting for if the central government was negotiating behind their backs." General Minh had appointed Khiem as his go-between with the Americans.

As the generals still hesitated, the junior officers in touch with Do Mau went ahead with their own conspiracy against Diem. Weeks afterward, when the activities of these officers were revealed to the press after the generals' coup had succeeded, General Don threatened the young officers with arrest. He seemed to think that by diverting attention to their own well-organized plot they had diminished the triumph of the generals; they had sullied the honor of General Minh. On that occasion it was Do Mau who intervened to shield them, as in the time of their plotting he had shielded them from Nhu.

As late as mid-October, when these officers approached the generals to work out details for a joint coup, the generals wavered; they could not make up their minds to act. To the highly motivated younger officers, they seemed indecisive and opportunistic—as indeed they were.

It was during this time that a CIA agent sought out a prominent civilian reputed for keeping a private army to protect his extensive business interests. It was a front for three thousand Catholics organized in units that fought the Viet Cong on their own terrain. The American agent who kept these counterinsurgents supplied with arms assumed mistakenly that their enterprising leader was a part of the conspiracy against Diem and told him, "The generals are all agreed on a coup but they don't seem able to get going." He then proposed that the startled Vietnamese take over leadership of the plotters. If the coup were successful, the American promised that the United States would recognize the new regime within twelve hours.

The talk on Radio Catinat was of rising prices and food shortages, the displeasure of the Americans with Diem, and the coup that seemed imminent even though people could only guess at its leaders. Then, on October 24, a mission from the United Nations arrived in Saigon to find out for itself what was happening to the Buddhists in the Vietnam of Ngo Dinh Diem.

Educated Vietnamese had been awaiting the mission with great interest, "coupled with a general belief that GVN will not permit delegation to function freely," Ambassador Lodge wired President Kennedy. In September, Roger Hilsman and his colleagues had looked to the United Nations to make its contribution to the battery of pressures directed against Diem, by condemning his treatment of the Buddhists. Fifteen nations of Asia and Africa requested that the subject of "the violation of human rights in South Vietnam" be inscribed on the agenda of the forthcoming meeting of the General Assembly, and the United States made no move to stop them. But then it dawned on at least some American officials that in their zeal to intimidate Diem they had opened a Pandora's box: a full-scale debate would never stop at the Buddhist question; many countries would welcome a chance to attack the American presence in the South and call for a reunified and neutral Vietnam and an end to the war. Then the Kennedy administration, and not just the government of President Diem, would be in the dock at the United Nations.

If the delegates assembled in the glass building on the East River in New York had not yet profited from the occasion to turn on the United States, that was because the Saigon government had surprised the Americans by mounting a defensive action of its own; American policymakers, not for the first time, had underestimated the Vietnamese.

The Americans had started off by assuming that Madame Nhu would be the representative of the Saigon regime, promising a display of vituperation that could only backfire against its American ally. Then the Americans had picked up published comments by Diem's sister-in-law that her government would welcome a mission of inquiry and abide by its findings. *The New York Times* dismissed the idea as a ploy of Madame Nhu, advanced only because she thought it would be rejected in New York. Ambassador Lodge cabled Washington that in the opinion of the embassy the Saigon government "would strongly resist resolution calling for UN representative or commission to examine on-the-spot facts concerning violation of human rights in Vietnam."

The Americans did not know that the decision to invite a mission to Saigon was made at the end of August when Buu-Hoi went to Gia Long Palace to see Ngo Dinh Nhu. The scientist-diplomat, having made sure that the leaders of the activist bonzes did not intend to let his mother immolate herself for Buddha, spent many hours talking with Tri Quang and other monks at Xa Loi pagoda. He had tried to mediate between them and the government and had failed. At the end of the month he prepared to return to his laboratory in Paris and had called on Nhu to say good-bye.

"*Tu me laisse dans la merde,*" Nhu had said to his old friend, the comrade of his university days in Paris. At Nhu's insistence, Buu-Hoi agreed to take on the job of defending the Saigon government in New York, but only on condition that he would be free to invite the United Nations to send a mission to see the truth for themselves.

Buu-Hoi arrived in New York in mid-September to find the American public in the grip of a nightmare fantasy of Vietnam—a horrifying land of burning monks and ravaged pagodas where the desperate population struggled to defend themselves against diabolical rulers. According to U Thant, the Buddhist secretary general of the United Nations, there was no country so chaotic as South Vietnam and it was getting worse. It completely lacked the two virtues of democracy, the capacity for changing governments by constitutional procedures and the ability to conduct affairs by persuasion instead of force.

The Saigon radio responded, "The Secretary General of the United Nations, who is a Burmese, seems to be completely oblivious of the fact that in his own country the army has thrown a duly elected government in jail."

At the United Nations, the delegate of Ceylon was leading an emotional campaign against the Saigon regime. But the Vietnamese felt the Cambodians were their real enemies, working against them among the Asian and African delegates. Prince Sihanouk had broken off diplomatic relations with Saigon on August 27, after the latest in a long series of border incidents and the pagoda raids.

The General Assembly opened its session on September 17, and Buu-Hoi called at the American mission to the United Nations to see Ambassador Charles Yost two days later. As a Buddhist who had been intimately involved in the recent events, he believed the Buddhists had had good reason to protest in Hue, Buu-Hoi told Yost. But in Saigon, their protest had been transformed into a political attempt to overthrow the government. The highly colored accounts in the American press were inaccurate and would have been ridiculed at home, even by Buddhists.

All the same, it was widely believed that an intolerable situation had developed in Vietnam, Yost said. The government had to take steps to redress the situation.

The Vietnamese envoy did not disagree. He was well aware of discriminatory practices in Vietnam and thought foreign pressure on behalf of the Buddhists could be useful—but inside the country, not abroad. The key to the crisis was to make sure that Diem faithfully implemented the terms of the five-point accord he had signed with the Buddhists in June.

Lodge was unimpressed when he read the report of this interview in Saigon. The American ambassador was launched on a bold plan to change the government of Vietnam at the top. He was not interested in trying to defuse tensions in the country, least of all by resort to patient and low-key diplomacy. "It is clear, in embassy's judgment, that GVN [Government of Vietnam]'s repressive acts of August 21 have taken problem beyond Buu-Hoi's oversimplified solution."

At the American mission in New York, Buu-Hoi outlined a plan to avoid a full-scale debate on Vietnam in the General Assembly. His government obviously would have to reject a formal mission of inquiry imposed on it by the United Nations as unacceptable interference in its internal affairs. But the Saigon government was ready to take the initiative and invite the General Assembly to send a fact-finding mission to Vietnam to see for itself that the Buddhist crisis was over, and they had already sounded out interested delegates. The arrival of such a mission would help to ease the situation of the Buddhists. And the General Assembly might be persuaded to hold off its debate in New York until it had facts at its disposal provided by the members of its own mission on their return. Privately, Buu-Hoi asked the Americans to tell Tri Quang at the embassy in Saigon that he would do nothing in New York to hurt the Buddhist cause.

The Vietnamese envoy made a brief visit to Washington, and for the first time since Ambassador Nolting had left Vietnam in August there was a direct, though short-lived, link between Gia Long Palace and the State Department.

Harlan Cleveland, assistant secretary for international organization affairs, found the position of the Saigon government "sophisticated and gauged just right to cope with this kind of situation in UN." He said that under the circumstances the Americans would try to help, following the lead of the Vietnamese. "We believe Buu-Hoi's presence in New York should give GVN tremendous assist in presenting its case. He is an individual of considerable intellect, stature, dignity and sophistication. He possesses obvious diplomatic talents which should serve him well at UN. In addition, he already knows a number of African diplomats as result his current assignment as GVN ambassador to six African states."

Under Secretary of State Harriman and Assistant Secretary of State Hilsman, the two men in the forefront of the campaign to dislodge Diem, were less enthusiastic about meeting his ambassador.

The Vietnamese envoy used his visit to Washington to try to break the deadlock that had paralyzed relations between the two governments, to salvage the independent nationalist regime in Saigon. But Harriman was not willing to have Diem either explained or justified in his presence. He made no effort to hide his hostility to the Vietnamese president and removed his hearing aid when Buu-Hoi suggested that former ambassador Nolting might still play a useful role in Vietnam.

Hilsman spoke of the effect on American opinion of the repression of religious and student groups. The image of Vietnam in the United States was unfavorable, and the only way to improve it was to begin by releasing the imprisoned students and Buddhists. President Kennedy had already explained what needed to be done. Diem should make changes in policy, and perhaps personnel, to gain the widest possible political support for the war. The United States favored whatever furthered the war and opposed whatever hindered it.

The emissary from Saigon responded that the religious part of the crisis had been over even before the pagoda raids. The crisis had become entirely political; the bonzes had overextended their position to the point where the government had to force a showdown to survive. Of course, as a Buddhist and a humanist, he personally deplored the manner of the raids. He told Hilsman about letters he had received from Buddhist leaders, showing that not only the patriarch Khiet but also Tam Chau, the chairman of the former Intersect Committee for the Defense of Buddhism, now deplored the political use that had been made of the Buddhists. Copies of these letters were being distributed to delegates at the General Assembly.

But Buu-Hoi did agree that changes had to be made in Saigon. The government needed to start over on a new basis. It had to be broadened and reformed even though few trained people were available. The problem was to find the right people and then let them do the job without constant interference and favoritism. He did not think it would be hard to overhaul the government; the difficulty, as always, would be convincing people outside the capital that the changes were real. Too many projects never got much further than the paper they were written on.

And then Buu-Hoi raised the question that had embittered Saigon's dealings with Washington for so long: what did the American government think about Nhu and his departure? Hilsman weighed his words. Despite the important contribution of Nhu to the strategic hamlet program, he would seem to have become a political symbol to many Vietnamese. If this were true, Diem ought to consider the future of his brother very carefully.

But the country simply could not dispense with Nhu's great talents, Buu-Hoi answered. All Nhu really wanted was to work in the field of his own particular interest. His job could be something like "government planning director." Buu-Hoi indicated that President Diem himself was ready to withdraw from the day-to-day affairs of government to play an "increasingly more distant leader role." It would be useful if American officials made specific suggestions to him for reforming the structure and the performance of the government. In particular, the Americans ought to encourage the appointment of Secretary Thuan as prime minister to take over direction of the affairs of government. On this subject, at least, the Vietnamese emissary agreed with the American ambassador in Saigon.

Hilsman spoke scornfully of the rumors about negotiations with Hanoi, saying he did not believe a word. Nhu was only bluffing, and the United States could not be blackmailed like that. Hilsman discoursed on a favorite subject, counterinsurgency. Accompanying Buu-Hoi to this meeting was Tran Van Dinh, the chargé d'affaires of the Vietnamese Embassy in Washington. The two men listened courteously, Buu-Hoi who had represented the Ho Chi Minh government on the military commission that nego-

tiated with the French at Fontainebleau, and Dinh who had led
guerrilla forces against the French in the jungles of Laos. As they
left Hilsman's office, Buu-Hoi turned to Dinh with a smile. "See,"
he said. "Now you know how to fight a guerrilla war."

In New York, time was running out. The delegate from Ceylon was scheduled to speak in favor of a draft resolution expressing
serious concern about "the continuing violation of human rights in
Vietnam." The South Vietnamese had no right of reply on the
General Assembly floor because their country was not a member
of the United Nations. But Buu-Hoi had brought together a team
of dynamic young diplomats, members of leading Confucian families in Hue, as it happened, most of whom had represented their
country in Africa or Asia; and they were already at work, talking
with old friends and making new ones behind the scenes at the
General Assembly.

The delegate from Ceylon delivered a diatribe against the
Saigon regime on October 7, but no one was willing to take up the
attack where he left off. The Soviet Union had wanted to use
the International Control Commission to investigate the situation
in Vietnam but changed its position overnight. Without a single
dissenting vote, the General Assembly agreed to accept the invitation from Saigon to send a fact-finding mission to South Vietnam.

It was a rare example of South Vietnamese diplomacy, averting
a vote of censure against the Saigon government and staving off an
international debate on the role of the United States in South
Vietnam. The strategy espoused by Buu-Hoi of seeking friends for
South Vietnam in the Third World had paid off; but this, its most
important success, would also be its last.

In Saigon, Ambassador Lodge did not understand why the
American mission to the United Nations wished to avoid a debate
in the General Assembly and a resolution that condemned the
Diem government. "I should think there would be considerable
concern over possibility of report favorable to GVN, given true
facts of situation and our established policy based on these facts."

The president of the General Assembly announced the members of the fact-finding mission: Afghanistan, Brazil, Ceylon, Costa
Rica, Dahomey, Morocco, Nepal. Buu-Hoi had assured Secretary

of State Rusk that his invitation to the mission was not intended as a stalling device, the mission would be free to move around in Vietnam and see anyone it wished to see. But Lodge thought the mission was naïve to believe that; the government would never allow any unfavorable information to reach it.

He informed Kennedy that student leaders were being arrested. "All evidence to date points to concentrated GVN attempt to cow potential adverse witnesses and prevent their appearing before the delegation and to keep delegation busy on a Cook's tour."

When the mission reached Saigon, its Afghan president, who was personally a strong believer in a policy of nonalignment with any of the great powers, issued a statement to the press. The intention of the mission was to carry out on-the-spot investigations, to hear witnesses, and receive petitions. "We are here with our minds open to the truth and determined to report the facts."

By this time, several hundred Buddhist monks had been released; there were still some two to three hundred in prison, including most of the activist leaders. Thirty or forty people had been arrested since the mission left New York, Nhu told the visiting diplomats—few Buddhists, but some members of one of the various Dai Viet party groups.

The mission established its headquarters at the Hotel Majestic and considered the tentative program drawn up for it by the government. The schedule for the first two days was approved: calls on high officials, visits to three pagodas to meet representatives of Buddhist associations. An invitation to attend the parade marking the National Day, October 26, was also accepted.

That Sunday, October 27, a Buddhist monk sat down in front of the Saigon cathedral and burned himself to death. *The New York Times* reported that this shocking event convinced the mission to break away from the constraints of the government program and strike out on its own. This was a good story and would have been a better one had it been true. In reality, the mission had notified the government the previous day that it intended to follow its own schedule after the national holiday.

During the next few days, the mission visited young people

who were held in camps and talked with Buddhists in prisons and in pagodas—but not with Tri Quang, still a guest at the American Embassy. His hosts had been unable to convince the Vietnamese authorities to broaden their interpretation of the status of political asylum granted to him, to allow his meeting with the mission.

Several of the diplomats left for Hue to go to Tu Dam and other pagodas and hear witnesses whose names had already been communicated to them, while other witnesses were received in Saigon. The mission planned to complete its work in time to leave Vietnam on Monday, November 4.

Henry Cabot Lodge once again had misjudged the intentions of the Diem regime. On October 30, he had to admit to President Kennedy that the government "appears to be off to a good start with the U.N. mission. So far they have allowed them to meet everyone, including imprisoned Buddhists."

But by that time Lodge was more interested in other events that affected him personally. For one thing, he had recently spent a day in the company of President Diem.

The invitation from Gia Long Palace had arrived before the National Day, October 26, which fell on Saturday this year. The ambassador was planning to put in an appearance for the occasion and then withdraw into the same splendid isolation in which he had passed the previous weeks.

Although John Kennedy complained privately to his brother Robert about Lodge's refusal to make any overtures to Diem, the American president seemed unwilling or unable to do anything about it; he was no more successful than Diem had been with the father of Madame Nhu in Washington, in calling his ambassador to order. Kennedy was reduced to using other intermediaries, such as Vice-President Lyndon Johnson, who had taken to Madame Nhu when they met in Saigon in 1961 and was employed as one emissary to the Ngo family. Another was Torbert MacDonald, a congressman from Massachusetts, Kennedy's intimate friend, who brought messages to Diem from Kennedy, urging him to save himself before it was too late.

On Thursday, October 24, the same day the mission from the

United Nations arrived in the Vietnamese capital, Lodge received a telephone call from Foreign Minister Cuu. President Diem had learned that Lodge and his wife were going to Dalat after the parade on Saturday. They meant to remain in that pleasant highland resort town until the inauguration of the Atomic Energy Center near Dalat on Monday. Diem had asked the minister to warn Lodge to be very careful: there was a real problem of security at the rather isolated inn where they planned to stay. Diem particularly wished to invite the Lodges to fly to Dalat with him Sunday morning and visit an agricultural project and a strategic hamlet on the way. He proposed that they spend the night at one of the presidential villas in Dalat. Lodge accepted both invitations.

It was too late to include this news in his personal report to President Kennedy. In that report, dispatched on Wednesday, Lodge had mused on such questions as what is a fact and what is victory. He had said the Viet Cong was gaining in the delta and "when it comes to defeating the Viet Cong, time is not working for us as long as the government is run by brother Nhu in the way in which he is now doing it." Lodge thought all this could be quickly changed, but as things stood, "in the contest with the Viet Cong we are not doing much more than holding our own."

As for the three other questions Kennedy had put to him previously, Lodge noted General Harkins's report that in no case had the government resisted any military recommendations of the Americans. But he found no improvement in the political situation. "Atmosphere in Saigon still one of unrest and discontent but inability to move beyond verbalizing for fear of arrest. Most people still waiting for us to clarify situation and bring about a change," according to Lodge.

He added that urban discontent had not spilled over to the countryside, and Diem and Nhu were "sitting tight, reacting to U.S. pressure by counterpressure and implying through public statements that they can go it alone."

Lodge told Kennedy that he would be surprised if the Vietnamese president said anything about the suspension of the Commodity Import Program when they met at the National Day ceremonies on Saturday or at the dedication of the Atomic Energy

Center on Monday. Foreign Minister Cuu had telephoned the next day. "Diem's invitation to you may mean that he has finally decided to come to you," the State Department commented, not unreasonably.

Lodge was advised to use the occasion to press the American point of view on Diem. Military matters came first: the need for clear and hold operations; increasing combat units to full strength; and speeding up the training and arming of hamlet militia, especially in the delta. The strategic hamlet program needed to be consolidated in the delta and future hamlets should not be built before they could be protected and civic action programs started. There was advice to Diem on how to handle the United Nations mission and conciliate the Buddhists. Lodge might also like to bring up the anti-American statements by Nhu and others and the articles in the *Times of Vietnam* attacking Americans.

But first, the ambassador was expected to attend the ceremonies marking the eighth anniversary of the founding of the Republic, which was also the eighth anniversary of the Diem regime.

NATIONAL DAY, OCTOBER 26, 1963

In a speech broadcast to the nation, Diem proclaimed the goals of his government that he and Nhu had been preaching for weeks: "Self-sufficiency and reliance on our own strength to lead us toward economic independence."

High officials and notables arrived at Gia Long Palace to honor the president, but the usual laudatory speeches had a hollow sound this year. With French ambassador Lalouette gone, the ambassador of Nationalist China was dean of the diplomatic corps and delivered the congratulatory address to Diem on behalf of his colleagues. Lodge stood listening with the others.

Saigon had never known a National Day like this. Maximum security precautions were in effect, and the parade ground, an area of several blocks, was closed to the general public, so they could not watch the military parade. The United States showed its displeasure with Diem by not sending any of the planes or naval vessels it had provided in past years. But if there were few spectators, there were many Vietnamese troops, and would have been more if General Harkins had not intervened to limit the number of men brought in from other parts of the country.

Harkins sat for two hours with General Minh and General Don during the parade, "and no one mentioned coups," he wired General Taylor. And yet a coup had been planned for that very Saturday. Unknowingly, Harkins himself may have given the generals cause to change their plans.

Four days earlier, he had dealt the conspirators a rude shock when he complained to General Don, at a party given by the British military attaché on Tuesday evening, that two American officers had been approached by a Vietnamese colonel asking whether their government would back a coup. Harkins went on to tell Don that he personally was against a coup and had told his officers to forget about changing the government and concentrate on fighting Communists.

General Don, though horrified, had managed to register no stronger feeling than mild surprise. I thought we had stopped all that, he said calmly. But as soon as he could, he hurried to call Conein and summon him to a meeting.

They met the following day. Had the United States government changed its mind about favoring a coup? Don needed to know at once. Conein did his best to reassure the shaken general that Harkins had only expressed his personal opinion and did not speak for the government. (Harkins, in fact, had not known about the American contacts with the generals, and was informed of them now only because he had unintentionally upset one of the key plotters.) American policy was still not to thwart a coup or deny support to a new regime.

Then Conein asked for proof that a generals' committee actually existed, as Don claimed, and the Vietnamese said he would try to get permission from the others to show their plans to the Americans. But when the two men met again in the evening of October 24, Don reported that the generals' committee had decided against giving a written plan to the Americans. They would try to have something to show Lodge two days before the coup took place.

According to one of the conspirators, the generals had planned to act on October 26, using the troops assembled for review, because they had heard rumors that their commands would be reshuffled after the holiday to cut their links with one another. But on October 23, the day after the Harkins run-in with Don about coups, military security units went around removing live ammunition from the assembled troops. Although this was commonly done on such occasions, the leaders became frightened that precise information about their plans had reached Diem. General Kim and others talked about kidnapping Diem and Nhu if they came to Dalat or of arranging a meeting with the brothers at the headquarters of the general staff or at a Republican Youth camp and kidnapping them there. But they did none of these things, and Colonel Thao, who had planned a coup of his own, was again persuaded to hold off by Conein and General Khiem.

National Day, October 26, came and went, and Ngo Dinh Diem retired for the night in his austere room at Gia Long Palace still president of the Republic of Vietnam. But for how much longer?

General Harkins had cabled General Taylor his reaction to the news, the first he had had since Taylor's visit to Saigon, "that the generals' group is still in business": "Though I am not trying to thwart a change in government, I think we should take a good hard look at the group's proposal to see if we think it would be capable of increasing the effectiveness of the military effort. There are so many coup groups making noises. Unless elements of all are included I'm afraid there will be a continuous effort to upset whoever gains control for sometime out and this to me will interfere with the war effort."

Taylor responded: "View here is that your actions in disengaging from the coup discussion were correct and that you should continue to avoid any involvement."

Washington policymakers wondered who really was behind General Don and worried about the lack of evidence that the generals could carry off a coup. The conspirators did not have a spokesman to make their case in American government councils but they did not need one; they had Henry Cabot Lodge.

The ambassador was confident that they were engaged in a serious attempt to change the government and deserved support. In the unlikely event that all this was simply a provocation set up by Nhu, the CIA station was ready to have Lodge disavow Conein. But Lodge thought there was little danger of that. "I feel sure that the reluctance of the generals to provide the United States with full details of their plans at this time, is a reflection of their own sense of security and a lack of confidence that in the large American community present in Saigon their plans will not be prematurely revealed." The detailed plans Don was going to give him before the coup ought to clear up any doubts in Washington.

When Lodge later discovered that his part in these events was not universally approved at home, he tried to play down his knowledge of what the generals were up to in the last days of October 1963. But in this cable sent to Bundy on October 25, Lodge had wanted it clearly understood that Conein, the American go-between with whom the conspirators shared so many secrets, was operating under his direct orders. The CIA station "has been punctilious in carrying out my instructions. I have personally approved each meeting between General Don and Conein who has carried out my orders in each instance explicitly."

Lodge argued that the United States should not thwart a coup because "it seems at least an even bet that the next government would not bungle and stumble as much as the present one has." And how else could the people in Vietnam possibly get a change of government? he wrote, as though the Viet Cong did not exist. We should not be in the position of "setting ourselves in judgment over the affairs of Vietnam." That the Americans had been in just that position ever since they had decided to sponsor a coup in Saigon seemed to have eluded the ambassador.

Even Lodge did not believe that General Don was realistic when he promised a democratic election after the generals had seized power. But the ambassador was already thinking about the new government they would set up when they had overthrown the present one and the people who should be in it, a "very broad range," he cabled Washington, that "might include Tri Quang and which should certainly include men of the stature of Mr. Buu, the labor leader."

But what of Ngo Dinh Diem, with whom Henry Cabot Lodge set off to spend the day on October 27?

OCTOBER 27, 1963

The noise made by the helicopter was so loud they could not hear each other speak. Diem had a large pad of paper and was constantly writing messages on it to explain the varied scenery that stretched beneath them on the way to Dalat. "I did this," he would say. "I did that." This was Diem at his best, dedicated to reclaiming land out of the wilderness, knowledgeable and deeply concerned about conditions of life of people in the underdeveloped highlands. To Lodge, who had never bothered to get to know the Vietnamese president, it was a revelation. He found Diem very likable. "One feels that he is a nice good man, leading a good life." But not good enough for Lodge to change his opinion of this man he dismissed as living in the past, indifferent to people, and simply unbelievably stubborn.

A sumptuous Vietnamese dinner, and then, finally, Diem allowed himself to touch on the matter of the frozen commodity import payments. Lodge was noncommittal. But supposing the policy did change, would Diem open the schools, liberate the Buddhists and the others in prison, change decree law No. 10 that treated Buddhism as an association?

The schools were already being reopened, Diem replied; they were all open in Hue, and the Buddhists were gradually being freed. Changing the decree law was a complicated affair, and that was up to the National Assembly.

Diem raised the question of what certain Americans were doing in Vietnam. A CIA agent had talked to government people about threats to assassinate Lodge and said the Seventh Fleet would come in if such a thing happened. But it was inconceivable; the rumor had been started to poison Lodge's mind. Anyone who knew Diem had to know that the safety of the ambassador was of vital concern to him.

Then Diem went on to accuse the United States Information Service of helping opponents of the regime and the CIA of intriguing against his government. Lodge said superbly, "Give me proof of any improper action by any employee of the United States government and I will see that he leaves Vietnam."

Lodge spoke at length about the impact of events in Vietnam on the United States, where public opinion was all-important. You want us to do something for you, he said, but what can you do for us? Diem did not understand why American newspapers printed such biased and inaccurate stories about his country. Or how his former ambassador in Washington could be permitted to attack the Vietnamese government freely in the United States, where Chuong was carrying on a highly public verbal duel with his daughter, Madame Nhu.

Diem said with a sigh, "I made a great mistake in leaving such a gap in Washington." The remark was self-evident and Lodge did not disagree or pretend to misunderstand his meaning "that if [he] had had another kind of ambassador, the press and the politicians could have been cultivated so that Vietnam would not now find itself with such an unfavorable public opinion." For Diem, it was a sobering moment to have to recognize his own responsibility in entrusting the defense of his government to a man he had come to despise.

Lodge congratulated himself that this conversation in Dalat at least had persuaded Diem that the state of American opinion was very bad—which for a man cut off as he is, is something, he reported to Washington. (A curious observation from the individual who had done more than anyone else to isolate the Vietnamese president.)

At the end, Lodge said, "Mr. President, every single specific suggestion which I have made, you have rejected. Isn't there some one thing you may think of that is within your capabilities to do and that would favorably impress American opinion?"

Diem did not reply but simply changed the subject.

Lodge was well aware that Diem "does not react on the spot to any initiative that is made to him." He had used those very words himself at the time of the visit of McNamara and Taylor to Saigon.

But now, he chose to take Diem's silence as a deliberate refusal to make any concession to the Americans.

At the dedication of the Atomic Energy Center the next day, the two men went through their ceremonial paces as ambassador and president, and no words of any importance passed between them. Buu-Hoi in his capacity of director general of the Office of Atomic Energy had invited members of the American press corps to Dalat for the occasion, but the capital was rife with rumors of an impending coup, and the newsmen refused to leave Saigon just to meet a group of scientists, Vietnamese and foreign, and watch the opening of a research center.

DALAT AND SAIGON, OCTOBER 28–30, 1963

Lunch that Monday in Dalat was a formal affair, but afterward Lodge had a chance to talk privately with Secretary Thuan and tell him about his "long and frustrating" conversation with Diem on Sunday. To Lodge's surprise, he found that Thuan saw no reason to write off the day as a failure.

Thuan did his best to explain that Lodge had missed the real meaning of the hours he had spent with Diem. It could well be a beginning, Thuan suggested. He thought Lodge would be hearing from Diem again. "Perhaps so," Lodge reported to Washington, "but taken by itself, it does not offer much hope that it is going to change."

The gulf between the American ambassador and the Vietnamese president had never been wider, for Diem was highly satisfied with the day he had spent in the company of Lodge, a new opening in his relationship with the American. "At last, Mr. Lodge understands what I am trying to do," he told a confidant.

And in his own way, and his own time, Diem proceeded to take action. The day after Lodge filed his gloomy report to Washington, the Vietnamese president received a trusted Vietnamese diplomat at Gia Long Palace. Tran Van Dinh had been waiting in the United States for the Americans to accept the credentials of Diem's new ambassador, Do Van Ly, so that Dinh could surrender his post as chargé d'affaires in Washington and replace Ly as chief of the Vietnamese diplomatic mission in India. It had been close to midnight in the American capital on Saturday; Dinh had said good-bye to the last of the guests come to celebrate the Vietnamese National Day, when he received the cable ordering him back to Saigon immediately.

Diem greeted him on Tuesday, October 29, with a question. Why had there been so much delay in permitting his ambassador to present his credentials to President Kennedy? The State Department, Harriman, Hilsman, or both, seemed to be blocking the ceremony, was the reply.

"Why does Washington insist on having more military and civilian control and yet refuse to satisfy our request for more aid in building strategic hamlets and arming the self-defense units and the national guard?" Diem asked the man who had just come from Washington; then answered his own question: He believed the Americans wanted to send in their regular troops even though that would only play into the hands of the Communists.

He talked about Secretary Thuan and spoke of creating a new post of prime minister. "But not because the Americans want it," he said.

Then Diem proceeded to give his instructions and Dinh took careful notes. He was to return to Washington in three days, on November 1, and immediately call a press conference, to announce that "agreements have been reached between the Vietnamese government and Ambassador Cabot Lodge regarding the best methods to combat the Viet Cong insurgency. These methods concern more efficient use of military and economic aid, a better administrative structure at the national and provincial level, in short, changes in both personnel and policies."

Dinh was directed not to go into any detail but to say only, "The next few days will see the materialization of these agreements." If possible, he was to convey the same message directly to President Kennedy.

As soon as this was done, Dinh had to go immediately to New Delhi. Because of what Diem called "new developments," he was needed in India to deal with "the highest person" the Hanoi government might choose to send for talks. It seemed that the North was willing to discuss constructive matters such as trade relations with the South and stopping infiltrations. The fact was that the situation of the North was bad, with the government caught in the conflict between Peking and Moscow and under pressure from Communist China. Diem said, "While Hanoi wants a period of real nonalignment, we can profit from it, too."

He added, "In the nonaligned world, we have more friends now, thanks to the diplomatic bases laid by Professor Buu-Hoi in Africa and your work [as consul general with the rank of minister plenipotentiary] in Burma." To the diplomat, it seemed that this changed standing of Vietnam among its natural allies in the Third World had convinced Diem to agree to negotiations.

Diem warned the younger man against overoptimism and said the negotiations might be protracted. But he himself seemed optimistic.

Ambassador Lodge was about to make a brief trip to Washington for consultations. It would be a chance to discuss conditions under which the Commodity Import Program could be resumed, he informed the State Department. Diem would have to be made to understand it had been suspended because the actions of his government and the public statements of Madame Nhu and others had weakened the support of the American public. The Saigon regime must "abandon any exaggerated concern for its own tenure of office and concentrate on winning the war."

But when Lodge sat down to write his third weekly letter to President Kennedy that same Wednesday, October 30, it was clear that Diem had the best of reasons to be concerned about his tenure of office.

Lodge repeated to Kennedy Secretary Thuan's comment that his talk with Diem might have been the start of a dialogue, but personally Lodge doubted that Diem would offer anything significant. "In any case, whatever they promise to do would be subject to delay and would be difficult to verify."

Lodge was simply not interested anymore, if he ever had been, in what Diem might choose to do to save his government. The ambassador had news for Kennedy, "the most noteworthy event which happened to me personally" in the last week, and it was not that President Diem at last had come to him or that the two men had spent a day together. Lodge's news was his encounter with General Don at the Dalat airport on Monday morning, October 28, and Don's "highly secret statement" to him. There was really going to be a coup d'état in Saigon.

Does Conein have authority to speak for you, Don had asked. Lodge said yes, he does. Don told him the coup had to remain purely Vietnamese. Lodge agreed and wanted to know when it would take place. He could not give that information, Don answered. But there was no doubt in Lodge's mind that Don was entirely serious about the plot. "If I am any judge of human nature, Don's face expressed sincerity and determination on the morning that I spoke to him," he cabled Washington.

Conein met briefly with General Don that evening and, according to Don, offered the conspirators money and weapons that he refused. The American agent tried to pin down Don to an exact date and time for the operation and raised the question of Lodge's forthcoming trip to Washington then scheduled for October 31. Don replied that he simply could not be more definite. Lodge should stand by his announced departure plan so as not to awaken the suspicions of President Diem. If necessary, the ambassador could always return to Saigon.

Don did say that Conein ought to hold himself in readiness from the night of October 30 on. (So it could be as early as Thursday, Bundy noted in Washington.) It would not be later than November 2. There was no longer any question of handing over the plans of the conspirators two days ahead of time. Four hours' notice was all they were prepared to give. They would call Conein as soon as the operation was under way.

Lodge cabled the State Department, "Action taken with respect to the Commercial Import Program [sic] and the severance of support of certain elements under Colonel Tung have created a coup atmosphere and some deterioration in the economic situation characterized by the fluctuation of the piastre value, the disappearance of gold on the market, and the rising prices of consumer commodities."

The plotters would need money from the Americans. "Although there have been no requests to date by the generals for material or financial support, we must anticipate that such requests may be forthcoming," the ambassador added. Conein already had received three million piastres—some forty-two thousand dollars—on October 24 for this purpose, money he kept in a safe in his house.

"In summary, it would appear that a coup attempt by the generals' group is imminent," Lodge reported. "No positive action by the U.S. Government can prevent a coup attempt short of informing Diem and Nhu with all the opprobrium that such an action would entail. . . . U.S. will not be able significantly to influence course of events."

On Tuesday, October 29, General Don went to Nha Trang to see General Dinh (no relation to Tran Van Dinh) and review their plans. In August, when Dinh was named military governor of Saigon and his troops controlled the capital, this writer had asked a high official how President Diem could risk giving so much power to a single man and a general at that. "The family trusts Dinh," was the reply. General Dinh's devotion to the president soured when Diem refused to take seriously his ambitions for advancement. But that October, American intelligence sources were still not sure General Dinh could be relied on for the coup. It was said that an astrologer had been enlisted to keep this volatile young man—the youngest of the generals—in line. (Don in his memoirs made a point of denying the story in the Pentagon Papers and other American accounts that Dinh had only joined the conspiracy at the end. In view of the final outcome, General Dinh may not have appreciated seeing his earlier contacts with Diem's enemies so carefully detailed.)

Wednesday, October 30, Don and Dinh returned to Saigon and went to meet General Minh and General Khiem at a private club in Cholon.

They no longer had to worry about Special Forces in the Saigon area. Colonel Tung, their commander, had been upset and angry when told the Americans would stop paying his men unless they were placed under the effective command of the Joint General

Staff. Yet, even this ultimatum from the United States had not convinced Diem and Nhu to deprive the palace of the protection of the several Special Forces companies that the president retained under his direct control. But the ubiquitous Do Mau, director of military security, succeeded where the Americans had failed. He persuaded Diem and Nhu that the Viet Cong was building up its strength outside Saigon and the Special Forces were ordered away from the city to deal with them.

In Hue, it was said, Ngo Dinh Can became suspicious of Do Mau and Diem finally acted on his brother's advice and ordered his arrest; General Khiem deliberately held up the order. But even if this story was true, neither Diem nor Nhu realized in time that Do Mau had fed them lies to get loyal Special Forces units out of the way of the conspirators.

For weeks the diplomatic corps had watched the intricate interplay between the Vietnamese and the Americans with little doubt of the outcome, and waited now, well aware that a coup threatened. The Indian ambassador saw the imminent collapse of the hopes he had shared with French ambassador Lalouette for a political settlement in Vietnam. He grasped at the last chance to try to heal the breach between Lodge and Nhu.

At Nhu's request, Goburdhun arranged a private meeting between the American ambassador and the brother of the president.

The two men took up their dialogue of the deaf. Nhu said he would leave if personally asked to do so by President Kennedy, the leader of the free world, whom it would be impossible to refuse. Lodge saw this as a sign of contempt for himself, the ambassador of Kennedy, and seemed not to understand when Goburdhun tried to explain the Asian need to save face. When the meeting was over, Nhu told Goburdhun that he had tried to convince Lodge of his loyalty to the American alliance but did not think he had succeeded.

WASHINGTON, OCTOBER 29–30, 1963

At 4:20 P.M. President Kennedy met with the National Security Council to consider the prospects for a coup d'état in Saigon. The

CIA had prepared a map that showed the lineup of Vietnamese military units for and against a coup. William Colby explained that they estimated that fewer than 38,000 troops would be involved and of that number 9,800 were still loyal to the government and 18,000 were neutral, leaving only another 9,800 men to overthrow the Diem regime.

Secretary of State Rusk feared that if a coup were undertaken now it might lead to civil war. Rusk nonetheless favored a coup although some others present did not. All these senior officials of the American government took for granted that the Americans were free to intervene at this late date and tell the generals to call off their plot, and even side with Diem against them if they appeared unable to overthrow him. But if the Americans did decide to support the rebels, then, said Rusk, "we will have to guarantee that they are successful."

President Kennedy said that before a coup it always looks as if pro- and antigovernment forces are evenly balanced; the rebels pick up support once the action begins. Still, it would be silly to engineer a coup if the CIA were right and the opposing forces were about equal. They would have to find out what Lodge thought about it.

Vietnam was not a football game, General Taylor said. There were a few people crucial to the success of a coup and it was they who mattered far more than their numbers.

"The president asked that we try to find out who these key people are." These words would inspire incredulity if they did not appear in the official summary of the meeting. American officials had been putting pressure of one sort or another on the Vietnamese government and courting the Vietnamese army, for months, yet John Kennedy had never before thought to inquire what men were crucial to the success of a coup in Saigon, and on this last Tuesday in October still did not know who they were.

Robert Kennedy said the present situation made no sense to him. "To support a coup would be putting the future of Vietnam and in fact all of Southeast Asia in the hands of one man not now known to us." And an attempted coup that failed would be too great a risk. If it did fail, Diem would throw the Americans out of the country.

In response the men from the State Department argued that the war could not be won with Diem. Harriman admitted they did not know whether a coup would succeed. Neither Rusk nor Harriman bothered any more than did Hilsman (who was not at this meeting) about the ability of the generals to rule Vietnam after the coup. The question was not raised by the president. They all seemed to regard South Vietnamese leaders as interchangeable, provided they did not belong to the Ngo family. They were ready to support anyone able to muster the military strength to dislodge Diem from power and who appeared amenable to American advice.

General Taylor and Director of Central Intelligence McCone both suggested that failure was not the only danger inherent in a coup. Even a successful coup d'état would slow the war effort because of the inexperience of the new central government, Taylor said. The entire administration of Vietnam would be disrupted because the province chiefs who administered the country under the direction of Diem probably would all be removed.

President Kennedy did not understand why they should be removed. He evidently had not given much thought to the practical consequences that the overthrow of Diem might have in Vietnam. General Taylor had to explain that officials appointed by Diem would naturally be distrusted by the rebels, who would want to replace them with their own men. McCone agreed with Taylor. True, a coup that failed would be a disaster, but the war effort would also suffer from a coup that succeeded.

Bundy did not look that far into the future. For him, the most unfortunate development would be a three-day war in Saigon set off by an attempted coup d'état. Lodge was getting ready to leave for Washington. (Harkins would replace him if a coup began during his absence.) The time remaining to instruct Lodge was very short; there were uncertain days ahead.

President Kennedy did not know whom to believe; he could not make up his mind. It was decided that more cables should be sent out, asking for more facts about what was going on in Saigon.

Telegrams arrived in Washington reporting the disposition of the forces available to the generals, the names of various civilians who might join the government after this one was overthrown. Most of the plotters seemed to have coalesced around the generals; others still followed Colonel Thao: Lodge reported that if the generals moved first, the Thao group would have to join them with whatever limited forces they still controlled.

The coup d'état in Saigon might be days, perhaps only hours, away so far as President Kennedy and his advisers knew, and for John Kennedy the moment of truth was at hand. He had never shared Lodge's certainty or Lodge's enthusiasm about the conspiracy against Diem. Now, Kennedy was shaken to learn that General Harkins, the senior American officer in Vietnam, was still at odds with the American ambassador and had not budged from his support of President Diem.

Lodge had been instructed to show the cables about the generals' plot to General Harkins, who read them with rising indignation and sent off three angry cables of his own to Washington on October 30. "Last week I said I was out of the coup business," but Lodge had promised to keep him informed of the progress of the conspiracy and had failed to do so. Harkins was "shocked" at "how imminent Don's plan is to implementation."

He objected to Lodge's use of the telegram about not thwarting a coup that they had received by way of the CIA on October 6, to justify encouraging the plot of the generals and making that official American policy in Saigon. Harkins disagreed with the unfavorable reports on the military situation that Lodge had sent to Washington without his knowledge. And he reiterated his own opposition to a coup. Harkins, who knew the generals as Lodge did not, was only confirmed in his opposition by the latest news of their plot. "In my contacts here I have seen no one with the strength of character of Diem, at least in fighting Communists. Clearly there are no generals qualified to take over in my opinion."

Harkins was not a Diem man per se, he assured General Taylor. He saw the faults in Diem's character but favored persuasion to try to get him to change his course. "After all, rightly or wrongly, we have backed Diem for eight long hard years. To me it seems incongruous now to get him down, kick him around and get rid of him. . . . Leaders of other underdeveloped countries will take a dim view of our assistance if they were led to believe the same fate lies in store for them."

Officials at the State Department and the White House were not moved by such arguments. But Harkins was also of the opinion that the generals did not control the forces necessary for a successful operation against the government; and this opinion caused deep concern at the White House, where all the questions had narrowed, finally, to one—were the generals capable of carrying off a coup?

Lodge was notified that the Defense Department was dispatching a berth-equipped military aircraft for him that would reach Vietnam on Thursday, October 31, allowing him to stay on in Saigon two extra days, until Saturday, and still arrive in Washington on Sunday as planned.

The Americans had no power to delay or discourage a coup without betraying the conspirators to Diem, Lodge repeated to Washington. This medieval country had to be brought into the twentieth century. He wanted funds for the generals to buy off potential opposition. And if the coup were to fail, the Americans had a commitment to the generals from "the August episode"— that same episode Lodge and others at the State Department would later claim had no connection with the pending coup—to help in evacuating dependents.

Bundy at the White House asked for assurances that the balance of forces was clearly favorable to the plotters, that there was no danger of defeat or even of prolonged fighting. They could not agree with Lodge that it was too late for the Americans to delay or courage the generals. On the contrary, it was up to him to do just that if the coup, "in your best judgment, does not clearly give high prospect of success."

But that Wednesday, October 30, Bundy left no doubt about what the White House wanted in Saigon: "Once a coup under responsible leadership has begun, . . . it is in the interest of the U.S. Government that it should succeed."

American naval forces would stand by in readiness off the Vietnamese coast as they had during the stillborn coup of August.

An amphibious group and a carrier task group were directed "to take up positions quietly and inconspicuously" and "be prepared to support the American commander [General Harkins] with security forces or assist in the evacuation of U.S. noncombatants."

SAIGON, OCTOBER 31, 1963

On Thursday, October 31, General Don went to Gia Long Palace and talked with both Diem and Nhu. He inquired about the petition he and General Dinh had given Diem in September, asking for cabinet posts and policy changes. He was told that since everything had returned to normal there was no need for changes.

Don had another purpose in going to the palace that morning. Admiral Felt was due to arrive for a twenty-four-hour visit. He had not been scheduled to call at the palace but the conspirators feared the president might decide to leave the city on Friday. Diem was rather surprised when General Don suggested that he receive Felt but readily agreed to see him. And so, according to Don's account, an American admiral, the commander of the American forces in the Far East, would be used as a decoy by the plotters to keep President Diem in the palace, where they wanted him to be on Friday morning.

General Don was busy on Thursday with last-minute preparations for the coming action. That was the day that Buu-Hoi went with two Buddhist monks to see Ngo Dinh Nhu. They asked him to intervene with Diem to set free "all Buddhist dignitaries, laymen and students still under detention," and Nhu "promised to obtain from the president a favorable answer to this request."

The news was announced in an official press release. It would be a banner headline on the front page of the *Times of Vietnam* the next day.

This was awkward news for the generals. The Buddhist issue, which had been slipping away ever since the arrival of the mission from the United Nations, seemed to be disappearing before their eyes, and a convenient excuse for their coup with it.

If images of burning monks still represented Saigon to the public in the United States, the concern of Washington policymakers was with the war, and they were tired of Diem's resistance to American advice. Kennedy had said it best—what helps the war effort we support—and now the generals were ready to take over with no inconvenient ideas of their own about how the war should be fought—no great enthusiasm about fighting the war either, but the Americans did not know that yet.

In the early morning of November 1, a message was brought from Gia Long Palace to Ambassador Lodge, who was going to accompany Admiral Felt to call on the president. Lodge was asked to remain at the palace for fifteen minutes after the admiral took his leave. President Diem wished to talk privately to the American ambassador.

10.
The
Death
of a
President

SAIGON, NOVEMBER 1, 1963

Friday, the first of November. Officially, a half holiday in Saigon
as Catholics marked All Saints Day and prepared to observe the
following day, the saddest in the Catholic calendar, All Souls Day
—in French, *la fête des morts,* the Day of the Dead. French was the
language spoken at Gia Long Palace that Friday morning after
Admiral Felt departed, leaving Ambassador Lodge alone with President Diem.

   The admiral had met with General Don and General Harkins
before he accompanied Lodge to the palace. Felt was surprised that
Don did not receive him at Joint General Staff headquarters, had
chosen instead to come to the headquarters of the American military assistance command. Within hours, JGS headquarters was
going to be transformed into a rebel command post; dissident troop

movements had already begun outside the city. But Don gave no hint of that to the two American officers.

To Admiral Felt, Don appeared cool and collected. But the conspirators were growing nervous. Whatever the later conventional wisdom that the coup could not fail, the plotters then felt far from assured of its success. General Minh had begun to doubt they commanded enough support in the army to carry off a successful coup d'état. He would have preferred a simpler operation, like the one he had mentioned to Conein on October 5—assassinating Ngo Dinh Nhu. Minh had actually put an assassination squad in place one October day but was forced to call it off because General Don happened to accompany Nhu that day and would have been in the line of fire.

The final decision to go ahead with the coup had been made only on Wednesday afternoon, when the four generals met at a private club in Cholon: October 30, the same day Lodge had told Bundy the Americans could not possibly intervene to stop the coup even had they wished to do so. On this occasion, General Dinh had insisted that Diem's life be spared, and Generals Khiem and Don echoed his concern. General Minh apparently did not disagree.

Even this meeting had not dispelled the distrust among these four. It was awkward that President Diem showed such confidence in Dinh and Khiem; neither was quite sure he could count on the other not to betray them all to the president. Early that Friday morning, November 1, Khiem told Don that he had deliberately reddened his eyes to look as if he had been crying and had gone to Dinh to suggest they give up the coup because he did not want any harm to come to President Diem. It was to test Dinh, Khiem explained, who to his relief, had refused.

Unsurprisingly, Don had been very cautious that morning with General Harkins, who he knew opposed a coup. Also with Admiral Felt, who might have passed on anything he learned to the president. Don could not know that Felt was already privy to Lodge's secret cables about the coup. Felt had inquired of the ambassador how it was going. But Lodge was not about to risk a leak at this late date. "There isn't a Vietnamese general with hair enough on his chest to make it go," he said.

The admiral and the ambassador found that President Diem, too, was thinking about coups d'état when they arrived at the palace at ten o'clock that morning. After recounting the achievements of his government for the benefit of Felt, as he had for McNamara and Taylor a month earlier, Diem spoke with what Lodge termed "unusual directness."

Lodge quoted Diem afterward as having said, "I know there is going to be a coup but I don't know who is going to do it." According to Felt, Lodge told the Vietnamese president that he did not think there was anything for him to worry about.

Diem protested to Felt about the Americans' sanctions directed against his government. The decision to hold back aid could hurt the war effort; it had led to shortages of milk, of flour, too. As to the cut in funds for the Special Forces, Colonel Tung's men were already under the General Staff. They should not be blamed for the pagoda raids because the senior officers of the army had unanimously agreed on the need for military action to deal with the bonzes. (In August, General Don had admitted to the CIA this embarrassing detail that Vietnamese generals and the American officials who supported them later preferred to forget.)

The visit of Felt to Gia Long Palace was over. A simple courtesy call on an allied leader. Lodge had already explained to Bundy that warning Diem his government (and perhaps his life) was in danger would have made "traitors" of the Americans—to the conspirators. Admiral Felt left for the airport still unaware of the role he himself had played in their unfolding scenario.

Alone with Lodge, Diem informed him that Buddhist monks had told the visiting mission from the United Nations that they were victims of "intoxication" by the Americans. "I would translate the French word 'intoxiquer' as having been bamboozled by the Americans," Lodge wrote in his cable to Washington. In fact Diem meant the bonzes had been brainwashed.

Once again, as on that day in August when the two men had encountered each other for the first time, Diem complained of American agents conspiring against his government, and promised to give the embassy their names. "I said that I hoped we would get the names." He could be sure that if any American committed an impropriety, I would send him out of the country, Lodge replied with a straight face.

Diem wished Lodge to know that the universities would be reopened after the United Nations mission left the country; they had been kept closed, he said, because it had been learned that small student groups under Communist influence intended to throw hand grenades and plastic bombs during the stay of the mission.

The trip Lodge was about to make to Washington was very much on Diem's mind. He had a particular message he wanted the ambassador to convey to President Kennedy. It was the same conciliatory message on which he had briefed Tran Van Dinh, the diplomat who expected to see Diem later that day before leaving for Washington himself.

Diem hoped the Americans would understand how much he needed his brother Nhu. When Lodge reached the American capital, Diem said, he ought to go to see Colby at the CIA and former ambassador Nolting and talk to them about Nhu, "who did not wish power but had such a flexible spirit and was always so full of good advice that people would ask him for advice." If there was a difficult problem he could always find a solution. When Colby was stationed in Vietnam (Diem said), he had told Diem one day that Nhu should not live in an ivory tower but go out more. Nolting had agreed, and it was "due to their pressure" that Nhu had started going out and making himself known, and then people had said he was usurping power and the bad publicity had begun.

Lodge got up to leave. "Please tell President Kennedy that I am a good and frank ally," Diem said, "that I would rather be frank and settle questions now than talk about them after we have lost everything. Tell President Kennedy that I take all his suggestions very seriously and wish to carry them out but it is a question of timing."

By now, even Lodge realized a dialogue was in progress. And "this is another step," he cabled Washington. "If U.S. wants to make a package deal, I would think we were in a position to do it.

. . . In effect, he said, Tell us what you want and we'll do it. . . . See Nhu's statement on release of all Buddhists and students now in jail."

But all the pressures and the prodding, the promises and the threats, directed at an army formed by the Americans and dependent on them, were finally about to bear fruit. It was too late for Ngo Dinh Diem.

The report of this, Lodge's last meeting with Diem, was sent by ordinary "priority" cable and only reached Washington hours after news of the outbreak of the coup had been flashed to the American capital.

For the conspirators it began inauspiciously and with a suggestion there would be more bloodshed than anyone bargained for. The first victim was Captain Ho Tan Quyen, the senior naval officer, who was loyal to President Diem, and whose thirty-sixth birthday was that Friday, November 1. After an early morning game of tennis with other officers, he refused an invitation to celebrate his birthday with them at lunch; his children were alone; his wife was away, studying in Japan; and he went home. But his deputy came after him and persuaded him to change his mind. They set off for a restaurant in the outskirts of Saigon, but they never reached it. The young naval commander was assassinated by his fellow officer, a member of the conspiracy against Diem.

At JGS headquarters, General Minh was immediately informed of this murder that the generals had not planned. Fearing it would alert the government to the coup before it started, he ordered rebel troops to move on the capital ahead of schedule.

General Don was still busy with the Americans. He went to the airport for a press conference with Admiral Felt and General Harkins after Felt's call on Diem and waited to see Felt off. Harkins invited Don to lunch, but the general had other plans and hurried back to Joint General Staff headquarters.

He found Lucien Conein already installed there, with a direct telephone line to the American Embassy. Don had sent word to him during the morning that the generals were about to act and needed all the money he had on hand. "In case we fail, you're going with us," General Minh told Conein when he arrived.

The American had brought three million piastres and a radio that cut him into a special network so that he was in touch with the CIA station and with other CIA officers. Thus, Conein stayed in communication with Washington by telephone and radio, as he had been from the beginning, ever since he had first become involved with the coup.

"During the whole reporting period," Conein said, "through my own channels, I was reporting every one of the developments leading up to and including the time of the coup. Every one of the meetings, every one of the negotiations, the discussions that were held with General Big Minh, with General Don and General Kim and any other military leaders who were participating in the coup was completely reported to Washington, D.C., and I received many times guidance of what I was to discuss with these individuals and the limits of which I could discuss these problems with them."

The coup leaders as well as the Americans counted on Conein to keep open this link between them in the dramatic hours that lay ahead, and he did not disappoint them. "Lt. Col. Conein's close contacts with the generals' group were of priceless value to us," Lodge would cable McCone, "and [his] tireless reporting and transmission of messages has been of greatest benefit."

The generals gathered at the JGS, convoked by General Don and Colonel Do Mau. They had been invited to attend a luncheon at the Officers' Club. A few well-known officers were absent: General Dinh, commander of the Third Army Corps, busy preparing the assault of the rebel troops; General Cao, commander of the Fourth Army Corps, on duty with his troops in the Mekong Delta and loyal to Diem; General Nguyen Khanh, commander of the Second Army Corps in the central highlands, who had been given little advance notice that this was to be the day of the coup. The First Army Corps commander, General Do Cao Tri, was in Da Nang, where he had gone on Tuesday when he learned the coup was imminent, to put as much distance as he could between himself and Ngo Dinh Can in Hue. General Tri had summoned the province chief and other officials to a meeting in Da Nang so they would not be able to call out the Republican Youth and other mass movements to defend the government on November 1.

At the JGS, the coup d'état was announced to the assembled officers by the coup committee. One by one, the other generals declared their support; their statements were taped for later use. The commanders of the various services and special units had also been summoned to the JGS and their escorts disarmed. Colonel Tung, commander of the Special Forces, was taken into custody. The air force, the airborne brigade, and the marines all participated in the coup led by rebel junior officers; their commanders, who were loyal to the government, were held under guard at the JGS.

By 1:30 P.M., the airport from which Admiral Felt had departed two hours earlier was occupied by dissident troops. The telephone rang at the headquarters of the American Military Assistance Command at 1:45. General Don announced to General Stilwell, Harkins's deputy, that the army had decided to move against the government. When? Stilwell asked. Immediately.

The insurgents seized police headquarters, the central post office that was the site of cable and telephone communications with the outside world, two radio stations, naval headquarters. They moved into position to attack the headquarters of the Special Forces, the barracks of the presidential guard, and Gia Long Palace.

Other units were deployed to prevent a counterattack from outside the city, from General Cao's Fourth Army Corps in the Mekong Delta to the south. But loyal troops never arrived from the delta. Cao's attempt to come to the aid of the president had been forestalled by the conspirators, who placed one of their own men in command of the key Seventh Division that prevented Cao's troops from crossing the river to move on Saigon. When a regiment of the Seventh Division eventually arrived in the capital, it was to join the attack on the palace.

The Fifth Infantry Division from Bien Hoa northwest of Saigon, part of General Dinh's Third Army Corps, played a major role in the coup. When rebel officers had risen against President Diem the first time, in 1960, the colonel in charge of this strategically placed division had immediately occupied the airfield at Bien Hoa to keep it out of the hands of the insurgents. But that particular officer had been replaced, reportedly because he had incurred the displeasure of Archbishop Thuc, the president's brother, and in November 1963, the Fifth Infantry Division was commanded by Colonel Nguyen Van Thieu.

Thieu had not become a supporter of Diem until 1961. He had even postponed his baptism as a Catholic for years after his wife converted him because he had not wished to seem to be currying favor with the president. In 1962, however, he had been inducted into the secret Can Lao government party at the home of a prominent Catholic civilian in Hue. But Thieu was an eager plotter in 1963. Years later, he would tell a press conference that General Minh and Colonel Do Mau had promised him they were going to establish a stronger, anti-Communist government supported by the United States, with Diem brought back as a figurehead president. Perhaps, during the early hours of the coup, General Minh still actually believed that possible.

There were persistent rumors that Nhu had been planning a false coup of his own, to flush out the conspirators and when they had revealed themselves allow General Dinh and Colonel Tung to destroy them. Whether Nhu ever seriously contemplated such an operation is a subject of controversy. In any case, the events of that Friday afternoon made the question academic. Colonel Tung was forced by the rebels to order the Special Forces to surrender and they did, after a short resistance. Diem and Nhu discovered General Dinh had changed sides when in vain they called on him for support.

At 3:00 P.M., Diem reached General Don by telephone and told him he was ready to announce reforms and a new government. But he had said nothing of that to Don the previous day at the palace and now his words sounded as empty as the promises he had made during the 1960 failed coup when he had pretended to negotiate while waiting for General Khiem to come to his aid. The conspirators could not know that this time he spoke the truth—and perhaps they no longer cared. "Why didn't you tell me that yesterday?" Don said. "It is too late now. All the troops are moving on the capital."

Don called on the president to surrender unconditionally and promised safe conduct to him and his family. Minh took the telephone to repeat the offer and other generals followed. No one in that room at Joint General Staff headquarters would agree to any further negotiations with the palace. When Nhu telephoned Don he received the same answer.

At 4:00 P.M., General Khiem spoke to Diem to tell him that the palace was being encircled by military units. Diem refused to believe it and suggested that the generals come to see him and talk things over. Fighting had already begun between the insurgents and the presidential guard. Don ordered two fighter planes to strafe their camp.

Ambassador Lodge was at home, where he had heard the first machine-gun fire during lunch. At 4:30, he received a telephone call from President Diem.

Lodge would give different versions of this conversation afterward. Not only had he offered Diem asylum and the chance to leave the country, he would say; he had even told Diem he thought an important place could be arranged for him in the new government.

But on November 1, Lodge reported the following dialogue to the State Department:

DIEM: Some units have made a rebellion and I want to know: what is the attitude of the United States?

LODGE: I do not feel well enough informed to be able to tell you. I have heard the shooting, but am not acquainted with all the facts. Also it is 4:30 A.M. in Washington and U.S. government cannot possibly have a view.

DIEM: But you must have some general ideas. After all, I am a chief of state. I have tried to do my duty. I want to do now what duty and good sense require. I believe in duty above all.

LODGE: You have certainly done your duty. As I told you only this morning, I admire your courage and your great contributions to your country. No one can take away from you the credit for all you have done. Now I am worried about your physical safety. I have a report that those in charge of the current activity offer you and your brother safe conduct out of the country if you resign. Had you heard this?

DIEM: No. *(and then after a pause)* You have my telephone number.

LODGE: Yes. If I can do anything for your physical safety, please call me.

DIEM: I am trying to reestablish order.

Diem never spoke to Henry Cabot Lodge again.

Lodge was in communication with other embassies as well as his own that afternoon. The acting papal delegate at first doubted it was the American ambassador speaking when Lodge called and asked the Vatican diplomat to persuade "Diem," not "President Diem," to come to the American Embassy. After the diplomat had established that it was indeed Lodge he was talking to, he said that Monsignor Asta was away and he did not think any call he personally might make would change Diem's mind about not wanting to take refuge in the embassy of the United States.

Italian ambassador d'Orlandi had spoken to Lodge earlier in the afternoon. The Italian had been awakened from his siesta to find Secretary Thuan and the ministers of finance and economy in his living room with their bags. They had come to request asylum. Lodge told d'Orlandi that he intended to call Diem to offer the two brothers a flight out of Vietnam on an American military plane. But it was Diem who eventually called Lodge at 4:30; and no one during the eighteen hours that the coup d'état lasted would ever be able to find an American plane for Diem and Nhu.

The American Embassy cabled Washington that Radio Saigon had returned to the air at 4:50 with a communiqué from the armed forces: "the Vietnamese army has completed its mission and controls the situation in Vietnamese territory. The army is unanimous in rising up to demand that Diem resign."

They said they had acted "because of the difficult economic situation and because Ngo Dinh Nhu, while pretending to fight the Communists, is trying to contact them."

This declaration was well received at the State Department.

They had been alerted to the news of the coup at 2:00 A.M. local time; Hilsman had gone to the "operations room" to study the cable traffic from Saigon. Lodge's statement to Diem that the American government could have no policy in the middle of the night was disingenuous. Of course, the Kennedy administration in general and Ambassador Lodge in particular did have a policy toward the coup but it was one they could only admit to in top secret meetings and "eyes only" telegrams.

Hilsman and Bundy drafted one of these telegrams to the Saigon embassy: "If coup succeeds, acceptance and understanding of its purpose here will be greatly increased if generals and their civilian associates continue to develop strongly and publicly the conclusion reported in one of their broadcasts that Nhu was dickering with Communists to betray the anti-Communist cause. High value of this argument should be emphasized to them at earliest opportunity."

A laconic reply was flashed back: "Point has been made to the generals."

At 4:45 P.M., the generals brought their prisoner, Colonel Tung, to the telephone and made him tell Diem that he and the Special Forces had capitulated and the situation was hopeless. Later, Tung and his brother, his second in command, were taken away and shot.

General Minh warned Nhu that Gia Long Palace would be bombarded if Diem did not resign in five minutes. But Nhu was unmoved by threats. An hour later, Minh called Diem, who showed his contempt by refusing to talk to him. Furious, Minh called again to say they would be blasted off the face of the earth if they did not surrender.

Only help from outside the city could save Diem now, as General Khiem had saved him in 1960. The two brothers isolated at Gia Long Palace telephoned throughout the country, trying to summon troop commanders to their aid. It was hard to reach anyone, and when they did manage to get through they talked to men who had already changed sides and whose only message to them was "Surrender." They called in vain on the Republican Youth and other organizations to act.

Southeast of Saigon, at the port of Vung Tau on the South China Sea, a loyal counterguerrilla leader heard them. He had tried to extend his operations against the Viet Cong northward to Dalat and persuaded General Dinh to support his request, but Diem would not permit it. Now, when he wanted to help the president, he was cut off in Vung Tau with his men, unable to do anything but listen to appeals from the palace that went unanswered.

At the American Embassy, six blocks from Gia Long Palace, the heavy iron grille gates were closed. Three foreign service officers who knew Vietnamese were monitoring radio broadcasts. Conein telephoned with the latest news from the JGS; other Americans reported by radio as they circulated by car around the city. Embassy officers sent and received "flash" cables to and from Washington.

At six that evening, they heard the first rounds of the heavy bombardment of the presidential guard barracks. It was already dark when the tapes made by the generals earlier in the day were played on the radio and each general was heard to say in his own words that he supported the coup.

At 9:30 Lodge telephoned from his residence. He was about to go to bed as he usually did at that hour. Trueheart told him to go ahead; there had been "no change."

At the embassy, they heard the announcement on the radio instructing all members of the government to surrender to the generals, with a promise of clemency if they turned themselves in before eleven that night. Anyone who failed to do so would be treated as an enemy of the new regime.

At 10:30 the telephone rang. Secretary Thuan was calling to ask what the Americans thought of the generals' ultimatum. Could they be trusted? He needed advice on what to do.

John Mecklin, who was present, realized that Thuan's call "implied that he believed the United States was somehow involved in the coup and has special access to the generals, if not indeed control over their actions." Thuan was too intelligent and sophisticated, and too well informed, to believe anything else.

But for the Americans, as Mecklin wrote, "there was still the possibility that the coup would fail, and whatever we said to a man in Thuan's influential position could be held against the United States."

The American diplomat, who was well acquainted with Thuan, spoke carefully. "Mr. Minister, we only know what we heard on the radio." Thuan would not be put off with such an answer. The American repeated, "We only know what we have heard on the radio." But Thuan persisted; not for the first time, he expected more from the Americans than they were able or willing to give. He continued to talk and the diplomat responded with the same formula he had used before. They went on like this for five or six minutes until the American had to cut him off. "Good night, Mr. Minister," he said firmly.

He put down the telephone and reached for a cup of bourbon without looking at anyone in the room. Nobody spoke.

Colonel Thieu began the direct assault on Gia Long Palace at 3:30 A.M. on November 2. Thieu turned artillery, tanks, and mortars against the palace, and the presidential guard brigade that had already put up a fierce defense of its camp until forced to abandon it, fought on doggedly through the night.

At 6:45, it was all over. The defenders were ordered to cease firing, and the victorious commander entered the devastated building. But Colonel Thao, whose plotting had helped to bring about this moment, had been there before him.

Thao had made his way into the palace at dawn, to look for Diem and Nhu, and found them gone. They had left many hours before the start of the attack.

Thao hurried to report to General Khiem, who commanded troop movements before Gia Long Palace, and Khiem ordered him to go to look for Diem and when he found him, protect him. Both men knew that a faction of the generals wished the president dead.

During the long night, General Don had been told that the brothers might no longer be in the palace. He was impressed by the reaction of the CIA agent at Joint General Staff headquarters. "Conein seemed irritated by this news, saying Diem and Nhu must be found at any cost."

The brothers had departed after nightfall at about seven-thirty the previous evening. American reports spoke of a secret tunnel they had used to slip away, but they did not need a secret tunnel. The palace was not yet under siege; people were going in and out. Diem and Nhu had simply walked past the tennis courts and left the palace grounds through a small gate at Le Thanh Ton Street where a car waited. They were accompanied by Cao Xuan Vy, who headed the Republican Youth under Nhu, and Do Tho, Diem's young aide-de-camp, an air force lieutenant who happened to be the nephew of Colonel Do Mau, the archplotter who was director of military security.

Nhu had wanted the president to leave without him. Their chances would be better if they set off separately, he argued: one to the Mekong Delta to rally General Cao and the Fourth Army Corps to the defense of the regime, while the other could make for the headquarters of General Nguyen Khanh and the Second Army Corps in the central highlands. Even if one brother were captured they would not dare kill him as long as the other remained free.

It was sound advice but this was one time when Diem would not listen to his brother. Just now no political scheme was so real to Diem as the deep feeling he had for Nhu. According to one account, he said to Nhu, "You cannot leave alone. They hate you too much; they will kill you. Stay with me and I will protect you." Another story had Diem saying, "We have always been together during these last years. How could we separate in this critical hour?"

Nhu bowed to the inevitable; they would stay together until the end.

They drove to the Chinese quarter of Cholon, avoiding the main road that was held by rebel troops, to the house of Ma Tuyen, a leader of the Chinese community. He invited them in to rest and offered them tea.

Colonel Thao succeeded in tracing the brothers to Cholon, but he was too late. They had left the house of Ma Tuyen by the time he arrived.

Do Tho drove them to the church of Father Tam that Diem had frequented over the years. The young flier, a witness to these grave and historic events, died in a mysterious plane crash several months later, and his diary was kept secret until 1970. In it, he recorded the words of Diem to him as they left the house of Ma Tuyen. "I don't know whether I will live or die and I don't care, but tell Nguyen Khanh that I have great affection for him and he should avenge me."

Diem had decided to surrender. Do Tho would blame himself for not advising them to get away from the Saigon-Cholon area and save their lives. Instead, he had urged Diem to give himself up, saying he was sure they could rely on General Khiem and General Dinh and his uncle, Colonel Do Mau, to guarantee the safety of both brothers. "I consider myself responsible for having led them to their death," Do Tho wrote.

Diem telephoned General Staff headquarters at 6:20 A.M. and spoke to General Don. He was ready to surrender, with "military honors" from the troops. But the resistance at the palace had gone on too long, the rebels had taken losses, and Don told him his surrender had to be unconditional but assured him that he and his family would be safe. Diem accepted a half hour later after telephoning the presidential guard to cease firing. He wanted General Khiem to come personally and escort them back. Another call had been made to the junta earlier, presumably by Do Tho, to tell his uncle where they were. Yet when General Minh dispatched a party to pick them up, it started for the palace before instructions were received to go to the church in Cholon.

General Minh and General Don had asked Conein for an American plane to fly Diem and Nhu out of the country. According to Don, he personally had made the request two hours after the coup started. Conein would say it had been many hours later, between six and seven on the morning of November 2 during the surrender negotiations, when he called the acting CIA station chief. Ten minutes later, Conein was informed that there was no plane available and would not be for twenty-four hours, the time required to bring from Guam an aircraft with the range to fly directly to Europe.

Roger Hilsman had written in his memorandum of August 30: "Under no circumstances should the Nhus be permitted to remain in Southeast Asia in close proximity to Vietnam because of the plots they will mount to try to regain power. If the generals decide to exile Diem, he should also be sent outside Southeast Asia."

In that same memorandum, Hilsman had anticipated what he called a "Götterdämmerung in the palace": "We should encourage the coup group to fight the battle to the end and destroy the palace if necessary to gain victory. Unconditional surrender should be the terms for the Ngo family since it will otherwise seek to outmaneuver both the coup forces and the US. If the family is taken alive, the Nhus should be banished to France or any other country willing to receive them. Diem should be treated as the generals wish."

During the night of the coup d'état, the conspirators had come to Conein to tell him they were bogged down because a unit that was supposed to be in place was delayed. He had advised them, "Once you are into the attack, you must continue. If you hesitate you're going to be lost." He also had made it clear that the brothers must not be allowed to get away. They had to be found at any cost, he had told Don.

Roger Hilsman and other Washington officials had planned for so many contingencies. They had the imagination to work out a battery of selective pressures against the regime; the prudence to have American marines waiting beyond the horizon to safeguard American lives that were never in danger; the foresight to think of what Diem and Nhu might attempt from outside the country. But for the time when the fighting stopped and Diem and Nhu, still alive, were about to deliver themselves into the hands of the rebels, there was no plan; the generals were left to do as they pleased.

When Conein told him they would have to wait twenty-four hours for a plane, General Minh said, "We can't hold them that long."

General Minh was given to speaking frankly. On October 5, he had talked to Conein about assassinating Diem's brothers, Can and Nhu, and the acting director of the CIA station had seen a certain merit in the plan and recommended to Ambassador Lodge that the American government should not set itself irrevocably against assassinations that might prevent a bloodbath or a protracted struggle. The first reaction of the Director of Central Intelligence was that the best approach would be "hands off." "We would be interested in intelligence on any such plan," but "we could not approve or support assassination and certainly would not favor the assassination of Diem."

But the following day, McCone had directed Colby to draft an order to the CIA station withdrawing this recommendation to the ambassador so that "we would not be in the position of condoning an assassination and thereby engaging our responsibility therefore." Lodge was duly informed (and expressed his agreement). He waited some two weeks before instructing Conein to tell General Don the American government opposed assassination; it was sometime after October 20 that Conein told Don that he personally was not even permitted to discuss the subject. "All right," Don said. "You don't like it. We won't talk about it."

Now it was the early morning of November 2 and Diem was discussing surrender with the generals while American officials in Saigon remained carefully aloof. Richard Nixon was convinced that a secret order must have been sent from Washington that somehow implicated President Kennedy in the murder of Diem, and once in the White House he initiated an investigation by the notorious E. Howard Hunt into the murders. But with all the resources at his command, Nixon never could find this telegram, and there is no evidence that such a telegram ever existed.

American policy in these crucial hours, it would seem, was made more by omission than by commission. In none of the cables that have been declassified, in whole or in part, is there any message from Washington making the security of Diem (and Nhu) a prerequisite to American support of the generals. This writer has seen the working copy of one cable dated November 1 from Washington when the coup was already well advanced, addressed to the Saigon embassy. After approving names the generals had decided on for a provisional government, the draft cable emphasized the importance of the reaction of the American public and the Congress toward the coup in progress. "Realize you acutely aware problem this respect we face here and through wise counsel you doing what possible to assure Generals take right steps. . . . We realize this Vietnamese affair and Generals appear to know where and how they wish to proceed and may not seek advice or take it if requested. Nevertheless for guidance following are points we hope Generals will bear in mind." The second point was "Exile for the Ngo family."

Such a qualified and tentative recommendation, coming so late, could not be expected to restrain the fears and passions unleashed among the rebels by the coup. At this writing, more than twenty years afterward, no cable has surfaced to dispel the appearance of chilling indifference to the fate of Diem and Nhu that was epitomized by the failure to have a plane waiting for them.

November 2, about 7:00 A.M. General Minh had called a meeting at the JGS to decide what to do with the two brothers. Even now, after all these years, lacunae and discrepancies mark accounts of what was said and done by men who were there—still fearful that their part in these events be revealed. For Diem and Nhu were powerful and respected men, leaders and patriots; if Nhu had become a controversial figure, Diem was still held in high esteem by many of his countrymen, including some of the rebel generals.

Not all the senior officers attended this meeting. General Don left early to make arrangements for lodging Diem and Nhu at General Staff headquarters. There was no formal vote taken at the end; had there been a vote, a majority of those present might not have agreed on what was finally done. But a small group of generals wanted Diem and Nhu dead and they had their way. "To kill weeds, you must pull them up at the roots," said one general. General Khiem had promised Diem decent treatment when they had talked on the telephone earlier that morning, but Khiem made no move to prevent what was about to happen and did not try to join the convoy General Minh ordered to go to the church in Cholon.

Lucien Conein had left for his own house by this time, after his long vigil at Joint General Staff headquarters.

Two jeeps and an armored personnel carrier were dispatched for Diem and Nhu. The nominal head of the convoy was Colonel Lam, commander of the civil guard, who had joined the coup after it started. But the officer General Minh placed in charge was Mai

Huu Xuan, a sometime policeman in the French colonial adminis-tration, a veteran of the fight against the Binh Xuyen whom Diem had made a general. In addition to Colonel Quan, a subordinate of General Minh, two other men made up the convoy. In the days when it was not safe in Saigon to be too precise about these matters, they were described in one newspaper as "two officers whose name began with N"—Major Duong Hieu Nghia, a member of the Dai Viet, and Captain Nhung, General Minh's bodyguard, a profes-sional assassin who liked to keep a record of the people he killed by scratching a mark on his pistol for each victim.

To this man, Nhung, General Minh made a prearranged sign with his hand as they set off at 7:30.

The brothers waiting at the church were surprised that there was no car for them, that they were expected to board a personnel carrier. Nhu protested that it was unseemly for the president to travel in this fashion. They had to be shown how to bend their heads and climb into the vehicle. Then their hands were tied behind their backs. Nhung, Minh's bodyguard, was in the car with them. Above them, at the turret from which he could look into the car and fire his submachine gun directly at them, was Major Nghia.

The cortège set off. It stopped only once, briefly, at a railroad crossing, then proceeded to Joint General Staff headquarters. It arrived at 8:30 and the car was opened. The brothers were dead. They had both been shot; Nhu had also been knifed several times.

Colonel Quan threw himself on a table at the JGS, looking pale and sick. But General Xuan was very professional when he re-ported to General Minh. *"Mission accomplie,"* he said in French.

"Why are they dead?" General Don asked Minh.

"And what does it matter that they are dead?" was Minh's reply.

General Minh would try to fob off the responsibility for what had happened on others, profiting from the secrecy to which the conspirators had pledged themselves. If Diem and Nhu had not escaped they probably would not have died, he would say in 1971. It was Thieu who had caused their deaths by delaying the attack on the palace. (During that fateful night, one of the conspirators, Colonel Chuan, had heard General Don phoning Thieu to urge him to speed up the attack on the palace. "Why are you so slow in doing it? Do you need more troops? If you do, ask Dinh to send more troops—and do it quickly because after taking the palace you will be made a general.")

Thieu did become a general and was chief of state in 1971 when Minh tried to blame him for Diem's murder. President Thieu had the last word then and Minh, confronted with the truth, did not deny it. "Duong Van Minh has to assume entire responsibility for the death of Ngo Dinh Diem."

Conein returned to Joint General Staff headquarters at 10:30 A.M. on November 2. He had received a message from the embassy that President Kennedy had given orders to locate Diem. The generals informed him the brothers had committed "accidental suicide." They offered to show him the bodies but Conein thought it best to refuse. He would say that he had not wanted to compromise the United States.

A Vietnamese arrested because of his loyalty to Diem was visited at Joint General Staff headquarters by friends in the CIA. They told him that Lodge's policy was not to intervene in favor of people closely identified with the late president.

He said, "If you felt that President Diem was inefficient I can see that you have to replace him, but why assassinate him?"

"They had to kill him" was the reply. "Otherwise his supporters would gradually rally and organize and there would be civil war."

This was the same argument the acting CIA station chief had given on October 5 for not opposing the assassination of Ngo Dinh Can and Ngo Dinh Nhu.

Although General Minh tried to hide the extent of his personal responsibility for the murder of Diem and Nhu, he told an American months after their death: "We had no alternative. They had to be killed. Diem could not be allowed to live because he was too much respected among simple, gullible people in the countryside, especially the Catholics and the refugees. We had to kill Nhu because he was so widely feared—and he had created organizations that were arms of his personal power."

A civilian who was one of the few political figures to command respect among his fellow Southerners had no illusions about why the generals had acted as they did. Tran Van Huong had been a critic of Diem, a signatory of the Caravelle declaration who had been imprisoned for his hostility to the regime; he served briefly as prime minister in the post Diem era. Huong said: "The top generals who decided to murder Diem and his brother were scared to death. The generals knew very well that having no talent, no moral virtues, no political support whatsoever, they could not prevent a spectacular comeback of the president and Mr. Nhu if they were alive."

Henry Cabot Lodge failed to understand why Washington officials did not share his satisfaction with what had been done in Saigon. He thought it had been a "remarkably able performance in all respects." He was gratified and proud despite a cable from Bundy requesting an explanation of the deaths "that have caused shock here" and warning that the reputation of the new regime would be "significantly damaged" if people believed the assassinations had been ordered by one or more of its senior members.

During the night of November 2, the American journalist Marguerite Higgins asked Roger Hilsman, "How does it feel to have blood on your hands?" She was calling at the request of Madame Nhu, who was still in the United States and wanted the three children she had left behind brought out of Vietnam. "Oh, come on, Maggie," Hilsman said. "Revolutions are rough. People get hurt." Secretary Rusk dispatched an enthusiastic cable to Ambassador Lodge. "I want to express my highest esteem for your superb handling of a very complex and difficult series of events."

But President Kennedy took the news of the murders hard. He was seated at the round table in the cabinet room of the White House, discussing the coup d'état in Saigon with his advisers, when a staff member brought in a flash message from the Situation Room. It reported the deaths of the two brothers that the generals were still trying to pass off as suicides. Kennedy paled and jumped up, and General Taylor saw on his face "a look of shock and dismay . . . which I had never seen before" as the president rushed out of the room.

Director of Central Intelligence McCone, who also witnessed this scene, described it to a group of unsympathetic CIA officials the next day. Kennedy had insisted at meetings in the rarefied atmosphere of the White House that Diem should suffer nothing worse than exile but it seemed inconceivable that he had not realized that if the Americans unleashed a coup d'état in Saigon it could lead to murder. Apparently, Kennedy had persuaded himself that he could make and break governments in South Vietnam on his own terms. The deaths in Saigon "troubled him really deeply," according to Michael Forrestal, "bothered him as a moral and religious matter —shook his confidence in the kind of advice he was getting about South Vietnam."

Years earlier, the young senator from Massachusetts had made the acquaintance of the visiting patriot from Vietnam and had been impressed by Diem's single-minded dedication to the cause of the independence of his country. Now, the first Catholic ever to become a Vietnamese chief of state was dead, assassinated as a direct result of a policy authorized by the first American Catholic president. Kennedy was still shaken and depressed days afterward. A friend tried to rally his spirits by saying Diem and Nhu after all had been tyrants. "No," he said. "They were in a difficult position. They did the best they could for their country."

It was a fitting epitaph from the president of the United States.

On November 3, Henry Cabot Lodge had CIA agent Conein summon the leading generals to the American Embassy to brief him on the new situation in Vietnam and discuss their plans for the future. General Minh was busy with Nguyen Ngoc Tho, Diem's vice-president, who had joined the generals and would provide a semblance of legal continuity with the old regime. Minh sent General Don and his brother-in-law, General Kim, to call on Lodge. They did more business at the embassy in fifteen minutes than Lodge had done at Gia Long Palace in four hours, the ambassador reported triumphantly to Washington.

General Don remarked on Lodge's enthusiasm as he congratulated them on what he called "the masterful performance" of the generals. True, there was the awkwardness about the two murders, but Lodge suggested the way to handle that was to say that the fate of the Ngo brothers had "not only not been in any way ordered by them but was contrary to their wishes and was, unfortunately, the kind of thing which will happen in a coup d'état when order cannot be guaranteed everywhere."

Lodge in his euphoria seemed actually to have believed that this was true. "I am sure the assassination was not at their direction," he informed Washington.

He asked his visitors if they had any ideas about relations between the United States and the government of Vietnam, and reported that Don said "with a big grin." "Certainly and we would like to start getting milk and flour for free sale immediately [the American sanctions had forced the Diem government to restrict the sale of milk] and, of course, the restoration of economic aid."

They talked of the provisional government they intended to have, with General Minh president of a committee of generals and under them a cabinet headed by former Vice-President Tho as prime minister. General Don asked Lodge what he thought of Secretary Thuan. Thuan had turned himself in to the generals after his unsatisfactory call to the American Embassy the night of the coup. Lodge now praised him highly, his character, his intelligence, his understanding of other countries. But Thuan's talents did not commend him to the generals, who were suspicious of his American ties and his past loyalty to Diem. Thuan's vendetta against Ngo Dinh Nhu had in the end turned against Thuan himself. Had there been no coup, he probably would have become prime minister and perhaps might have had a chance to try his hand at long overdue reforms. Instead, his career in government ended with the deaths of Diem and Nhu. The new regime would place Thuan under house arrest.

That day at the American Embassy, the generals told Lodge that the father of Madame Nhu, the former ambassador to Washington, wanted a post in their government. He deserved one, after all that he and his wife had done to undermine the Diem regime in the American capital and at the United Nations. But it seemed that Tran Van Chuong and his wife had changed sides once too often; the generals told Lodge there would be no place for Chuong in the government because they did not want his wife in the country. Ironically, the coup that the Chuongs helped to prepare from abroad would condemn them to exile as surely as it did their daughter, Madame Nhu.

Lodge was pleased to learn that the freeze of the Commodity Import Program had been of great psychological importance in bringing about the coup d'état. The two generals thanked him warmly for all he had done to help them.

Before they left, he took them downstairs to see Tri Quang, who had been a guest of the American government for the past two months. The presence at the embassy of this highly publicized monk, a well-known adversary of the Diem government, had also been a source of encouragement to the generals, they told the ambassador, another sign of American support for their plot.

This first meeting with representatives of the new regime in Saigon was evidently a most satisfactory experience for Henry Cabot Lodge. But Washington officials were not pleased. The State Department cabled: "Reports of manner death of Diem and Nhu (shot and stabbed with gory details) carried in press headlines and causing considerable shock here. When pictures [of] bodies reach U.S. effect will be even worse. . . . We do not think there should be any suggestion that this is just the sort of thing you have to expect in a coup."

While John Kennedy grappled with the reality of these "suicides" that he as a Catholic had known from the start could not have been self-inflicted, American officials shrank from the prospect of negative and embarrassing publicity. It was bad enough that Madame Nhu had publicly blamed the Americans when the State Department denied they had anything to do with the coup. She had given vent to her bitterness and despair in a long statement accusing the United States of "cruel treachery," "treason," a "dirty crime."

Lodge was instructed to have the generals "emphasize extensive efforts we understand they made to prevent this result." And he was to repeat what he had already told Don and Kim that they could help counteract this unfortunate publicity by taking measures to assure the safety of the fatherless children of Ngo Dinh Nhu.

With Conein in attendance, Lodge saw General Minh and General Don the next day, November 4, and passed on these messages.

But he objected to the attitude of Washington officials, the "divergence between ourselves and yourselves on significance and merit of coup." At home they did not seem to understand what a remarkable operation it had been, so secret and so efficient. He quoted approvingly the opinion of an observer: if the military can perform like this when their hearts are in it, isn't it reasonable to assume they can do equally well against the Viet Cong? Lodge said, "We should not overlook what the coup can mean in the way of shortening the war and enabling Americans to come home."

He had found General Minh tired and somewhat frazzled. "Obviously a good and well-intentioned man." (Lodge had informed Washington a week earlier that Diem, whose murder had just been ordered by Minh, was a good man, too.) But will Minh, he wondered "be strong enough to get on top of things?"

After Hilsman read Lodge's report of his meeting with General Minh and General Don, he cabled the ambassador: "Urgent that Nhu children be evacuated from South Vietnam immediately. Separate DOD [Department of Defense] message instructing Harkins make his airplane available to the children."

That same evening, November 4, the three children left on General Harkins's plane for Bangkok, where they boarded a Pan American flight to Rome. They were accompanied by an American diplomat from the Saigon embassy, and the State Department directed that their uncle, Archbishop Thuc, be notified to expect them in the Italian capital.

They left one other uncle still alive in Vietnam. On November 3, priests from the Redemptorist Seminary in Hue had gone to the American consulate in the former imperial capital to inquire whether the United States were willing to grant political asylum to Ngo Dinh Can.

· · ·

Two separate emissaries from Ngo Dinh Can had approached the American consulate the day his brothers were killed. On that occasion the State Department instructed the consul: "Asylum should be granted to Ngo Dinh Can if he is in physical danger from any source. If asylum granted explain to Hue authorities further violence would harm international reputation new regime. Also recall to them that U.S. took similar action to protect Tri Quang from Diem government and can do no less in Can case."

After these first feelers to the consulate, Ngo Dinh Can delayed making direct contact with the Americans. On November 3, he telephoned General Do Cao Tri, the commander of the First Army Corps, who had carried out the repression of Buddhist activists in the former imperial capital. Some Hue people, bemused to see General Tri still in power, thought he must be plotting a countercoup with Ngo Dinh Can.

General Tri told Can he had nothing to fear, the council of generals had agreed to let him come to Saigon and would send him abroad. Can at this time was staying with the Canadian Redemptorist priests with whom he had taken refuge after the coup.

On November 4, a "flash" cable was sent to the Saigon embassy; the text of the cable had been received from the White House: "agree that harm to Ngo Dinh Can must be avoided. Believe we should make every effort to get him and his mother, if necessary, out of country soonest, using our own facilities if this would expedite their departure. In meantime, we should do all within our power to ensure their protection." As a statement of Washington policy this cable was unexceptionable, but in Vietnam it would mean only what the American ambassador chose to make it mean.

The morning of November 5, Ngo Dinh Can appeared alone at the American consulate. But General Tri had received new orders from Saigon and informed the consul that he could not guarantee the security of the consulate; Can was to be sent to Saigon immediately. All that Tri would promise was his safe passage to the capital in an American plane.

The consul cabled Washington that Ngo Dinh Can had to be

removed from the building and from the city as soon as possible. "Provided embassy Saigon concurs and confirms coup generals guarantee of Can safety you may at your discretion release Can to General Tri," was the reply. The consul telephoned to Saigon for instructions and was authorized by Lodge to do as Tri requested.

Ngo Dinh Can left the consulate that same afternoon intending to ask for asylum in Japan where in other times his dead brother Nhu had advised him to retire. He departed from Hue in an American plane accompanied by an American vice-consul, two American military policemen, and an American lieutenant colonel.

When Can reached Saigon, he was turned over to the Vietnamese military authorities on instructions from Henry Cabot Lodge.

Lodge explained his decision to Washington. He had found that the generals did not want Can to leave the country as they had let the children of Nhu leave, which should have come as no surprise to the ambassador. But General Don had personally given Lodge assurances of Can's physical safety and the promise that he would be dealt with "legally and judicially." "It seems to me that our reason for giving him asylum therefore no longer exists. I also consider that we would be subject to justified criticism if we attempted to obstruct the course of justice here, particularly as Can is undoubtedly a reprehensible figure who deserves all the loathing which he now receives."

Several days after Can left the former imperial capital Father Luan, the rector who had been dismissed from the university by the Diem government, made a triumphant return to Hue and was received by an enthusiastic crowd. Father Luan had joined the opposition to Diem after the outbreak of the Buddhist affair in Hue and his futile protests against the behavior of Archibishop Thuc. But the rector, who knew Thuc's younger brother well, did not regard him with loathing but with sympathy, enough to go to see the ambassador and ask his help on behalf of Ngo Dinh Can. In his memoir of this period, Father Luan recorded the promise Lodge made to him that Can would not be condemned to death.

Henry Cabot Lodge was still ambassador to South Vietnam when Can was executed in May 1964. By that time General

Nguyen Khanh had seized power in Saigon and it was reported by reliable sources that he had offered Can safe-conduct out of the country if he turned over the funds he was believed to hold abroad, Can refused, saying he had nothing left. General Don later suggested that even if Can had paid he knew too much about the illegal financial dealings of the generals and their civilian friends for them to have allowed him to live.

By the time Can was executed, his ailing and bedridden mother had already died. The diabetes from which Can suffered had worsened during the months he spent in jail and he had a heart attack during his trial. At sundown on May 9, 1964, he was brought on a stretcher into the prison courtyard and half carried by guards and two Roman Catholic priests to the post to which he was tied. He had asked not to be blindfolded but his request was ignored. He was shot by a firing squad before an audience of some two hundred spectators.

Henry Cabot Lodge would say the United States had done all it could to prevent the execution. Had Can only come to the embassy he would have been granted asylum like Tri Quang, Lodge said, but did not explain how Can could have reached the embassy from Hue. Lodge blamed the generals, who would not permit Can to leave the country. But he took no responsibility for his own failure to insist that Can be immediately evacuated from Vietnam on his arrival in Saigon and not delivered by the American government into the hands of his enemies.

Can's lawyers had taken advantage of the provision in the legal code that permitted an appeal to the chief of state for clemency; their appeal had been rejected. As the post of chief of state was still held by General Minh, he thus had the questionable satisfaction of ordering a third death in the Ngo family.

The editorial writer of *The New York Times* was impressed by the argument that Hilsman and Bundy had told the generals to emphasize during the coup. *The Times* saw new, improved perspectives opened up by their deaths. "Fortunately the new Vietnamese rulers are pledged to stand with the free world. It is significant that one of their charges against Mr. Nhu is that he tried to make a deal with

Communist North Vietnam along the lines hinted at by President de Gaulle."

On November 4, the State Department directed the American ambassador in Paris to make this point to de Gaulle, "our feeling that change in regime ends any thought in Saigon of accommodation with North Vietnam on basis of neutralization which idea previous regime may have toyed with." The deaths of Diem and Nhu were regrettable but had not been intended or ordered by the coup leaders. "We feel that generals committed to vigorous prosecution of the war and will reenergize struggle not only in military but civilian aspects. There [was] now far greater hope for success than was the case under Diem and the U.S. intended to support the Vietnamese effort."

For de Gaulle, the overthrow of Diem and the independent nationalist regime in South Vietnam was a blow to French influence in Saigon, an end to prospects for a peaceful settlement of the conflict, a personal affront to de Gaulle himself. The French president did not share the American view of the Hanoi government and the Viet Cong as pawns of international communism, and of Communist China as inevitably an enemy of the West. De Gaulle speeded up his plans to open diplomatic relations with the Peking government, which was recognized by France in January 1964, despite objections from Washington.

The American ambassador was also instructed to tell de Gaulle that the new regime in Saigon might improve South Vietnamese relations with Laos and Cambodia, the latter particularly; and to ask that the French use their influence in Phnom Penh to help. The Kennedy administration needed help in Cambodia. Prince Norodom Sihanouk did not pretend to be sorry that Ngo Dinh Diem was dead, but he was terrified by the murders in Saigon and believed the United States was responsible for them.

On November 20, two days before President Kennedy was killed in Dallas, the Phnom Penh government informed the American government that it would no longer accept economic aid from the United States because "any such aid, however small, would be considered an affront to the national dignity." That same day in Washington, in the Oval Office of the White House, and just before he took off for his Texas trip, Kennedy told Michael Forrestal he wanted him to make a trip to Cambodia, to reassure Sihanouk that the American government was not planning to have him killed.

Death—in Texas and Saigon—certainly would preoccupy Lyndon Johnson in the days immediately after he became president. The day after Kennedy's funeral—and before he moved into the White House—Johnson showed Hubert Humphrey a portrait of Ngo Dinh Diem hanging in the hallway of his house. "We had a hand in killing him," he said. "Now it's happening here."

When the first news of the fall of Ngo Dinh Diem reached members of the Viet Cong, there were some who thought it must be an American trick to catch them off guard; they could not believe that the Americans would allow the South Vietnamese government to be disrupted by a coup d'état in Saigon. But American critics of Diem and Nhu in and out of the government and the press were so gratified by the overthrow of the Ngo brothers that they did not think about the reaction of people who knew Diem's strength far better than they did—his Vietnamese adversaries in the Viet Cong and Hanoi.

Before long, some of the Saigon generals would make a second coup d'état. "They were gifts from heaven for us," Nguyen Huu Tho, the president of the National Liberation Front, said of the two coups. "Our enemy has been seriously weakened from all points of view, military, political and administrative. The special shock troops which were an essential support for the Diem regime have been eliminated. The military command has been turned upside down and weakened by purges.

"For the same reasons, the coercive apparatus, set up over the years with great care by Diem, is utterly shattered, specially at the base. The principal chiefs of security and the secret police, on which mainly depended the protection of the regime and the repression of the revolutionary movement, have been eliminated, purged.

"Troops, officers and officials of the army and administration are completely lost; they have no more confidence in their chiefs and have no idea to whom they should be loyal. . . .

"From the political point of view the weakening of our adversary is still clearer. Reactionary political organizations like the Labor and Personalism party, the National Revolutionary Movement, the Republican Youth, the Women's Solidarity Movement, etc. . . . which constituted an appreciable support for the regime have been dissolved, eliminated."

In the North, the Hanoi radio quoted the official newspaper, *Nhan Dan*: "By throwing off Ngo Dinh Diem and his brother Ngo Dinh Nhu, the U.S. imperialists have themselves destroyed the political bases they had built up for years. The deaths of Diem and Nhu were followed by the disintegration of big fragments of the . . . [government] machine."

From Peking, Mao Tse-tung looked back on these events early in 1965 in a conversation with Edgar Snow: "Talking of South Vietnam, Mao said American forces there were still relatively small. Of course if they increased they could help speed up the arming of the people against them. But if he should tell that to the United States leaders they would not listen. Had they listened to Diem? Both Ho Chi Minh and he (Mao) thought that Ngo Dinh Diem was not so bad. . . . After all, following his assassination, was everything between Heaven and Earth more peaceful? . . . Diem had not wanted to take orders. . . ."

November 6 was a Wednesday, the first Wednesday after the coup d'état, when Henry Cabot Lodge wrote his fourth and last weekly report to President Kennedy. He noted that "The whole trend of the new crowd is to have warm and cordial relations with the American people and government." He repeated what he had insisted on in cables to Washington before November 1: "There is no doubt that the coup was a Vietnamese and a popular affair, which we could neither manage nor stop after it got started and which we could only have influenced with great difficulty." Lodge would fall back on this line when questioned about the overthrow of Diem in later years. But in this cable to President Kennedy he went ahead to demolish his own argument:

"But it is equally certain that the ground in which the coup seed grew into a robust plant was prepared by us and that the coup would not have happened when it did without our preparation.

General Don as much as said this to me on November 3. Our actions made the people who could do something about it start thinking hard about how to get a change of government.

"Another indication of this was the statement made on the radio by Vietnamese speakers on the day of the coup that the Diem-Nhu regime had deprived the country of U.S. aid without which the communists would gain and that the army's coup would enable the country to get this economic aid and thus survive. This . . . was widely said by nameless 'authorized spokesmen. . . .'

"All this may be a useful lesson in the use of U.S. power. . . ."

Lodge concluded: "The prospects now are for a shorter war, thanks to the fact that there is this new government, provided the generals stay together. Certainly officers and soldiers who can pull off an operation like this should be able to do very well on the battlefield if their hearts are as much in it."

Epilogue

The mirage that American policymakers had pursued in Vietnam with such assiduity—of a strong and democratic government that would rally the population behind it and defeat the Communists—dissolved in the harsh light of autumn 1963.

John Kennedy was shot to death in Dallas on November 22, three weeks after the murder of Diem and Nhu in Saigon. Lyndon Johnson had been president for two days when Henry Cabot Lodge came to see him, to tell him (according to Johnson) that South Vietnam was going to hell in a handbasket. The Vietnamese will to fight seemed to have died with Diem. Their morale needed stiffening; soon Lodge would want the United States to bomb North Vietnam. Johnson was not yet ready for that.

Yet Director of Central Intelligence John McCone noted that

Lodge was still optimistic that day in Washington, when McCone himself made a gloomy report on the Vietnamese situation to the new president.

The ambassador went back to Saigon where he did his best to insulate the already weak regime of the generals from outside pressures that threatened to weaken it further. From the American newsmen, whom he had courted when Diem was alive and now feared lest they turn their batteries on the generals. From the French, too. When General de Gaulle issued a new pronouncement in favor of a unified and independent Vietnam, Lodge appealed to Washington to do something, anything, to persuade the French president to keep silent before the entire South was converted to neutralism.

In Saigon, the seat of political power had shifted from Gia Long Palace to the American Embassy.

The government established by General Minh and his fellow conspirators—Generals Don, Kim, and Dinh—lasted three months. It was overthrown on January 30, 1964, by General Nguyen Khanh abetted by the Dai Viet, whose plans for a coup had been preempted by the generals on November 1. At American insistence, General Minh was allowed to keep the title, though little of the authority, of chief of state, to preserve the illusion of continuity.

Maxwell Taylor and John McCone had understated the case when they had warned Kennedy that a coup would lead to a turn-over in province chiefs. The army and the administration were paralyzed by purges. Posts changed hands not just once, but two or three times. Some members of the Special Forces defected to the Viet Cong.

General Khanh disappointed the expectations of those Vietnamese and Americans who had looked to him to reverse the decay that had set in after the first coup. He justified the worst fears of others about his character, his judgment, and his ambition.

It was Nguyen Khanh who designated a new National Day for South Vietnam, November 1, a day that would be observed by the Saigon regime until it fell to the Communists. Neither Khanh nor any of his successors could ever find any other political legitimacy on which to base their rule than the destruction of the first Republic of Vietnam and the assassination of Ngo Dinh Diem and his brother Nhu.

The self-immolation of Buddhists did not stop with the overthrow of Diem: already within four months more had died than under Diem. Some died to proclaim their faith in Buddha, others for personal reasons, and the practice went on. "Of course, nobody writes about them any more," Robert Kennedy said in April 1964. Before, the self-immolations were "used to show that Diem was so bad but . . . I don't know what they prove now."

Neither Madame Nhu nor Archbishop Thuc, her brother-in-law, ever returned to Vietnam. Secretary Thuan managed to elude the surveillance of the generals in 1964 and escaped to France. Buu-Hoi went back to Vietnam on the occasion of the death of his mother from natural causes, then returned to the scientific research in Paris that he had never abandoned.

Ambassador Nolting resigned from the foreign service in protest against the American role in the death of Diem in February 1964. "That my decision has been influenced by my strong disapproval of certain actions which were taken last fall in relation to Vietnam, with predictable adverse consequences, I do not deny," he wrote to President Johnson. Roger Hilsman also left the government soon after Lyndon Johnson became president. Like Diem's former ambassador in Washington, the father of Madame Nhu, he would say he resigned over differences on policy. But that was not what Johnson said: "When I became president, the first man I instructed to be fired was Hilsman. . . . It took three–four months, but it was one of the first things I did."

Henry Cabot Lodge resigned during the summer of 1964 to participate in the Republican presidential campaign, then returned as ambassador to Saigon a year later. During his absence he was replaced by General Maxwell Taylor. When Nguyen Khanh overreached himself in a bid for absolute power, it was Taylor who passed the word to the other generals that Khanh was no longer acceptable to the United States, and in 1965 Khanh was eventually forced out of the government, and left the country, never to return.

A series of coups and attempted coups had started under

Khanh and continued after him. The structure of authority was crumbling in the South. The Viet Cong made huge gains. Buddhist leaders fanned popular hopes for peace.

In Washington, policymakers did not consider withdrawing from Vietnam. The mood in Washington was still for military action against the Communists, not political accommodation, and by General Taylor's account, "there was the memory of Diem to haunt those of us who were aware of the circumstances of his downfall. By our complicity we Americans were responsible for the plight in which the South Vietnamese found themselves . . . when the political turbulence in South Vietnam offered the United States an excuse to withdraw from its involvement, the realization of our role in creating the Vietnamese predicament was a strong deterrent to anyone inclined to make such a proposal."

Johnson ordered the bombing of North Vietnam in January 1965. Two months later, the first American marine infantry unit of thirty-five hundred men landed at Da Nang. The Americans were sucked into the vacuum created by Diem's violent overthrow and its aftermath. American troops, technology, and material wealth vastly escalated the level of warfare.

In 1966, Tri Quang launched a full-scale Buddhist revolt in the central provinces against the American-backed regime of the generals. Eleven Buddhists immolated themselves in support of his campaign. The government with the approval of the American Embassy sent troops against the Buddhists in Da Nang and Hue, and hundreds were killed; Tri Quang was jailed. He did not return to Hue until 1973, for the funeral of the aged patriarch Thich Tinh Khiet.

American officials no longer seemed to care that the regime in Saigon was neither democratic nor popular; all they asked for was stability—a government that would remain in power to supply the indigenous base necessary for the war against the Viet Cong. This stability was achieved with General Thieu, who became chief of state in 1965, and president of the Republic two years later.

During Tet, 1968, five years after the last Tet of Ngo Dinh Diem, the Viet Cong launched a major offensive. They failed to break through the American and Vietnamese defenses, and much of the Viet Cong organization was destroyed in the attempt. Yet this was a resounding political victory for the Viet Cong because it revealed their strength to the American public and broke the American will to carry on the war.

Later that year, President Johnson sent a negotiating team to Paris led by Averell Harriman to begin long drawn-out negotiations with the North. The war went on. It spread to Cambodia, secretly at first, with bombing raids, then openly, after a coup d'état in Phnom Penh.

The coup d'état that overthrew Norodom Sihanouk came in 1970, six years after he rejected American economic and military aid following the death of Ngo Dinh Diem. That decision turned against him the rightist elements that had profited most from the American aid program—the military, government officials, the rising business community, certain members of the royal family. These were the people, alienated by Sihanouk's policies, who supported the coup d'état of General Lon Nol.

There have been persistent reports that some Americans were implicated in the coup against Sihanouk because of his help to the Vietnamese Communists. He had permitted them to use Cambodian territory as a sanctuary since the early 1960s, having lacked the military strength to keep them out. But when he turned to Communist China to replace American aid, he went further: he acceded to the personal request of Chou En-lai to allow Chinese ships to use the port of Kompong Som (then Sihanoukville) to supply arms and munitions to the Vietnamese Communists on both sides of the Cambodian-Vietnamese border. Sihanouk kept one-third of what the Chinese brought for his own army. "That way I didn't have to provide in my budget for military equipment, arms and ammunition," he would explain. The rest was transported by the Royal Cambodian Army to the Vietnamese Communists (who paid the Khmer military for this service), on a road that had been financed by the American economic aid program.

Sihanouk was out of the country when General Lon Nol seized the government in March 1970. With a pro-American, anti-Communist regime installed in Phnom Penh, Hanoi sent its troops against the Khmer army. American forces came to the aid of the Lon Nol government, and the war engulfed the country.

Thousands of Khmer Communists who had gone to North Vietnam after the Geneva Accords in 1954, and remained there, returned to Cambodia to fight alongside the Vietnamese against Lon Nol. These Communists clashed with other, more extremist Khmer revolutionaries, who seized control of the resistance movement. Brutal and xenophobic, they would unleash a reign of terror against which even the horrors of the war in Vietnam paled, so that the Khmer Rouge would be condemned before the world for practicing genocide against their own people.

On November 2, 1971, several thousand people gathered at the grave of Ngo Dinh Diem in Saigon for religious services in his memory. A yellow-robed Buddhist monk offered a Buddhist "remembrance" and Catholic prayers were said in Latin. Banners proclaimed Diem a savior of the South. The previous day, All Saints Day, Catholics had come to the cemetery from the refugee villages outside Saigon, carrying portraits of the slain president.

This was the third year that public services had been allowed to mark Diem's death, the first year they had been held with government approval. Madame Thieu, the wife of the president, who came to the grave, was seen crying at a requiem mass for Diem held at the Saigon basilica. Several members of the cabinet were also at the grave. A general gave the eulogy. President Diem, he said, had died because he had resisted the domination of foreigners and their schemes to bring great numbers of troops to Vietnam and widen the war that was going to destroy North and South. The speaker evoked a more peaceful time when there had been at most 16,000 American military advisers in Vietnam, and few, if any, of the assembled Vietnamese doubted that if Diem had lived he would never have allowed the Americans to bring 500,000 men to fight on their soil and ravage the country.

The Saigon regime never regained the independence it had lost with Diem. The American presence corroded the social fabric, and corruption was all-pervasive. The war effort was controlled by

Americans; and it was the Americans, not the Vietnamese, who decided the time had come to seek an agreement with the Hanoi regime. General Don, who had become a senator, now claimed that the coup against Diem had been intended to end the war and adopt a policy of nonalignment with any of the great powers! He noted that the Communist countries "voluntarily removed themselves . . . completely from the Paris peace talks and left them entirely in the hands of the North. Meanwhile, South Vietnam, in the eyes of the entire world, can hardly claim the leading role. . . ."

The day was long past when Americans blamed everything that went wrong in the South on Diem; and much of the American press had shifted its dislike of the dead leader and his brother to non-Communist Vietnamese in general.

During the presidency of Richard Nixon, the Americans gradually withdrew their troops, leaving the fighting to the Vietnamese. Under Nixon relations were opened with Communist China, and in the end Washington came to see South Vietnam as just another piece of real estate that the United States no longer needed. This was the point at which the Nixon administration abandoned the Saigon government to Hanoi.

Although the Thieu regime had its own delegation at the Paris Peace Conference—as did the provisional government established by the National Liberation Front—it was left with no choice but to accept the cease-fire agreement reached by the Nixon administration and the Hanoi government. The accord signed in Paris in January 1973 allowed Hanoi's divisions to remain in the South. The only protection for the Saigon regime were promises from Nixon to intervene in case of North Vietnamese aggression. Congress, however, made clear its opposition to any further American military intervention in Indochina. In any case, the Watergate scandal intervened, and Richard Nixon was no longer president when the Hanoi leaders launched their offensive against the Saigon government in January 1975.

The Southern army was demoralized without the American direction it had learned to depend on, and unable to survive without American military and economic assistance, which was not forthcoming despite appeals from Saigon.

The interval between the signature of the Paris cease-fire accord and the collapse of the non-Communist South had lasted less than two and a half years.

Thirteen Communist divisions were closing in on Saigon in April when officials at the American Embassy decided that General Minh should become chief of state once again. For the past several years, the general had been speaking out in favor of peaceful coexistence between North and South. French officials chose to believe against all reason that the Hanoi regime would still settle for that. The French ambassador convinced his gullible American colleague that with General Minh a peace could be negotiated even then with the North. But first, it was up to the Americans to dislodge Thieu from power.

The long shadow of the events that marked the death of the first Republic of Vietnam twelve years before touched the car that drove through the outskirts of Saigon after curfew during the night of April 25, 1975. A CIA agent was at the wheel; another CIA officer accompanied him. They did not know who or what might lie in wait for their passenger, General Thieu, until four days earlier president of the Republic. Thieu had finally bowed to American pressure and resigned in favor of the vice-president, Tran Van Huong.

Thieu was lucky; he escaped the fate of Diem and Nhu. This time an American plane was waiting when his CIA escort brought him to Tan Son Nhut airport, and the American ambassador was on hand to bid him farewell before he boarded the aircraft that would take him to safety.

Three days later, General Minh took office. He gave the American ambassador twenty-four hours to get everyone attached to the American Defense Attaché's Office—the vestigial survival of the American Military Advisory Command—out of the country. The new government broadcast an appeal to all Americans to leave Vietnam.

Ambassador Graham Martin, the successor of Lodge and other

would-be proconsuls, made an inglorious escape by helicopter from the roof of his embassy, like many other Americans. General Don, who had only just joined Minh's cabinet as minister of defense, was among the well-connected Vietnamese for whom the Americans found places in their overcrowded aircraft. Countless thousands of other Vietnamese, desperate to leave because they, too, had collaborated with the Americans, were left behind.

On April 30, North Vietnamese tanks entered the city and drew up in a half-circle in front of the palace. General Minh was waiting for them. He had nothing left to offer except unconditional surrender.

And the city for which the men in Hanoi had sacrificed and fought, planned and intrigued, for thirty years became the prize and the symbol of their victory—Saigon no longer, but Ho Chi Minh City.

Notes

The literature on the history, politics, and culture of Vietnam is extensive, and the people with whom I have discussed these matters —many of them protagonists in the history of the first Republic of Vietnam—are far too numerous to be listed. Only conversations, documents, and books directly related to events in 1963, or essential to an understanding of their background, are cited here. Sometimes reference is made to my conversations with one person over the years; I have noted when a fact or opinion can be traced to a particular conversation or interview and have specified when someone else was the interviewer. In some instances I am bound by a promise of confidentiality, and that has been indicated.

The American documents declassified in whole or in part under the Freedom of Information Act and Executive Order

12065, now superseded by Executive Order 12356, have been invaluable in the writing of this book. To simplify these notes, the technical designation *Deptel* is used for telegrams from the State Department and *Embtel* for telegrams from the embassy to the State Department. Unless otherwise noted, these telegrams were sent to and from the American Embassy in Saigon.

1: THE PRESIDENT'S BIRTHDAY

8–9   instructions from President . . . Kennedy: Frederick E. Nolting, "The Turning Point," *Foreign Service Journal* (July 1968), p. 20.

9   Diem was no dictator: Embtel 70, July 14, 1961.

10   The previous summer: Conversation with Roger Lalouette, Paris, June 1970.

10   "If the French would . . .": Ibid.

11   the man he replaced had been kidnapped: Colonel Hoang Thuy Nam was murdered in October 1961. His successor, Colonel Nguyen Van An, had been serving as acting chief of the liaison mission.

11   evacuate its members: Hanoi radio broadcasts, Foreign Broadcast Information Service (FBIS), *Daily Report: Asia and Pacific* (Washington, D.C.), May 14, 15, 19, 21, 22, 1958.

11   doctors of the Southern: Source for this is Dr. Nguyen Ba Giao.

11   Rice was sold unofficially: A series of secret telegrams from President Diem to his brother Ngo Dinh Can, giving him full power to sell rice to the North, was made public during the trial of Can. The first telegram was dated September 5, 1957; the last in the series was dated September 7, 1959. *Hoa Binh* (Saigon), August 1971.

14   two conservative Vietnamese nationalists: Interview with Vu Hong Khanh and Pham Thai of the VNQDD in Paris,

January 3, 1970. Vu Hong Khanh, VNQDD leader, was one of the two nationalists who vouched for Ho Chi Minh. The other was Nguyen Hai Than.

15   American officials refused: Source is Buu-Hoi, one of the Vietnamese who called at the embassy.

16   Americans arrived to join: "Some of us may have suspected that in the future the weapons and training might be used against the French, but no one dreamed that they would ever be used against Americans," Archimedes L. A. Patti, *Why Viet Nam?* (Berkeley: University of California Press, 1980), p. 129. Patti, a major in the Office of Strategic Services, arrived in Hanoi on August 22, 1945.

17   The nationalist politicians: Interview with Vu Hong Khanh and Pham Thai.

17   did manage to seize territory: Ibid. Viet Minh forces drove them out of the citadel at Mon Cay and seized the arms and machine guns stored there. In the border province of Ha Giang, the Viet Minh captured two hundred important VNQDD cadres.

18   The Viet Minh leaders: Vo Nguyen Giap, *Unforgettable Days* (Hanoi: Foreign Languages Publishing House, 1975), p. 19.

20   Their praise: *Times of Vietnam,* January 4, 1963.

20   "The Diem regime . . .": Conversation with Nguyen Dinh Thuan, Paris, December 1969.

21   In later years he would wonder: Ibid.

21   knowledgeable Americans dismissed him: Maxwell D. Taylor, *Swords and Plowshares* (New York: W.W. Norton, 1972), p. 248; Paul Kattenberg, *The Vietnam Trauma in American Foreign Policy, 1945–1975* (New Brunswick, N.J.: Transaction Books, 1980), p. 118.

22   in the small town of Tra Bong: *Le Courrier du Vietnam* (Hanoi), September 2, 1967.

22–23 For the regroupment of Viet Minh forces and their activities in the South, see the Communist radio broadcasts for this period, FBIS, *Daily Report: Asia and Pacific.*

23   . . . to make ready for the coming struggle: "The Party left in the South many cadres to engage in secret work. In October 1954, the Nam Bo Party Committee was set up to lead the revolutionary movement there. The Party Committees in districts and provinces were reorganized. . . ." Commission for the Study of the History of the Party, *Fifty Years of Activities of the Communist Party of Vietnam* (Hanoi: Foreign Languages Publishing House, 1980), p. 140.

2: THE EAGER AMERICANS

27   a message from President Diem: Letter to President Kennedy, June 9, 1961, *United States–Vietnam Relations, 1945–1967* [The Pentagon Papers, Department of Defense edition] (Washington, D.C.: U.S. Government Printing Office, 1971), Book 11, p. 167.

27–28   "We have not become accustomed": Letter to President Kennedy, May 16, 1961, ibid., p. 155.

28   "the key to the entire area": Memorandum of Conference on January 19, 1961, ibid., Book 10, p. 1362.

28   South Vietnam was seen: Maxwell D. Taylor, *Swords and Plowshares* (New York: W.W. Norton, 1972), p. 223.

28   ". . . had little bearing on the situation": Ibid.

29   G. M. Pushkin: "Whether indeed Pushkin ever informed his own Government of his compact with Harriman will probably never be known for certain. Pushkin died of a heart attack not long after the Laos talks, and Moscow has never admitted to any knowledge of the arrangement." Chester L. Cooper, *The Lost Crusade* (New York: Dodd, Mead & Co., 1970), p. 190.

29   approached the delegation from Hanoi: William H. Sullivan recorded interview by Dennis J. O'Brien, June 16, August 5, 1970, p. 32, John F. Kennedy Library Oral History Project.

30   under pressure from the Soviet Union: When Harriman, years later, was negotiating with the North Vietnamese in Paris, they told him that the provision against infiltrating into the South through Laos had been forced on them by the Soviets and they would not abide by something the Soviets had forced down their throats. Roger Hilsman recorded interview by Dennis J. O'Brien, August 14, 1970, p. 25, John F. Kennedy Library Oral History Project.

31   the meeting . . . was "stormy": Frederick E. Nolting, *U.S. News & World Report* (July 26, 1971).

31   "They took a violent dislike": Conversation with Nguyen Dinh Thuan, Paris, December 1969.

31   ". . . Harriman Memorial Highway": Frederick E. Nolting, "The Turning Point," *Foreign Service Journal* (July 1968), p. 19.

31   Harriman went to Moscow: Sullivan, Oral History, p. 27.

32   "It became an emotional": Robert F. Kennedy recorded interview by John Bartlow Martin, April 30, 1964, p. 393, John F. Kennedy Library Oral History Project.

32   ". . . and in fact, his advice": Ibid., February 29, 1964, pp. 121–22.

32   Khrushchev's speech: The schism between China and the Soviet Union was not yet understood in Washington at this time.

32   Kennedy himself . . . "repeatedly emphasized": Taylor, *Swords and Plowshares,* p. 202.

32–33 In May 1961, the president had ordered: National Security Action Memorandum No. 52, May 11, 1961, as cited in Department of Defense, *United States–Vietnam Relations: 1945–1967,* Book 11, p. 136.

33   Laos was a special case: Deptel 28, July 9, 1962.

34   Lansdale's report, *United States–Vietnam Relations,* Book 11, pp. 1–12.

34   Diem wanted his old friend: Lansdale did serve as a member of the Taylor mission to Vietnam that fall. But afterward he was assigned to Operation MONGOOSE, the

supersecret operation ordered by Kennedy to try to oust Castro, which proved ill suited to his special talents (and where he outraged a CIA colleague by putting into writing a program that included "liquidation of leaders"). See Senate Select Committee to Study Governmental Operations, *Alleged Assassination Plots Involving Foreign Leaders* (Washington, D.C.: U.S. Government Printing Office, 1975), p. 162.

34   "This is the worst one": Walt W. Rostow, An NBC News White Paper. Vietnam Hindsight Part I: How It Began, December 21, 1971. Transcript.

34   Nolting remarked . . .: "Turning Point," p. 19.

34–35 In his report to Kennedy: *United States–Vietnam Relations,* p. 164. When Johnson became president of the United States he did not forget his esteem for the Vietnamese president who was murdered in Saigon in 1963. Robert Kennedy, trying to explain the rancor of his brother's successor against Averell Harriman, said, "I think it goes back somewhat to the dislike Harriman had of Diem," Robert Kennedy Oral History, p. 125.

35   "We just can't . . .": John Kenneth Galbraith, NBC White Paper.

35   Ever since May: On May 10, the Joint Chiefs of Staff recommended that Diem be encouraged to request the immediate deployment of "appropriate U.S. forces to South Vietnam . . . in view of the new threat now posed by the Laotian situation," *United States–Vietnam Relations,* Book 2, IV.B.1, p. 43.

35   When the president met: Gilpatric memorandum for record, ibid., Book 11, pp. 322–23.

35   . . . interdepartmental mission headed by . . .: Walt Rostow, deputy special assistant to the president for national security, was a member of the mission that included representatives of the State Department, AID, the Department of Defense, the Joint Chiefs of Staff, and the Central Intelligence Agency.

35–36   Taylor was instructed: *United States–Vietnam Relations,* p. 327.

36   Diem seemed ready to accept: "The report Nolting sent on Taylor's final meeting with Diem . . . leaves the impression that Diem was still not really anxious to get American troops deeply involved in his country. . . . Taylor came to the conclusion that some sort of ground troop commitment was needed mainly because of what he heard from Diem's colleagues and his military people, rather than from Diem himself," ibid., Book 2, IV.B.1, p. 112.

36–37   ". . . was prepared to join": Deptel 619, November 15, 1961.

37   Nolting was instructed: Ibid.

37   "Vietnam does not want . . .": Embtel 678, November 18, 1961.

37–38   Vice-President Tho . . . : Interview of Arthur J. Dommen with Nguyen Ngoc Tho in Saigon, December 6, 1969.

38   Nolting reported to Washington: Embtel 687, November 22, 1961.

38   "Should he not do so": Embtel 1151, December 4, 1960.

38   on December 4, Nolting cabled: Embtel 756, December 4, 1961.

39   . . . and "began to . . .": Taylor, *Swords and Plowshares,* pp. 251, 257. General Taylor became chairman of the Joint Chiefs of Staff in October 1962.

39   "The debate in the Kennedy administration": Roger Hilsman, *To Move a Nation* (Garden City, N.Y.: Doubleday, 1967), p. 565.

39   . . . a "political approach": Ibid., p. 426.

39   ". . . protect the people . . .": Hilsman Oral History, pp. 21–22.

39–40   "Perhaps the highest . . .": William Colby, *Honorable Men* (New York: Simon & Schuster, 1978), p. 175.

40–41   Yet, ". . . hundreds of thousands": Dennis J. Duncanson, *Government and Revolution in Vietnam* (London: Oxford University Press, 1968), p. 339.

41 ". . . a relatively clearheaded conclusion": Nguyen Chi Thanh, "Who Will Win in South Vietnam?" *Hoc-Tap* (July 1963), translated in *Vietnamese Studies* no. 1 (Hanoi, 1964), p. 15. A version of this article published as a pamphlet in Peking (Foreign Languages Press, 1963) and circulated in the West omits this significant passage.

41 "The point is . . .": Hilsman Oral History, pp. 21, 27.

3: WHY CAN'T A PUPPET ACT LIKE A PUPPET?

43 ". . . like it always is . . .": David Halberstam, *The Making of a Quagmire* (New York: Random House, 1965), p. 154.

43 Another officer who was respected: Interview with Lt. Col. Jonathan (Fred) Ladd in Washington, May 1974.

43 "I consider it a victory": Halberstam, *Quagmire,* p. 158.

44 "The American press representatives": Memorandum for the President, February 1963, in *The Pentagon Papers* (Gravel Edition) (Boston: Beacon Press, 1971), vol. 2, p. 724.

44 ". . . perhaps one of only five or six": Halberstam, *Quagmire,* p. 319.

44 not even "a strong . . .": Ibid., p. 72.

44–45 "Whether they intended . . .": Pierre Salinger, *With Kennedy* (Garden City, N.Y.: Doubleday, 1966), p. 325.

46 a man . . . "revered . . .": William O. Douglas, *North from Malaya* (New York: Doubleday, 1954), pp. 180–81.

46–47 "I wanted some important": William O. Douglas recorded interview by John F. Stewart, November 9, 1967, pp. 15, 16, John F. Kennedy Library Oral History Project. The meeting is described in U.S. Department of State, *Foreign Relations of the United States (FRUS), 1952–1954* (Washington, D.C.: U.S. Government Printing Office, 1982), vol. 13, pp. 553–54.

47 "Only one man could . . .": Interview with this writer in Paris, October 1948.

48   "... the seemingly ridiculous prospect": U.S. Department of State, *FRUS, 1952–1954,* pp. 1608–1609.

48   One of the three . . .: Source is Dr. Erich Mosettig, the scientist who went to Paris.

50   ... three Vietnamese emperors: Two of the three had led rebellions against France. Only when the Americans decided to intervene in Vietnamese affairs was a Vietnamese chief of state who stood up to them murdered, in 1963.

52   the elderly Prince Cuong De: Phan Boi Chau had been forced to move his base to China before World War I when the Japanese signed a treaty with France, but Prince Cuong De had remained in Japan.

53   a quotation from the teachings: Marguerite Higgins, *Our Vietnam Nightmare* (New York: Harper & Row, 1965), p. 178.

53   asked an American correspondent: Source is David Schoenbrun, the correspondent who was approached by Diem's supporters.

56   Diem was greeted with indifference: Georges Chaffard, *Indochine: Dix Ans d'Indépendence* (Paris: Calmann-Lévy, 1964), p. 33.

56   An American watched Diem: Edward G. Lansdale, *In the Midst of Wars* (New York: Harper & Row, 1972), pp. 154–59; Robert Shaplen, *The Lost Revolution* (New York: Harper & Row, 1965), pp. 103–104.

56   President Eisenhower had congratulated: Joseph B. Smith, *Portrait of a Cold Warrior* (New York: G.P. Putnam's Sons, 1976), pp. 112–14.

56–57   the government could be made: Lansdale, *In the Midst,* pp. 157–58.

57   "... when the right . . .": Lansdale, "Vietnam: Do We Understand Revolution?" *Foreign Affairs* (October 1964), p. 78.

59   A "crisis of inertia": U.S. Congress, Senate, Committee on Foreign Relations, *Report on Indochina,* Report of Senator Mike Mansfield on a Study Mission to Vietnam, Cambodia and Laos, October 15, 1954, Committee Print, 83d Cong.,

2d Sess. (Washington, D.C.: U.S. Government Printing Office, 1964), pp. 10, 11.

59 ". . . the current of nationalism": Quoted in *Report on Indochina,* p. 3.

60 An American CIA team: This CIA group reflected Washington thinking more accurately than the beleaguered consul whom the United States insisted on maintaining in Hanoi against the wishes of the Ho Chi Minh government, after the departure of the French and the Bao Dai regime. Although even at this late date there was still some sensible talk in Washington about trying to keep Hanoi from falling irrevocably into the hands of the Soviet Union, it remained just that, talk. Reality was these CIA agents and high-ranking American officials in Washington and Saigon for whom the Ho Chi Minh government had become "the Enemy."

61 the last French ship: B. S. N. Murti, *Vietnam Divided* (New York: Asia Publishing House, 1964), p. 42.

65 "at their own request . . .": "These mature and responsible news correspondents performed a valuable service to their country," Lansdale reported to Washington. *The Pentagon Papers,* vol. 1, p. 581.

66 the Cao Dai who suffered most: Roger Pinto, *Aspects de l'Évolution Gouvernementale de l'Indochine Française* (Saigon, Paris: Librairie du Recueil Sirey, 1946), pp. 102–105.

68 "The man's a scoundrel": Lansdale, *In the Midst,* p. 177.

69 an article for the Paris . . .: *L'Express,* November 6, 1954.

70 "I believe that the United States": *Report on Indochina,* p. 14.

70 a diplomat from the American Embassy: U.S. Department of State, *FRUS, 1952–1954,* p. 2237.

71 a letter from President Eisenhower: Ibid., p. 2167.

71 Collins announced: *The New York Times,* November 18, 1954.

71 Dulles had warned: General J. Lawton Collins, *Lightning Joe* (Baton Rouge: Louisiana State University Press, 1979), p. 379.

71   "... able, forceful, resourceful ...": Embtel 2250, December 13, 1954.

72   "I see no repeat": Embtel 4663, April 19, 1955.

72–73   but only "unless and until . . .": Deptel (Saigon) 4757; Deptel (Paris) 3829.

73   ". . . any change in leadership": Quoted by Kenneth T. Young, *United States–Vietnam Relations,* vol. 10, p. 947.

76   "There were elections": Halberstam, *Quagmire,* p. 58.

76   ". . . a government that had . . .": Ibid.

76   "Show me a single": Higgins, *Nightmare,* p. 173.

79   Can had his own . . . his brother Nhu): The two brothers were said to compete for power when their jurisdictions overlapped. Their eldest brother, Monsignor Thuc, also had a network of informants.

79   his pretty sharp-tongued wife: She forced a ban on both polygamy and divorce through the National Assembly— in time to prevent her brother-in-law from divorcing her sister. Madame Nhu's attempt to legislate private morality contributed to the unpopularity of the regime, while the reputation for unsavory financial dealings of her brother Tran Van Khiem fueled charges of corruption against the family.

82   However, Cooper recommended: Chester Cooper recorded interview by Joseph E. O'Connor, May 6, 1966, p. 37, John F. Kennedy Library Oral History Project.

82   ". . . very withdrawn, very secluded . . .": Michael Charlton and Anthony Moncrieff, *Many Reasons Why* (London: Scolar Press, 1978), p. 83.

82   ". . . calmer, more self-possessed": Hilsman, *To Move a Nation,* p. 461.

82   He made Hilsman squirm: Ibid.

82–83   Hilsman and Forrestal reported to President Kennedy: Memorandum for the President, February 1963, *The Pentagon Papers,* vol. 2, pp. 717–25.

83   "We are once again": U.S. Congress, Senate, *Two Reports on Vietnam and Southeast Asia to the President of the United States by Senator Mike Mansfield,* Report No. 1 To President

John F. Kennedy—Southeast Asia—Vietnam—December 18, 1962, 93d Cong., 1st Sess. (Washington, D.C.: U.S. Government Printing Office, 1973), pp. 7, 9.

83   "... the first nails ...": Interview with Frederick Nolting, December 7, 1978. U.S. Congress, Senate, Committee on Foreign Relations, *The U.S. Government and the Vietnam War*, Part II 1961–1964, by the Congressional Research Service, Library of Congress, December 1984, Committee Print, 98th Cong., 2d Sess. (Washington, D.C.: U.S. Government Printing Office, 1985), p. 132.

83   "... a great deal of Buddhist": *World Buddhism* (Colombo) (September 1962), p. 19.

84   "O merciful Buddha": *Times of Vietnam Magazine,* March 17, 1963.

84–85   For David Halberstam ...: *Times Talk* 16, no. 9 (October 1963), p. 2.

4: A CHECKERED HISTORY, A FRAGILE BALANCE

86   One spring day ...: This writer was a member of the party. The trip is described by Georges Chaffard, *Les Deux Guerres du Vietnam* (Paris: La Table Ronde, 1969), pp. 295–97.

89   A delegate from the Nam Bo: Duong Bach Mai, *Conférence Préparatoire de Dalat, Compte rendu de la séance d'ouverture du 19 avril 1946.* Typescript.

89–90   Then General Giap: Ibid., *Texte de l'intervention de M. Vo Nguyen Giap au cours de la séance de la Commission politique du 22-4-46.*

90   "We signed ...": *Conférence Franco-Vietnamienne Commission plénière politique: Séance du 26 juillet 1946.* Transcript mimeograph, p. 27.

90   "As long as Cochinchina": Duong Bach Mai, ibid., p. 28.

90   That October, Ho Chi Minh: Ho Chi Minh, *Oeuvres Choisies* (Paris: François Maspero, 1967), p. 107.

91 Ho Chi Minh issued a declaration: Ibid., pp. 110–11.

92 See Buu-Hoi, "Ma Mission Auprès du Viet-Minh en 1953," *L'Express* (Paris), March 6, 1954.

94 Viet Minh resentment . . .: Ministry of Foreign Affairs, *The Truth About Vietnam-China Relations over the Last Thirty Years,* White Paper (Hanoi, 1979). A condensed version appears in *Journal of Contemporary Asia* 10, no. 3 (1980). The full text was published by FBIS, *Daily Report: Asia and Pacific,* October 19, 1979. See also François Joyaux, *La Chine et le Règlement du Premier Conflit d'Indochine* (Paris: Publications de la Sorbonne, 1979).

94 But high-level Communist cadres: See, for example, Jeffrey Race, *War Comes to Long An* (Berkeley: University of California Press, 1972), p. 34.

96 . . . political action did not seem to exclude political terror: A resolution of the Political Bureau of the Party Central Committee in June 1956 pointed out that "armed struggle was also used in definite circumstances . . . it was necessary to strengthen our armed and semi-armed forces, set up resistance bases and secure strong popular support, which were primordial conditions to maintain and develop the armed forces. . . . Tens of thousands of firearms were hidden in many regions. . . . Armed struggles against ruffians and traitors also gained momentum. . . . At the end of 1957 . . . the first concentrated armed units were set up, . . . the nucleus for the future regular army in Nam Bo." Commission for the Study of the History of the Party, *Fifty Years of Activities of the Communist Party of Vietnam* (Hanoi: Foreign Languages Publishing House, 1980), pp. 140–42.

97 When Tra published his memoir: This was intended to be volume 5 of his *History of the Bulwark B2 Theatre,* but it was the first volume published.

97 "The period 1956–59 . . .": Aubrac report to Kissinger, *United States–Vietnam Relations* [The Pentagon Papers, Department of Defense], VI, C.4., microfiche.

97 "If . . . Nhu had only": Conversation with Nguyen Van Chi in Paris, August 1971.

97   The Chinese Communists had tried to hold back: In 1958, the Chinese had told the Lao Dong Party Central Committee that the time was not ripe for an armed struggle against the Diem government. They later reversed themselves and agreed to support an armed struggle. Ho Chi Minh went to China to request military assistance for the South in 1962, and the Chinese supplied over ninety thousand rifles and machine guns to the South Vietnamese revolutionaries that year, according to Hoang Van Hoan, a comrade of Ho Chi Minh and ambassador to China, who later defected to the Chinese. The Hanoi government had accused the Chinese, among other points, of exerting pressure on them to accept a policy of "prolonged ambush" in the South, *The Truth About Vietnam-China Relations.* Hoan's articles in reply to the White Paper in *Renmin Ribao* (Peking) were reprinted in *Beijing Review* (Peking), November 30, 1979, and December 7, 1979.

97   The new line was adopted: "it was stressed that *the revolution in the South must be carried out through violence.*" The Nam Bo Party Committee met in November 1959 and the Party Committee in Central Nam Bo met the following month to carry out the instructions from Hanoi. The Party Committee of Ben Tre province organized a "week of concerted uprisings" in January 1960. At Tra Bong, in Quang Ngai province, the local Party Committee had led an uprising in August 1959. Commission for the Study of the History of the Party, *Fifty Years,* pp. 143–45.

97   . . . infiltrated back to participate: In Hanoi, in January 1961, the Political Bureau of the Party Central Committee "decided to entrust the Army Party Committee and the Reunification Committee with the task of helping the Central Committee guide the military work in the South. It was also decided to strengthen the Central Office for South Vietnam and the Party committees, send more cadres and supplies . . . and expand communications to the South. . . ." Ibid,. pp. 160–61.

99   "I suspected I was seeing in them": Truong Nhu Tang,

A Vietcong Memoir (San Diego/New York: Harcourt Brace Jovanovich, 1985), p. 72.

100   "We would even accept": Georges Chaffard, *Les Deux Guerres,* p. 267.

101   They met at the Perle du Lac: Ibid., p. 261f.

101   He had been warned: Source is Buu-Hoi, ambassador to Morocco and other African states.

101   an invitation from . . . Nasser: *Vietnam Presse,* July 10, 1961.

101   In Burma, Diem had authorized: Source is Tran Van Dinh, then consul general in Rangoon with the rank of minister plenipotentiary.

5: INCIDENT IN HUE

105   "But my hands are tied": *Hoa Binh,* March 31, 1970.

106   To one visiting Catholic: "L'Église au Sud-Vietnam," *Informations Catholiques Internationales,* March 15, 1963, p. 17.

109   He ought to pay a visit: Conversation with Nguyen Van Buu, Paris, January 1970. Mr. Buu was Nhu's emissary to his brother.

110   "Why are there Vatican flags?": Conversation with Nguyen Dinh Thuan, Paris, December 1969.

110   "Why did my brother": Ibid.

111   they were still subject to a regulation: Ordinance No. 10 of August 6, 1950.

112   "Why does he attack me?": *Hoa Binh,* March 31, 1970.

114   . . . American diplomats echoed their disbelief: The CIA reported that the "weight of evidence" indicates "government cannon-fire caused the deaths in Hue." Central Intelligence Agency, "Buddhist Demonstrations in South Vietnam," June 3, 1963.

114–15   For Dang Sy's trial, see *Saigon Post,* June 3, 5, 8, 1964. The events of May 8, 1963, are discussed in detail in United Nations General Assembly Eighteenth session, A/5630,

The Violation of Human Rights in South Viet-Nam, Report of the United Nations Fact-Finding Mission to South Viet-Nam, December 7, 1963. See also Marguerite Higgins, *Our Vietnam Nightmare* (New York: Harper & Row, 1965), pp. 89–100.

115   "It was a price": Ibid., p. 98.

115   The London *Economist,* May 7, 1966.

115   George A. Carver, "The Real Revolution in South Viet Nam," *Foreign Affairs* (April 1965), p. 396. General Maxwell Taylor wrote in 1972 that "government forces reportedly fired . . . I say 'reportedly' because to this day the facts are in dispute . . .": Taylor, *Swords and Plowshares* (New York: W.W. Norton, 1972), p. 289.

116   "Dang Sy is totally innocent": *Hoa Binh,* March 31, 1970.

117–   The only way to do that: Embtel 1038, May 18, 1963.
18

118–   Two messengers from Ngo Dinh Can: Conversation with
19   Le Trong Quat, one of the two messengers.

119   "Tell my brother": Conversation with Nguyen Dinh Thuan.

119   "My brother . . .": Ibid.

6. ATTEMPTED COUPS AND RUMORS OF COUPS

120   the Vietnamese were approaching "repudiation": Embtel 888, April 6, 1963.

120   Nolting cabled Washington: Ibid.

121   advised Diem to ask "gently": Marianna P. Sullivan, *France's Vietnam Policy* (Westport, Conn.: Greenwich Press, 1978), p. 67.

121   Lalouette himself would: Conversation with Roger Lalouette, Paris, June 1970.

121   "Everyone close to Ngo Dinh Diem": Dr. Tran Kim Tuyen, *Hoa Binh,* August 8, 1970.

121   a permanent military establishment: of about fifty thousand men, according to well-informed Vietnamese sources.

121	"The Americans want a base": Do Tho, *Hoa Binh,* July 5, 1970.
122–23	Interview with Warren Unna, *The Washington Post,* May 12, 13, 1963; editorial comment, ibid., May 14, 1963.
123	"Counterinsurgency projects will continue": Embtel 1032, May 17, 1963.
123	"In any case," Hilsman . . .: Deptel 1104, May 17, 1963.
123–24	Nolting's report on interview with Nhu: Embtel 1056, May 23, 1963.
124	Tho was "more bullish": Ibid.
124	"We would withdraw troops": *The Washington Post,* May 23, 1963.
125	"Vietnamese soldiers who are incorporated": Georgette Elgey, *La République des Contradictions 1951–1954* (Paris: Fayard, 1968), p. 431.
125	". . . a little strange that he survived": Tran Van Don, *Our Endless War* (San Rafael, Calif.: Presidio Press, 1978), p. 78.
126	"We know that Big Minh": *United States–Vietnam Relations: 1945–1967* [The Pentagon Papers, Department of Defense edition] (Washington, D.C.: U.S. Government Printing Office, 1971), Book 11, p. 427.
127	the CIA now had "contacts": William Colby, *Honorable Men* (New York: Simon & Schuster, 1978), p. 178.
128	"meaningless when in reality": Robert Thompson, *Defeating Communist Insurgency* (London: Chatto & Windus, 1966), pp. 58–59.
128	Colby decided against "Big Minh": Colby, *Honorable Men,* pp. 179.
128	they could find a refuge: Don, *Our Endless War,* p. 93.
129	"a warlord outlook": Thompson, *Defeating Communist Insurgency,* p. 59.
130	"President Diem . . . was forced to devote": Ibid., p. 58. "That he [Diem] lasted for nine years through several attempted coups was a great tribute both to his own political sagacity and to that of his brother Ngo Dinh Nhu," ibid., p. 59.

131   a strong cable from Washington: Deptel 775, November 11, 1960. In a memorandum for Deputy Secretary of Defense Douglas, Lansdale was sharply critical of Ambassador Elbridge Durbrow for urging Diem "at the most critical moment of the coup attempt . . . to give in to rebel demands to avoid bloodshed. . . . The invitation to engage in this badly-timed and demoralizing meddling in Vietnam's affairs was given the Ambassador by the Southeast Asia desk staff in State message 775," *United States–Vietnam Relations,* Book 10, p. 1331.

133   "The least you can say": Warren Unna, *The Washington Post,* May 13, 1963.

7: FROM HUE TO SAIGON

135   "Don't coddle the bonzes": Interview with Nguyen Dinh Thuan, Paris, December 1969.

136   blister gas: Embtel 1100, 1104, June 4, 1963.

138   the French colonial authorities had encouraged: Mai Tho Truyen, interviewed by Jean Lacouture, *Le Monde,* December 7, 1963.

138   certain Americans . . . seeking a justification: Roger Hilsman would call him "a Frenchified Catholic . . . who began to beat up the pagodas and kill Buddhist priests and Buddhist nuns." Michael Charlton and Anthony Moncrieff, *Many Reasons Why* (London: Scolar Press, 1978), p. 84.

139   Buddhism, Giap noted: *Dossier Sud Vietnamien 1945–1965, Études Vietnamiennes,* no. 8, p. 17.

143   At this interview with the president: Embtel 1136, June 9, 1963.

145   her young daughter had heard American photographers: Marguerite Higgins, *Our Vietnam Nightmare* (New York: Harper & Row, 1965), p. 72.

145   "Such grisly scenes": *The New York Times,* September 13, 1963.

146   Different strands of tradition had combined to produce the death of Thich Quang Duc. The story of the Bodhisattva Bhaisajyaraja, who set fire to himself as an offering to Buddha, was told in the Lotus Sutra, where it was written that his body would burn for twelve thousand years. According to the same sutra, even the sacrifice of a finger or a toe to Buddha must earn merit for the giver. In India, where this scripture was written, it was read as allegory and not put into practice. But Mahayana Buddhists like those in Vietnam chose to take it literally. However, as early as the mid-nineteenth century, the Buddhist scholar who became King Mongkuk of Siam had called religious self-immolation "an expression of worthless credulity . . . gruesome sacrifices described in the translations of the original Pali texts that were made by ignorant and superstitious priests to deceive ignorant and superstitious people." King Mongkuk had not only forbidden such sacrifices in his own Buddhist country; he had threatened punishment for anyone who did not try to prevent such a suicide. See Heinz Bechert, *Buddhismus, Staat und Gesellschaft*, vol. 2 (Wiesbaden: Otto Harrassowitz, 1967), who provides a bibliography on the subject for Thailand and Vietnam, pp. 198ff, 347ff; Walpole Rahula Thera, "Self Immolation an Ancient Buddhist Custom," *World Buddhism* (December 1963), pp. 6–7; and the letter from Pierre Rondet, *Le Monde,* August 25, 1966.

146   In 1948 in the Chinese city: Holmes H. Welch, *The Practice of Chinese Buddhism 1900–1950* (Cambridge, Mass.: Harvard University Press, 1967), p. 327.

150   the people who wanted Diem to hang himself: Frederick E. Nolting, *U.S. News & World Report* (July 26, 1971).

151   "If we make a concession now": Father Cao Van Luan, *Ben Giong Lich Su: Hoi Ky 1940–65* (Saigon: Tri Dung, 1972), p. 339.

152   ". . . a weak, third-rate bigot": George Ball, *The Past Has Another Pattern* (New York: W.W. Norton, 1982), p. 370.

153   a State Department briefing for the president: Department of State Memorandum of Conversation July 4, 1963.

156   the CIA had been openly: *The New York Times,* July 2, 1963.

157   "has begun a campaign": Pierre Salinger, *With Kennedy* (New York: Doubleday, 1966), p. 402.

157   ". . . the revolutionary spirits of 1776": Dang Van Sung quoted by Edward Lansdale, "Vietnam: Do We Understand Revolution?" *Foreign Affairs* (October 1964), p. 82.

158   Nolting's report on his meetings with Diem: Embtel 85, July 15, 1963.

162   Nolting's last interview with Diem: Embtel 226, August 14, 1963.

162–   "Does your departure": Nolting, *Foreign Service Journal*
63   (July 1968), p. 20, and *U.S. News & World Report.*

163   "Mr. Ambassador, I believe": Ibid.

164   Tri Quang had told an American official: Higgins, *Our Vietnam Nightmare,* p. 101.

164   To certain visitors . . . at Xa Loi pagoda: Source is Buu-Hoi, who was one of these visitors. See also Higgins, *Our Vietnam Nightmare,* pp. 28, 33–34.

165   They would either have to leave: Mieczyslaw Maneli, *War of the Vanquished* (New York: Harper & Row, 1971), p. 134.

166   The evening of August 18: Gen. Tran Van Don in conversation with Lucien Conein, August 23, 1963, Central Intelligence Agency, Information Report No. TDCS DB-3/656, 252, August 24, 1963.

166–   on August 20: The meeting of the generals with Nhu and
67   Diem was described by Don to Conein, ibid. On August 21, Gen. Tran Thien Khiem, chief of staff of the general staff, "said that all [the] general officers, in unison, had lately become convinced that if [the] situation were to continue [a] few weeks longer, morale of army would seriously deteriorate. As [a] result, they had decided [to] request (at this point and later Khiem reiterated that generals 'had requested') that martial law be imposed in [the]

nation and that free hand be given to the army to run the affairs of [the] country and prosecute [the] war against [the] Viet Cong with vigor. [The] President had acceded to their request yesterday . . . .": Embtel 292, August 21, 1963.

167 Some of these men were in army uniform: On the morning of August 21, the Americans learned from General Khiem that "assaults on pagodas had been made by regular civilian security components, that no one was killed, and that army had taken no part. Army's job was to fight Viet Cong." Embtel 292, August 21, 1963.

168 the CIA reported: Memorandum for Mr. Michael V. Forrestal, National Security Council, September 6, 1963.

168 found all four alive: United Nations General Assembly, Eighteenth session, A/5630, *The Violation of Human Rights in South Viet-Nam,* Report of the United Nations Fact-Finding Mission to South Viet-Nam, December 7, 1963.

168 "Where are the gentlemen of the press?": David Halberstam, *The Making of a Quagmire* (New York: Random House, 1965), p. 239. Lodge had radioed ahead that he did not want to talk to the press on arrival. But seeing the newsmen waiting, he made them a five-minute speech "about the vital role of the press in American democracy and how much he welcomed any opportunity to help the newsmen do their job. . . . As far as the U.S. Embassy was concerned, the so-called press problems ended then and there," John Mecklin, *Mission in Torment* (Garden City, N.Y.: Doubleday, 1965), p. 190.

8: WASHINGTON DECIDES FOR A COUP

170 John Kennedy replied: Robert Kennedy Oral History, April 13, 1964, p. 223, John F. Kennedy Oral History Project.

171 According to Arthur Schlesinger: Arthur Schlesinger, Jr.,

Robert Kennedy and His Times (Boston: Houghton Mifflin, 1978), p. 712.

172   a cable from Hilsman: Deptel 235, August 22, 1963.

172   Ngo Dinh Nhu had told Warren: Warren Unna, *The Washington Post,* May 13, 1963.

172–   In an Associated Press: *The New York Times,* October 8,
73   1963.

173   "The young people must have some means": Gen. Tran Van Don in conversation with Lucien Conein, Central Intelligence Agency, Information Report No. TDCS DB-3/656, 252, August 23, 1963.

174   Paul Kattenberg's report of his interview with Vo Van Hai, Embtel 316, August 24, 1963.

175   "Under no circumstances should the Americans": Embtel 324, August 24, 1963.

176–   interview that . . . Rufus Phillips had: Memorandum of
77   Conversation between Rufus Phillips and Gen. Le Van Kim, Embtel 320, August 24, 1963.

177   Roger Hilsman . . . would write that the generals: Roger Hilsman, *To Move a Nation* (Garden City, N.Y.: Doubleday, 1967), pp. 484–85. Hilsman would later say the approaches of the generals had been initiated by Khiem and Kim. Roger Hilsman recorded interview by Dennis J. O'Brien, August 14, 1970, p. 31, John F. Kennedy Library Oral History Project. According to Thomas Powers, *The Man Who Kept the Secrets: Richard Helms and the CIA* (New York: Alfred A. Knopf, 1979), p. 164, there had been a CIA report that the dissident generals feared they were about to become the target of Diem's "assassination teams."

178   "Averell [Harriman] and Roger [Hilsman] now agree": Memo for the President's "Weekend Reading File," August 24, 1963.

178   Lodge advised against it: Embtel 329, August 24, 1963.

178–   "Harriman, Hilsman, and I": White House telegram CAP
79   63460, August 24, 1963.

179   It stated that the American government: Deptel 243, August 24, 1963.

179–   Ball telephoned Rusk: Firsthand accounts of the events of
80   that day, the details of which did not always agree with
Roger Hilsman's account (*To Move a Nation,* pp. 487–88),
have been given by other participants, in memoirs—
George Ball, *The Past Has Another Pattern* (New York:
W.W. Norton, 1982), pp. 370–72; Maxwell Taylor,
Swords and Plowshares (New York: W.W. Norton, 1972),
p. 292—and in interviews—see Geoffrey Warner, "The
United States and the Fall of Diem, Part I," *Australian
Outlook* (December 1974); Michael Charlton and Anthony
Moncrieff, *Many Reasons Why* (London: Scolar Press,
1978); An NBC News White Paper, Vietnam Hindsight,
Part II, The Death of Diem, December 22, 1971; "The
Untold Story of the Road to War in Vietnam," *U.S. News
& World Report* (October 10, 1983)—and the book version
—William J. Rust and the Editors of U.S. News Books,
Kennedy in Vietnam (New York: Charles Scribner's Sons,
1985).

Dean Rusk has denied ("has no recollection") he
added a "crucial extra paragraph" (in Hilsman's words) to
the cable calling for American logistic support to anti-
Communist rebel forces, if necessary through some other
port than Saigon; and General Taylor has denied ever
approving the telegram, as Hilsman has said he did.

180   With the president's approval: When informed by Forrestal that the agencies involved had agreed with the telegram, Kennedy replied without comment, "Send it out."
"The Untold Story of the Road to War in Vietnam" *U.S.
News & World Report* (October 10, 1983); Rust, *Kennedy in
Vietnam,* p. 116.

180   "He had passed it off too quickly": Robert Kennedy Oral
History, February 29, 1964, p. 122.

180   He was thunderstruck: Charlton and Moncrieff, *Many Reasons Why,* p. 195; ". . . they were asking me to": *Interna-*

tional Herald Tribune, July 26, 1975; . . . ill-advised, reprehensible: Charlton and Moncrieff, *Many Reasons Why;* . . . insane . . . *International Herald Tribune.*

180   "I am personally in full agreement": Embtel 375, August 29, 1963.

181   "I can read English": Charlton and Moncrieff, *Many Reasons Why,* p. 96.

181   Lodge was authorized to tell the generals: Forrestal informed the president, "Ball, Harriman and Hilsman have answered Department approves modification." Forrestal to General McHugh for President. CAP 63461. Ball would later come to see his approval of Lodge's proposal as "a tactical error." Ball, *The Past Has Another Pattern,* p. 372.

181   He decided the "American official hand": *The Pentagon Papers* (Gravel Edition), (Boston: Beacon Press, 1971), vol. 2, p. 735.

181   the CIA . . . instructed to take its orders on policy from the ambassador: William Colby, *Honorable Men* (New York: Simon & Schuster, 1978), pp. 210–11.

181–   the 8 A.M. broadcast of Voice of America: John Mecklin,
82   *Mission in Torment* (Garden City, N.Y.: Doubleday, 1965), p. 193.

182   "The United States must not appear publicly": Senate Select Committee to Study Governmental Operations, *Alleged Assassination Plots Involving Foreign Leaders* (Washington, D.C.: U.S. Government Printing Office, 1975), p. 219.

182   "Paul, perhaps you had better not": Mecklin, *Mission in Torment,* p. 194.

182–   . . . a private conversation with Diem: Embtel 340, August
83   26, 1963.

184   ". . . a highly intelligent and effective man": Embtel 346, August 27, 1963.

185   ". . . nobody was behind it": Kennedy Oral History, interviewed by Arthur M. Schlesinger, Jr., February 27, 1965, p. 944.

185   "The government split in two": Ibid., interviewed by John Bartlow Martin, April 30, 1964, pp. 381–82.

187   In his emotion, Nolting: Frederick E. Nolting, *U.S. News & World Report* (July 26, 1971).

187–
88   the meeting of the National Security Council: Memorandum of Conference with the president, August 27, 1963.

188   Colby called "frantic . . .": Colby, *Honorable Men,* p. 211.

189   encouraged "to take some hand": William H. Sullivan recorded interview by Dennis O'Brien, June 16, 1970, p. 41, John F. Kennedy Library Oral History Project.

191   "The game had started": Embtel 375, August 29, 1963.

191   "The chance of bringing off": Ibid.

192   "I know from experience that": Telegram "personal for the Ambassador from the President," August 29, 1963.

192   "The best chance of doing it": Telegram to Rusk, August 30, 1963.

192   "I am contemplating": Ibid.

192–
93   Roger Hilsman sat at his desk: Hilsman memorandum, Possible Diem-Nhu Moves and U.S. Responses, August 30, 1963.

193   "The days come and go and nothing": Telegram to Rusk, August 30, 1963.

193   ". . . the absence of bone and muscle": Deptel 284, August 30, 1963.

194   The whiff of Saigon: Memo for the record from Brigadier General Lansdale, August 27, 1963.

195   Diem told Paul Kattenberg: Embtel 371, August 29, 1963.

195–
96   "More than on earlier occasions": Ibid.

196   Nhu pleaded with them: Entries for August 28 and 30 in d'Orlandi's unpublished diary, Warner, *Australian Outlook,* p. 257.

197   He had the proof: Henry Cabot Lodge, *The Storm Has Many Eyes* (New York: W.W. Norton, 1973), p. 208; Ball, *The Past Has Another Pattern,* p. 374.

198   "The result . . . is we started down a road": Robert Kennedy Oral History, February 29, 1964, p. 122.

198   "The policy he . . . was following": Ibid., interviewed by Arthur M. Schlesinger, Jr., February 27, 1965, p. 954.

198   "When the spaghetti was pushed": Deptel 294, August 31, 1963.

198   "The generals are not willing": Conversation with Roger Lalouette, Paris, June 1970.

198–   "We are prepared to continue": Department of State Bul-
99   letin, September 30, 1963.

199   Kennedy had rejected more innocuous language: Hilsman, *To Move a Nation*, p. 497.

199   a partial distortion, a disservice: Salinger, *With Kennedy*, p. 114; letters to the editor, *The New York Times Magazine*, Walter Cronkite, February 14, 1971, and Pierre Salinger, March 14, 1971. To make clear to Diem that the broadcast had not been intended as a personal attack on him, Kennedy had the entire CBS transcript, part of which was not broadcast, sent to Lodge. Memorandum of Conference with the President, September 3, 1963.

199   "That he would support any change": Charlton and Moncrieff, *Many Reasons Why*, p. 99.

200   He saw no future for the Diem government: Memorandum for the Record by General Krulak, August 31, 1963.

200   He wanted to go secretly: Embtel 399, September 2, 1963.

201   ". . . was destroying Vietnamese society": Ball, *The Past Has Another Pattern*, p. 374.

203   "You have to tell the president": Conversation with Nguyen Van Buu, Paris, January 1970. Buu was the Catholic layman who received this message for Diem.

205   Nhu had declared he was ready to resign: Embtel 403, September 2, 1963. The previous evening the papal delegate had told d'Orlandi that Nhu had agreed to withdraw from public life on condition that this served to reestablish relations of trust between Diem and the Americans, and Madame Nhu would leave the country altogether. September 1 entry in d'Orlandi unpublished diary, Warner, "The

United States and the Fall of Diem, Part II," *Australian Outlook* (April 1975), p. 3.

205   When the two Italian diplomats had pressed Nhu: September 6, ibid., p. 4.

205–   "What they really want is a protectorate": *Times of Vietnam,*
206   September 8, 1963; *The New York Times,* September 6, 1963.

206   "The president is very authoritarian": *The New York Times,* ibid.

206   "I make the decisions": Ibid.

206   "We have to be tough": Memorandum of Conference with the President, September 6, 1963.

207   "Why, it would be out of the question": Embtel 455, September 9, 1963.

208   "There were some things going wrong": Al Santoli, *To Bear Any Burden* (New York: E.P. Dutton, 1985), p. 86.

209   ". . . the time has arrived": Embtel 478, September 11, 1963.

209–   . . . urging him to resume talks: Draft telegram "eyes only"
10   for Ambassador from Secretary, September 12, 1963; White House telegram to Lodge CAP 63516, September 17, 1963.

210   dinner with the Indian ambassador: Embtel 541, September 19, 1963.

210   "I believe that for me to press Diem": Embtel 544, September 19, 1963.

210   ". . . whatever sanctions we may discover": Ibid.

211   "What helps to win the war": *Public Papers of the Presidents of the United States: John F. Kennedy,* 1963, p. 673.

212   Taylor on General Minh: Taylor, *Swords and Plowshares,* p. 234.

213   Lodge was again authorized: White House telegram to Lodge CAP 63516, September 17, 1963.

215   "So we now have the secretary of defense": Embtel 542, September 19, 1963.

215   denied there was any truth: Conversation with this writer.

215   Thuan told General Harkins: Harkins cable to Felt and Taylor, September 20, 1963.

215   "his obvious ruthlessness": Embtel 541, September 19, 1963.

215–   Lodge forbade him to renew: Colby, *Honorable Men,* pp.
16   212f.

216   and had been sending to Washington their own reports: Colby, *Honorable Men,* p. 206.

217–   McNamara and Taylor call on Diem: Embtel 612, Septem-
19   ber 29, 1963; Taylor, *Swords and Plowshares,* pp. 298–99.

219   They call on Vice-President Tho.: Embtel 613, September 30, 1963.

9: THE LAST WEEKS

220–   A diplomatic reception: Mieczyslaw Maneli, *War of the*
21   *Vanquished* (New York: Harper & Row, 1971), pp. 136–39.

221–   When Goburdhun had visited Hanoi: Sources are Ram-
22   chundur Goburdhun and Roger Lalouette.

223   not until July . . .: A coalition government would have been set up in the South. "I asked if such a government could be headed by Mr. Diem. In the summer of 1963 the answer was finally yes." Mieczyslaw Maneli, *The New York Times,* January 27, 1975.

223   "He would have had to change the system": Conversation with Roger Lalouette, Paris, June 1970.

223   Nhu was certainly capable of thinking logically: Maneli, *War of the Vanquished,* pp. 122, 127–28.

223   He believed negotiations were feasible: Conversation with Lalouette, Paris, June 1970.

223–   the worst drought it had known: Hanoi radio, Foreign
24   Broadcast Information Service (FBIS), February 4, 1964. Vo Nhan Tri, *Croissance Économique de la République Démocratique du Vietnam 1945–1965* (Hanoi: Editions en

Langues Etrangères, 1966), p. 421; Tran Dang Khoa, "Les problèmes hydrauliques au Nord Vietnam," *Etudes Vietnamiennes* (Hanoi), Cahier no. 2 (1964), p. 53.

224   contacts between the two sides: *Hoa Binh*, August 21, 1970.

224   A North Vietnamese ambassador: Encountered by Lalouette in Czechoslovakia during the time he served as French ambassador to Prague, after leaving Vietnam. Conversation with Lalouette, Paris, June 1970.

224   Maneli learned that direct talks had already begun: They were carried on with the help of the French—"at least technical help at this stage," according to Maneli, *War of the Vanquished*, p. 127.

224–   They dealt with parallel actions: Conversation with La-
25   louette, Paris, June 1970. See also Geoffrey Warner's interview with Lalouette, "The United States and the Fall of Diem," *Australian Outlook* (December 1974), p. 249.

226   "The relationship between France and Vietnam": Maneli, *War of the Vanquished*, p. 202.

227   He told Maneli one evening: Ibid., pp. 140–41.

228   "In the near future I do not foresee": Ibid., p. 146.

228   "If he does not rid himself of these illusions": Ibid., pp. 140–41.

228–   the talks . . . were already under way: Embtel 403, Septem-
29   ber 2, 1963; d'Orlandi, September 2 diary entry, Warner, *Australian Outlook* (April 1975), pp. 3–4.

229   "I urged Lodge not to make the coup": Conversation with Roger Lalouette, Paris, June 1970.

229   Lodge's account of his meeting with Lalouette on September 10: Embtel 460, September 10, 1963. "They had made up their minds": Conversation with Lalouette, Paris, June 1970.

230   he met secretly with the South Vietnamese ambassador: Georges Chaffard, *Les Deux Guerres du Vietnam* (Paris: La Table Ronde, 1969), p. 336.

231   he told visitors: See, for example, Warner, *Australian Outlook* (April 1975), p. 11.

231   a public denial . . .: Tran Van Don, *Our Endless War* (San Rafael, Calif.: Presidio Press, 1978), p. 54.

232   it seemed to him that "Nhu's request": Conversation with Roger Lalouette, Paris, June 1970.

232–   "Report of McNamara-Taylor Mission to South Vietnam,"
36   October 2, 1963.

233   "Many of the reporters had long since": Taylor, *Swords and Plowshares,* p. 300.

238   "He talked to newspapers all the time": Robert Kennedy Oral History, interviewed by John Bartlow Martin, April 30, 1964, p. 388.

239   American newsmen spurned suggestions: Madame Nhu, who was on her way to the United States, asked, "If a girl in France announced she was going to jump out of a window, what would you think of newspaper correspondents who instead of calling the police and firemen contented themselves with standing at the scene with a camera?" Madame Nhu was in Paris at the time, where, as it happened, the correspondents would probably have been arrested, because it was against the law not to go to the aid of a person in danger of death.

240   Kennedy intervened personally: Deptel 576, October 14, 1963.

243   "Mr. President, if I was manager": Senate Select Committee to Study Governmental Operations, *Alleged Assassination Plots Involving Foreign Leaders* (Washington, D.C.: U.S. Government Printing Office, 1975), p. 221.

243   "By that I was saying that": Ibid.

245   Escape routes were studied: Embtel 692, October 12, 1963.

246   he "wouldn't communicate": Robert Kennedy Oral History, interviewed by Schlesinger, p. 962.

246   "You've come to talk about the Special Forces": Embtel 731, October 18, 1963.

247   Thuan and Lodge met at a reception: Embtel 745, October 19, 1963.

251   "what the devil were they fighting for": An NBC News

White Paper, Vietnam Hindsight, Part II, "The Death of Diem."

252   "The generals are all agreed": Interview with a confidential Vietnamese source.

252   Educated Vietnamese had been awaiting the mission: Embtel 768, October 23, 1963.

253–   but only on condition that he would be free: Source is
54   Buu-Hoi; Chaffard, *Les Deux Guerres,* p. 317.

254   ". . . a duly elected government in jail": This was a reference to the fact that General Ne Win had seized power in Rangoon in 1962 and jailed Prime Minister U Nu and the cabinet. The new government had been no more successful than the old in stamping out the insurrections that had become endemic in several parts of Burma.

255   "It is clear, in embassy's judgment": Embtel 583, September 23, 1963.

255–   "sophisticated and gauged just right to cope": Deptel
56   (USUN, New York) 894, (Saigon) 510, October 1, 1963.

256   Harriman was not willing: Sources are Buu-Hoi, Tran Van Dinh.

256–   Conversation with Hilsman (and "subsequent private con-
58   versation with Department officer"): Deptel (USUN, New York) 105, (Saigon) 509, October 1, 1963; also source is Tran Van Dinh.

258   "I should think there would be considerable": Embtel 738, October 18, 1963.

259   In reality, the mission had notified: United Nations, General Assembly, *Violation of Human Rights,* p. 11.

260   the government "appears to be off . . .": Embtel 821, October 30, 1963.

260   Kennedy was reduced to using other intermediaries . . . a congressman from Massachusetts: Herbert S. Parmet, *JFK: The Presidency of John Kennedy* (New York: Dial Press, 1983), p. 335.

261   Lodge accepted both invitations: Embtel 776, October 24, 1963.

263– According to one of the conspirators: Memoirs of former
64 general Nguyen Van Chuan, *Hoa Binh,* August 1971.

266– Lodge's day with President Diem: Embtel 805, October
67 28, 1963.

268 It could well be a beginning: Embtel 804, October 28,
1963.

269– The source for the meeting between Diem and Tran Van
70 Dinh is Tran Van Dinh, based on the notes he made at Gia
Long Palace.

273 The two men took up their dialogue: Interview with Goburdhun, Warner, *Australian Outlook* (April 1975), p. 15.
Also a confidential Vietnamese source.

273– President Kennedy met with the National Security Coun-
75 cil: Memorandum of Conference with the President, October 29, 1963, by Bromley Smith.

278 according to Don's account: Don, *Our Endless War,* pp. 99,
101.

279 a message was brought from Gia Long Palace: Embtel 841,
November 1, 1963.

10: THE DEATH OF A PRESIDENT

280 Felt was surprised: "The Untold Story of the Road to War
in Vietnam," *U.S. News & World Report* (October 10,
1983).

281 Minh had actually put an assassination squad: Tran Van
Don, *Our Endless War* (San Rafael, Calif.: Presidio Press,
1978), p. 102.

281 The final decision to go ahead: Ibid., p. 99.

281 he had deliberately reddened his eyes: Ibid., pp. 103–104.

281 "There isn't a Vietnamese general with hair": "Untold
Story," *U.S. News & World Report* (October 10, 1983).

282 "unusual directness": Embtel 854, November 1, 1963.

282 According to Felt, Lodge . . .: "Untold Story," *U.S. News
& World Report* (October 10, 1983); and the book version,

William J. Rust and the Editors of U.S. News Books, *Kennedy in Vietnam* (New York: Charles Scribner's Sons, 1985), p. 162.

283   "Please tell President Kennedy that I am": Deptel 841, November 1, 1963.

283–   "If U.S. wants to make a package deal": Ibid.
84

284   Captain Ho Tan Quyen: Letter from his widow to the *Hoa Binh,* August 6, 1971.

285   "In case we fail": "Untold Story," *U.S. News & World Report* (October 10, 1983); and Rust, *Kennedy in Vietnam,* p. 163.

285   "During the whole reporting period," Conein: An NBC News White Paper, Vietnam Hindsight, Part II, "The Death of Diem."

287   he would tell a press conference: *Vietnam Presse,* July 21, 1971.

289   The acting papal delegate: Stephen Pan and Daniel Lyons, *Vietnam Crisis* (New York: Twin Circle Publishing, 1966), p. 129.

289   Lodge told d'Orlandi: D'Orlandi diary entry, November 1; Geoffrey Warner, "The United States and the Fall of Diem, Part II" *Australian Outlook* (April 1975), pp. 15–16.

290   "If coup succeeds": Deptel 674, November 1, 1963.

291   Lodge telephoned from his residence: John Mecklin, *Mission in Torment* (Garden City, N.Y.: Doubleday, 1965), pp. 262–63.

291–   Secretary Thuan was calling: Ibid., p. 265.
92

292   "Conein seemed irritated by this news": Don, *Our Endless War,* p. 107.

294   "I don't know whether I will live or die": Do Tho memoir, *Hoa Binh,* July 28, 1970.

294   "I consider myself responsible": Ibid.

295   "Once you are into the attack": NBC White Paper, Part II, "Death of Diem."

295   "We can't hold them that long": "Untold Story," *U.S.*

News & World Report (October 10, 1983); and Rust, *Kennedy in Vietnam,* p. 171.

296 McCone had directed Colby to draft an order: *Alleged Assassination Plots Involving Foreign Leaders* (Washington, D.C.: U.S. Government Printing Office, 1975), p. 221.

296 "All right," Don said: Ibid.

297 appearance of chilling indifference: This indifference contrasted with the concern shown in State Department telegram 770, which was dispatched to Saigon during the abortive coup of 1960: "In view his great services to his own country and cause of freedom, we do hope that at this difficult hour President Diem and family will be treated with all due respect." U.S. Department of State, *Foreign Relations of the United States (FRUS), 1958–1960* (Washington, D.C.: U.S. Government Printing Office, 1986), vol. 1, p. 633.

298 "And what does it matter": Don, *Our Endless War,* p. 111.

299 "Why are you so slow": Chuan memoir, *Hoa Binh,* August 6, 1971.

299 "Duong Van Minh has to assume": *Vietnam Presse,* July 24, 1971.

299 "If you felt that President Diem": A confidential source.

299 "We had no alternative": Marguerite Higgins, *Our Vietnam Nightmare* (New York: Harper & Row, 1965), p. 215. Yet long after Saigon had fallen to the Communists and Duong Van Minh had taken refuge in France, he would tell a Vietnamese he knew well, as he had told the same man years earlier in Saigon, that it was not he who had ordered the death of Diem. He had not even wanted the coup but had gone ahead with it only to forestall Colonel Thao, whom he believed to be a Communist. Source is Ton That Thien.

300 "The top generals who decided": Higgins, *Our Vietnam Nightmare,* p. 215.

300 "Oh, come on, Maggie": Ibid., p. 225.

300 ". . . a look of shock and dismay": Taylor, *Swords and Plowshares,* p. 301.

301   ". . . troubled him really deeply": NBC White Paper, Part II, "Death of Diem."

301   "They were in a difficult position": Peter Collier and David Horowitz, *The Kennedys* (New York: Summit, 1984), p. 309.

302   General Don remarked: Don, *Our Endless War*, p. 109.

302   Lodge suggested that the way to handle: Embtel 900, November 3, 1963.

303   Lodge was pleased to learn: Ibid.

303   he took them downstairs to see: Don, *Our Endless War*, p. 109.

303   "Reports of manner death": Deptel 704, November 3, 1963.

304   the "divergence between ourselves and yourselves": Embtel 917, November 4, 1963.

305   "Asylum should be granted": Deptel (Hue) 5, (Saigon) 698, November 2, 1963.

305   On November 4, a "flash" cable: Deptel 714.

306   intending to ask for asylum in Japan: Cable from U.S. Consulate, Hue, No. 17, November 4, 1963.

306   Lodge explained his decision to Washington: Embtel 930, November 5, 1963.

306   Father Luan recorded the promise: Father Cao Van Luan, *Ben Giong Lich Su: Hoi Ky 1940–65* (Saigon: Tri Dung, 1972), p. 405.

307–   "Fortunately the new Vietnamese rulers": *The New York*
308   *Times,* November 3, 1963.

308   On November 4, the State Department directed: Deptel (Paris) 2333.

309   "We had a hand in killing": Hubert Humphrey, *The Education of a Public Man* (Garden City, N.Y.: Doubleday, 1976), p. 265.

309–   "They were gifts from heaven": *Bulletin du Vietnam,*
10   July 5, 1964.

310   the Hanoi radio quoted the official newspaper: FBIS, *Daily Report: Asia and Pacific,* March 9, 1964.

310   "Talking of South Vietnam": *Sunday Times* (London), February 14, 1965.

EPILOGUE

312   . . . going to hell in a handbasket: Johnson's account of his meeting with Lodge. Bill Moyers, *Newsweek* (February 10, 1975).

312–   Yet Director of Central Intelligence: Memorandum for
13   the Record by John McCone, November 25, 1963.

313   From the American newsmen: Lodge's views were reported as follows: "The U.S. press should be induced to leave the new government alone. They have exerted great influence on events in Vietnam in the past, and can be expected to do so again. Extensive press criticism, at this juncture, could be disastrous." Department of Defense, *United States–Vietnam Relations: 1945–1967* (Washington, D.C.: U.S. Government Printing Office, 1971), Book 7, pp. 4–5.

314   "Of course, nobody writes": Robert Kennedy Oral History, April 30, 1946, p. 396.

314   Ambassador Nolting resigned: Nolting, *Foreign Service Journal* (July 1968), p. 18.

314   "When I became president": "Talk with President Johnson," August 12, 1969, interviewed by William J. Jorden. Transcript, Lyndon B. Johnson Library, pp. 7–8.

315   "there was the memory of Diem": Maxwell Taylor, *Swords and Plowshares* (New York: W.W. Norton, 1972), p. 407.

316   a sanctuary since the early 1960s: Norodom Sihanouk, *L'Indochine Vue de Pékin* (Paris: Seuil, 1972), p. 94.

316   the personal request of Chou En-lai: Sihanouk to resident correspondents in Peking, *The Guardian* (London), December 8, 1971.

316   "That way I didn't have to provide": Sihanouk to Henry Kamm in Romania, *The New York Times*, June 30, 1973.

316   road . . . financed by the American: This road was built at a cost of $30 million at a time when Diem was pleading with the Americans to furnish the Vietnamese Army with bulldozers to push strategic roads through the central highlands. No such strategic roads were ever built. U.S. Department of State, *Foreign Relations of the United States* (*FRUS*), *1958–1960* (Washington, D.C.: U.S. Government Printing Office, 1986), vol. 1, p. 253.

318   General Don . . . now claimed: Speech commemorating the coup delivered in 1969. Transcript (n.d.) provided by Arthur J. Dommen.

318   He noted that the Communist countries: Ibid.

Index

Index

United States
  abandoned South Vietnam to Hanoi
    regime, 318–19
  aid to Cambodia, 316–17
  aims in Vietnam intervention, 124,
    211
  anti-Communism, 32, 46, 211, 244
  attitude toward Diem's trouble with
    Buddhists, 136, 139, 162, 168,
    173, 179, 181, 182–83, 200
  canceled plan for coup, 197–98
  capability to install desired regime in
    Saigon, 186, 315, 316
  concern if war could be won without
    Diem, 206–207, 208, 275
  criticism of Vietnamese conduct of
    war, 122, 123
  decision for coup, 169–219
  decision to abandon Diem, 121, 122,
    139, 152, 153, 232
  foreign policy, 46, 184
  and Geneva Conference, 96
  intelligence agencies operating in
    Vietnam, 172–73
  intervention in Vietnamese internal
    affairs, 6, 32–33, 53, 120–21, 183,
    211, 219, 318
  lack of understanding of Vietnamese,
    4–5, 6, 41, 67, 245, 253, 267–68
  and plans to remove Nhu, 175–76
  policy to replace Diem, 127, 128,
    191–92, 235
  and post-Diem South Vietnam, 315,
    317–18
  pressured Diem for policy/personnel
    changes, 37–38, 56–57, 198–99,
    204, 208, 213, 229, 234–35,
    236–37, 256–57, 262, 266, 269
  pursued mirage of democracy in
    Vietnam, 56–57, 312–13, 315, 316
  relations with Diem, 9, 20, 21,
    27–41, 52–53, 171, 213–14
  relations with postcoup regime, 302
  relations with Vietnam, 2–3, 4–6, 12,
    13
  role in Cambodian coup, 316–17
  role in overthrow of Diem, 32, 38,
    72–73, 242–43, 263, 273–78, 285,
    288–89, 290, 291–92, 295–97,
    299, 301, 309, 310–11, 314, 315
  selective pressures (leverages) on
    Diem government, 208, 234–35,
    236–38, 240–41, 243, 246, 247
  sought peace negotiations with North
    Vietnam, 316, 318

support for Diem, 36, 59, 70–71,
    82–83, 101, 133, 170–71, 213–14
support for generals plotting against
    Diem, 177–78, 181, 186, 189–90,
    193, 197, 252, 264–66, 271–72
suspicion of implication in coup
    attempts, 154
threats to withdraw support from
    Diem, 150, 158, 162–63, 179
urged to take stand against Nhu, 176,
    177
Vietnam policy, 70, 229 (see also
    Kennedy administration, Vietnam
    policy)
will to carry on the war broken, 316
see also American advisers in Vietnam
U.S. aid to South Vietnam, 21, 33–34,
    35, 36–37, 73, 97, 120–21, 219,
    225, 228, 269
  administration of, 215
  cuts in, 234–35, 244–45, 282, 302,
    311
  effects of cuts in, 237–38, 240–41
  end of, desired by generals, 197
  graft, corruption in, 214, 215
  levels of, 122–24
  military, 9, 27, 36, 38–39, 87,
    318–19 (see also American military
    advisers; U.S. troops in Vietnam)
  promised to generals, 181, 189–90,
    193, 197, 252
  suspension of, 190, 192
  threats to discontinue, 102, 122, 206,
    208, 209, 210, 213
U.S. Congress, 204, 213
  House Foreign Affairs Committee, 73
  need to enlist support of, 182, 184
  opposition to further U.S. intervention
    in Vietnam, 318
U.S. Department of Defense, 33, 212
  and coup plans, 178–79, 180, 186,
    277–78
  support for Diem, 217, 218, 219
U.S. Department of State, 34, 38, 69,
    72, 133, 168, 202, 212, 215, 217,
    218, 234, 269
  and Can's request for asylum, 305
  communication with Diem, 255–56
  and coup, 178, 180, 289–90, 308
  and coup plans, 186, 275, 277
  and cuts in aid, 240
  displeasure with Diem, 207
  and murder of Diem and Nhu,
    303–304
  and Nhu's dealing with North,
    231–32

371